The Study of Language
SEVENTH EDITION

This bestselling textbook provides an engaging and user-friendly introduction to the study of language. Assuming no prior knowledge of the subject, Yule presents information in bite-sized sections, clearly explaining the major concepts in linguistics and all the key elements of language.

This seventh edition has been revised and updated throughout, with substantial changes to the chapters on phonetics and semantics, and 40 new study questions. To increase student engagement and to foster problem-solving and critical thinking skills, the book includes over 20 new tasks.

An expanded and revised online study guide provides students with further resources, including answers and tutorials for all tasks, while encouraging lively and proactive learning. This is the most fundamental and easy-to-use introduction to the study of language.

GEORGE YULE has taught linguistics at the University of Edinburgh, the University of Hawai'i, the University of Minnesota and Louisiana State University.

The Study of Language

SEVENTH EDITION

GEORGE YULE

CAMBRIDGE
UNIVERSITY PRESS

CAMBRIDGE
UNIVERSITY PRESS

University Printing House, Cambridge CB2 8BS, United Kingdom

One Liberty Plaza, 20th Floor, New York, NY 10006, USA

477 Williamstown Road, Port Melbourne, VIC 3207, Australia

314–321, 3rd Floor, Plot 3, Splendor Forum, Jasola District Centre, New Delhi – 110025, India

79 Anson Road, #06–04/06, Singapore 079906

Cambridge University Press is part of the University of Cambridge.

It furthers the University's mission by disseminating knowledge in the pursuit of
education, learning, and research at the highest international levels of excellence.

www.cambridge.org
Information on this title: www.cambridge.org/9781108499453
DOI: 10.1017/9781108582889

First published 1985
Second edition 1996
Third edition 2006
Fourth edition 2010
Fifth edition 2014
Sixth edition 2017
Seventh edition 2020

Printed in Singapore by Markono Print Media Pte Ltd

A catalogue record for this publication is available *from the British Library.*

Library of Congress Cataloging-in-Publication Data
Names: Yule, George, 1947– author.
Title: The study of language / George Yule.
Description: Seventh edition. | New York, NY : Cambridge University Press, [2019] | Includes
bibliographical references and index.
Identifiers: LCCN 2019020553 | ISBN 9781108499453 (alk. paper)
Subjects: LCSH: Language and languages. | Linguistics.
Classification: LCC P107 .Y85 2019 | DDC 401–dc23
LC record available at https://lccn.loc.gov/2019020553

ISBN 978-1-108-49945-3 Hardback
ISBN 978-1-108-73070-9 Paperback

Additional resources for this publication at www.cambridge.org/yule7

Contents

Preface

In This New Edition

Thanks to a number of constructive reviews by instructors familiar with earlier editions, I received some good advice and suggestions for improvements to this new edition. Detailed revisions and additions have been made to Chapter 3 (Phonetics) and Chapter 9 (Semantics), along with additional material on a possible musical source for language, phonetic transcription, manner of articulation, the pronunciation of diphthongs, componential analysis, corpus studies, concordances, right brain specializations, PET scans, infant gestures, Nicaraguan Sign Language, an epenthetic vowel, *terribly* and *literally*, non-standard grammatical features, the future in Aymara and singular *they*.

In addition, there are forty new study questions and twenty-six new tasks. The majority of the tasks are data based and designed to help develop analytic, problem-solving and critical-thinking skills. There are new examples from languages as diverse as Arabana, Arabic, Daga, Dong, Hausa, Jamaican Creole, Lotuko, Maninka, Nahuatl, Setswana, Spanish, Wangkajunga, Wolaytta and Yoruba. Additional topics explored in the study of English include causatives, collocation, conversational features, developmental sequences, dissimilation, impoliteness, rhotic and non-rhotic varieties, palimpsests, the *Peterborough Chronicle*, semantic maps of the brain and word play. An expanded and revised Study Guide providing answers and tutorials for all the tasks can be found on the book's website, along with other resources including the full IPA chart: www.cambridge.org/yule7

To the Student

In *The Study of Language*, I have tried to present a comprehensive survey of what is known about language and also of the methods used by linguists in arriving at that knowledge. There continue to be interesting developments in the study of language, but it is still the case that any mature speaker of a language has a more comprehensive "unconscious" knowledge of how language works than any linguist has yet been able to describe. Consequently, as you read each of the following chapters, take a critical view of the effectiveness of the descriptions, the analyses and the generalizations by measuring them against your own intuitions about how your language works. By the end of the book, you should feel that you do know quite a lot about both the internal structure of language (its form) and the varied uses of language in human life (its function), and also that you are ready to ask more of the kinds of questions that professional linguists ask when they conduct their research.

At the end of each chapter, there is a section where you can test and apply what you have learned. This section contains:

- **Study questions** that you can use to check if you have understood some of the main points and important terms introduced during that chapter
- **Tasks** that extend the topics covered in the chapter, mostly through exercises in data analysis, with examples from English and a wide range of other languages
- **Discussion topics/projects** that offer opportunities to consider some of the more general, sometimes controversial, language-related topics and to develop your own opinions on issues involving language
- **Further reading** suggestions provided to help you find more detailed treatments of all the topics covered in that chapter

The origins of this book can be traced to introductory courses on language taught at the University of Edinburgh, the University of Minnesota and Louisiana State University, and to the suggestions and criticisms of hundreds of students who forced me to present what I had to say in a way they could understand. An early version of the written material was developed for Independent Study students at the University of Minnesota. Later versions have had the benefit of expert advice from a lot of teachers working with diverse groups in different situations. I am particularly indebted to Professor Hugh Buckingham, Louisiana State University, for sharing his expertise and enthusiasm over many years as a colleague and friend. I must also acknowledge the support of the excellent production team at Cambridge University Press, with special thanks to Andrew Winnard, Charlie Howell and Jane Adams.

For feedback and advice in the preparation of recent editions of the book, I would like to thank Jean Aitchison (University of Oxford), Linda Blanton (University of New Orleans), Karen Currie (Federal University of Espíritu Santo), Mary Anna Dimitrakopoulos (Indiana University, South Bend), Thomas Field (University of Maryland, Baltimore), Anthony Fox (University of Leeds), Agustinus Gianto (Pontifical Biblical Institute), Gordon Gibson (University of Paisley), Katinka Hammerich (University of Hawai'i), Raymond Hickey (Essen University), Richard Hirsch (Linköping University), Mohammed Hosseini-Maasum (University of Copenhagen), Fiona Joseph (University of Wolverhampton), Eliza Kitis (Aristotle University), Mairead MacLeod, Terrie Mathis (California State University, Northridge), Megan Melançon (Georgia College), Stephen Matthews (University of Hong Kong), Robyn Najar (Flinders University), Eric Nelson (University of Minnesota), Mana Overstreet, Jens Reinke (Christian Albrechts Universität zu Kiel), Philip Riley (Université de Nancy 2), Rick Santos (Fresno City College), Joanne Scheibman (Old Dominion University), Robert Sinclair, Royal Skousen (Brigham Young University), Michael Stubbs (Universität Trier), Mary Talbot (University of Sunderland), Sherman Wilcox (University of New Mexico) and Jay Yule.

For my own introductory course, I remain indebted to Willie and Annie Yule, and, for my continuing enlightenment, to Maryann Overstreet.

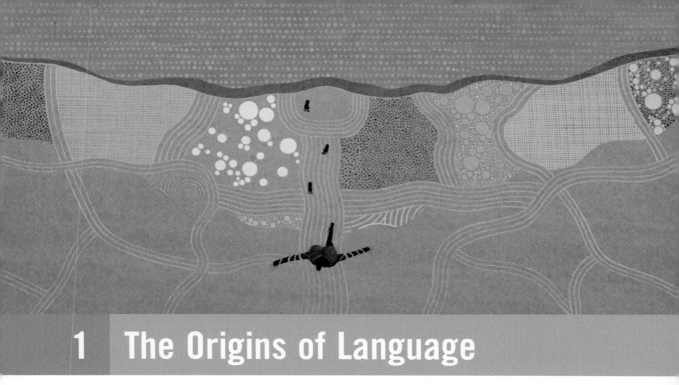

1 The Origins of Language

The first person to set foot on the continent of Australia was a woman named Warramurrungunji. She emerged from the sea onto an island off northern Australia, and then headed inland, creating children and putting each one in a specific place. As she moved across the landscape, Warramurrungunji told each child, "I am putting you here. This is the language you should talk! This is your language!"

Erard (2016)

This origin story from the Iwaidja people of Australia, illustrated in the painting above, offers an explanation of not only where language came from, but also why there are so many different languages. Among the English-speaking people, there have been multiple attempts to provide a comparable explanation, but not much proof to support any of them. Instead of a belief in a single mythical earth mother, we have a variety of possible beliefs, all fairly speculative.

We simply don't have a definitive answer to the question of how language originated. We do know that the ability to produce sound and simple vocal patterning (a hum versus a grunt, for example) appears to be in an ancient part of the brain that we share with all vertebrates, including fish, frogs, birds and other mammals. But that isn't human language.

We suspect that some type of spoken language must have developed between 100,000 and 50,000 years ago, well before written language (about 5,000 years ago). Yet, among the traces of earlier periods of life on earth, we never find any direct evidence or artifacts relating to the speech of our distant ancestors that might tell us how language was back in the early stages, hence the multiple speculations. Closest to the Iwaidja story are tales of gods blessing humans with the power of language.

The Divine Source

In the biblical tradition, as described in the book of Genesis, God created Adam and "whatsoever Adam called every living creature, that was the name thereof." Alternatively, following a Hindu tradition, it is Sarasvati, wife of Brahma, who is credited with bringing language to humanity. In most religions, there appears to be a divine source who provides humans with language. In an attempt to rediscover this original divine language, a few experiments have been carried out, with rather conflicting results. The basic hypothesis seems to have been that, if human infants were allowed to grow up without hearing any language around them, then they would spontaneously begin using the original God-given language.

The Greek writer Herodotus reported the story of an Egyptian pharaoh named Psammetichus (or Psamtik) who tried the experiment with two newborn babies more than 2,500 years ago. After two years of isolation except for the company of goats and a mute shepherd, the children were reported to have spontaneously uttered, not an Egyptian word, but something that was identified as the Phrygian word *bekos*, meaning "bread." The pharaoh concluded that Phrygian, an older language spoken in part of what is modern Turkey, must be the original language. That seems very unlikely. The children may not have picked up this "word" from any human source, but as several commentators have pointed out, they must have heard what the goats were saying. (First remove the *-kos* ending, which was added in the Greek version of the story, then pronounce *be-* as you would the English word *bed* without *-d* at the end. Can you hear a goat?)

King James the Fourth of Scotland carried out a similar experiment around the year 1500 and the children were reported to have spontaneously started speaking Hebrew, confirming the king's belief that Hebrew had indeed been the language of the Garden of Eden. About a century later, the Mogul emperor Akbar the Great also arranged for newborn babies to be raised in silence, only to find that the children produced no speech at all. It is unfortunate that Akbar's result is more in line with the real-world outcome for children who have been discovered living in isolation, without coming into contact with human speech. Very young children living without access to human language in their early years grow up with no language at all. This was true of Victor, the wild boy of Aveyron in France, discovered near the end of the eighteenth century, and also of Genie, an American child whose special life circumstances came to light in the 1970s (see Chapter 12). From this type of evidence, there is no "spontaneous" language. If human language did emanate from a divine source, we have no way of reconstructing that original language, especially given the events in a place called Babel, "because the Lord did there confound the language of all the earth," as described in Genesis (11: 9).

The Natural Sound Source

A quite different view of the beginnings of language is based on the concept of natural sounds. The human auditory system is already functioning before birth (at around seven months). That early processing capacity develops into an ability to identify sounds in the environment, allowing humans to make a connection between a sound and the thing producing that sound. This leads to the idea that primitive words derive from imitations of the natural sounds that early men and women heard around them. Among several nicknames that he invented to talk about the origins of speech, Jespersen (1922) called this idea the "bow-wow" theory.

The "Bow-Wow" Theory

In this scenario, when different objects flew by, making a caw-caw or coo-coo sound, the early human tried to imitate the sounds and then used them to refer to those objects even when they weren't present. The fact that all modern languages have some words with pronunciations that seem to echo naturally occurring sounds could be used to support this theory. In English, in addition to *cuckoo*, we have *splash, bang, boom, rattle, buzz, hiss, screech* and of course *bow-wow*.

Words that sound similar to the noises they describe are examples of **onomatopeia**. While a number of words in any language are onomatopoeic, it is hard to see how most of the soundless things (e.g. "low branch") as well as abstract concepts (e.g. "truth") could have been referred to in a language that simply echoed natural sounds. We might also be rather skeptical about a view that seems to assume that a language is only a set of words used as "names" for things.

The "Pooh-Pooh" Theory

Another of Jespersen's nicknames was the "pooh-pooh" theory, which proposed that speech developed from the instinctive sounds people make in emotional circumstances. That is, the original sounds of language may have come from natural cries of emotion such as pain, anger and joy. By this route, presumably, *Ouch!* came to have its painful connotations. But *Ouch!* and other interjections such as *Ah!, Ooh!, Phew!, Wow!* or *Yuck!* are usually produced with sudden intakes of breath, which is the opposite of ordinary talk. We normally produce spoken language as we breathe out, so we speak while we exhale, not inhale. In other words, the expressive noises people make in emotional reactions contain sounds that are not otherwise used in speech production and consequently would seem to be rather unlikely candidates as source sounds for language.

The Musical Source

Part of the problem with the discussion of natural sounds is the assumption that they were used to create "words." However, before we utter words, we can produce a wide range of sounds that aren't word forms at all. Let's go back to the observation that human infants can process sounds early on, and then soon begin to produce sounds in a way that may provide some clues to how language developed. There is a prolonged period in early infant development during which adults and infants interact via single sounds then through more extended sound sequences as the child uses intonation as a means of non-verbal communication. For some scholars, this is consistent with the idea that musical ability developed before the ability to create words. One famous scholar, Charles Darwin, made the following proposal in 1871:

> The suspicion does not appear improbable that the progenitors of man, either the males or females, or both sexes, before they acquired the power of expressing their mutual love in articulate language, endeavored to charm each other with musical notes and rhythm.

The idea that early humans spent their time trying "to charm each other" may not match the typical image that we have of our early ancestors as rather rough characters wearing animal skins and certainly not very charming. However, setting "charm" aside, we do have evidence that intonation, and hence the ability to create melody, develops in the human infant before other aspects of language. We might say that our first musical instrument was the human voice, or more specifically, control of the vibration of the vocal folds. Control of the respiratory system to produce extended sound was also required.

Studies of newborn infants have found that they can recognize the intonation of their mother's voice and orient to that voice more than any other. They also show a preference for the intonation of their mother's language, even when spoken by others. These observations suggest that early humans may indeed have learned and used melody to express themselves before they added words to their songs. However, other creatures, from songbirds to humpback whales, also produce songs. We have to wonder what prompted humans to go beyond melody and develop a more elaborated means of interacting with each other. One motivation may have been the need to cooperate.

The Social Interaction Source

A source that Jespersen (1922) nicknamed the "yo-he-ho" theory involves the utterance of sounds in physical effort, or more specifically, the sounds needed to coordinate a physical activity involving several people. So groups of early humans might have developed not just songs, but some distinct grunts and curses that were used when lifting and carrying large bits of trees or lifeless hairy mammoths.

The appeal of this proposal is that it places the development of human language in a social context. Early people must have lived in groups, if only because larger groups offered better protection from attack. Groups are necessarily social organizations and, to maintain those organizations, some form of communication is required, even if it is just grunts and curses. Sounds, then, would have some principled use in the social interaction of early human groups. This is an important idea involving the uses of humanly produced sounds. It does not, however, reveal the origins of the sounds produced. Apes and other primates live in social groups and use grunts and social calls, but they have not developed the capacity for speech.

The Physical Adaptation Source

Instead of looking at types of sounds as the source of human speech, we can look at the types of physical features humans possess, especially those that may have supported speech production. We can start with the observation that, at an early stage, our ancestors made a major transition to an upright posture, with bi-pedal (on two feet) locomotion. This really changed how we breathe. Among four-legged creatures, the rhythm of breathing is closely linked to the rhythm of walking, resulting in a one pace – one breath relationship. Among two-legged creatures, the rhythm of breathing is not tied to the rhythm of walking, allowing long articulations on outgoing breath, with short in-breaths. It has been calculated that "human breathing while speaking is about 90% exhalation with only about 10% of time saved for quick in-breaths" (Hurford, 2014: 83).

Other physical changes have been found. The reconstructed vocal tract of a Neanderthal man from around 60,000 years ago suggests that some consonant-like sound distinctions were possible. Around 35,000 years ago we start to find features in fossilized skeletal structures that resemble those of modern humans. In the study of evolutionary development, there are certain physical features that are streamlined versions of features found in other primates. By themselves, such features would not guarantee speech, but they are good clues that a creature with such features probably has the capacity for speech.

Teeth and Lips

Human **teeth** are upright, not slanting outwards like those of apes, and they are roughly even in height. They are also much smaller. Such characteristics are not very useful for ripping or tearing food and seem better adapted for grinding and chewing. They are also very helpful in making sounds such as f or v. Human **lips** have much more intricate muscle interlacing than is found in other primates and their resulting flexibility certainly helps in making sounds like p, b and m. In fact, the b and m sounds are the most widely attested in the vocalizations made by human infants during their first year, no matter which language their parents are using.

Mouth and Tongue

The human **mouth** is relatively small compared to other primates and can be opened and closed rapidly. It is also part of an extended vocal tract that has more of an L-shape than the straight path from front to back in other mammals. In contrast to the fairly thin flat tongue of other large primates, humans have a shorter, thicker and more muscular **tongue** that can be used to shape a wide variety of sounds inside the oral cavity. In addition, unlike other primates, humans can close off the airway through the nose to create more air pressure in the mouth. The overall effect of these small differences taken together is a face with more intricate muscle interlacing in the lips and mouth, capable of a wider range of shapes and a more rapid and powerful delivery of sounds produced through these different shapes.

Larynx and Pharynx

The human **larynx** or "voice box" (containing the vocal folds) differs significantly in position from the larynx of other primates such as monkeys. In the course of human physical development, the assumption of an upright posture moved the head more directly above the spinal column and the larynx dropped to a lower position. This created a longer cavity called the **pharynx**, above the vocal folds, which acts as a resonator for increased range and clarity of the sounds produced via the larynx. Other primates have almost no pharynx. One unfortunate consequence of this development is that the lower position of the human larynx makes it much more possible for the human to choke on pieces of food. Monkeys may not be able to use their larynx to produce speech sounds, but they do not suffer from the problem of getting food stuck in their windpipe. In evolutionary terms, there must have been a big advantage in getting this extra vocal power (i.e. a larger range of sounds) to outweigh the potential disadvantage from an increased risk of choking to death.

The Tool-Making Source

In the physical adaptation view, one function (producing speech sounds) must have been superimposed on existing anatomical features (teeth, lips) previously used for other purposes (chewing, sucking). A similar development is believed to have taken place with human hands and some believe that manual gestures may have been a precursor of language. By about two million years ago, there is evidence that humans had developed preferential right-handedness and had become capable of making stone tools. Tool making, or the outcome of manipulating objects and changing them using both hands, is evidence of a brain at work.

The Human Brain

The human **brain** is not only large relative to human body size, it is also **lateralized**, that is, it has specialized functions in each of the two hemispheres. (More details are presented in Chapter 12.) Those functions that control the motor movements involved in complex vocalization (speaking) and object manipulation (making or using tools) are very close to each other in the left hemisphere of the brain. That is, the area of the motor cortex that controls the muscles of the arms and hands is next to the articulatory muscles of the face, jaw and tongue. It may be that there was an evolutionary connection between the language-using and tool-using abilities of humans and that both were involved in the development of the speaking brain.

A recent study kept track of specific activity in the brains of experienced stonecutters as they crafted a stone tool, using a technique known to have existed for 500,000 years. The researchers also measured the brain activity of the same individuals when they were asked to think (silently) of particular words. The patterns of blood flow to specific parts of the brain were very similar, suggesting that aspects of the structure of language may have developed through the same brain circuits established earlier for two-handed stone tool creation.

If we think in terms of the most basic process involved in primitive tool-making, it is not enough to be able to grasp one rock (make one sound); the human must also bring another rock (other sounds) into contact with the first in order to develop a tool. In terms of language structure, the human may have first developed a naming ability by consistently using one type of noise (e.g. *bEEr*). The crucial additional step was to bring another specific noise (e.g. *gOOd*) into combination with the first to build a complex message (*bEEr gOOd*). Several thousand years of development later, humans have honed this message-building capacity to a point where, on Saturdays, watching a football game, they can drink a sustaining beverage and proclaim *This beer is good*. As far as we know, other primates are not doing this.

The Genetic Source

We can think of the human baby in its first few years as a living example of some of these physical changes taking place. At birth, the baby's brain is only a quarter of its eventual weight and the larynx is much higher in the throat, allowing babies, like chimpanzees, to breathe and drink at the same time. In a relatively short period of time, the larynx descends, the brain develops, the child assumes an upright posture and starts walking and talking.

This almost automatic set of developments and the complexity of the young child's language have led some scholars to look for something more powerful than small physical adaptations over time as the source of language. Even children who are born deaf (and do not develop speech) become fluent sign language users, given appropriate circumstances, very early in life. This seems to indicate that human offspring are born with a special capacity for language. It is innate, no other creature seems to have it and it is not tied to only one specific variety of language. Is it possible that this language capacity is genetically hard-wired in the newborn human?

The Innateness Hypothesis

As a solution to the puzzle of the origins of language, the **innateness hypothesis** would seem to point to something in human genetics, possibly a crucial mutation or two, as the source. In the study of human development, a number of gene mutations have been identified that relate to changes in the human diet, especially those resulting in an increase in calorie intake, possibly tied to the ability to digest starch in food and a substantial increase in glucose production. These changes are believed to have enhanced blood flow in the brain, creating the conditions for a bigger and more complex brain to develop. We are not sure when these genetic changes might have taken place or how they might relate to the physical adaptations described earlier. However, as we consider this hypothesis, we find our speculations about the origins of language moving away from fossil evidence or the physical source of basic human sounds toward analogies with how computers work (e.g. being pre-programmed or hard-wired) and concepts taken from the study of biology and genetics. The investigation of the origins of language then turns into a search for the special "language gene" that only humans possess. In one of the tasks at the end of this chapter (Task G on page 10), you can investigate the background to the discovery of one particular gene (FOXP2) that is thought to have a role in language production.

If we are indeed the only creatures with this special capacity for language, then will it be completely impossible for any other creature to produce or understand language? We will try to answer that question in Chapter 2.

Study Questions

1 When did written language develop?

2 When can we say the human auditory system has begun working?

3 What did Darwin think early human communication was first based on?

4 What two things did early humans need to take control of in order to produce intonation?

5 What percentage of human breathing while speaking normally consists of in-breaths?

6 What is the difference between the position of the larynx in humans and other primates?

7 Why are interjections such as *Ooh!* or *Yuck!* considered to be unlikely sources of human speech sounds?

8 What is the basic idea behind the "bow-wow" theory of language origin?

9 Why is it difficult to agree with Psammetichus that Phrygian must have been the original human language?

10 Where is the pharynx and how did it become an important part of human sound production?

11 Why do you think that young deaf children who become fluent in sign language would be cited in support of the innateness hypothesis?

12 With which of the seven "sources" would you associate the following quotation?

Chewing, licking and sucking are extremely widespread mammalian activities, which, in terms of casual observation, have obvious similarities with speech. (MacNeilage, 1998)

Tasks

A What is the connection between the Heimlich maneuver and the development of human speech?

B What exactly happened at Babel and why is it used in explanations of language origins?

C What are the arguments for and against a teleological explanation of the origins of human language?

D The Danish linguist Otto Jespersen, who gave us the terms "bow-wow" and "pooh-pooh" for theories about language origins, dismissed both of these ideas in favor of another theory. What explanation did Jespersen (1922, chapter 21) favor as the likely origin of early speech?

E In the study of the relationship between brain, tools and language in human development, two distinct types of stone tools are typically mentioned. They are described as Oldowan tools and Acheulean tools. What is the difference between them, when were they used, and which of them was investigated in the recent study involving blood flow in the brain, as described in the chapter?

F The idea that "ontogeny recapitulates phylogeny" was first proposed by Ernst Haeckel in 1866 and is still frequently used in discussions of language origins. Can you find a simpler or less technical way to express this idea?

G When it was first identified, the FOXP2 gene was hailed as the "language gene." What was the basis of this claim and how has it been modified?

H In his analysis of the beginnings of human language, William Foley comes to the conclusion that "language as we understand it was born about 200,000 years ago" (1997: 73). This is substantially earlier than the dates (between 100,000 and 50,000 years ago) that other scholars have proposed. What kinds of evidence and arguments are typically presented in order to choose a particular date "when language was born"?

I What is the connection between the innateness hypothesis, as described in this chapter, and the idea of a Universal Grammar?

Discussion Topics/Projects

I In this chapter we didn't address the issue of whether language has developed as part of our general cognitive abilities or whether it has evolved as a separate component that can exist independently (and is unrelated to intelligence, for example). What kind of evidence do you think would be needed to resolve this question?

(For background reading, see chapter 4 of Aitchison, 2000.)

II A connection has been proposed between language, tool-using and right-handedness in the majority of humans. Is it possible that freedom to use the hands, after assuming an upright bipedal posture, resulted in certain skills that led to the development of language? Why did we assume an upright posture? What kind of changes must have taken place in our hands?

(For background reading, see Beaken, 2011.)

Further Reading

Basic Treatments

Aitchison, J. (2000) *The Seeds of Speech* (Canto edition) Cambridge University Press

Hurford, J. (2014) *The Origins of Language* Oxford University Press

Kenneally, C. (2007) *The First Word* Viking Press

More Detailed Treatments

Beaken, M. (2011) *The Making of Language* (2nd edition) Dunedin Academic Press

McMahon, A. and R. McMahon (2013) *Evolutionary Linguistics* Cambridge University Press

Human Physical Development

Harari, Y. (2015) *Sapiens: A Brief History of Humankind* Harper Collins

Onomatopoeia

Haiman, J. (2018) *Ideophones and the Evolution of Language* Cambridge University Press

Music before Language

Mithen, S. (2006) *The Singing Neanderthals* Harvard University Press

Patel, A. (2008) *Music, Language and the Brain* Oxford University Press

A Hum Versus a Grunt

Bass, A., E. Gilland and R. Baker (2008) "Evolutionary origins for social vocalization in a vertebrate hindbrain-spinal compartment" *Science* 321 (July 18): 417–421

Victor, Genie and Feral Children

Lane, H. (1976) *The Wild Boy of Aveyron* Harvard University Press

Newton, M. (2002) *Savage Girls and Wild Boys: A History of Feral Children* Picador

Rymer, R. (1993) *Genie* HarperCollins

"Bow-Wow" Theory, etc.

Jespersen, O. (1922) *Language: Its Nature, Development and Origin* George Allen & Unwin

The Early Sounds Made by Infants

Locke, J. (1983) *Phonological Acquisition and Change* Academic Press

Mother's Intonation

Mampe, B., A. Friederici, A. Christophe and K. Wermke (2009) "Newborns' cry melody is shaped by their native language" *Current Biology* 19: 1994–1997

McGilchrist, I. (2009) *The Master and His Emissary* (chapter 3) Yale University Press

Vaneechoutte, M. and J. Sloyles (1998) "The memetic origin of language: modern humans as musical primates" *Journal of Memetics* 2: 84–117

Social Interaction

Burling, R. (2005) *The Talking Ape* Oxford University Press

Physical Development

Blake, J. (2000) *Routes to Child Language* Cambridge University Press
Lieberman, P. (1998) *Eve Spoke: Human Language and Human Evolution* Norton

Gesture

Corballis, M. (2002) *From Hand to Mouth* Princeton University Press
McNeill, D. (2012) *How Language Began: Gesture and Speech in Human Evolution* Cambridge
University Press

Brain Development

Loritz, D. (1999) *How the Brain Evolved Language* Oxford University Press

Stone Tools

Balter, M. (2013) "Striking patterns: skill for forming tools and words evolved together" *Science/
AAAS*/News (August 30, 2013) and news.sciencemag.org
Uomini, N. and G. Meyer (2013) "Shared brain lateralization patterns in language and Acheulean
stone tool production: a functional transcranial Doppler ultrasound study" *PLoS ONE* 8(8): e72693

Innateness

Pinker, S. (1994) *The Language Instinct* William Morrow

Against Innateness

Sampson, G. (2005) *The "Language Instinct" Debate* (revised edition) Continuum

Genetics and Bigger Brains

Fiddes, I., G. Lodewijk, M. Mooring, S. Salama, F. Jacobs and D. Haussler (2018) "Human specific
NOTCH2NL genes affect notch signaling and cortical neurogenesis" *Cell* 173: 1356–1369
https://doi.org/10.1016/j.cell.2018.03.051

Other References

Erard, M. (2016) "Why Australia is home to one of the largest language families in the world" www
.sciencemag.org/news/2016/09/why-australia-home-one-largest-language-families-world
September 21, 2016
Foley, W. (1997) *Anthropological Linguistics* Blackwell
MacNeilage, P. (1998) "The frame/content theory of evolution of speech production" *Behavioral
and Brain Sciences* 21: 499–546

2 | Animals and Human Language

One evening in the mid-1980s my wife and I were returning from an evening cruise around Boston Harbor and decided to take a waterfront stroll. We were passing in front of the Boston Aquarium when a gravelly voice yelled out, "Hey! Hey! Get outa there!" Thinking we had mistakenly wandered somewhere we were not allowed, we stopped and looked around for a security guard or some other official, but saw no one, and no warning signs. Again the voice boomed, "Hey! Hey you!" As we tracked the voice we found ourselves approaching a large, glass-fenced pool in front of the aquarium where four harbor seals were lounging on display. Incredulous, I traced the source of the command to a large seal reclining vertically in the water, with his head extended back and up, his mouth slightly open, rotating slowly. A seal was talking, not to me, but to the air, and incidentally to anyone within earshot who cared to listen.

Deacon (1997)

There are a lot of stories about creatures that can talk. We usually assume that they are fantasy or fiction or that they involve birds or animals simply imitating something they have heard humans say (as Terrence Deacon discovered was the case with the loud seal in Boston Aquarium). Yet we believe that creatures can communicate, certainly with other members of their own species. Is it possible that a creature could learn to communicate with humans using language? Or does human language have properties that make it so unique that it is quite unlike any other communication system and hence unlearnable by any other creature? To answer these questions, we first look at some special properties of human language, then review a number of experiments in communication involving humans and animals.

Communication

We should first distinguish between specifically **communicative signals** and those that may be unintentionally **informative signals**. Someone listening to you may become informed about you through a number of signals that you have not intentionally sent. She may note that you have a cold (you sneezed), that you are not at ease (you shifted around in your seat), that you are disorganized (non-matching socks) and that you are from somewhere else (you have a strange accent). However, when you use language to tell this person, *I'm one of the applicants for the vacant position of senior brain surgeon at the hospital*, you are normally considered to be intentionally communicating something. Humans are capable of producing sounds and syllables in a stream of speech that appears to have no communicative purpose, as in **glossolalia**, or "speaking in tongues," which is associated with the religious practices of Pentecostal Christian churches. These outpourings sound like language, but with no speaker control it is not intentional communication. We might say the same thing about some of the chirping and singing produced by birds. We also don't assume that the blackbird is communicating anything by having black feathers and sitting on a branch. However, the bird is considered to be sending a communicative signal with the loud squawking produced when a cat appears on the scene. So, when we talk about distinctions between human language and animal communication, we are considering both in terms of their potential for intentional communication.

Properties of Human Language

While we tend to think of communication as the primary function of human language, it is not its only distinguishing feature. All creatures communicate in some way, even if it is not through vocalization. However, we suspect that other creatures are not reflecting on the way they create their communicative messages or reviewing how they work (or not). That is, one barking dog is probably not offering advice to another barking dog along the lines of "Hey, you should lower your bark to make it sound more menacing." They're not barking about barking. Humans are clearly able to reflect on language and its uses (e.g. "I wish he wouldn't use so many technical terms"). This is **reflexivity**. The property of reflexivity (or "reflexiveness") accounts for the fact that we can use language to think and talk about language itself, making it one of the distinguishing features of human language. Indeed, without this general ability, we wouldn't be able to reflect on or identify any of the other distinct properties of human language. We willl look in detail at another five of them: displacement, arbitrariness, productivity, cultural transmission and duality.

Displacement

When your pet cat comes up to you calling *meow*, you are likely to understand this message as relating to that immediate time and place. If you ask your cat what it has been up to, you will probably get the same *meow* response. Animal communication seems to be designed exclusively for the here and now. It isn't used to relate events that are removed in time and place. When your dog says *GRRR*, it means *GRRR, right now*, because dogs aren't capable of communicating *GRRR, last night, over in the park*. In contrast, human language users are normally capable of producing messages equivalent to *GRRR, last night, over in the park*, and then going on to say *In fact, I'll be going back tomorrow for some more*. Humans can refer to past and future time. This property of human language is called **displacement**. It allows language users to talk about things not present in the immediate environment. Displacement allows us to talk about things and places (e.g. angels, fairies, Santa Claus, Superman, heaven, hell) whose existence we cannot even be sure of.

We could look at bee communication as a small exception because it seems to have some version of displacement. When a honeybee finds a source of nectar and returns to the beehive, it can perform a dance routine to communicate to the other bees the location of this nectar. Depending on the type of dance (round dance for nearby and tail-wagging dance for further away), the other bees can work out where this newly discovered feast can be found. Doesn't this ability of the bee to indicate a location some distance away mean that bee communication has at least some degree of displacement as a feature? Yes, but it is displacement of a very limited type. It just doesn't have the range of possibilities found in human language. Certainly, the bee can direct other bees to a food source. However, it must be the most recent food source. It cannot be *that delicious rose bush on the other side of town that we visited last weekend*, nor can it be, as far as we know, possible future nectar in bee heaven.

Arbitrariness

It is generally the case that there is no "natural" connection between a linguistic form and its meaning; the connection is quite arbitrary. We can't just look at the Arabic word كلب and from its shape determine that it has a natural and obvious meaning any more than we can with its English translation form *dog*. The linguistic form has no natural or "iconic" relationship with that hairy four-legged barking object out in the world. This aspect of the relationship between words and objects is described as **arbitrariness**. It is possible to make words "fit" the concept they indicate, as in Figure 2.1, but this type of game only emphasizes the arbitrariness of the connection that normally exists between a word and its meaning.

Figure 2.1 Words made to "fit" concepts

There are some words in language with sounds that seem to "echo" the sounds of objects or activities and hence seem to have a less arbitrary connection. English examples are *cuckoo, crash, slurp, squelch* or *whirr*. However, these onomatopoeic words are relatively rare in human language.

For the majority of animal signals, there does appear to be a clear connection between the conveyed message and the signal used to convey it. This impression may be closely connected to the fact that, for any animal, the set of signals used in communication is finite. Each variety of animal communication consists of a limited set of vocal or gestural forms. Many of these forms are only used in specific situations (to establish territory) or at particular times (to find a mate).

Cultural Transmission

While we inherit physical features such as brown eyes and dark hair from our parents, we do not inherit their language. We acquire a language in a culture with other speakers and not from parental genes. An infant born to Korean parents in Korea, but adopted and brought up from birth by English speakers in the United States, will have physical characteristics inherited from his or her natural parents, but will inevitably speak English. A kitten, given comparable early experiences, will produce *meow* regardless.

This process whereby a language is passed on from one generation to the next is described as **cultural transmission**. It is clear that humans are born with some kind of predisposition to acquire language in a general sense. However, we are not born with the ability to produce utterances in a specific language such as English. We acquire our first language as children in a culture.

The general pattern in animal communication is that creatures are born with a set of specific signals that are produced instinctively. There is some evidence from studies of birds as they develop their songs that instinct has to combine with learning (or exposure) in order for the right song to be produced. If those birds spend their first seven weeks without hearing other birds, they will instinctively produce songs or calls, but those songs will be abnormal in some way. Human infants, growing up in isolation, produce no "instinctive" language.

Productivity

Humans are continually creating new expressions by manipulating their linguistic resources to describe new objects and situations. This property is described as **productivity** (or "creativity" or "open-endedness") and essentially means that the potential number of utterances in any human language is infinite.

The communication systems of other creatures are not like that. Cicadas have four signals to choose from and vervet monkeys have thirty-six vocal calls. Nor does it seem possible for creatures to produce new signals for novel experiences or events. The honey-bee, normally able to communicate the location of a nectar source to other bees, will fail to do so if the location is really "new." In one experiment, a hive of bees was placed at the foot of a radio tower and a food source placed at the top. Ten bees were taken to the top, given a taste of the delicious food, and sent off to tell the rest of the hive. The message was conveyed via a bee dance and the whole gang buzzed off to get the free food. They flew around in all directions, but couldn't locate the food. (It's probably one way to make bees really mad!) The problem seems to be that bee communication has a fixed set of signals for communicating location and they all relate to horizontal distance. The bee cannot manipulate its communication system to create a "new" message for vertical distance. According to Karl von Frisch (1993), who conducted the experiment, "the bees have no word for *up* in their language" and they can't invent one.

This lack of productivity in animal communication can be described in terms of **fixed reference**. Each signal in the communication system of other creatures seems to be fixed in terms of relating to a particular occasion or purpose. This is particularly true of scent based signaling, as in the pheromones (a chemical substance) released by insects such as female moths as they try to contact a mate. It's a case of one scent, one meaning.

Among our closer relatives, there are lemurs (similar to small monkeys) in Madagascar that have only three basic calls. In the vervet monkey's repertoire, there is one danger signal *CHUTTER*, which is used when a snake is around, and another *RRAUP*, used when an eagle is spotted nearby. These signals are fixed in terms of their reference and cannot be manipulated. What might count as evidence of productivity in the monkey's communication system would be an utterance of something like *CHUTT-RRAUP* when a flying creature that looked like a snake came by. Despite a lot of laboratory research involving snakes suddenly appearing in the air above them (among other weird experiences), the vervet monkeys didn't produce a new danger signal. The human, given similar circumstances, is quite capable of creating a "new" signal, after initial surprise perhaps, by saying something never said before, as in *Hey! Watch out for that flying snake!*

Duality

Human language is organized at two levels simultaneously. This property is called **duality** (or "double articulation"). When we speak, we have a physical level at which we produce individual sounds, like *n, b* and *i*. As individual sounds, none of these discrete forms has any intrinsic meaning. In a combination such as *bin*, we have another level with a meaning that is different from the meaning of the combination in *nib*. So, at one level, we have distinct sounds, and, at another level, we have distinct meanings. This duality of levels is one of the most economical features of human language because with a limited set of sounds we are capable of producing a very large number of sound combinations (e.g. words) that are distinct in meaning.

Among other creatures, each communicative signal appears to be a single fixed form that cannot be broken down into separate parts. Although your dog may be able to produce *woof* ("I'm happy to see you"), it does not seem to do so on the basis of a distinct level of production combining the separate elements of *w + oo + f*. If the dog was operating with the double level (i.e. duality), then we might expect to hear different combinations with different meanings, such as *oowf* ("I'm hungry") and *foow* ("I'm really bored").

Talking to Animals

If these properties make human language such a unique communication system, then it would seem extremely unlikely that other creatures would be able to understand it. Some humans, however, do not behave as if this is the case. Riders can say *Whoa* to horses and they stop, we can say *Heel* to dogs and they will follow at heel (well, sometimes . . .), and a variety of circus animals go *Up, Down* and *Roll over* in response to spoken commands. Should we treat these examples as evidence that non-humans can understand human language? Probably not. The standard explanation is that the animal produces a particular behavior in response to a sound stimulus, but does not actually "understand" what the noise means.

If it seems difficult to conceive of animals understanding human language, then it appears to be even less likely that an animal would be capable of producing human language. After all, we do not generally observe animals of one species learning to produce the signals of another species. You could keep your horse in a field of cows for years, but it still won't say *Moo*. And, in some homes, a new baby and a puppy may arrive at the same time. Baby and puppy grow up in the same environment, hearing the same things, but two years later, the baby is making lots of human speech sounds and the puppy is not. Perhaps a puppy is a poor example. Wouldn't it be better to work with a closer relative such as a chimpanzee?

Chimpanzees and Language

The idea of raising a chimp and a child together may seem like a nightmare, but this is basically what was done in an early attempt to teach a chimpanzee to use human language. In the 1930s, scientists Luella and Winthrop Kellogg reported on their experience of raising an infant chimpanzee together with their baby son. The chimpanzee, called Gua, was reported to be able to understand about a hundred words, but did not "say" any of them. In the 1940s, a chimpanzee named Viki was reared by another scientist couple, Catherine and Keith Hayes, in their own home, as if she was a human child. These foster parents spent five years attempting to get Viki to "say" English words by trying to shape her mouth as she produced sounds. Viki eventually managed to produce some words, rather poorly articulated versions of *mama, papa* and *cup*. In retrospect, this was a remarkable achievement since it has become clear that non-human primates do not actually have a physically structured vocal tract that is suitable for articulating the sounds used in speech. Apes and gorillas can, like chimpanzees, communicate with a wide range of vocal calls, but they just can't make human speech sounds.

Washoe

Recognizing that a chimpanzee was not likely to learn spoken language, Beatrix and Allen Gardner set out to teach a female chimpanzee called Washoe to use a version of American Sign Language. As described later in Chapter 15, this sign language has all the essential properties of human language and is learned by many congenitally deaf children as their natural first language. Moreover, in the wild, chimpanzees have been recorded using up to sixty-six distinct gesture types.

From the beginning, the Gardners and their research assistants raised Washoe like a human child in a comfortable domestic environment. Sign language was always used when Washoe was around and she was encouraged to use signs, even her own incomplete "baby-versions" of the signs used by adults. In a period of three and a half years, Washoe came to use signs for more than a hundred words, ranging from *airplane, baby* and *banana* through to *window, woman* and *you*. Even more impressive was Washoe's ability to take these forms and combine them to produce "sentences" of the type *gimme tickle, more fruit* and *open food drink* (to get someone to open the refrigerator). Some of the forms appear to have been inventions by Washoe, as in her novel sign for *bib* and in the combination *water bird* (referring to a swan), which would seem to indicate that her communication system had the potential for productivity. Washoe also demonstrated understanding of a much larger number of signs than she produced and was capable of holding rudimentary conversations, mainly in the form of question–answer sequences.

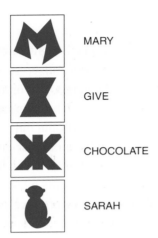

MARY

GIVE

CHOCOLATE

SARAH

Figure 2.2 Shapes representing words used by chimpanzee Sarah

Sarah and Lana

At the same time as Washoe was learning sign language, another chimpanzee was being taught by Ann and David Premack to use a set of plastic shapes for the purpose of communicating with humans. These plastic shapes represented "words" that could be arranged in sequence to build "sentences." This chimpanzee was called Sarah and she preferred to arrange the shapes into a vertical order, as shown in Figure 2.2. The basic approach was quite different from that of the Gardners. Sarah was not treated like a human child in a domestic environment. To begin with, she was over five years old when the training began. She was systematically trained to associate the plastic shapes with objects or actions. She remained an animal in a cage, being trained with food rewards to manipulate a set of symbols. Once she had learned to use a large number of the plastic shapes, Sarah was capable of getting an apple by selecting the correct plastic shape (a blue triangle) from a large array. Notice that this symbol is arbitrary since it would be hard to argue for any natural connection between an apple and a blue plastic triangle. Sarah was also capable of producing "sentences" such as *Mary give chocolate Sarah* and had the impressive capacity to understand complex structures such as *If Sarah put red on green, Mary give Sarah chocolate*. Sarah would get the chocolate.

A similar training technique with another artificial language was used by Duane Rumbaugh to train a chimpanzee called Lana. The language she learned was called Yerkish and consisted of a set of symbols on a large keyboard linked to a computer. When Lana wanted some water, she had to find and press four symbols to produce the message *please machine give water*, as illustrated in Figure 2.3.

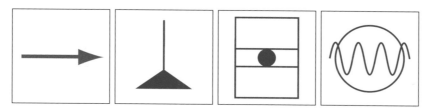

Figure 2.3 "Please machine give water" in Yerkish

The Controversy

Both Sarah and Lana demonstrated an ability to use what look like word symbols and basic structures in ways that superficially resemble the use of language. There is, however, a lot of skepticism regarding these apparent linguistic skills. It has been pointed out that when Lana used the symbol for "please," she did not have to understand the meaning of the English word *please*. The symbol for "please" on the computer keyboard might simply be the equivalent of a button on a vending machine and, so the argument goes, we could learn to operate vending machines without necessarily knowing language. This is only one of the many arguments that have been presented against the idea that the use of signs and symbols by these chimpanzees is similar to the use of language.

On the basis of his work with another chimpanzee called Nim, the psychologist Herbert Terrace argued that chimpanzees simply produce signs in response to the demands of people and tend to repeat signs those people use, yet they are treated as if they are taking part in a "conversation." As in many critical studies of animal learning, the chimpanzees' behavior is viewed as a type of conditioned response to cues provided (often unwittingly) by human trainers. Terrace's conclusion was that chimpanzees are clever creatures who learn a certain type of behavior (signing) in order to get rewards and are essentially performing sophisticated "tricks."

In response, the Gardners argued that they were not animal trainers, nor were they eliciting conditioned responses from Washoe. In complex experiments, designed to eliminate any visual cues, they showed that in the absence of any human, Washoe could produce correct signs to identify objects in pictures. They also emphasize a major difference between Washoe and Nim. While Nim was a research animal in a complex environment, dealing with a lot of different researchers who were often not fluent signers, Washoe lived in a more limited domestic environment with a lot of opportunity for imaginative play and interaction with fluent signers who were also using sign language with each other. They also report that another group of younger chimpanzees learned sign language and occasionally used signs with each other and with Washoe, even when there were no humans present.

Kanzi

In a more recent set of studies, an interesting development relevant to this controversy came about almost by accident. While Sue Savage-Rumbaugh was attempting to train a bonobo (a pygmy chimpanzee) called Matata how to use the symbols of Yerkish, Matata's adopted baby, Kanzi, was always with her. Although Matata did not do very well, her son Kanzi spontaneously started using the symbol system with great ease. He had learned not by being taught, but by being exposed to, and observing, a kind of language in use at a very early age. Kanzi eventually developed a large symbol vocabulary (over 250 forms). By the age of eight, he was reported to be able to demonstrate understanding of spoken English at a level comparable to a two-and-a-half-year-old human child. There was also evidence that he was using a consistently distinct set of "gentle noises" as words to refer to things such as bananas, grapes and juice. Kanzi could also use Yerkish to ask for his favorite movie, *Quest for Fire*, and even learned how to collect wood, make a fire and cook his own food, as shown in the photo at the beginning of this chapter.

Using Language

Important lessons have been learned from attempts to teach chimpanzees how to use forms of language. Were Washoe and Kanzi capable of taking part in interaction with humans by using a symbol system chosen by humans and not chimpanzees? The answer is clearly "Yes." Did Washoe and Kanzi go on to perform linguistically like a human child about to begin pre-school? The answer is just as clearly "No." Yet, even as we arrive at these answers, we still don't seem to have a non-controversial definition of what "using language" means.

One solution might be to stop thinking of language, at least in the phrase "using language," as a single thing that one can either have or not have. We could then say there are (at least) two ways of thinking about "using language." In a broad sense, language serves as a type of communication system in different situations. In one situation, we look at the behavior of a two-year-old human child interacting with a caregiver as an example of "using language." In another situation, we observe very similar behavior from chimpanzees when they are interacting with humans. It has to be fair to say that, in both cases, we observe the participants "using language."

However, there is a difference. Underlying the two-year-old's communicative activity is the capacity to develop a complex system of sounds and structures, plus computational procedures, that will allow the child to produce extended discourse containing a potentially infinite number of novel utterances. No other creature has been observed "using language" in this sense. It is in this more comprehensive and productive sense that we say that language is uniquely human.

Study Questions

1 What is displacement?

2 What is the difference between a communication system with productivity and one with fixed reference?

3 Why is reflexivity considered to be a special property of human language?

4 What kind of evidence is used to support the idea that language is culturally transmitted?

5 How do we think the harbor seal was able to yell "Hey! Hey you!"?

6 Why isn't glossolalia considered to be communicative language use?

7 Which English words was Viki reported to be able to say?

8 What property did Washoe's language seem to have when she used an expression such as "water bird" to refer to a swan?

9 How did the Gardners try to show that Washoe was not simply repeating signs made by interacting humans?

10 If Sarah could use a gray plastic shape to convey the meaning of the word *red*, which property does her "language" seem to have?

11 What was the name of the "language" that Lana learned?

12 What was considered to be the key element in Kanzi's language learning?

Tasks

A In studies of communication involving animals and humans, there is sometimes a reference to "the Clever Hans phenomenon." Who or what was Clever Hans, why was he/she/it famous and what exactly is the "phenomenon"?

B We recognized a distinction early in the chapter between communicative and informative signals. How would "body language" be characterized? Also, what kind of signaling is involved in "distance zones"? What about "eye contact" and "eyebrow flashes"?

C What is meant by "sound symbolism"? How does it relate to arbitrariness?

D (i) In the study of animal communication, what are "playback experiments"?

(ii)   Which forms of animal communication described in this chapter were discovered as a result of playback experiments?

E   It has been claimed that "recursion" is a key property of human language, and of human cognition in general. What is recursion? Could it still be a universal property of human language if one language was discovered that had no evidence of recursion in its structure?

F   We reviewed studies involving chimpanzees and bonobos learning to communicate with humans. Can only African apes accomplish this task? Are there any studies involving the Asian great ape, the orangutan, learning how to use a human communication system?

G   What was the significance of the name given to the chimpanzee in the research conducted by the psychologist Herbert Terrace (1979)?

H   Consider these statements about the symbol-using abilities of chimpanzees in animal language studies and decide if they are correct or not. What evidence can be used to argue for or against the accuracy of these statements?

(1)   They can create combinations of signs that look like the telegraphic speech produced by young children.

(2)   They can invent new sign combinations.

(3)   They can understand structures with complex word order, such as conditionals (i.e. *if X, then Y*).

(4)   They overgeneralize the references of signs, using one sign for many different things, just as human children do in the early stages.

(5)   They don't use signs spontaneously and only produce them in response to humans.

(6)   They have complex concepts such as time because they produce sign combinations such as *time eat*.

(7)   They use signs to interact with each other, just as three-year-old children do with speech.

(8)   They steadily increase the length of their utterances, so that their average utterance length of 3.0 is equivalent to that of a three-and-a-half-year-old child.

Discussion Topics/Projects

I   Listed below are six other properties (or "design features") that are often discussed when human language is compared to other communication systems.

vocal–auditory channel use	(language signals are sent using the vocal organs and received by the ears)
specialization	(language signals do not serve any other type of purpose such as breathing or feeding)
non-directionality	(language signals have no inherent direction and can be picked up by anyone within hearing, even unseen)
rapid fade	(language signals are produced and disappear quickly)
reciprocity	(any sender of a language signal can also be a receiver)
prevarication	(language signals can be false or used to lie or deceive)

(i)   Are these properties found in all forms of human communication via language?

(ii) Are these special properties of human language or can they be found in the communication systems of other creatures?

(For background reading, see chapter 17 of O'Grady *et al.*, 2017.)

II The most persistent criticism of the chimpanzee language-learning projects is that the chimpanzees are simply making responses like trained animals for rewards and are consequently not using language to express anything. Read over the following reports and try to decide how the different behaviors of these chimpanzees (Dar, Washoe and Moja) should be characterized. Signs are represented by words in capital letters.

> *After her nap, Washoe signed OUT. I was hoping for Washoe to potty herself and did not comply. Then Washoe took my hands and put them together to make OUT and then signed OUT with her own hands to show me how.*
>
> *Greg was hooting and making other sounds, to prevent Dar from falling asleep. Dar put his fist to Greg's lips and made kissing sounds. Greg asked WHAT WANT? and Dar replied QUIET, placing the sign on Greg's lips.*
>
> *Moja signed DOG on Ron and me and looked at our faces, waiting for us to "woof." After several rounds I made a "meeow" instead. Moja signed DOG again, I repeated "meeow" again, and Moja slapped my leg harder. This went on. Finally, I woofed and Moja leapt on me and hugged me.*
>
> *Moja stares longingly at Dairy Queen as we drive by. Then for a minute or more signs NO ICE CREAM many times, by shaking her head while holding fist to mouth, index edge up.*

(For background reading, see Rimpau *et al.*, 1989, which is the source of these examples. There is also a film with the title *Project Nim* (Lionsgate) that describes the unfortunate experiences of the chimpanzee Nim.)

Further Reading

Basic Treatments

Aitchison, J. (2011) *The Articulate Mammal* (chapter 2) Routledge Classics

Friend, T. (2005) *Animal Talk* Simon and Schuster

More Detailed Treatments

Anderson, S. (2004) *Doctor Doolittle's Delusion* Yale University Press

Rogers, L. and G. Kaplan (2000) *Songs, Roars and Rituals* Harvard University Press

General Properties of Language

Hockett, C. (1960) "The origin of speech" *Scientific American* 203: 89–96

Glossolalia

Newberg, A., N. Wintering, D. Morgan and M. Waldman (2006). "The measurement of regional cerebral blood flow during glossolalia: a preliminary SPECT study" *Psychiatry Research: Neuroimaging* 148: 67–71

Samarin, W. (1972) *Tongues of Men and Angels: The Religious Language of Pentecostalism* Macmillan

Animal Communication and Consciousness

Griffin, D. (2001) *Animal Minds* University of Chicago Press

Hauser, M. (1996) *The Evolution of Communication* MIT Press

Bee Communication

von Frisch, K. (1993) *The Dance Language and Orientation of Bees* Harvard University Press

Lemur and Vervet Monkey Communication

Cheney, D. and R. Seyfarth (1990) *How Monkeys See the World* University of Chicago Press

Jolly, A. (1966) *Lemur Behavior* University of Chicago Press

Chimpanzee Gestures

Hobaiter, C. and R. Byrne (2014) "The meaning of chimpanzee gestures" *Current Biology* 24: 1596–1600 http://dx.doi.org/10.1016/j.cub.2014.05.066

Individual Chimpanzees and Bonobos

(Gua) Kellogg, W. and L. Kellogg (1933) *The Ape and the Child* McGraw-Hill

(Viki) Hayes, C. (1951) *The Ape in Our House* Harper

(Washoe) Gardner, R., B. Gardner and T. van Cantfort (eds.) (1989) *Teaching Sign Language to Chimpanzees* State University of New York Press

(Sarah) Premack, A. and D. Premack (1991) "Teaching language to an ape" In W. Wang (ed.) *The Emergence of Language* (16–27) W. H. Freeman

(Lana) Rumbaugh, D. (ed.) (1977) *Language Learning by a Chimpanzee: The LANA Project* Academic Press

(Nim) Hess, E. (2008) *Nim Chimpsky: The Chimp Who Would Be Human* Bantam Books

(Kanzi) Savage-Rumbaugh, S. and R. Lewin (1994) *Kanzi: The Ape at the Brink of the Human Mind* John Wiley

Other References

Deacon, T. (1997) *The Symbolic Species* W.W. Norton

O'Grady, W., J. Archibald, M. Aronoff and J. Rees-Miller (2017) *Contemporary Linguistics* (7th edition) Bedford/St. Martins Press

Rimpau, J., R. Gardner and B. Gardner (1989) "Expression of person, place and instrument in ASL utterances of children and chimpanzees" In R. Gardner, B. Gardner and T. van Cantfort (eds.) *Teaching Sign Language to Chimpanzees* (240–268) State University of New York Press

Terrace, H. (1979) *Nim: A Chimpanzee Who Learned Sign Language* Knopf

3 The Sounds of Language

I take it you already know
Of tough and bough and cough and dough?
Others may stumble but not you
On hiccough, thorough, lough and through.
Well done! And now you wish, perhaps,
To learn of less familiar traps?
Beware of heard, a dreadful word,
That looks like beard and sounds like bird.
And dead: it's said like bed, not bead–
For goodness sake don't call it "deed"!
Watch out for meat and great and threat
(They rhyme with suite and straight and debt).

T. S. Watt (1954)

In Chapter 1, we noted some of the basic features of the human vocal tract and the intricate muscle interlacing in and around the mouth that give humans the ability to produce a wide range of sounds with great speed. Yet, as they chatter away, humans do not simply produce a random selection of these sounds. Only certain sounds are selected on a regular basis as significant for communicative activity. In order to identify and describe those sounds, we have to slow down the chatter of everyday talk and focus on each individual sound segment within the stream of speech. This may seem straightforward, but it is not an easy task.

Phonetics

Fortunately, there is an already established analytic framework for the study of speech segments that has been developed and refined for over a hundred years and is known as the **International Phonetic Alphabet**, or **IPA**. In this chapter, we will look at how some of the symbols of this alphabet can be used to represent the sounds of English words and what physical aspects of the human vocal tract are involved in the production of those sounds. The full IPA chart can be found at internationalphoneticalphabet.org and on the website: www.cambridge.org/yule7

The general study of the characteristics of speech sounds is called **phonetics**. Our main interest will be in **articulatory phonetics**, which is the study of how speech sounds are made, or articulated. Other areas of study are **acoustic phonetics**, which deals with the physical properties of speech as sound waves in the air, and **auditory phonetics** (or perceptual phonetics), which deals with the perception, via the ear, of speech sounds.

Consonants

We are not generally aware of how we produce speech sounds and it takes a certain amount of concentration on what we are doing with our mouths to become capable of describing the individual sounds produced. We will begin with the consonants. When we describe the articulation of a consonant, we focus on three features: the voiced/voiceless distinction, the place of articulation and the manner of articulation.

Voiced and Voiceless Sounds

To make a consonant sound, we start with the air pushed out by the lungs up through the trachea (or windpipe) to the larynx. Inside the larynx are your **vocal folds (or vocal cords)**, which take two basic positions.

1 When the vocal folds are spread apart, the air from the lungs passes between them with no obstruction, producing **voiceless sounds**.
2 When the vocal folds are drawn together, the air from the lungs repeatedly pushes them apart as it passes through, with a vibration effect, producing **voiced sounds**.

The distinction can be felt physically if you place a fingertip gently on the top of your Adam's apple (i.e. that part of your larynx you can feel in your neck below your chin), then produce sounds such as Z-Z-Z-Z or V-V-V-V. Because these are voiced sounds, you should be able to feel some vibration. Keeping your fingertip in the same position, now make the sounds S-S-S-S or F-F-F-F. Because these are voiceless sounds, there should be no vibration. Another trick is to put a finger in each ear, not too far, and produce the voiced sounds (e.g. Z-Z-Z-Z) to hear and feel some vibration, whereas no vibration will be heard or felt if you make voiceless sounds (e.g. S-S-S-S) in the same way.

Place of Articulation

Once the air has passed through the larynx, it enters the vocal tract and comes up via the pharynx, an extended tube shape about five inches (13 centimeters) long. It is then pushed out through the mouth (the oral tract) and/or the nose (the nasal tract). As noted in Chapter 1, we typically produce speech as we are breathing out and generally find it quite difficult to do very much talking while breathing in. Most consonant sounds are produced by using the tongue and other parts of the mouth to constrict, in some way, the shape of the oral tract through which the air is passing. The terms used to describe many sounds are those that denote the place of articulation of the sound: that is, the location inside the mouth at which the constriction takes place.

What we need is a slice of head. If we crack a head right down the middle, we will be able to see those parts of the oral cavity that are crucially involved in speech production. In Figure 3.1, in addition to lips and teeth, a number of other physical features are identified. To describe the place of articulation of most consonant sounds, we can start at the front of the mouth and work back. We can also keep the voiced–voiceless distinction in mind and begin using the symbols of the IPA for specific sounds. These symbols will be enclosed within square brackets [ ].

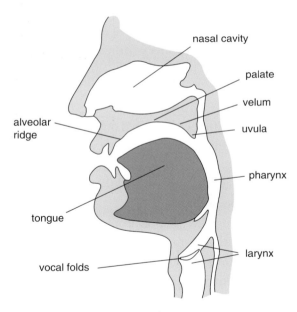

Figure 3.1 The human vocal tract

Familiar Symbols

Many of the symbols used in phonetics to describe consonant sounds will be familiar. We use [p] for the voiceless consonant in _pop_. We use [b] in _Bob_, [m] in _mom_ and [w] in _wet_ for the voiced versions. These are **bilabial** consonants, made with both lips.

We use [f] and [v] for the **labiodentals**, which are formed using the upper front teeth and the lower lip at the beginning of _fat_ and _vat_. The voiceless [f] is at the beginning and the voiced [v] is at the end of the pronunciation of _five_.

Behind the upper teeth is a rough area called the alveolar ridge. We raise the front of the tongue to this area when we make the **alveolar** sounds of [t] in _tot_, [d] in _dad_, [s], [z] in _size_, [r], [l] in _rail_ and [n] in _nun_; [t] and [s] are voiceless, [d], [z], [r], [l] and [n] are voiced.

 ## Unfamiliar Symbols

Other symbols may be much less familiar, as in the two ways of representing the "th" sounds in English. We use [θ], called "theta," for the voiceless version, as in _thin_ and _wrath_, and at the beginning and end of the phrase _three teeth_. We use [ð], called "eth," for the voiced version, as in _thus_, _then_, _feather_ and _loathe_. Because the teeth are involved in creating these sounds, they are called **dentals**. If these sounds are made with the tongue tip between (= inter) the teeth, they are described as **interdentals**.

There are some special symbols used for the sounds made in the middle area of the mouth, involving the tongue and the palate (the roof of the mouth). We use [ʃ] for the "sh" sound, as in _shout_ and _shoe-brush_, and [tʃ] for the "ch" sound, as in _child_ and _church_. These are voiceless consonants. Their voiced counterparts are [ʒ] for the sound in _treasure_ and _rouge_, and [dʒ] for the sound in _judge_ and _George_. Because they are produced in an area where the alveolar ridge meets the palate, these sounds ([ʃ], [tʃ], [ʒ], [dʒ]) are sometimes described as "post-alveolar" or "palato-alveolar," but we will just refer to them as **palatals**. Another palatal is the voiced sound [j], which often represents the sound of the written letter "y," as in _yes_, _yoyo_ and _lawyer_.

The sounds produced toward the back of the mouth, involving the velum, are represented by the **velars** [k], as in _kick_ (voiceless), and [g], as in _gag_ (voiced). Note that phonetic [g] is different from typewritten "g." Another velar consonant is [ŋ], called "angma," as in _thong_ and _ringing_. There is no [g] sound at the end of these words.

There is one consonant sound produced without the active use of the tongue. It is the [h] sound in _have_ and _hold_, and the first sound in _who_ and _whose_. This sound is described as a voiceless **glottal**. The "glottis" is the space between the vocal folds in the larynx. When the glottis is open, as in the production of other voiceless sounds, and there is no manipulation of the air passing out of the mouth, the sound produced is [h].

A summary of the place of articulation for each consonant is presented in Table 3.1.

TABLE 3.1 PLACE OF ARTICULATION

Consonants	Voiceless	Voiced	Place of articulation
Bilabials	[p]	[b], [m], [w]	both (=bi) lips (=labia)
	pet, tape	bet, met, wet	
Labiodentals	[f]	[v]	upper teeth with lower lip
	fat, safe	vat, save	
Dentals	[θ]	[ð]	tongue tip behind upper teeth
	thin, bath	then, bathe	
Alveolars	[t], [s]	[d], [z], [n], [l], [r]	tongue tip to alveolar ridge
	top, sit	dog, zoo, nut, lap, rap	
Palatals	[ʃ], [tʃ]	[ʒ], [dʒ], [j]	tongue and palate
	ship, chip	casual, gem, yet	
Velars	[k]	[g], [ŋ]	back of tongue and velum
	cat, back	gun, bang	
Glottals	[h]		space between vocal folds
	hat, who		

 Transcribing Sounds (Not Letters)

It is important to remember that written English is often a poor guide to pronunciation. We have already seen that words such as _bang_ and _tongue_ end with [ŋ] only, and there is no [g] sound despite the spelling. As shown in Table 3.1, there are some single sounds in English that are represented in spelling by two letters. We don't pronounce an [s] sound followed by an [h] sound at the beginning of _ship_; we use the single sound [ʃ]. Some sounds can have very different spellings, as in the underlined forms in _photo_ and _enough_. Both are pronounced as [f].

There are also words with letters that are not pronounced at all, as in the first and last letters of _write_ and the middle two letters of _right_. Both these words are pronounced as [raɪt]. Perhaps more tricky are letters that suggest one sound, but are pronounced with another. Try pronouncing the pairs _face_ versus _phase_ and _race_ versus _raise_. If you listen carefully, you will hear [s] at the end of the first word of each pair and [z] in the second.

Manner of Articulation

When we focus on the place of articulation for consonants, as in Table 3.1, we can see that [t] and [s] are similar in that they are both voiceless alveolars. But they are clearly different sounds. The difference is in how they are pronounced, or their manner of articulation. The [t] sound is a **stop** consonant. We produce stops by blocking the airflow very briefly, then letting it go abruptly. The sound [p] is another stop consonant. Go to a mirror and look at your lips as you say the word *pop*. That initial [p] is pronounced like a small explosion, so that in some descriptions the term "plosive" is used instead of stop for this type of articulation.

The [s] sound is a **fricative** consonant, produced by almost blocking the airflow, then letting the air escape through a narrow gap, creating friction. If you place the back of your hand against your chin while making a [sss] sound, you'll feel the air pushing downward after squeezing past the alveolar ridge behind the upper teeth. Other terms used to describe manner of articulation are included in Table 3.2. Note that "glides" may also be described as "approximants" or "semi-vowels."

 TABLE 3.2 MANNER OF ARTICULATION

Consonants	Voiceless	Voiced	Manner of articulation
Stops	[p], [t], [k]	[b], [d], [g]	block airflow, let it go abruptly
	*pe**t**, ta**lk***	*be**d**, do**g***	
Fricatives	[f], [θ], [s], [ʃ], [h]	[v], [ð], [z], [ʒ]	almost block airflow, let it escape through a narrow gap
	*fa**ith**, hou**se**, **sh**e,*	*va**se**, **the**, rou**ge***	
Affricates	[tʃ]	[dʒ]	combine a brief stop with a fricative
	ch**eap, ri**ch	***j**eep, ra**ge***	
Nasals		[m], [n], [ŋ]	lower the velum, let air flow out through nose
		*morni**ng**, **n**ame*	
Liquids		[l], [r]	raise and curl tongue, let airflow escape round the sides
		***l**oad, **l**ight, **r**oad, **wr**ite*	
Glides		[w], [j]	move tongue to or from a vowel
		***w**e, **w**ant, **y**es, **y**ou*	

A Consonant Chart

Having described the most common consonant sounds used by English speakers, we can summarize the information in a chart (Table 3.3). Along the top are the terms for place of articulation, as well as –V (voiceless) and + V (voiced). On the lefthand side are the terms for manner of articulation.

TABLE 3.3 CONSONANT CHART

	Bilabial		Labiodental		Dental		Alveolar		Palatal		Velar		Glottal	
	–V	+V	–V	+V	–V	+V	–V	+V	–V	+V	–V	+V	–V	+V
Stops	p	b					t	d			k	g		
Fricatives			f	v	θ	ð	s	z	ʃ	ʒ			h	
Affricates									tʃ	dʒ				
Nasals		m						n				ŋ		
Liquids								l r						
Glides		w								j				

Glottal Stops and Flaps

Missing from Table 3.3 are two ways of pronouncing consonants that may also be heard in English, usually in casual speech situations. The **glottal stop**, represented by the symbol [ʔ], is produced when the space between the vocal folds (the glottis) is closed completely very briefly, then released. Many speakers produce a glottal stop in the middle of *Uh-uh* (meaning "no"), when they say the name *Harry Potter* as if it didn't have the "H" or the "tt," or in the words *bottle* or *butter* without the "tt" part.

If, however, you are someone who pronounces the word *butter* in a way that is close to "budder," you are making a **flap**. It is represented by [ɾ]. This sound is produced by the tongue tip tapping the alveolar ridge briefly. Many American English speakers have a tendency to "flap" [t] and [d] consonants between vowels with the result that the pairs *latter/ladder*, *metal/medal* and *writer/rider* do not have distinct middle consonants. Those young students who were told about the importance of *Plato* in class and wrote it in their notes as *playdough* were clearly victims of a misinterpreted flap.

🔊 Vowels

While the consonant sounds are mostly articulated via obstruction in the vocal tract, **vowel** sounds are produced with a relatively free flow of air. They are all typically voiced. To describe vowel sounds, we consider the way in which the tongue influences the shape through which the airflow must pass. To talk about a place of articulation, we think of the space inside the mouth as having a front versus a back and a high versus a low area. Thus, in the pronunciation of *heat* and *hit*, we talk about "high, front" vowels because the sound is made with the front part of the tongue in a raised position.

In contrast, the vowel sound in *hat* is produced with the tongue in a lower position and the sound in *hot* can be described as a "low, back" vowel. The next time you're facing the bathroom mirror, try saying the words *heat, hit, hat, hot*. For the first two, your mouth will stay fairly closed, but for the last two, your tongue will move lower and cause your mouth to open wider. (The sounds of relaxation and pleasure typically contain lower vowels.)

We can use a vowel chart, like Table 3.4 (based on Ladefoged and Johnson, 2015), to help classify the most common vowel sounds in English, as illustrated in the words below.

 TABLE 3.4 VOWEL CHART

	Front	Central	Back
High	i		u
	ɪ		ʊ
Mid	e	ə	o
	ɛ	ʌ	ɔ
Low	æ		
		a	ɑ

Front vowels	Central vowels	Back vowels
[i] *bead, beef, key, me*	[ə] <u>a</u>bove, ov<u>e</u>n, s<u>u</u>pport	[u] *boo, move, two, you*
[ɪ] *bid, myth, w<u>o</u>men*	[ʌ] *butt, blood, dove, tough*	[ʊ] *book, could, put*
[ɛ] *bed, dead, said*		[ɔ] *born, caught, fall, raw*
[æ] *bad, laugh, wrap*		[ɑ] *Bob, cot, swan*

◀))) Diphthongs

In addition to single vowel sounds, we regularly create sounds that consist of a combination of two vowel sounds, known as **diphthongs**. When we produce diphthongs, our vocal organs move from one vocalic position [a] to another [ɪ] as we produce the sound [aɪ], as in *Hi* or *Bye*. The movement in this diphthong is from low toward high front. Alternatively, we can use movement from low toward high back, combining [a] and [ʊ] to produce the sound [aʊ], which is the diphthong repeated in the traditional speech training exercise [haʊ naʊ braʊn kaʊ]. In some descriptions, the movement is interpreted as involving a glide such as [j] or [w], so that the diphthongs we are representing as [aɪ] and [aʊ] may sometimes be seen as [aj] or [aw].

While the vowels [e], [a] and [o] are used as single sounds in other languages, and by speakers of different varieties of English, they are more often used as the first sounds of diphthongs in American English. Figure 3.2 provides a rough idea of how diphthongs are produced and is followed by a list of the sounds, with examples to illustrate some of the variation in the spelling of these sounds.

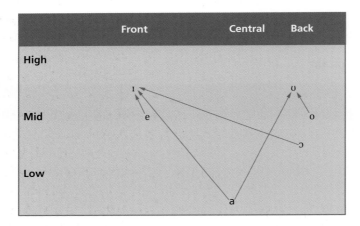

Figure 3.2 Diphthongs

[aɪ] *buy, eye, I, my, pie, sigh*   [oʊ] *boat, home, owe, throw, toe*
[aʊ] *bough, doubt, cow*   [ɔɪ] *boy, noise, royal*
[eɪ] *bait, eight, great, late, say*

American and British Diphthongs

The pronunciation of some diphthongs in Southern British English, following Roberts (2017), is noticeably different from North American English, as shown in Table 3.5. Note that the final [r] sound, normally pronounced in American varieties, is typically omitted in Southern British English, especially among higher social status speakers (see Table 19.1, page 297).

TABLE 3.5 DIFFERING DIPHTHONGS

	poor	*peer*	*pair*	*pour*	*pyre*	*power*
American	[pʊr]	[pir]	[peɪr]	[pour]	[paɪər]	[paʊər]
British	[pʊə]	[pɪə]	[pɛə]	[pɔə]	[paɪə]	[paʊə]

🔊 Subtle Individual Variation

Vowel sounds are notorious for varying between one variety of English and the next, often being a key element in what we recognize as different accents. It may be, for example, that you make no distinction between the vowels in the words *caught* and *cot* and use [ɑ] in both. You may also be used to seeing the vowel sound of *pet* represented as [e] in dictionaries rather than with [ɛ] as used here. For many speakers, [e] is the short vowel in words like *came* and *make*.

You may not make a significant distinction between the central vowels [ə], called "schwa," and [ʌ], called "wedge." If you're trying to transcribe, just use schwa [ə]. It is the unstressed vowel (underlined) in the everyday use of words such as a*fford*, *collapse, photograph, wanted*, and in those very common words *a* and *the* in casual speech. You can check the transcription in Task A on page 39 to see how often the schwa sound occurs. There are many other variations in the physical articulation of speech sounds. We didn't even mention the **uvula** ("little grape"), hanging at the end of the velum. It is used with the back of the tongue to produce **uvular** sounds, such as the "r" sound, usually represented by [ʀ], in the French pronunciation of *rouge* and *lettre*. The more we focus on the subtle differences in each sound, the more likely we are to find ourselves describing the pronunciation of a group or an individual speaker. Such differences help us to recognize a person's voice as soon as he or she speaks. But those differences do not explain how we understand what total strangers with unfamiliar voices are saying.

We are able to disregard variation in phonetic detail and identify each underlying sound type as part of a word with a particular meaning. Trying to understand how we do that takes us into phonology.

Study Questions

1   What different aspects of language are studied in articulatory phonetics, acoustic phonetics and auditory phonetics?

2   What do we call the space between the vocal folds?

3   How would you transcribe the final sound in the English word *tongue*?

4   Which of these words begins with a glottal in normal pronunciation?

    chip, photo, shoe, thus, who, yet

5   How many fricatives are there in the pronunciation of *mechanic*?

6   How do we describe the vowel in the normal pronunciation of *hot*?

7   In casual speech what is the most common vowel sound?

8   Which of the following words normally end with voiceless (–V) sounds and which end with voiced sounds (+ V) sounds?

    (a) bash _____   (d) fizz_____   (g) splat _____
    (b) clang _____   (e) rap_____   (h) thud _____
    (c) din _____   (f) smack _____   (i) wham _____

9   Try to pronounce the initial sounds of the following words and identify the place of articulation of each one (e.g. bilabial, alveolar, etc.).

    (a) calf _____   (e) hand _____   (i) shoulder _____
    (b) chin _____   (f) knee _____   (j) stomach _____
    (c) foot _____   (g) mouth _____   (k) thigh _____
    (d) groin _____   (h) pelvis _____   (l) toe _____

10   Identify the manner of articulation of the initial sounds in the following words (stop, fricative, etc.).

    (a) cheery _____   (d) funny _____   (g) merry _____
    (b) crazy _____   (e) jolly _____   (h) silly _____
    (c) dizzy _____   (f) loony _____   (i) wimpy _____

11   Which English words are usually pronounced as they are transcribed here?

    (a) baɪk _____   (e) haʊl_____   (i) maɪn _____
    (b) bædʒ _____   (f) hoʊpɪŋ _____   (j) pɪs _____
    (c) əndʒɔɪ _____   (g) hu _____   (k) tʃeɪndʒ _____
    (d) feɪs _____   (h) kloʊk _____   (l) ʃɪp _____

12   Using symbols introduced in this chapter, write a basic phonetic transcription of the most common pronunciation of the following words.

(a) catch _____   (e) noise _____   (i) thought _____
(b) doubt _____   (f) phone _____   (j) tough _____
(c) gem _____   (g) shy _____   (k) would _____
(d) measure_____   (h) these _____   (l) wring _____

Tasks

A   The following transcription was made by Peter Ladefoged of a speech sample of "a 21-year-old speaker who has lived all her life in Southern California" and included in the *Handbook of the International Phonetic Association* (1999: 41). Most of the phonetic symbols should be familiar, with the exception of [ɹ], which is close to [r], and [ɚ] which identifies the sound made when combining a schwa [ə] and [r]-type sound, often written in English as "er" or "ir."

Can you produce a written English version of this text?

ðə noɹθ wind ən ðə sʌn wɚ dɪspjutɪŋ wɪtʃ wəz ðə stɹɑŋgɚ, wɛn ə tɹævələ kem əlaŋ ɹæpt ɪn ə woɹm klok. ðe əgɹid ðət ðə wʌn hu fɚst səksidəd ɪn mekɪŋ ðə tɹævələ tek ɪz klok af ʃud bi kənsɪdəd stɹɑŋgɚ ðən ðɪ əðɚ. ðɛn ðə noɹθ wind blu əz haɹd əz i kud, bət ðə moɹ hi blu ðə moɹ klosli dɪd ðə tɹævlɚ fold hɪz klok əɹaund ɪm; æn ət læst ðə noɹθ wind gev ʌp ðɪ ətɛmpt. ðɛn ðə sʌn ʃaɪnd aʊt woɹmli, ənd ɪmidiətli ðə tɹævlɚ tuk af ɪz klok. ən so ðə noɹθ wɪnd wəz əblaɪʒ tɪ kənfɛs ðət ðə sʌn wəz ðə stɹɑŋgɚ əv ðə tu.

B   We noted that the relationship between the spelling and pronunciation of English words is not always simple. Keeping this in mind, try to provide a basic phonetic representation of the following words.

although, beauty, bomb, ceiling, charisma, choice, cough, exercise, hour, light, phase, quiche, quake, sixteen, thigh, tongue, whose, writhe

C   Using a dictionary if necessary, try to decide how each of the following words is usually pronounced. Then, put the words in five lists as illustrations of each of the sounds [eɪ], [i], [f], [k] and [ʃ]. Some words will be in more than one list.

air, belief, critique, crockery, Danish, gauge, giraffe, headache, keys, meat, mission, nation, ocean, pear, people, philosopher, queen, receipt, scene, Sikh, sugar, tough, weight

D   We can create a definition for each consonant (e.g. [k]) by using the distinction between voiced and voiceless plus the terms for place (i.e. velar) and manner of articulation (i.e. fricative). So we say that [k] is a voiceless velar fricative. Write similar definitions for the initial sounds in the normal pronunciation of the following words.

fan, lunch, goal, jail, mist, shop, sun, tall, yellow, zoo

Are there any definitions in which the voiced/voiceless distinction is actually unnecessary and could be omitted?

E   In some phonetic descriptions, particularly in traditional North American studies, the following four symbols are used: [š], [ž], [č], [ǰ]. The small v-shaped mark, called haček ("little hook") or caron, indicates some common feature in the pronunciation of these sounds. Based on the following examples, can you work out what that common feature is? What are the four equivalent symbols used in the International Phonetic Alphabet, as illustrated in Table 3.3 on page 34?

[eɪǰ], [ǰɪn], [trɛžər], [ruž], [čip], [roʊč], [šu], [fɪš]

F   The terms "obstruent" and "sonorant" are sometimes used in descriptions of how consonants are pronounced. Among the types of consonants already described (affricates, fricatives, glides, liquids, nasals, stops), which are obstruents, which are sonorants and why?

G   (i)   How would you make a retroflex sound?
        (ii)   How are retroflex sounds identified in phonetic transcription?
        (iii) With which varieties of English are retroflex sounds generally associated?

H   What is forensic phonetics?

I   When we change the English word *secret* [sikrət] to *secrecy* [sikrəsi], the pronunciation of the final consonant changes ([t] > [s]). This type of change is an example of lenition ("softening" or "weakening" from Latin *lenis* ("soft")).

    (i)   Look at the four sets of examples presented here and try to describe the change that takes place in the pronunciation of the final consonant in each set.
    (ii)   Thinking in terms of manner of articulation, can you provide a general description of the pattern of change found in all four sets?

    (a) *democrat > democracy*   (b) *act > action*
        diplomat > diplomacy   *inert > inertia*
        patient > patience   *integrate > integration*
    (c) *electric > electrician*   (d) *conclude > conclusion*
        magic > magician   *decide > decision*
        music > musician   *explode > explosion*

J The examples below are from Maninka, spoken in Guinea and surrounding countries in West Africa (based on Bird and Shopen, 1979). In some words, *-li* is added to a base form (e.g. *bo*) to create *boli*. In others, *-ni* is added to a base form (e.g. *don*) to create *donni*. Which one of the following analyses (a)–(d) best describes the phonetic basis of this difference?

boli	("going out")	*sigili*	("sitting down")
donni	("coming in")	*tali*	("going")
foli	("greeting")	*dumuni*	("eating")
minni	("drinking")	*tobili*	("cooking")
menni	("hearing")	*famuni*	("understanding")

(a) If the base form begins with a stop, use *-li*.
  If the base form begins with a fricative, use *-ni*.

(b) If there's a vowel at the end of the base form, use *-li*.
  If there's a consonant at the end of the base form, use *-ni*.

(c) If there isn't a nasal in the base form, use *-li*.
  If there is a nasal in the base form, use *-ni*.

(d) If there's a liquid in the base form, use *-li*.
  If there's a glide in the base form, use *-ni*.

Discussion Topics/Projects

I When we concentrate on the articulation of sounds, it's easy to forget that people listening to those sounds often have other clues to help them recognize what we're saying. In front of a mirror (or enlist a cooperative friend to be the speaker), say the following pairs of words. As you are doing this, can you decide which are rounded or unrounded vowels and which are tense or lax vowels? What clues are you using to help you make your decision?

   bet/bought coat/caught feed/food late/let mail/mole neat/knit

(For background reading, see chapter 5 of Ashby and Maidment, 2012.)

II English has a number of expressions such as *chit-chat* and *flip-flop* which never seem to occur in the reverse order (i.e. not *chat-chit* or *flop-flip*). Perhaps you can add examples to the following list of similar expressions.

criss-cross	*hip-hop*	*riff-raff*
dilly-dally	*knick-knacks*	*see-saw*
ding-dong	*mish-mash*	*sing-song*
fiddle-faddle	*ping-pong*	*tick-tock*
flim-flam	*pitter-patter*	*zig-zag*

(i)   Can you think of a phonetic description of the regular pattern of sounds in these expressions?

(ii) What kind of phonetic description might account for these other common pairings?

fuddy-duddy	*hocus-pocus*	*namby-pamby*
fuzzy-wuzzy	*hurly-burly*	*razzle-dazzle*
hanky-panky	*lovey-dovey*	*roly-poly*
helter-skelter	*mumbo-jumbo*	*super-duper*

(For background reading, see chapter 6 of Pinker, 1994.)

Further Reading

Basic Treatments

Knight, R-A. (2012) *Phonetics: A Coursebook* Cambridge University Press

Ladefoged, P. and K. Johnson (2015) *A Course in Phonetics* (7th edition) Wadsworth, Cengage Learning

More Detailed Treatments

Ashby, M. and J. Maidment (2012) *Introducing Phonetic Science* (2nd edition) Cambridge University Press

Ogden, R. (2017) *An Introduction to English Phonetics* (2nd edition) Edinburgh University Press

On Acoustic and Auditory Phonetics

Johnson, K. (2011) *Acoustic and Auditory Phonetics* (3rd edition) Wiley-Blackwell

On Phonetic Symbols

Ashby, P. (2005) *Speech Sounds* (2nd edition) Routledge

Pullum, G. and W. Ladusaw (1996) *Phonetic Symbol Guide* (2nd edition) University of Chicago Press

Phonetic Transcription of English

Tench, P. (2011) *Transcribing the Sound of English* Cambridge University Press

Phonetic Descriptions of Other Languages

Handbook of the International Phonetic Association (1999) Cambridge University Press www .ipachart.com

A Phonetics Dictionary

Crystal, D. (2008) *A Dictionary of Linguistics and Phonetics* (6th edition) Blackwell

On Pronunciation

Cox, F. (2012) *Australian English: Pronunciation and Transcription* Cambridge University Press

Cruttenden, A. (2008) *Gimson's Pronunciation of English* (7th edition) Hodder Arnold

Jones, D., P. Roach, J. Setter and J. Esling (2011) *Cambridge English Pronouncing Dictionary* (18th edition) Cambridge University Press

Kreidler, C. (2004) *The Pronunciation of English* (2nd edition) Blackwell

Pronunciation of Other Varieties of British English

Culpeper, J., P. Kerswill, R. Wodak, T. McEnery and F. Katamba (2018) *English Language* (chapters 2–3) (2nd edition) Palgrave Macmillan

Other References

Bird, C. and T. Shopen (1979) "Maninka" In T. Shopen (ed.) *Languages and Their Speakers* (59–111) Winthrop

Pinker, S. (1994) *The Language Instinct* William Morrow

Roberts, I. (2017) *The Wonders of Language* Cambridge University Press

See also soundsofspeech.uiowa.edu

4 The Sound Patterns of Language

Uans appona taim uas tri berres; mamma berre, pappa berre, e beibi berre. Live inne contri nire foresta. NAISE AUS. No mugheggia. Uanna dei pappa, mamma, e beibi go bice, orie e furghetta locche di dorra. Bai ene bai commese Goldilocchese. Sci garra natingha tu du batte meiche troble. Sci puscia olle fudde daon di maute; no live cromma. Den sci gos appesterrese enne slipse in olle beddse.

Bob Belviso, quoted in Espy (1975)

In the preceding chapter, we investigated the physical production of speech sounds in terms of the articulatory mechanisms of the human vocal tract. That investigation was possible because of some rather amazing facts about the nature of language. When we considered the human vocal tract, we didn't have to specify whether we were talking about a fairly large person, over 6 feet tall, weighing over 200 pounds, or about a rather small person, about 5 feet tall, weighing less than 100 pounds. Yet those two physically different individuals would inevitably have physically different vocal tracts, in terms of size and shape. In a sense, every individual has a physically different vocal tract. Consequently, in purely physical terms, every individual will pronounce sounds differently. There are, then, potentially millions of physically different ways of saying the simple word *me*.

🔊 Phonology

In addition to the millions of different individual vocal tracts that belong to humans all over the world, each individual will not pronounce the word *me* in a physically identical manner on every occasion. Obvious differences occur when that individual is shouting, or has just woken from a deep sleep, or is suffering from a bad cold, or is trying to ask for a sixth martini, or any combination of these. Given this vast range of potential differences in the actual physical production of a speech sound, how do we manage consistently to recognize all those versions of *me* as the form [mi], and not [ni] or [si] or [mæ] or [mo] or something else entirely? The answer to that question is provided to a large extent by the study of phonology.

Phonology is essentially the description of the systems and patterns of speech sounds in a language. It is, in effect, based on a theory of what every adult speaker of a language unconsciously knows about the sound patterns of that language. Because of this theoretical status, phonology is concerned with the abstract or mental aspect of the sounds in language rather than with the actual physical articulation of speech sounds. If we can make sense of Bob Belviso's comic introduction to the Goldilocks story at the start of this chapter, we must be using our phonological knowledge of sounds in English words to overcome some very unusual spellings. We can use various different ways of spelling the words in the first and second lines below, but the underlying phonological representation in the third line is constant. (See the end of the chapter for a full translation of the story.)

> Uans appona taim uas tri berres
> Ones up on atam waz theree bars
> /wʌns əpan ə taim wəz θri berz/

Phonology is about the underlying design, the blueprint of each sound type, which may vary in different physical contexts. When we think of the [t] sound in the words *tar, star, writer, butter* and *eighth* as being "the same," we actually mean that, in the phonology of English, they would be represented in the same way. In actual speech, these [t] sounds are all potentially very different from each other because they can be pronounced in such different ways in relation to the other sounds around them.

However, all these articulation differences in [t] sounds are less important to us than the distinction between the [t] sounds in general and the [k] sounds, or the [f] sounds, or the [b] sounds, because there are meaningful consequences related to the use of one rather than the others. These sounds must be distinct meaningful sounds, regardless of which individual vocal tract is being used to pronounce them, because they are what make the words *tar, car, far* and *bar* meaningfully distinct. Considered from this point of view, we can see that phonology is concerned with the abstract representation of sounds in our minds that enables us to recognize and interpret the meaning of words on the basis of the actual physical sounds we say and hear.

 **Phonemes**

Each one of these meaning-distinguishing sounds in a language is described as a **phoneme**. When we learn to use alphabetic writing, we are actually using the concept of the phoneme as the single stable sound type that is represented by a single written symbol. It is in this sense that the phoneme /t/ is described as a sound type, of which all the different spoken versions of [t] are tokens. Note that slash marks are conventionally used to indicate a phoneme, /t/, an abstract segment, as opposed to the square brackets, as in [t], used for each phonetic or physically produced segment.

An essential property of a phoneme is that it functions contrastively. We know there are two phonemes /f/ and /v/ in English because they are the only basis of the contrast in meaning between the words *fat* and *vat*, or *fine* and *vine*. This contrastive property is the basic operational test for determining the phonemes in a language. If we change one sound in a word and there is a change of meaning, the sounds are distinct phonemes.

Natural Classes

The descriptive terms we used to talk about sounds in Chapter 3 can be considered "features" that distinguish each phoneme from the next. If the feature is present, we mark it with a plus sign (+) and if it is not present, we use a minus sign (−). Thus /p/ can be characterized as [− voice, + bilabial, + stop] and /k/ as [− voice, + velar, + stop]. Because these two sounds share some features, they are sometimes described as members of a **natural class** of phonemes. Phonemes that have certain features in common tend to behave phonologically in some similar ways. Table 4.1 presents an analysis of some of the distinctive features of four English phonemes. Only /p/ and /k/ have sufficient features in common to be members of a natural class. They are both voiceless stops.

In contrast, /v/ has the features [+ voice, + labiodental, + fricative] and so cannot be in the same natural class of sounds as /p/ and /k/. Although other factors will be involved, this feature analysis could lead us to suspect that there may be a good phonological reason why words beginning with /pl-/ and /kl-/ are common in English, but words beginning with /vl-/ or /nl-/are not. This type of feature analysis allows us to describe not only individual phonemes, but also the possible sequences of phonemes in a language.

TABLE 4.1 DISTINCTIVE FEATURES OF FOUR ENGLISH PHONEMES

/p/	/k/	/v/	/n/
−voice	−voice	+voice	+voice
+bilabial	+velar	+labiodental	+alveolar
+stop	+stop	+ fricative	+nasal

◀))) Phones and Allophones

While the phoneme is the abstract unit or sound type ("in the mind"), there are many different versions of that sound type regularly produced in actual speech ("in the mouth"). We can describe those different versions as **phones**, which are phonetic units, in square brackets. When we have a set of phones, all of which are versions of one phoneme, we add the prefix "allo-" (meaning one of a closely related set) and call them **allophones** of that phoneme.

For example, the phoneme /t/ can be pronounced in a number of physically different ways as phones. The [t] sound in the word *tar* is normally pronounced with a stronger puff of air than is present in the [t] sound in the word *star*. If you put the back of your hand in front of your mouth as you say *tar*, then *star*, you should feel some physical evidence of **aspiration** (the puff of air) accompanying the [t] sound at the beginning of *tar* (but not in *star*). This aspirated phone is represented more precisely as [tʰ].

In the last chapter, we noted that the [t] sound between vowels in a word like *writer* often becomes a flap, which we can represent as [ɾ]. That's another phone.

We also saw that a word like *butter* can have a glottal stop as the middle consonant in the pronunciation, so the part written as "t" may be pronounced as [ʔ], which is yet another phone. In the pronunciation of a word like *eighth* (/eɪtθ/), the influence of the final dental [θ] sound causes a dental articulation of the [t] sound. This can be represented more precisely as [t̪]. That's yet another phone. There are even more variations of this sound which, like [tʰ], [ɾ], [ʔ] and [t̪], can be represented in a more precise way in a detailed, or narrow phonetic transcription. Because these variations are all part of one set of phones, they are referred to as allophones of the phoneme /t/, as shown in Table 4.2.

The crucial distinction between phonemes and allophones is that substituting one phoneme for another will result in a word with a different meaning (as well as a different pronunciation), but substituting allophones only results in a different (and perhaps unusual) pronunciation of the same word.

TABLE 4.2 ALLOPHONES

Phoneme	Allophones	
	[tʰ]	(*tar*)
	[ɾ]	(*writer*)
/t/		
	[ʔ]	(*butter*)
	[t̪]	(*eighth*)

Complementary Distribution

When we have two different pronunciations (allophones) of a sound type (phoneme), each used in different places in words, they are said to be in **complementary distribution**. That is, the [t^h] pronunciation of the phoneme /t/ with aspiration is used word-initially, as in *tar*, but never after another consonant in initial position, as in *star*. The places where /t/ occurs with aspiration, and without aspiration, never overlap and so the different pronunciations are in complementary distribution.

Minimal Pairs and Sets

Phonemic distinctions in a language can be tested via pairs and sets of words. When two words such as *fan* and *van* are identical in form except for a contrast in one phoneme, occurring in the same position, the two words are described as a **minimal pair**. When a group of words can be differentiated, each one from the others, by changing one phoneme (always in the same position in the word), they are described as a **minimal set**. Examples of contrasting pairs and sets are presented in Table 4.3.

TABLE 4.3 MINIMAL PAIRS AND SETS

Minimal pairs		Minimal sets
fan – van	bath – math	big – pig – rig – fig – dig – wig
bat –beat	math – myth	fat – fit – feet –fete – foot – fought
sit –sing	myth –Mick	cat –can – cap – cab – cash – cadge

Phonotactics

This type of exercise with minimal sets also allows us to see that there are definite patterns in the types of sound combinations permitted in a language. The first minimal set in Table 4.3 does not include forms such as *lig* or *vig*. According to my dictionary, these are not English words, but they could be viewed as possible English words. That is, our phonological knowledge of the pattern of sounds in English words would allow us to treat these forms as acceptable if, at some future time, they came into use. They might, for example, begin as invented abbreviations (*I think Bubba is one very ignorant guy.* ~ *Yeah, he's a big vig!*). Until then, they represent "accidental" gaps in the vocabulary of English. It is, however, no accident that forms such as [fsɪg] or [rnɪg] do not exist or are unlikely ever to exist. They have been formed without obeying some constraints on the sequence or position of English phonemes. Such constraints are called the **phonotactics** (i.e. permitted arrangements of sounds) in a language and are obviously part of every speaker's phonological knowledge. Because these constraints operate on a unit that is larger than the single segment or phoneme, we have to move on to a consideration of the basic structure of that larger phonological unit called the syllable.

Syllables

A **syllable** must contain a vowel or vowel-like sound, including diphthongs. The most common type of syllable also has a consonant (C) before the vowel (V) and is represented as CV. The basic elements of the syllable are the **onset** (one or more consonants) followed by the **rhyme**. The rhyme (sometimes written as "rime") consists of a vowel, which is treated as the **nucleus**, plus any following consonant(s), described as the **coda**.

Syllables like *me, to* or *no* have an onset and a nucleus, but no coda. They are known as **open syllables**. When a coda is present, as in the syllables *up, cup, at* or *hat*, they are called **closed syllables**. The basic structure of the kind of syllable found in English words like *green* (CCVC), *eggs* (VCC), *and* (VCC), *ham* (CVC), *I* (V), *do* (CV), *not* (CVC), *like* (CVC), *them* (CVC), *Sam* (CVC), *I* (V), *am* (VC) is shown in Figure 4.1.

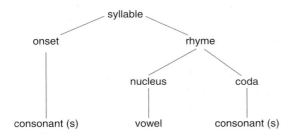

Figure 4.1 Syllable structure

 Consonant Clusters

Both the onset and the coda can consist of more than a single consonant, also known as a **consonant cluster**. The combination /st/ is a consonant cluster (CC) used as onset in the word *stop*, and as coda in the word *post*. There are many CC onset combinations permitted in English phonotactics, as in *black, bread, trick, twin, flat* and *throw*. Note that liquids (/l/, /r/) and a glide (/w/) are used in second position.

English can actually have larger onset clusters, as in the words *stress* and *splat*, consisting of three initial consonants (CCC). When we study the phonotactics of these larger onset consonant clusters, we can find a fairly regular pattern. The first consonant must always be /s/, followed by one of the natural class of voiceless stops (/p/, /t/, /k/), plus a liquid or a glide (/l/, /r/, /w/). We can check if this description is adequate for the combinations in *splash, spring, strong, scream* and *squeeze* (/skwiz/). Does the description also cover the second syllable in the pronunciation of *exclaim*? How about /ɛk-skleɪm/? Remember that it is the onset of the syllable that is being described, not the beginning of the word. See Task D on page 53 for more syllables and clusters.

Coarticulation Effects

It is quite unusual for languages to have large consonant clusters of the type just described. In English, large clusters may be reduced in casual conversational speech, particularly if they occur in the middle of a word. This is just one example of a process that is usually discussed in terms of **coarticulation effects**.

In much of the preceding discussion, we have been describing speech sounds in syllables and words as if they are always pronounced carefully in slow motion. Speech is not normally like that. Mostly our talk is fast and spontaneous, and it requires our articulators to move from one sound to the next without stopping. The process of making one sound almost at the same time as the next sound is called coarticulation.

 ### Assimilation

When two sound segments occur in sequence and some aspect of one segment is taken or "copied" by the other, the process is known as **assimilation**. In the physical production of speech, this regular process happens simply because it is quicker, easier and more efficient for our articulators as they do their job. Think of the word *have* /hæv/ by itself, then think of how it is pronounced in the phrase *I have to go* in everyday speech. In this phrase, as we start to say the /t/ sound in *to*, which is voiceless, we tend to produce a voiceless version of the preceding sound, resulting in what sounds more like /f/ than /v/. So, we typically say [hæftə] in this phrase and you may even see it written informally as "hafta," showing how the assimilation from a voiced to a voiceless sound is perceived.

 ### Nasalization

Vowels are also subject to assimilation. In isolation, we would typically pronounce [ɪ] and [æ] with no nasal quality at all. However, when we say the words *pin* and *pan* in everyday talk, the anticipation of the final nasal consonant makes it easier to go into the nasalized articulation in advance. This process is known as **nasalization** and can be represented with a small diacritic (~), called "tilde," over the vowel symbol. The vowel sounds in those words will be, in more precise transcription, [ĩ] and [æ̃]. This process is such a regular feature of English that a phonological rule can be stated in the following way: "Any vowel becomes nasal whenever it immediately precedes a nasal."

This type of assimilation process occurs in a variety of different contexts. By itself, the word *can* may be pronounced as [kæn], but, when we say *I can go*, the influence of the following velar [g] in *go* will typically make the preceding nasal sound come out as [ŋ] (velar) rather than [n] (alveolar). The most commonly observed conversational version of the phrase is [aɪkəŋgoʊ]. Notice that the vowel in *can* has also changed to schwa [ə] from the isolated-word version [æ]. We may also pronounce *and* as [ænd] by itself, but in the normal use of the phrase *you and me*, we usually say [ən], as in [juənmi].

Elision

In the last example, illustrating the normal pronunciation of *you and me*, the [d] sound of the word *and* was not included in the transcription. That is because it is not usually pronounced in this phrase. In the environment of a preceding nasal [n] and a following nasal [m], we simply don't devote speech energy to including the stop sound [d].

There is also typically no [d] sound included in the everyday pronunciation of a word like *friendship* [frɛnʃɪp]. This process of not pronouncing a sound segment that might be present in the deliberately careful pronunciation of a word in isolation is described as **elision**. In consonant clusters, especially in coda position, /t/ is a common casualty in this process, as in the typical pronunciation [æspɛks] for *aspects*, or in [himəsbi] for the phrase *he must be*. We can, of course, slowly and deliberately pronounce each part of the phrase *we asked him*, but the process of elision (of /k/) in casual conversation is likely to produce [wiæstəm].

Vowels also disappear through elision, with the result that sometimes a whole syllable may not be pronounced, as in [ɛvri] for *every*, [ɪntrɪst] for *interest*, [kæbnət] for *cabinet*, [kæmrə] for *camera*, [prɪznər] for *prisoner* and [spoʊz] for *suppose*.

These processes are summarized in Table 4.4. We use a pair of symbols (/ ____) to indicate "in the context of" or "under the influence of" the following element.

TABLE 4.4 COARTICULATION EFFECTS

Assimilation:	making a sound segment more similar to the next one
	voiced (→ voiceless) /____ + voiceless: hæv + tu → hæftə
Nasalization:	adding a nasal quality to a sound segment before a nasal sound
	non-nasal (→ nasal) /____ + nasal: pæ + n → pæ̃n
Elision:	leaving out a sound segment
	consonant cluster (→ reduced) / ____ + consonant: məst + bi → məsbi
	three syllables (→ two syllables) /____ + syllable: prɪzənər → prɪznər

Normal Speech

These processes of assimilation, nasalization and elision occur in everyone's normal speech and should not be regarded as some type of sloppiness or laziness in speaking. In fact, consistently avoiding the regular patterns of assimilation, nasalization and elision used in a language would result in extremely artificial-sounding talk. The point of investigating these phonological processes is not to arrive at a set of rules about how a language should be pronounced, but to try to come to an understanding of the regularities and patterns that underlie the actual use of sounds in language.

Study Questions

1   Is phonology mainly concerned with sound tokens, sound types or sound spelling relationships?

2   Which of these phonemes are members of a natural class?

/b/, /f/, /g/, /m/

3   In French, the words /bo/ for *beau* ("handsome") and /bõ/ for *bon* ("good") seem to have different vowels. Are these two vowels allophones or phonemes in French?

4   Which English phoneme has the features: –voice, +velar, +stop?

5   What is an aspirated sound and which of the following words would normally be pronounced with one?

kill, pool, skill, spool, stop, top

6   Does this phrase (*big black bag*) contain a minimal pair, a minimal set, or neither?

7   Which of the following words would be treated as minimal pairs?

ban, fat, pit, bell, tape, heat, meal, more, pat, tap, pen, chain, vote, bet, far, bun, goat, heel, sane, tale, vet

8   What is meant by the phonotactics of a language?

9   In the pronunciation of *track*, which sound(s) would be the nucleus?

10   What is the difference between an open and a closed syllable?

11   Is the nasal consonant in the everyday pronunciation of *I can go* alveolar or velar?

12   Which segments in the pronunciation of the following words are most likely to be affected by elision?
    (a) *government*   (b) *postman*   (c) *pumpkin*   (d) *sandwich*   (e) *victory*

Tasks

A   What are diacritics and which ones were used in this chapter to identify sounds?

B   Individual sounds are described as segments. What are suprasegmentals?

C   (i)   In the phonology of the Hawaiian language there are only open syllables. Using this information, can you work out how English "Merry Christmas" became

"Mele Kalikimaka" for people in Hawai'i? Also, based on this slender evidence, which two English consonants are probably not phonemes in Hawaiian?

(ii) Including the glottal stop /ʔ/, described in Chapter 3, Hawaiian has eight consonant phonemes. Looking at the list of Hawaiian names below, can you identify the other seven Hawaiian consonants?

(iii) Can you pair each Hawaiian name with its matching English name from the second list (e.g. *Henele = Henry*)?

Henele, Kala, Kalona, Kania,   *Bev, David, Fabian, Fred,*

Kawika, Keoki, Kimo, Likeke,   *George, Henry, Jim, Richard,*

Lopaka, Papiano, Peleke, Pewi   *Robert, Sarah, Sharon, Tanya*

D The word *central* has a consonant cluster (*-ntr-*) in the middle and two syllables. What do you think is the best way to divide the word into two syllables (*ce + ntral, centr + al, cen + tral, cent + ral*) and why?

E The English words *lesson* and *little* are typically pronounced with syllabic consonants.

(i) What exactly is a syllabic consonant and how would it appear in a phonetic transcription?

(ii) Which of these words would most likely be pronounced with a syllabic consonant?

bottle, bottom, button, castle, copper, cotton, paddle, schism, wooden

F We can use the phonology of English as a guide to some regularities in spelling, based on a distinction between shorter vowels and longer vowels (including diphthongs).

(i) Complete Table 4.5 by adding the minimal pairs to appropriate columns to illustrate differences in spelling that match differences in pronunciation here. Can you also add the appropriate phonological forms of the three diphthongs at the top of each column?

(ii) Can you state a general principle connecting spelling to phonology (in these examples)?

back, bake, cock, coke, dame, damn, diner, dinner, dole, doll, hoping, hopping, later, latter, Mick, Mike, mile, mill

TABLE 4.5 ENGLISH PHONOLOGY AND SPELLING

/æ/	/ /	/ɑ/	/ /	/ɪ/	/ /
back					

G In addition to assimilation, as described in the chapter, there is another phonological process known as **dissimilation**, in which a sound or syllable changes to become less like a nearby sound. An everyday example is the typical pronunciation of *February*, where two /r/ sounds are in close proximity. Speakers tend to change the first /r/ to a glide /j/, resulting in something like "Febuary" /fɛbjuəri/.

(i)   This process occurs in the pronunciation of some adverbs with *-ly*, derived from adjectives like *able* (but not **ablely*). What is the typical pronunciation of the adverbs formed from these adjectives plus *-ly: gentle, humble, probable*?

(ii) How does dissimilation operate in the everyday pronunciation of these words: *authoritative, deteriorate, fifth, library*?

H In the Spanish words *mi<u>s</u>mo* ("same") and *i<u>s</u>la* ("island"), the "s" is pronounced as [z], but in the words *e<u>s</u>te* ("this") and *pe<u>s</u>cado* ("fish"), the "s" is pronounced [s].

(i)   Based on these and the following examples, what is the rule for choosing [z] or [s]?

(<u>s</u> = [z])	(<u>s</u> = [s])
béi<u>s</u>bol ("baseball")	*E<u>s</u>paña* ("Spain")
de<u>s</u>de ("from")	*ca<u>s</u>a* ("house")
ra<u>s</u>gado ("torn")	*si<u>s</u>tema* ("system")
sociali<u>s</u>mo ("socialism")	*sociali<u>s</u>ta* ("socialist")

(ii) Based on this (rather slim) evidence, would you say that the difference is phonemic or allophonic?

I A general distinction can be made among languages depending on their basic rhythm, whether they have syllable-timing or stress-timing. How are these two types of rhythm distinguished and which type characterizes the pronunciation of English, French and Spanish?

J The following examples are from Cree, a Native American or Aboriginal language spoken in many areas across Canada. It has been noted that voiced and voiceless stops have different distributions in Cree than in English.

(i)   Can you describe the distribution of [p] and [b] by analyzing the places they occur in the following words (from Cowan and Rakušan, 1999)?

(ii) Based on this limited evidence, would you say that [p] and [b] are likely to be phonemes or allophones in Cree?

(1) *peyak*	("one")	(5) *asabap*	("thread")
(2) *nistosap*	("twelve")	(6) *kiba*	("soon")
(3) *tanispi*	("when")	(7) *mibit*	("tooth")
(4) *ospuagan*	("pipe")	(8) *nabeu*	("man")

K The following examples are from Dong, a Sino-Tibetan language spoken in southern China, based on Long and Zheng (1998), and adapted here from Yule and Overstreet (2017: 15). This language is also known as Kam.

(i) Choose words from this list to fill the spaces (1)–(6).

wen wjan wjen wang wut wju wo√ wəi√

(ii) What is the regular phonological relationship between the initial sounds of the syllables for "two" compared to "one" of the items?

ja po ("two bowls")	ji <u>wo</u> ("one bowl")
ja məi ("two coats")	ji <u>wəi</u> ("one coat")
(1) ja pjen ("two pages")	ji _____ ("one page")
(2) ja mju ("two lines")	ji _____ ("one line")
(3) ja wut ("two tufts")	ji _____ ("one tuft")
(4) ja men ("two slices")	ji _____ ("one slice")
(5) ja pang ("two buckets")	ji _____ ("one bucket")
(6) ja mjan ("two months")	ji _____ ("one month")

Discussion Topics/Projects

I We can form negative versions of words such as *audible* and *edible* in English by adding *in* to produce *inaudible* and *inedible*. How would you describe the special phonological processes involved in the pronunciation of the negative versions of the following words?

balance, compatible, complete, decent, glorious, gratitude, legal, literate, mature, per-fect, possible, rational, responsible, sane, tolerant, variable

(For background reading, see chapter 3 (pages 75–78) of Payne, 2006.)

II The use of plural *-s* in English has three different, but very regular, phonological alternatives:

We add /s/ to words like bat, book, cough and ship.
We add /z/ to words like cab, cave, lad, rag and thing.
We add /əz/ or /ɪz/ to words like bus, bush, church, judge and maze.

(i)   Can you identify the sets of sounds that regularly precede each of these alternative pronunciations of the plural ending?

(ii)   What are the features that each of these sets has in common?

(For background reading, see chapter 2 (pages 55–56) of Jeffries, 2006.)

Bob Belviso Translated

One attempt to interpret those very unusual spellings on page 44 might be as follows:

Once upon a time was three bears; mama bear, papa bear and baby bear. Live in the country near the forest. NICE HOUSE. No mortgage. One day papa, mama and baby go beach, only they forget to lock the door.

By and by comes Goldilocks. She got nothing to do but make trouble. She push all the food down the mouth; no leave a crumb. Then she goes upstairs and sleeps in all the beds.

Further Reading

Basic Treatments

Davenport, M. and S. Hannahs (2013) *Introducing Phonetics and Phonology* (3rd edition) Routledge

McCully, C. (2009) *The Sound Structure of English: An Introduction* Cambridge University Press

McMahon, A. (2002) *An Introduction to English Phonology* (16–17) Edinburgh University Press

More Detailed Treatments

Carr, P. (2013) *English Phonetics and Phonology* (2nd edition) Wiley-Blackwell

Odden, D. (2014) *Introducing Phonology* (2nd edition) Cambridge University Press

Roach, P. (2009) *English Phonetics and Phonology* (4th edition) Cambridge University Press

Syllables

Duanmu, S. (2008) *Syllable Structure* Oxford University Press

Ladefoged, P. and K. Johnson (2015) *A Course in Phonetics* (7th edition) (chapter 10) Wadsworth, Cengage

Phonotactics

Bauer, L. (2015a) "English phonotactics" *English Language and Linguistics* 19: 437–475

Herbst, T. (2010) *English Linguistics* (chapter 5) De Gruyter

Coarticulation

Hardcastle, W. and N. Hewlett (2006) *Coarticulation: Theory, Data and Techniques* Cambridge University Press

Assimilation and Elision

Brown, G. (1990) *Listening to Spoken English* (2nd edition) Longman

Other References

Cowan, W. and J. Rakušan (1999) *Source Book for Linguistics* (3rd edition) John Benjamins

Jeffries, L. (2006) *Discovering Language* Palgrave Macmillan

Long, Y. and G. Zheng (1998) *The Dong Language in Guizhou Province, China* Translated by D. Leary. The Summer Institute of Linguistics, The University of Texas at Arlington, Publication 126

Payne, T. (2006) *Exploring Language Structure* Cambridge University Press

Yule, G. and M. Overstreet (2017) *Puzzlings* Amazon Books

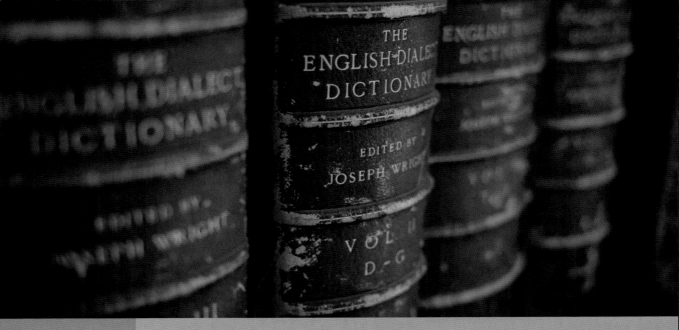

5 | Word Formation

Autocorrect I could do without. It thinks I am stupid and clumsy, and while it's true that I don't know how to disable it and I can't text with thumbs like a teenager (though I am prehensile), why would I let a machine tell me what I want to say? I text someone "Good night" in German, and instead of "Gute Nacht" I send "Cute Nachos." I type "adverbial," and it comes out "adrenal," which is like a knife to my adverbial gland. Invited to dinner, I text my friend to ask whether I can bring anything, and she replies that the "food and dissertation" are under control.

Norris (2015)

The creation of new words in a language never stops and English is one language that is particularly fond of adding to its large vocabulary. Traditionally, we would check in a dictionary to be sure that we were using the right word, with correct spelling, but technological advances have provided us with programs that do the checking for us, or, even more insidiously, as in the situation described by Mary Norris above, try to choose the words for us. Unfortunately, at the moment, these programs do not seem to have any way of knowing if the words that are chosen are appropriate or if it is quite normal to send someone a communication out of the blue that reads "cute nachos." In this chapter, we won't solve the problem of inappropriate choice of words, but we will look in some detail at how those words came to be part of the language.

Neologisms

Around 1900, in New Berlin, Ohio, a department-store worker named J. Murray Spangler invented a device that he called an *electric suction sweeper*. This device eventually became very popular and could have become known as a *spangler*. People could have been *spanglering* their floors or they might even have *spanglered* their rugs and curtains. The use could have extended to a type of person who droned on and on (and really sucked), described as *spanglerish*, or to a whole style of behavior called *spanglerism*. However, none of that happened. Instead, Mr. Spangler sold his new invention to a local business-man called William H. Hoover, whose Hoover Suction Sweeper Company produced the first machine called a "Hoover." Not only did the word *hoover* (without a capital letter) become as familiar as *vacuum cleaner* all over the world, but in Britain, people still talk about *hoovering* (and not *spanglering*) their carpets.

The point of this small tale is that, although we had never heard of Mr. Spangler before, we really had no difficulty coping with the new words: *spangler, spanglerish, spanglerism, spanglering* or *spanglered*. That is, we can very quickly understand a new word, a **neologism**, and accept the use of different forms of that new word in the language. This ability must derive in part from the fact that there is a lot of regularity in the word-formation processes in a language. In this chapter, we will explore some of the basic processes by which new words are created.

Etymology

The study of the origin and history of a word is known as its **etymology**, a term which, like many of our technical words, comes to us through Latin, but has its origins in Greek (*étymon* "original form" + *logia* "study of"), and is not to be confused with *entomology*, also from Greek (*éntomon* "insect"). Greek and Latin are the sources of many English words, often providing alternative ways to describe things, such as *mono-* from Greek (*mono-cycle*) and *uni-* from Latin (*uni-cycle*). The other major source, Germanic, provides an alternative form *one-* (*one-wheeled cycle*).

When we look closely at the etymologies of everyday words, we soon discover that there are many different ways in which new words can enter the language. We should keep in mind that a lot of words in daily use today were, at one time, considered barbaric misuses of the language. It is difficult now to understand the views expressed in the early nine-teenth century over the "tasteless innovation" of a word like *handbook*, or the horror expressed by a London newspaper in 1909 over the use of the newly coined word *aviation*. Yet many new words can cause similar outcries as they come into use today. Rather than act as if the language is being debased, we might prefer to view the constant evolution of new words and new uses of old words as a reassuring sign of vitality and creativeness in the way a language is shaped by the needs of its users.

Borrowing

One of the most common sources of new words in English is the process simply labeled **borrowing**, that is, the taking over of words from other languages. (Technically, it's more than just borrowing, because English doesn't give them back.) Throughout its history, the English language has adopted a vast number of words from other languages, including these examples:

dope (Dutch)   *piano* (Italian)   *tattoo* (Tahitian)
jewel (French)   *pretzel* (German)   *tycoon* (Japanese)
glitzy (Yiddish) *ski* (Norwegian)   *yogurt* (Turkish)
lilac (Persian)   *sofa* (Arabic)   *zebra* (Bantu)

Sometimes a new sound comes along along with new words. The voiced fricative /ʒ/ became part of English through borrowed French words such as *mea<u>s</u>ure* and *rou<u>ge</u>*.

Other languages, of course, borrow terms from English, as in the Japanese use of *suupaa* or *suupaamaaketto* ("supermarket") and *taipuraitaa* ("typewriter"). We can also hear of people in Finland using a *šekki* ("check") to pay their bills, Hungarians talking about *sport*, *klub* and *futbal*, or the French discussing problems of *le stress*, over a glass of *le whisky*, during *le weekend*.

In Brazilian Portuguese, the English words *up* and *nerd* have been borrowed and turned into verbs for the new activities *upar* ("to upload") and *nerdear* ("to surf the internet"). In some cases, the borrowed words are used with quite novel meanings, as in the contemporary German use of the English words *partner* and *look* in the phrase *im Partnerlook* to describe two people who are together and wearing similar clothing. Other German uses of English words are illustrated in Task F on page 69.

Loan-Translation

A special type of borrowing is described as **loan-translation** or **calque** (/kælk/). In this process, there is a direct translation of the elements of a word into the borrowing language. Interesting examples are the French term *gratte-ciel*, which literally translates as "scrape-sky," the Dutch *wolkenkrabber* ("cloud scratcher") or the German *Wolkenkratzer* ("cloud scraper"), all of which were calques for the English *skyscraper*.

The English word *superman* is thought to be a loan-translation of the German *Übermensch*, and the term *loanword* itself is believed to have come from the German *Lehnwort*. The English expression *moment of truth* is believed to be a calque from the Spanish phrase *el momento de la verdad*, though not restricted to the original use as the final thrust of the sword to end a bullfight. Nowadays, some Spanish speakers eat *perros calientes* (literally "dogs hot") or *hot dogs*, which have nothing to do with those four-legged *perros*. The American concept of "boyfriend" was borrowed, with sound change, into Japanese as *boyifurendo*, but as a calque into Chinese as "male friend" or *nan pengyu*.

Compounding

In some of the examples we have just considered, there is a joining of two separate words to produce a single form. Thus, *Lehn* and *Wort* are combined to produce *Lehnwort* in German. This combining process, technically known as **compounding**, is very common in languages such as German and English, but much less common in languages such as French and Spanish. Common English compounds are *bookcase, doorknob, fingerprint, sunburn, textbook, wallpaper, wastebasket* and *waterbed*. All these examples are nouns, but we can also create compound adjectives (*good-looking, low-paid*) and compounds of adjective (*fast*) plus noun (*food*) as in *a fast-food restaurant* or *a full-time job*.

This very productive source of new terms has been well documented in English and German, but can also be found in totally unrelated languages, such as Hmong (spoken in Laos and Vietnam), which has many recently created compounds. (More examples can be found in Task I, on page 70.)

hwj ("pot")	+ *kais* ("spout")		= *hwjkais* ("kettle")
paj ("flower")	+ *kws* ("corn")		= *pajkws* ("popcorn")
hnab ("bag")	+ *rau* ("put")	+ *ntawv* ("paper")	= *hnabrauntawv* ("schoolbag")

Blending

The combination of two separate forms to produce a single new term is also present in the process called **blending**. However, in blending, we typically take only the beginning of one word and join it to the end of the other word. To talk about the combined effects of *smoke* and *fog*, we can use the word *smog*. In places where they have a lot of this stuff, they can jokingly make a distinction between *smog, smaze* (smoke + haze) and *smurk* (smoke + murk). In Hawai'i, near the active volcano, they have problems with *vog*. Some common examples of blending are *bit* (binary/digit), *brunch* (breakfast/lunch), *motel* (motor/hotel), *telecast* (television/broadcast), *Oxbridge* (Oxford/Cambridge) for both universities considered together and the *Chunnel* (Channel/tunnel) connecting England and France.

The activity of fund-raising on television that feels like a marathon is typically called a *telethon*, while *infotainment* (information/entertainment) and *simulcast* (simultaneous/broadcast) are other new blends from life with television. To describe the mixing of languages, some people talk about *Franglais* (Français/Anglais) and *Spanglish* (Spanish/English). In a few blends, we combine the beginnings of both words, as in terms from information technology, such as *telex* (teleprinter/exchange) or *modem* (modulator/demodulator). A blend from the beginnings of two French words *velours croché* ("hooked velvet") is the source of the word *velcro*. How about the word *fax*? Is that a blend? No, see next category.

Clipping

The element of reduction that is noticeable in blending is even more apparent in the process described as **clipping**. This occurs when a word of more than one syllable (*facsimile*) is reduced to a shorter form (*fax*), usually beginning in casual speech. The term *gasoline* is still used, but most people talk about *gas*, using the clipped form. Other common examples are *ad* (advertisement), *bra* (brassiere), *cab* (cabriolet), *condo* (condominium), *fan* (fanatic), *flu* (influenza), *perm* (permanent wave), *phone, plane, porn* and *pub* (public house). English speakers also like to clip each other's names, as in *Al, Ed, Liz, Mike, Ron, Sam, Sue* and *Tom*. There must be something about educational environments that encourages clipping because so many words get reduced, as in *chem, exam, gym, lab, math, phys-ed, poly-sci, prof* and *typo*.

Hypocorisms

A particular type of reduction, favored in Australian and British English, produces forms technically known as **hypocorisms**. In this process, a longer word is reduced to a single syllable, then *-y* or *-ie* is added to the end. This is the process that results in *movie* ("moving pictures") and *telly* ("television"). It has also produced *Aussie* ("Australian"), *barbie* ("barbecue"), *bickie* ("biscuit"), *bookie* ("bookmaker"), *brekky* ("breakfast"), *hankie* ("handkerchief") and *toastie* ("toasted sandwich"). You can probably guess what *Chrissy pressies* are. By now, you may be ready to *take a sickie* ("a day of sick leave from work, whether for real sickness or not").

Backformation

A very specialized type of reduction process is known as **backformation**. Typically, a word of one type (usually a noun) is reduced to form a word of another type (usually a verb). A good example of backformation is the process whereby the noun *television* first came into use and then the verb *televise* was created from it. Other examples of words created by this process are: *donate* (from "donation"), *emote* (from "emotion"), *enthuse* (from "enthusiasm") and *liaise* (from "liaison"). Indeed, when we use the verb *backform* (*Did you know that "opt" was backformed from "option"?*), we are using a backformation. Here are some other recent creations.

automation → automate	*bulldozer → bulldoze*
choreography → choreograph	*mixture → mix*
syllabification → syllabify	*orientation → orientate → orient*

One very regular source of backformed verbs in English is based on the common pattern *work – worker*. The assumption seems to have been that if there is a noun ending in *-er* (or something close in sound), then we can create a verb for what that noun-*er* does. Hence, an *editor* will *edit*, a *sculptor* will *sculpt* and *babysitters, beggars, burglars, peddlers* and *swindlers* will *babysit, beg, burgle, peddle* and *swindle*.

Conversion

A change in the function of a word, as for example when a noun comes to be used as a verb (without any reduction), is generally known as **conversion**. Other labels for this very common process are "category change" and "functional shift." A number of nouns such as *bottle, butter, chair* and *vacation* have come to be used, through conversion, as verbs: *We bottled the home-brew last night*; *Have you buttered the toast?*; *Someone has to chair the meeting*; *They're vacationing in Florida*. These forms are readily accepted, but some conversions, such as the noun *impact* used as a verb, seem to *impact* some people's sensibilities rather negatively.

The conversion process is very productive in Modern English, with new uses occurring frequently. The conversion can involve verbs becoming nouns, with *guess, must* and *spy* as the sources of *a guess, a must* and *a spy*. Phrasal verbs (*to print out, to take over*) also become nouns (*a printout, a takeover*). One complex verb combination (*want to be*) has become a new noun, as in *He isn't in the group, he's just a wannabe*. Some other examples of conversion are listed here.

Noun →	Verb	Verb →	Noun
dust	*Did you dust the living room?*	*to cheat*	*He's a cheat.*
glue	*I'll have to glue it together.*	*to doubt*	*We had some doubts.*
referee	*Who will referee the game?*	*to hand out*	*I need a handout.*
water	*Would you water my plants?*	*to hire*	*We have two new hires.*

Verbs (*see through, stand up*) can also become adjectives, as in *see-through material* or a *stand-up comedian*. A number of adjectives, as in a *dirty floor, an empty room, some crazy ideas* and *those nasty people*, have become the verbs *to dirty* and *to empty*, or the nouns *a crazy* and *the nasty*.

Some compound nouns have assumed other functions, exemplified by *the ball park* appearing in a *ball-park figure* (as an adjective) or asking someone *to ball-park an estimate of the cost* (as a verb). Other nouns of this type are *carpool, mastermind, microwave* and *quarterback*, which are also used as verbs now. Other forms, such as *up* and *down*, can also become verbs, as in *They're going to up the price of oil* or *We downed a few beers at the Chimes*.

It is worth noting that some words can shift substantially in meaning when they go through conversion. The verb *to doctor* often has a negative sense, not normally associated with the source noun *a doctor*. A similar kind of reanalysis of meaning is taking place with the noun *total* and the verb *run around*, which do not have negative meanings. However, if you *total* (= verb) your car, and your insurance company gives you the *runaround* (= noun), you will have a double sense of the negative.

Coinage

The invention and general use of totally new terms, or **coinage**, is not very common in English. Typical sources are trade names for commercial products that become general terms (usually without capital letters) for any version of that product. Older examples are *aspirin, nylon, vaseline* and *zipper*; more recent examples are *granola, kleenex, teflon* and *xerox*. It may be that there is an obscure technical origin (e.g. *te(tra)-fl(uor)-on*) for some of these invented terms, but after their first coinage, they tend to become everyday words in the language. The most salient contemporary example of coinage is the word *google*. Originally a misspelling for the word *googol* (= the number 1 followed by 100 zeros), in the creation of the word *Googleplex*, which later became the name of a company (*Google*), the term *google* (without a capital letter) has since undergone conversion from a noun to become a widely used verb meaning "to use the internet to find information."

New words based on the name of a person or a place are called **eponyms**. When we talked about a *hoover* (or even a *spangler*), we were using an eponym. We use the eponyms *teddy bear*, derived from US president Theodore (Teddy) Roosevelt, and *jeans* (from the Italian city of Genoa where the type of cloth was first made). Another eponym dates from 1762 when John Montagu, the fourth Earl of Sandwich, insisted on having his salt beef between two slices of toasted bread while gambling. Apparently his friends started to ask "to have the same as Sandwich."

Acronyms

Acronyms are new words formed from the initial letters of a set of other words. These can be forms such as *CD* ("compact disk") or *SPCA* ("Society for the Prevention of Cruelty to Animals") where the pronunciation consists of saying each separate letter. More typically, acronyms are pronounced as new single words, as in *NATO, NASA* or *UNESCO*. These examples have kept their capital letters, but many acronyms simply become everyday terms such as *laser* ("light amplification by stimulated emission of radiation"), *radar* ("radio detecting and ranging"), *scuba* ("self-contained underwater breathing apparatus"), a *sim* ("subscriber identity module") card and *zip* ("zone improvement plan") code. You might even hear talk of a *snafu*, which is reputed to have its origins in "situation normal, all fouled up," though there is some dispute about the appropriate verb in there.

Names for organizations are often designed to have their acronym represent an appropriate term, as in "mothers against drunk driving" (*MADD*) and "women against rape" (*WAR*). Many speakers do not think of their component meanings. Innovations such as the *ATM* ("automatic teller machine") and the required *PIN* ("personal identification number") are regularly used with one of their elements repeated, as in *I sometimes forget my PIN number when I go to the ATM machine*. The *ATM* example is also known as an "initialism" (see Task A, page 68).

Derivation

In our list so far, we have not dealt with what is by far the most common word-formation process to be found in the production of new words. This process is called **derivation** and it is accomplished by means of a large number of small "bits" of the English language that are not usually given separate listings in dictionaries. These small "bits" are generally described as **affixes**. Some familiar examples are the elements *un-*, *mis-*, *pre-*, *-ful*, *-less*, *-ish*, *-ism* and *-ness* which appear in words like u<u>n</u>happy, <u>mis</u>represent, <u>pre</u>judge, joy<u>ful</u>, care<u>less</u>, boy<u>ish</u>, terror<u>ism</u> and sad<u>ness</u>.

Prefixes and Suffixes

Looking more closely at the preceding group of words, we can see that some affixes are added to the beginning of the word (e.g. *un-*, *mis-*). These are called **prefixes**. Other affixes are added to the end of the word (e.g. *-less*, *-ish*) and are called **suffixes**. All English words formed by this derivational process have either prefixes or suffixes, or both. Thus, <u>mis</u>lead has a prefix, <u>dis</u>respect<u>ful</u> has both a prefix and a suffix, and fool<u>ishness</u> has two suffixes. According to Dixon (2014: 11), English has about 200 derivational affixes, divided into 90 prefixes and 110 suffixes. We will investigate the range of English affixes in more detail in Chapter 6.

Infixes

There is a third type of affix, not normally used in English, but found in some other languages. This is called an **infix**, which is an affix that is incorporated inside another word. It is possible to see the general principle at work in certain expressions, occasionally used in fortuitous or aggravating circumstances by emotionally aroused English speakers: *Halle**bloody**lujah!*, *Abso**goddam**lutely!*, *Ala**damn**bama* and *Un**fuckin**believable!*. We could view these examples of "expletive insertion" as a special version of infixing in English. However, a much better set of examples can be provided from Khmu (or Kamhmu), a language spoken in northern Laos and Vietnam.

	Verb	Noun	
("to drill")	*see*	*srnee*	("a drill")
("to chisel")	*toh*	*trnoh*	("a chisel")
("to eat with a spoon")	*hiip*	*hrniip*	("a spoon")
("to tie")	*hoom*	*hrnoom*	("a thing with which to tie")

From these examples, we can see that there is a regular pattern whereby the infix *-rn-* is added to verbs to form nouns. If we know that the form *srnal* is the Khmu noun for "an ear ornament," then we can work out the corresponding verb "to put an ornament in the ear." According to Merrifield *et al.* (2003), the source of these examples, it is *sal*.

For examples of another type of affix called a "circumfix," see Task G, on page 70.

Multiple Processes

Although we have concentrated on each of these word-formation processes in isolation, it is possible to trace the operation of more than one process at work in the creation of a particular word. For example, the term *deli* seems to have become a common American English expression via a process of first borrowing *delicatessen* (from German) and then clipping that borrowed form. If someone says that *problems with the project have snowballed*, the final word can be analyzed as an example of compounding in which *snow* and *ball* were combined to form the noun *snowball*, which was then turned into a verb through conversion. Forms that begin as acronyms can also go through other processes, as in the use of *lase* as a verb, the result of backformation from *laser*. In the expression *waspish attitudes*, the acronym *WASP* ("white Anglo-Saxon Protestant") has lost its capital letters and gained a suffix (*-ish*) in the derivation process.

An acronym that never seems to have had capital letters comes from "young urban professional," plus the *-ie* suffix, as in hypocorism, to produce the word *yuppie* (first recorded in 1984). The formation of this new word, however, was helped by a quite different process, known simply as **analogy**, whereby new words are formed that are similar in some way to existing words. *Yuppie* was made possible as a new word by analogy with the earlier word *hippie* and another short-lived analogy *yippie*. The word *yippie* also had an acronym basis ("youth international party") and was used for some students in the USA who were protesting against the war in Vietnam. One joke has it that *yippies* just grew up to be *yuppies*. And the process continues. Another analogy, with the word *yap* ("to make shrill noises"), helped label some of the noisy young professionals as *yappies*.

Many of these new words can, of course, have a very brief life-span. Perhaps the generally accepted test of the "arrival" of recently formed words in a language is their published appearance in a dictionary. In recent years, we have added *app* (from "application") and *vape* (from "vaporizer"), both via clipping, *blog* (from "web log") and *sexting* ("sexual texting") via blending, and *unfriend* and *mint* (= "cool") via conversion. Further examples are included in Task E, on page 69.

However, new additions can sometimes lead to protests from some conservative voices, as Noah Webster found when his first dictionary, published in 1806, was criticized for citing words like *advocate* and *test* as verbs, and for including such "vulgar" words as *advisory* and *presidential*. It would seem that Noah had a keener sense than his critics of which new word forms in the language were going to last.

Study Questions

1   When is an eponym a neologism?

2   Which word-formation process is the source of the English word *modem*?

3   Which two processes were involved in the creation of the verb *google*, as in *Have you ever googled yourself?*?

4   Which process is clearly involved in creating the new term *selfie*?

5   What do we call the process whereby a new word is formed to be similar to an existing word?

6   Which of the following pairs contains an example of calque? How would you describe the other(s)?

   (a)   *footobooru* (Japanese) – *football* (English)
   (b)   *tréning* (Hungarian) – *training* (English)
   (c)   *luna de miel* (Spanish "moon of honey") – *honeymoon* (English)
   (d)   *jardin d'enfants* (French "garden of children") – *Kindergarten* (German "children garden")

7   Can you identify the different word-formation processes involved in producing each of the underlined words in these sentences?

   (a)   *Don't they ever worry that they might get* <u>AIDS</u>?
   (b)   *That's really* <u>fandamntastic</u>!
   (c)   *These new* <u>skateboards</u> *from Zee Designs are* <u>kickass</u>.
   (d)   *When I'm ill, I want to see a* <u>doc</u>, *not a* <u>vet</u>.
   (e)   *The house next door was* <u>burgled</u> *when I was* <u>babysitting</u> *the Smiths' children.*
   (f)   *I like this old* <u>sofa</u> – *it's nice and* <u>comfy</u>.
   (g)   *I think Robyn said she'd like a* <u>toastie</u> *for* <u>brekky</u>.
   (h)   *You don't need to* <u>button</u> *it because it's got* <u>velcro</u> *inside.*

8   Identify the prefixes and suffixes used in these words:

   misfortune, terrorism, carelessness, disagreement, ineffective, unfaithful, prepackaged, biodegradable, reincarnation, decentralization

9   In Khmu, the word *kap* means "to grasp with tongs," and *tiap* means "to fold a small package." What would be the words for "tongs" and "a small package"?

10 Why are the expressions *my PIN number* and *the ATM machine* slightly odd?

11   The English phrase *road rage* has become the expression *vejvrede* ("way anger") among Danish speakers. What is this process called?

12   More than one process was involved in the creation of the forms underlined in these sentences. Can you identify the processes involved in each case?

(a)   *Can you <u>FedEx</u> the books to me today?*
(b)   *Police have reported an increase in <u>carjackings</u> in recent months.*
(c)   *Jeeves, could you tell the maid to be sure to <u>hoover</u> the bedroom carpet?*
(d)   *I had to <u>temp</u> for a while before I got a real job.*
(e)   *Is your friend Ian still <u>blogging</u>?*
(f)   *Would you prefer a <u>decaf</u>?*

Tasks

A   What are "initialisms"? Were there any examples in this chapter?

B   Who invented the term "portmanteau words"? How many examples were included in this chapter?

C   Using a dictionary with etymological information, identify which of the following words are borrowings and from which languages they were borrowed. Are any of them eponyms?

assassin, clone, cockroach, denim, diesel, frisbee, horde, kayak, kiosk, nickname, penguin, robot, shampoo, sherry, slogan, snoop, taboo, tea, tomato, tuxedo, umbrella, voodoo

D   When English words are borrowed into Japanese, they are subject to **nativization**, a process whereby they are typically given a syllabic pronunciation, as in *ingurishu* ("English"). Can you reverse the syllabification process to identify the following English words borrowed into Japanese? One list has items you can get at a place known as *makudonarudo*, the other has items connected to *supootsu*.

chikin nagetto	_____	*beesubouru*	_____
furaido poteto	_____	*booringu*	_____
hotto doggu	_____	*futtobouru*	_____
juusu	_____	*hoomuran*	_____
kechappu	_____	*jogingu*	_____
sheiku	_____	*shuuzu*	_____
sofuto kuriimu	_____	*sokkusu*	_____

E There are a lot of new words in English from IT (an acronym for "information technology") and the widespread use of the internet (a blend from "international" and "network"). Using a dictionary if necessary, try to describe the word-formation processes involved in the creation of the underlined words in these sentences.

(1)   *There are some teenage <u>netizens</u> who rarely leave their rooms.*
(2)   *How much <u>RAM</u> do you have?*
(3)   *I can't get some of the students to <u>keyboard</u> more carefully.*
(4)   *Your friend Jason is such a <u>techie</u>!*
(5)   *Doesn't every new computer have a <u>webcam</u> now?*
(6)   *You should <u>bookmark</u> that site.*
(7)   *I got a great new <u>app</u> for my phone.*
(8)   *We're paying too much attention to <u>bloggers</u>.*
(9)   *Subscribers have unlimited <u>downloads</u>.*
(10) *I tried to find the site, but I just got <u>googledygook</u>*
(11) *He never puts his phone down, he's <u>intexticated</u>.*
(12) *You should check the <u>faq</u> because the information is usually helpful.*
(13) *Some people will have to learn better <u>netiquette</u>.*
(14) *Hey, just heard about the accident, <u>ruok</u>?*

F In this chapter we noted an example (*Partnerlook*) of the creation of a new German word using one or more English words, yet with a meaning not found in English. In the following list, there are some more words in contemporary German that have been created from English words.

(i)   What is the technical term used to describe forms created in this way?
(ii) Can you work out which meanings from the set below go with which words?

der Barmixer   (= _____)
der Beamer   (= _____)
der Bodybag   (= _____)
der Flipper   (= _____)
das Handy   (= _____)
der Messie   (= _____)
der Oldtimer   (= _____)
die Peep Toes   (= _____)
der Shootingstar (= _____)
der Smoking   (= _____)
der Talkmaster   (= _____)
der Tramper   (= _____)

bartender	shoulder bag	tuxedo
cell phone/mobile	overnight success	women's open-toed shoes
hitchhiker	pinball machine	video projector
hoarder/pack rat	talk show host	vintage car

G Another type of affix is called a circumfix, as in these examples from Indonesian:

("big")	*besar*	*kebesaran*	("bigness")
("beautiful")	*indah*	*keindahan*	("beauty")
("healthy")	_____	*kesehatan*	("health")
("free")	_____	*kebebasan*	("freedom")
("kind")	*baik*	_____	("kindness")
("honest")	*jujur*	_____	("honesty")

1 Can you provide the missing forms in these examples?

2 What is the circumfix illustrated here?

3 For what type of word-formation process is the circumfix being used here?

4 Given the words *tersedia* ("available"), *sulit* ("difficult"), *sesuai* ("suitable") and *seimbang* ("balanced"), how would you translate these words?

_____ ("availability")

_____ ("difficulty")

_____ ("suitability")

_____ ("balance")

5 After analyzing the following examples, what do you think the corresponding Indonesian words would be for "happy," "just/fair" and "satisfied"?

ketidakjujuran ("dishonesty")

ketidaksenangan ("unhappiness")

ketidakadilan ("injustice")

ketidakpuasan ("dissatisfaction")

H Can you divide the following set of English compounds into nouns and verbs? How do you decide? Which part of the compound determines whether it is a noun or verb?:

crash helmet, crash land, freeze dry, freeze frame, hang glide, hang nail, kick boxer, kick start, skim milk, skim read, sleep mode, sleep walk

I When Hmong speakers (from Laos and Vietnam) settled in the USA, they had to create some new words for the different objects and experiences they encountered. Using the following translations (from Downing and Fuller, 1984), can you work out the English equivalents of the Hmong expressions listed below?

chaw ("place")   *kho* ("fix")   *hlau* ("iron")   *cai* ("right")
dav ("bird")   *muas* ("buy")   *hniav* ("teeth")   *daim* ("flat")
hnab ("bag")   *nres* ("stand")   *looj* ("cover")   *mob* ("sickness")
kev ("way")   *ntaus* ("hit")   *ntoo* ("wood")   *nqaj* ("rail")
kws ("expert")   *tos* ("wait")   *ntawv* ("paper")   *tshuaj* ("medicine")
tsheb ("vehicle")   *zaum* ("sit")   *tes* ("hand")

chawkhomob _____   *kwshlau* _____
chawnrestsheb _____   *kwskhohniav* _____
chawzaumtos _____   *kwsntausntawv* _____
davhlau _____   *kwsntoo* _____
hnabloojtes _____   *kwskhotsheb* _____
kevcai _____   *kwstshuaj* _____
kevkhomob _____   *tshebnqajhlau* _____
kevnqajhlau _____   *daimntawvmuastshuaj* _____

J The process of borrowing may result in words that have more than one source. Many English words came into the language from Latin via French (e.g. *flōr-* > *flour (fleur)* > *flower* and *flour*). Other sources may be more obscure.

For example, we get *tomato* from the Spanish version of *tomatl*, borrowed from Nahuatl, the language of the Aztecs in Mexico. Can you work out what contemporary English words came via the same route from the Nahuatl words *ahuacatl* and *ahuacamolli*?

K The following sets of words, based on Jaggar (2001: 113), are from Hausa, which is spoken in northern Nigeria and Niger in West Africa. They are **ethnonyms**, that is, nouns that identify a person based on ethnicity or origin. The first column has words for a male (singular), the second column is for a female (singular), and the third column is for people (plural). The fourth column has English ethnonyms. After analyzing how the first examples are formed, try to complete the rest.

Bà'amirké	*Bà'amirkiya*	*Amirkawa*	("American")
Bàjamushé	*Bàjamushiya*	*Jamusawa*	("German")
Bàfaranshé	1_____	*Faransawa*	("French")
Bàhaushé	*Bàhaushiya*	2 _____	("Hausa")
Bàturé	3 _____	4 _____	("European")
5_____	6 _____	*Larabawa*	("Arab")
7_____	*Bàyarabiya*	8 _____	("Yoruba")
Bàmasaré	9 _____	10 _____	("Egyptian")

Discussion Topics/Projects

I When we form compounds in English, how do we know whether to join the words (*hairspray*), join them with a hyphen (*hair-spray*) or leave a space between them (*hair spray*)? Using the examples below, and any others that you want to include in the discussion, try to decide if there are any typical patterns in the way we form compounds.:

backpack, back-pedal, back seat, blackboard, black hole, black-tie affair, bulletin board, double bed, double-cross, house husband, house-warming, housewife, life-saving, lifestyle, life insurance, mother-in-law, mother tongue, postcard, Postits, post office, workbook, work experience, work-to-rule

(For background reading, see chapter 3 of Denning, Kessler and Leben, 2007.)

II The sign in Figure 5.1 contains a word (*flushable*) that you may not have seen before. But it isn't hard to understand. However, when we derive new words with a suffix such as *-able*, there seems to be some type of constraint on what is permitted. The words in the left column below are "acceptable" (that's one!), but the forms in the other two columns don't seem to be current English words. They are marked with an asterisk * to show that we think they are "unacceptable" (there's another one!). From these examples, and any others that you think might be relevant to the discussion, can you work out what the rule(s) might be for making new adjectives with the suffix *-able*?

breakable	**carable*	**dieable*
doable	**chairable*	**disappearable*
downloadable	**diskable*	**downable*
inflatable	**hairable*	**pinkable*
movable	**housable*	**runnable*
understandable	**pencilable*	**sleepable*
wearable	**quickable*	**smilable*

(For background reading, see chapter 4 of *Language Files*, 2018.)

Figure 5.1 Not flushable

Further Reading

Basic Treatments

Denning, K., B. Kessler and W. Leben (2007) *English Vocabulary Elements* (2nd edition) Oxford University Press

Minkova, D. and R. Stockwell (2009) *English Words* (2nd edition) Cambridge University Press

More Detailed Treatments

Harley, H. (2006) *English Words: A Linguistic Introduction* Blackwell

Plag, I. (2018) *Word-formation in English* (2nd edition) Cambridge University Press

Etymology

Durkin, P. (2009) *The Oxford Guide to Etymology* Oxford University Press

Googling

Vise, D. and M. Malseed (2005) *The Google Story* Delacorte Press

Borrowing

Durkin, P. (2014) *Borrowed Words: A History of Loanwords in English* Oxford University Press

Hitchings, H. (2008) *The Secret Life of Words* John Murray

Miller, D. (2012) *External Influences on English: From Its Beginnings to the Renaissance* Oxford University Press

Borrowing in Brazilian Portuguese

Diniz de Figueiredo, E. (2010) "To borrow or not to borrow: the use of English loanwords as slang on websites in Brazilian Portuguese" *English Today* 26: 5–12

Compounding

Bauer, L. (2017) *Compounds and Compounding* Cambridge University Press
Lieber, R. and P. Stekauer (2009) *The Oxford Handbook of Compounding* Oxford University Press
Sanchez-Stockhammer, C. (2018) *English Compounds and Their Spelling* Cambridge University Press

Blending

Roig-Marín, A. (2016) "'Blended' cyber-neologisms" *English Today* 128 (32): 2–5

Hypocorisms

Allan, K. (2015) *Linguistic Meaning* (reprint) Routledge

Conversion

Aitchison, J. (2012) *Words in the Mind* (4th edition) (part 3) Wiley-Blackwell

Eponyms

Marciano, J. (2009) *Anonyponymous* Bloomsbury

Derivation

Dixon, R. (2014) *Making New Words* Oxford University Press

Infixes

Yu, A. (2007) *A Natural History of Infixation* Oxford University Press

Expletive insertion

Bauer, L. (2015b) "Expletive insertion" *American Speech* 90: 122–127

Analogy

Fertig, D. (2013) *Analogy and Morphological Change* Edinburgh University Press

Other References

Downing, B. and J. Fuller (1984) "Cultural contact and the expansion of the Hmong lexicon" Unpublished paper, Department of Linguistics, University of Minnesota
Jaggar, P. (2001) *Hausa* John Benjamins
Language Files (2016) (12th edition) Ohio State University Press
Merrifield, W., C. Naish, C. Rensch and G. Story (2003) *Laboratory Manual for Morphology and Syntax* (7th edition) Summer Institute of Linguistics
See also wordspy.com

6 Morphology

AMBIMOUSTROUS (adj.) able to use a computer mouse with both hands

Collins English Dictionary (2019)

Throughout Chapter 5, we approached the description of processes involved in word formation as if the unit called the "word" was always a regular and easily identifiable form, even when it is a form such as *ambimoustrous* that we may never have seen before. This new word is based on an established form, *ambidextrous* ("able to use either hand equally well"), with the middle element, *dext(e)r* ("right hand"), replaced by *mous(e)*. Clearly this single word has more than one element contributing to its meaning. Yet we don't normally think of a "word" as having internal elements. We tend to think of words as those individual forms marked in black with bigger spaces separating them in written English. In this chapter, we'll investigate ways of taking a closer look inside words.

Morphology

In many languages, what appear to be single forms actually turn out to contain a large number of "word-like" elements. For example, in Swahili (or Kiswahili, spoken throughout East Africa), the form *nitakupenda* conveys what, in English, would have to be represented as something like *I will love you*. Now, is the Swahili form a single word? If it is a "word," then it seems to consist of a number of elements that, in English, turn up as separate "words." A rough correspondence can be presented here:

> *ni-*   *ta-*   *ku-*   *penda*
> I   will   you   love

It would seem that this Swahili "word" is rather different from what we think of as a written English "word." Yet there clearly is some similarity between the languages, in that similar elements of the whole message can be found in both. Perhaps a better way of looking at linguistic forms in different languages would be to use this notion of "elements" in the message, rather than depend on identifying only "words."

The type of exercise we have just performed is an example of investigating basic forms in language, known as **morphology**. This term, which literally means "the study of forms," was originally used in biology, but is now also used to describe the study of those basic "elements" in a language. What we have been describing as "elements" in the form of a linguistic message are technically known as "morphemes."

Morphemes

We do not actually have to go to other languages such as Swahili to discover that "word forms" may consist of a number of elements. We can recognize that English word forms such as *talks, talker, talked* and *talking* must consist of one element *talk*, and the other four elements *-s, -er, -ed* and *-ing*. All these five elements are described as **morphemes**. The definition of a morpheme is "a minimal unit of meaning or grammatical function." Units of grammatical function include forms used to indicate past tense or plural, for example. So, we can take words apart, as shown in Table 6.1 with the verb *re-new-ed* and the noun *tour-ist-s*, to reveal the different elements in their morphology.

TABLE 6.1 MORPHEMES

Minimal units of meaning	Grammatical function
re- ("again") *new* ("recently made")	*-ed* (past tense)
tour ("travel for pleasure") *-ist* ("person who")	*-s* (plural)

Free and Bound Morphemes

Looking at the examples in Table 6.1, we can make a broad distinction between two types of morphemes. There are **free morphemes**, that is, morphemes that can stand by themselves as single words, for example, *new* and *tour*. There are also **bound morphemes**, which are those forms that cannot normally stand alone and are typically attached to another form, exemplified as *re-, -ist, -ed, -s*. These forms were described in Chapter 5 as affixes. So, we can say that all affixes (prefixes and suffixes) in English are bound morphemes. The free morphemes can generally be identified as the set of separate English word forms such as basic nouns, verbs, adjectives and adverbs. When they are used with bound morphemes attached, the basic word forms are technically known as **stems**. For example:

	undressed			*carelessness*	
un-	dress	-ed	care	-less	-ness
prefix	stem	suffix	stem	suffix	suffix
(bound)	(free)	(bound)	(free)	(bound)	(bound)

We should note that this type of description is a partial simplification of the morphological facts of English. There are a number of English words, typically derived from Latin, in which the element treated as the stem is not a free morpheme. In words such as *receive, reduce* and *repeat*, we can identify the bound morpheme *re-* at the beginning, but the elements *-ceive, -duce* and *-peat* are not separate word forms in English and hence cannot be free morphemes. These types of forms are sometimes described as "bound stems."

Lexical and Functional Morphemes

What we have described as free morphemes fall into two categories. The first category is that set of ordinary nouns (*girl, house*), verbs (*break, sit*), adjectives (*long, sad*) and adverbs (*never, quickly*) that we think of as the words that carry the "content" of the messages we convey. These free forms are called **lexical morphemes**. We can add new lexical morphemes to the language rather easily, so they are treated as an "open" class of words.

Other types of free morphemes are called **functional morphemes**. Examples are articles (*a, the*), conjunctions (*and, because*), prepositions (*on, near*) and pronouns (*it, me*). Because we almost never add new functional morphemes to the language, they are described as a "closed" class of words.

Derivational Morphemes

The set of affixes that make up the category of bound morphemes can also be divided into two types. One type is described in Chapter 5 in terms of the derivation of words. These are **derivational morphemes**. We use these bound forms to make new words or to make words of a different grammatical category from the stem. For example, the addition of the derivational morpheme -*ment* changes the verb *encourage* to the noun *encouragement*. The noun *class* can become the verb *classify* by the addition of the derivational morpheme -*ify*. Derivational morphemes can be suffixes like -*ment* and -*ify* and also prefixes, such as *re-*, *pre-*, *ex-*, *mis-*, *co-*, *un-*.

Inflectional Morphemes

The second set of bound morphemes contains **inflectional morphemes** (or "inflections"). These are not used to produce new words in the language, but rather to indicate the grammatical function of a word. Inflectional morphemes are used to show if a word is plural or singular, past tense or not, and if it is a comparative or possessive form. English has only eight inflectional morphemes, all suffixes.

> *Jim's two sisters are really different.*
> *One likes to have fun and is always laughing.*
> *The other enjoyed school as a child and has always been very serious.*
> *One is the loudest person in the house and the other is quieter than a mouse.*

In the first sentence, both inflections are attached to nouns, marking possessive (-'*s*) and plural (-*s*). There are four inflections attached to verbs: -*s* (3rd person singular, present tense), -*ing* (present participle), -*ed* (past tense) and -*en* (past participle). Two inflections attach to adjectives: -*er* (comparative) and -*est* (superlative).

There is some variation in the form of these inflectional morphemes. For example, the possessive sometimes appears as a plural form -*s'* (*those boys' bags*) and the past participle is often -*ed* (*they have talked already*). Table 6.2 has a summary.

TABLE 6.2 DERIVATIONAL AND INFLECTIONAL MORPHEMES

	Nouns	Verbs	Adjectives
Derivational	critic-**ism**	critic-**ize**	critic-**al**
	encourage-**ment**	class-**ify**	wonder-**ful**
Inflectional	Jim-**'s**	like-**s**, laugh-**ing**	quiet-**er**
	sister-**s**	enjoy-**ed**, be-**en**	loud-**est**

Morphological Description

The difference between derivational and inflectional morphemes is worth emphasizing. An inflectional morpheme never changes the grammatical category of a word. For example, both *old* and *older* are adjectives. The *-er* inflection here (from Old English *-ra*) simply creates a different version of the adjective. However, a derivational morpheme can change the grammatical category of a word. The verb *teach* becomes the noun *teacher* if we add the derivational morpheme *-er* (from Old English *-ere*). So, the suffix *-er* in Modern English can be an inflectional morpheme as part of an adjective and also a distinct derivational morpheme as part of a noun. Just because they look the same (*-er*) doesn't mean they do the same kind of work.

Whenever there is a derivational suffix and an inflectional suffix used together, they always appear in that order. First the derivational (*-er*) is attached to *teach*, then the inflectional (*-s*) is added to produce *teachers*. Armed with all these terms for different types of morphemes, we can now take most sentences of English apart and list all the "elements." For example, in the sentence *The teacher's wildness shocked the girls' parents*, we can identify thirteen morphemes.

The	*teach*	*-er*	*-'s*	*wild*	*-ness*
functional	lexical	derivational	inflectional	lexical	derivational

shock	*-ed*	*the*	*girl*	*-s'*	*parent*	*-s*
lexical	inflectional	functional	lexical	inflectional	lexical	inflectional

A useful way to remember all these different types of morphemes is presented in Figure 6.1.

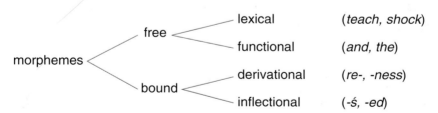

Figure 6.1 Types of morphemes

Morphs, Allomorphs and Special Cases

The rather neat chart presented in Figure 6.1 conceals a number of outstanding problems in the analysis of English morphology. The inflectional morpheme *-s* is added to *cat* and we get the plural *cats*. What is the inflectional morpheme that makes *sheep* the plural of *sheep*, or *men* the plural of *man*? These two words are clearly exceptions to the general pattern and have to be treated as special cases.

One way to describe more regular differences in inflectional morphemes is by proposing variation in morphological realization rules. In order to do this, we draw an analogy with processes already noted in phonology (Chapter 4, page 47). Just as we treated phones as the actual phonetic realization of phonemes, so we can propose **morphs** as the actual forms used to realize morphemes. For example, the form *cats* consists of two parts, /kæt/ + /-s/, with a lexical morpheme ("cat") and an inflectional morpheme ("plural"). The words *dogs* and *horses* also consist of two parts, /dɔg/ + /-z/ and /hɔrs/ + /-əz/, each consisting of a lexical morpheme and an inflectional morpheme ("plural"). So we have at least three forms (/-s/, /-z/ and /-əz/) used to realize the inflectional morpheme "plural." Just as we noted that there were "allophones" of a phoneme, so we can recognize the existence of **allomorphs** of a morpheme, again using the prefix "allo-" (= one of a closely related set). The three allomorphs of the one morpheme ("plural") are shown in Table 6.3.

TABLE 6.3 ALLOMORPHS

Morpheme	Allomorphs	
	/-s/	("cat<u>s</u>")
plural	/-z/	("dog<u>s</u>")
	/-əz/	("hors<u>es</u>")

Returning to our special cases, we could propose that there may be a "zero-morph" involved when we add the "plural" morpheme to a word like *sheep*, so that the plural of *sheep* can be analyzed as /ʃip/ + /∅/, adding another form (/∅/) to the set of allomorphs of "plural." When we add "plural" to /mæn/, we could have a vowel change in the word (æ → ɛ) as the morph that produces the "irregular" plural form *men*. However, it is more likely that we treat the two forms /mæn/ and /mɛn/ as two distinct lexical morphemes that we learn as separate words.

There is a similar pattern in the way "past tense" is realized in English. The inflectional suffix *-ed* is used in the typical derivation: *flirt<u>ed</u>, hugg<u>ed</u>* and *kiss<u>ed</u>*. The irregular forms are like separate lexical morphemes: *go/went, be/was/were*. See Task C, on page 84, for more on the allomorphs of past tense in English.

Other Languages

When we look at the morphology of other languages, we can find other forms and patterns realizing the basic types of morphemes we have identified. In the following examples, based on Gleason (1955), we can try to work out how different forms in the languages are used to realize morphological processes and features.

Kanuri

This first set of examples is from Kanuri, a language spoken in Nigeria.

	Adjective	Noun	
("excellent")	*karite*	*nəmkarite*	("excellence")
("big")	*kura*	*nəmkura*	("bigness")
("small")	*gana*	*nəmgana*	("smallness")
("bad")	*dibi*	*nəmdibi*	("badness")

From this set, we can propose that *nəm-* is a prefix, functioning as a derivational morpheme that is used to derive nouns from adjectives. The process is similar to the use of the suffix *-ness* in English, creating the noun *bigness* from the adjective *big*. Discovering a regular morphological feature of this type helps us to make certain predictions when we encounter other forms. For example, if the Kanuri word for "length" is *nəmkurugu*, then we can be reasonably sure that "long" is *kurugu*.

Ganda

Different languages also employ different means to produce inflectional marking on forms. Here are some examples from Ganda, a language spoken in Uganda.

	Singular	Plural	
("doctor")	*omusawo*	*abasawo*	("doctors")
("woman")	*omukazi*	*abakazi*	("women")
("girl")	*omuwala*	*abawala*	("girls")
("heir")	*omusika*	*abasika*	("heirs")

From this small sample, we can observe that there is an inflectional prefix *omu-* used with singular nouns, and a different inflectional prefix *aba-* used with the plural of those nouns. If we learn that *abalenzi* is a Ganda plural, meaning "boys," then we can be pretty sure that the singular form meaning "boy" must be *omulenzi*.

Ilocano

When we look at Ilocano, a language of the Philippines, we find a quite different way of marking plurals.

	Singular	Plural	
("head")	*úlo*	*ulúlo*	("heads")
("road")	*dálan*	*daldálan*	("roads")
("life")	*bíag*	*bibíag*	("lives")
("plant")	*múla*	*mulmúla*	("plants")

In these examples, there seems to be repetition of the first part of the singular form. When the first part is *bí-* in the singular, the plural begins with this form repeated *bibí-*. The process involved here is technically known as **reduplication** (= "repeating all or part of a form"). Having seen how plurals differ from singular forms in Ilocano, you should be able to take this plural form *taltálon* ("fields") and work out what the singular ("field") would be. If you follow the observed pattern, you should get *tálon*.

Tagalog

Here are some examples from Tagalog, another language of the Philippines.

basa ("read")	*tawag* ("call")	*sulat* ("write")
bumasa ("Read!")	*tumawag* ("Call!")	*sumulat* ("Write!")
babasa ("will read")	*tatawag* ("will call")	*susulat* ("will write")

If we assume that the first form in each column can be treated as a stem, then it appears that, in the second item in each column, an element *-um-* has been inserted after the first consonant, or more precisely, after the syllable onset. It is an example of an **infix** (described in Chapter 5, page 65).

In the third example in each column, the change involves a repetition of the first syllable, as *basa* becomes *babasa*. So, referring to the future in Tagalog is done via reduplication. Using this information, we can complete these examples:

lakad ("walk")	("Walk!") _____	("will walk") _____
lapit ("come here")	("Come here!") _____	("will come here") _____

In the second column, with the infix -um-, we would write *lumakad* and *lumapit*. In the third column, with reduplication, we would write *lalakad* and *lalapit*. So, next time you're enjoying a stroll through the streets of Manila and you hear *lumapit!*, you'll know what to do. Learn more about Tagalog in Task D, on page 85.

Study Questions

1 How many morphemes are there in the word *terrorists*?

2 What kind of morpheme is the suffix in *slowly*?

3 What are the functional morphemes in the following sentence?

When she walked into the room, the doctor asked me if I had a sore throat or an annoying cough.

4   (i) List the bound morphemes in these words: *fearlessly, happier, misleads, previewer, shortening, unreconstructed*
   (ii) Which of these words has a bound stem: *consist, deceive, introduce, repeat*?
   (iii) Which of these words contains an allomorph of the morpheme "past tense": *are, have, must, sitting, waits*?

5   (i) Which word(s) in the following sentence would you put in a closed class?
       Bob brought hot donuts to class.
   (ii) Which word(s) in the following sentence would you put in an open class?
       I put it on the shelf near you and him.

6 How many regular inflectional morphemes are there in English?

7 What are the inflectional morphemes in these expressions?

   (a) *Have you eaten yet?*
   (b) *Do you know how long I've been waiting?*
   (c) *She's younger than me and always dresses in the latest style.*
   (d) *We looked through my grandmother's old photo albums.*
   (e) *My parents' parents were all from Scotland.*

8 What is the difference between the *-er* morphemes in the words *smaller* and *singer*?

9 What are the allomorphs of the morpheme "plural" in the following set of English words?

   criteria, dogs, oxen, deer, judges, stimuli

10 In Indonesian, the singular form translating "child" is *anak* and the plural form ("children") is *anakanak*. What is the technical term used to describe this relationship?

11 When she heard some exciting news, one British English speaker exclaimed, "Fanflamingtastic!" What is the morphological process involved here?

12   Provide equivalent forms, in the languages listed, for the English translations shown on the right below.

Ganda	*omuloŋgo*	("twin")	–	("twins")	_____
Ilocano	*tawtáwa*	("windows")	–	("window")	_____
Ilocano	*tálon*	("field")	–	("fields")	_____
Kanuri	*nəmkaǰi*	("sweetness")	–	("sweet")	_____
Tagalog	*bili*	("buy")	–	("will buy")	_____
Tagalog	*kain*	("eat")	–	("Eat!")	_____

Tasks

A   What is "suppletion"? Were there any examples of English suppletive forms described in this chapter?

B   What are enclitics and proclitics? Does English have both? What are some typical English examples? Why aren't they just called affixes?

C   The regular past tense suffix (*-ed*) has three different pronunciations that illustrate a connection between the morphology and phonology of English, an area of investigation described as "morphophonology."

  (i)   Can you complete Table 6.4 (similar to Table 6.3, on page 80), listing the following verbs in the past tense as examples of each of the three pronunciations?

      cherish, detest, flirt, hug, kiss, like, loathe, love, offend

  (ii) Can you state the phonological conditions that determine how the past tense morpheme is pronounced?

TABLE 6.4 PAST TENSE ALLOMORPHS

Morpheme	Allomorphs	Examples		
	/-t/	*kiss<u>ed</u>*		
past tense	/ /			
	/ /			

D   Using what you learned about Tagalog, plus information from the set of examples here, create appropriate forms of these verbs for (1)–(10) below.

basag ("break"), bili ("buy"), hanap ("look for"), kain ("eat")

("Write!")	sumulat	("Call!")	tumawag
("was written")	sinulat	("was called")	tinawag
("is writing")	sumusulat	("is calling")	tumatawag
("is being written")	sinusulat	("is being called")	tinatawag

(1) ("Buy!") _____   (6) ("is eating") _____

(2) ("was bought") _____   (7) ("is breaking") _____

(3) ("was broken") _____   (8) ("is being broken") _____

(4) ("was looked for") _____   (9) ("is being looked for") _____

(5) ("is looking for") _____   (10) ("is being eaten") _____

E   Look over the following examples from Hungarian (based on Frommer and Finegan, 2015) and try to answer the questions that follow.

(1) te szép vagy   "you're beautiful" (singular)

(2) én beteg vagyok   "I'm ill"

(3) te magas vagy   "you're tall" (singular)

(4) mi lankadtak vagyunk   "we're tired"

(5) ti kedvesek vagytok   "you're nice" (plural)

(6) ti betegek vagytok   "you're ill" (plural)

(7) mi magasak vagyunk   "we're tall"

(8) te kedves vagy   "you're nice" (singular)

(9) én lankadt vagyok   "I'm tired"

(10) __ _____ _____   "you're beautiful" (plural)

  (i)   Complete example (10).

  (ii)   Which are the five free (adjective) morphemes in the data?

  (iii)   Which are the four pronouns? Are these lexical or functional morphemes?

  (iv)   Which are the three verb suffixes? Are these derivational or inflectional suffixes?

  (v)   Which are the two adjective suffixes? What do you think is the basis for choosing one or the other?

F   Using what you learned about Swahili and information provided in the set of examples below, create appropriate forms as translations of the English expressions (1)–(6) that follow.

nitakupenda ("I will love you")   alipita ("She passed by")

watanilipa ("They will pay me")   uliwapika ("You cooked them")

tutaondoka ("We will leave")   walimpiga ("They beat him")

(1) _____ ("She loved you")   (4) _____ ("We paid him")

(2) _____("I will cook them")   (5) _____ ("She will beat me")

(3) _____ ("You will pass by")   (6) _____ ("They left")

G These examples are from Samoan, as reported in Yu (2007: 24), and based on Mosel and Hovdhaugen (1992). (The consonant represented by ʔ is a glottal stop, as described in Chapter 3.)

	Singular	Plural
("love")	*alófa*	*alolófa*
("clever")	*atamái*	*atamamái*
("work")	*galúe*	*galulúe*
("brave")	*tóa*	*totóa*

(i) What is the morphological process involved here and where exactly does it take place in the word form?

(ii) What would be the plural of *avága* ("elope"), *má* ("ashamed"), *maʔalíli* ("cold") and *toʔúlu* ("fall")?

H Regular nouns in Tamasheq (spoken in north-west Africa) have different forms when they are singular or plural, masculine or feminine.

(i) Using the general patterns in the examples listed here (based on Sudlow, 2001), fill in the missing words to complete the chart.

(ii) Can you describe the general patterns found here relating singular to plural forms of the same noun?

(iii) Are the affixes involved derivational or inflectional? Is there a special term for affixes that have the structure illustrated in most of the plural nouns here?

	Singular		Plural
amadray	("younger brother")	*imadrayan*	("younger brothers")
amanokal	("chief")	*imanokalan*	("chiefs")
amawad	("adolescent boy")	*imawadan*	("adolescent boys")
amaqqar	("older brother")	_____	("older brothers")
amaraw	("parent")	_____	("parents")
anharag	("male neighbor")	_____	("male neighbors")
enhad	("craftsman")	*inhadan*	("craftsmen")
esed	("donkey")	*isedan*	("donkeys")
esen	("tooth")	_____	("teeth")
tabarart	("female child")	*tibararen*	("female children")
tagolayt	("stepdaughter")	*tigolayen*	("stepdaughters")

tahayawt	("female descendant")	_____	("female descendants")
tamadrayt	("younger sister")	_____	("younger sisters")
tamagart	("female guest")	_____	("female guests")
tamaqqart	("older sister")	_____	("older sisters")
_____	("spoon")	*tisokalen*	("spoons")
_____	("concubine")	*tiwayhaten*	("concubines")
_____	("road")	*zabotan*	("roads")
_____	("market")	*hebutan*	("markets")
bahu	("lie")	*bahutan*	("lies")
bokəti	("bucket")	*bokətitan*	("buckets")

I The following examples are from Manambu, a language spoken in northern Papua New Guinea, as reported in Aikhenvald (2008). (There is also a basic description in Aikhenvald and Genetti, 2014.) They illustrate a derivational process in which noun-like forms are created from verb stems. After studying the first set of examples and the additional verb stems, can you add appropriate forms to the sentences below?

Verb stem	Noun-like form
kawar ("to take up")	*kawarkawar* ("carrying and going up")
yawi kur ("to do work")	*yawi kurkur* ("doing work")
nas[ə] ("to count")	*nasənas* ("counting")
warya ("to fight")	*waryawari* ("fighting")

kə ("to eat")   *wali* ("to walk around")   *wuk[ə]* ("to hear")
təməl ("to roll")   *war* ("to go up")   *wukəmar* ("to forget")
və ("to stare")   *warsam* ("to be angry")   *yi* ("to talk")

(1) *kasan* _____ *vyakəta*
peanut-going up-good
("Peanuts going up/growing fine")

(2) *adi pato* _____ *tənadi*
those-ducks-walking around-they are
("Those ducks keep wandering around")

(3) _____ *ata nal*
rolling-then-there was
("Then there was a noise of rolling and rolling")

(4) *nagw* _____ *bər bətay lakubra*
sago-eating-they-already-knew
("They already knew about eating sago")

(5) *dayak* _____ *tənad*
at them-being very angry-he is
("He is very angry at them")

(6) _____ *akəs təkwanawun*
forgetting-never-I stand
("I'm never forgetful")

(7) *lə wuna takwam* _____ *ma*
she-my-wife-staring at-not
("She is not staring at my wife")

(8) _____ *wukəna* _____ *suan yina*
hearing-she hears-talking-hard-she talks
("She hears (and understands), (but) talking is hard")

J   Singular and plural nouns take different forms in Setswana (or Tswana), spoken in Botswana and South Africa. Think about how these words are formed, based on Cole (1955), then try to complete the sentences that follow.

motho ("person")   *moruti* ("teacher")

batho ("people")   *dikwele* ("schools")

setilo ("chair")   *mosetsana* ("girl")

ditilo ("chairs")   *dilo* ("things")

bosigo ("night")   *banna* ("men")

masigo ("nights")   *moapei* ("cook")

balemi ("farmers")   *marokwe* ("pairs of trousers")

(1) _____ *barata* _____.

"(The) teachers like (the) school."

(2) _____ *batshaba* _____.

"(The) girls fear (the) thing."

(3) _____ *obatla* _____.

"(The) man wants (a) pair of trousers."

(4) _____ *othusa* _____.

"(The) farmer helps (the) cooks."

K   Daga is spoken in the Central District of Papua New Guinea. The following examples are based on Murane (1974), cited in Mithun (2014). Try to work out how possession and location are marked by affixes in the first set of examples, then complete (1)–(6) below.

inana ("my mother")   *mamanu* ("our father")

pusiya ("your feet")   *noga* ("your mouth")

nanimu ("their hands")   *garinap* ("on my back")

evenga ("your friend")   *onep* ("on his shoulder")

yame ("his eye")   *pusip* ("on foot")

(1) *naniya* _____   (4) _____ ("his friend")
(2) *inanu* _____   (5) _____ ("on their feet")
(3) *mamana* _____   (6) _____ ("on your back")

L We can look at how some plural nouns are formed in Arabic to illustrate **non-concatenative morphology** (i.e. not adding affixes to words). Think about these examples, adapted from Yule and Overstreet (2017: 49), and try to choose the appropriate plural forms from the list to fill the spaces.

> 'aflam   'aqlām   'arbā'   'atfāl   'asbāb   'asdiqā
> 'ashjār   'ashur   'awlād   'awrāq   'ayādi✓   'ayām✓

yad ("hand")   ("hands") *'ayādi*_____
yawm ("day")   ("days") *'ayām*_____
(1) *walad* ("boy")   ("boys") _____
(2) *qalam* ("pen")   ("pens") _____
(3) *waraqa* ("paper")   ("papers") _____
(4) *shajara* ("tree")   ("trees") _____
(5) *film* ("film")   ("films") _____
(6) *sabab* ("cause")   ("causes") _____
(7) *sadīq* ("friend")   ("friends") _____
(8) *shahr* ("month")   ("months") _____
(9) *tifl* ("child")   ("children") _____
(10) *rub'* ("quarter")   ("quarters") _____

Discussion Topics/Projects

I In English, plural forms such as *mice* appear to be treated in a different way from plurals such as *rats*. If you tell people that a place is infested with mice or rats, they will accept the compounds *mice-infested* and *rat-infested*, but not **rats-infested*. This would suggest that the forms with the regular plural affix (*-s*) follow a different rule in compounding than irregular plural forms such as *mice*. Can you think of a way to state a rule (or sequence of rules) that would accommodate all the examples given here? (The asterisk * designates an unacceptable form.)

teethmarks   *the feet-cruncher*   *lice-infested*   *a people-mover*
clawmarks   *the finger-cruncher*   *roach-infested*   *a dog-mover*
*clawsmarks   **the fingers-cruncher*   **roaches-infested*   **a dogs-mover*

(For background reading, see chapter 6 of Pinker, 1999.)

II In Turkish, there is some variation in the plural inflection

	Singular		Plural	
("man")	*adam*	–	*adamlar*	("men")
("gun")	_____	–	*toplar*	("guns")
("lesson")	*ders*	–	_____	("lessons")
("place")	*yer*	–	*yerler*	("places")
("road")	_____	–	*yollar*	("roads")
("lock")	_____	–	*kilitler*	("locks")
("arrow")	*ok*	–	_____	("arrows")
("hand")	*el*	–	_____	("hands")
("arm")	*kol*	–	_____	("arms")
("bell")	_____	–	*ziller*	("bells")
("friend")	_____	–	*dostlar*	("friends")
("apple")	*elma*	–	_____	("apples")

(i) Can you provide the missing forms?

(ii) What are the two plural morphs exemplified here?

(iii) Treat the written forms of *a* and *o* as representing back vowels and *e* and *i* as representing front vowels. Using this information, can you state the conditions under which each of the plural morphs is used?

(iv) On the basis of the following phrases, how would you describe the Turkish translation equivalents of *your* and the conditions for their use?

dishin ("your tooth") *topun* ("your gun")
okun ("your arrow") *dersin* ("your lesson")
kushun ("your bird") *kibritlerin* ("your matches")

(v) While English usually marks location with prepositions (*in a house* or *at a place*), Turkish has postpositions (*house-in* or *place-at*). After looking at the following examples, try to identify the three versions of the "location" suffix and the conditions for their use.

("book")	*kitap*	–	*kitapta*	("in a book")
("chair")	*koltuk*	–	*koltukta*	("in a chair")
("room")	*oda*	–	*odada*	("in a room")
("restaurant")	*lokanta*	–	*lokantada*	("in a restaurant")
("house")	*ev*	–	*evde*	("in a house")
("place")	*yer*	–	*yerlerde*	("in places")
("hand")	*el*	–	*ellerimde*	("in my hands")
("road")	*yol*	–	*yollarda*	("in roads")

(vi)   When Turkish speakers borrowed (from French) the word *randevu*, meaning "an appointment," how do you think they expressed "in an appointment"?

(For more examples, see Gleason, 1955. For more on Turkish, see Lewis, 2000.)

Further Reading

Basic Treatments

Aronoff, M. and K. Fudeman (2011) *What Is Morphology?* (2nd edition) Blackwell
Payne, T. (2006) *Exploring Language Structure* (chapters 1–3) Cambridge University Press

More Detailed Treatments

Bauer, L. (2003) *Introducing Linguistic Morphology* (2nd edition) Edinburgh University Press
Booij, G. (2012) *The Grammar of Words: An Introduction to Morphology* (3rd edition) Oxford University Press

Specifically on English Morphology

Carstairs-McCarthy, A. (2018) *An Introduction to English Morphology* (2nd edition) Edinburgh University Press

Reduplication

Inkelas, S. and C. Zoll (2009) *Reduplication: Doubling in Morphology* Cambridge University Press

Morphology Exercises

Language Files (2016) (12th edition) Ohio State University Press
Lieber, R. (2016) *Introducing Morphology* (2nd edition) Cambridge University Press

Other References

Aikhenvald, A. (2008) *The Manambu Language of East Sepik, Papua New Guinea* Oxford University Press
Aikhenvald, A. and C. Genetti (2014) "Language profile 10: Manambu" In C. Genetti (ed.) *How Languages Work* (530–550) Cambridge University Press
Cole, D. (1955) *An Introduction to Tswana Grammar* Longmans
Frommer, P. and E. Finegan (2015) *Looking at Languages* (6th edition) Wadsworth
Gleason, H. (1955) *Workbook in Descriptive Linguistics* Holt
Lewis, G. (2000) *Turkish Grammar* (2nd edition) Oxford University Press
Mithun, M. (2014) "Morphology: what's in a word?" In C. Genetti (ed.) *How Languages Work* (71–99) Cambridge University Press
Mosel, U. and E. Hovdhaugen (1992) *Samoan Reference Grammar* Scandinavian University Press
Murane, E. (1974) *Daga Grammar: From Morpheme to Discourse* SIL Publications
Pinker, S. (1999) *Words and Rules* HarperCollins
Sudlow, D. (2001) *The Tamasheq of North-East Burkina Faso* R. Köppe Verlag
Yu, A. (2007) *A Natural History of Infixation* Oxford University Press
Yule, G. and M. Overstreet (2017) *Puzzlings* Amazon Books

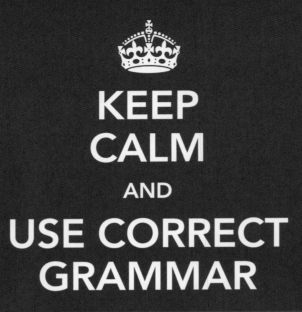

Diagramming sentences is one of those lost skills, like darning socks or playing the sackbut, that no one seems to miss. When it was introduced in an 1877 text called *Higher Lessons in English* by Alonzo Reed and Brainerd Kellogg, it swept through American public schools like measles, embraced by teachers as the way to reform students who were engaged in (to take Henry Higgins slightly out of context) "the cold-blooded murder of the English tongue."

Florey (2006)

We have already looked at two levels of description used in the study of language. We have described linguistic expressions as sequences of sounds that can be represented in the phonetic alphabet and described in terms of their features. That is, we can identify a voiced fricative /ð/, a voiceless stop /k/ and a diphthong /ɔɪ/ as segments in the transcription of a phrase such as /ðəlʌkibɔɪz/.

We can take the same expression and describe it as a sequence of morphemes:

the	*luck*	*-y*	*boy*	*-s*
functional	lexical	derivational	lexical	inflectional

With these descriptions, we could characterize all the words and phrases of a language in terms of their phonology and morphology.

English Grammar

However, we have not accounted for the fact that the three words in this phrase can only be combined in a particular sequence. We recognize that the phrase *the lucky boys* is a well-formed phrase in contemporary English, but that the following two "phrases" are not at all well-formed.

boys the lucky   *lucky boys the*

(We use an asterisk * to indicate that a form is unacceptable or ungrammatical.)

From these examples, we can see that English has strict rules for combining words into phrases. The article (*the*) must go before the adjective (*lucky*), which must go before the noun (*boys*). So, in order to be grammatical, this type of phrase must have the sequence article + adjective + noun (and not *noun + article + adjective, for example).

The process of describing the structure of phrases and sentences in such a way that we account for all the grammatical sequences in a language and rule out all the ungrammatical sequences is one way of defining the **grammar** of a language. It is the kind of definition assumed when we talk about the grammar of English as opposed to the grammar of Swahili, Tagalog or Turkish. As illustrated in Chapter 6, each of these languages has different ways of forming grammatical phrases and sentences. Studying grammar in this way has a very long tradition.

Traditional Grammar

The terms "article," "adjective" and "noun" that we use to label the grammatical categories of the words in the phrase *the lucky boys* come from traditional grammar, which has its origins in the description of languages such as Latin and Greek. Indeed, the expression "grammar school" was originally used exclusively for an institution where Latin was taught. Since there was a well-established grammatical description of Latin, based on earlier analyses of Greek, it seemed appropriate to adopt the existing categories from this description and apply them in the analysis of newer languages such as English. Because Latin and Greek were the languages of philosophy, religion and scholarship, the description of the grammatical components of these languages was taken to be the best model for other grammars. We have inherited a number of terms from the model that are used in describing those basic grammatical components, known as the "parts of speech," and how they connect to each other in terms of "agreement."

The Parts of Speech

Each part of speech, or word class, is illustrated in the following sentence and simple definitions of each technical term are listed below.

The	*lucky*	*boys*	*found*	*a*	*backpack*	*in*
article	adjective	noun	verb	article	noun	preposition

the	*park*	*and*	*they*	*opened*	*it*	*carefully*
article	noun	conjunction	pronoun	verb	pronoun	adverb

Nouns
are words used to refer to people (*boy*), objects (*backpack*), creatures (*dog*), places (*school*), qualities (*roughness*), phenomena (*earthquake*) and abstract ideas (*love*) as if they were all "things." We begin **proper nouns** with a capital letter (*Cathy, Latin, Rome*).

Articles
are words (*a, an, the*) used with nouns to form noun phrases classifying those "things" (*You can have **a** banana or **an** apple*) or identifying them as already known (*I'll take **the** apple*).

Adjectives
are words used, typically with nouns, to provide more information about the things referred to (**large** *objects, a* **strange** *experience*).

Verbs
are words used to refer to various kinds of actions (*go, talk*) and states (*be, have*) involving people and things in events (*Jessica **is** ill and **has** a sore throat so she can't **talk** or **go** anywhere*).

Adverbs
are words used, typically with verbs, to provide more information about actions, states and events (*slowly, yesterday*). Some adverbs (*really, very*) are also used with adjectives to modify information about things (***Really** large objects move **slowly**. I had a **very** strange experience **yesterday***).

Prepositions
are words (*at, in, on, near, with, without*) used with nouns in phrases providing information about time (***at** five o'clock, **in** the morning*), place (***on** the table, **near** the window*) and other connections (***with** a knife, **without** a thought*) involving actions and things.

Pronouns
are words (*she, herself, they, it, you*) used in place of noun phrases, typically referring to people and things already known (***She** talks to **herself**. **They** said **it** belonged to **you***).

Conjunctions
are words (*and, but, because, when*) used to make connections and indicate relationships between events (*Chantel's husband was so sweet **and** he helped her a lot **because** she couldn't do much **when** she was pregnant*).

Agreement

In addition to the terms used for the parts of speech, traditional grammatical analysis has also given us a number of other categories, including "number," "person," "tense," "voice" and "gender." These categories can be discussed in isolation, but their role in describing language structure becomes clearer when we consider them in terms of **agreement**. For example, we say that the verb *loves* "agrees with" the noun *Cathy* in the sentence *Cathy loves her dog*.

This agreement is partially based on the category of **number**, that is, whether the noun is singular or plural. It is also based on the category of **person**, which covers the distinctions of first person (involving the speaker), second person (involving the hearer) and third person (involving any others). The different forms of English pronouns can be described in terms of person and number. We use *I* for first person singular, *you* for second person singular, and *he, she, it* (or *Cathy*) for third person singular. So, in the sentence *Cathy loves her dog*, we have a noun *Cathy*, which is third person singular, and we use the verb *loves* (not *love*) to "agree with" the noun.

In addition, the form of the verb must be described in terms of another category called **tense**. In this case, the verb *loves* is in the present tense, which is different from the past tense (*loved*). The sentence is also in the **active voice**, describing what Cathy does (i.e. she performs the action of the verb). An alternative would be the **passive voice**, which can be used to describe what happens to Cathy (i.e. she doesn't perform the action), as in *Cathy is loved by her dog* or just *Cathy is loved*.

Our final category is **gender**, which helps us describe the agreement between *Cathy* and *her* in our example sentence. In English, we have to describe this relationship in terms of **natural gender**, mainly derived from a biological distinction between male and female. The agreement between *Cathy* and *her* is based on a distinction made in English between reference to female entities (*she, her*), male entities (*he, his*) and things or creatures, when the sex is unknown or irrelevant (*it, its*).

Figure 7.1 shows the basis of the agreement between *Cathy* and *loves*, and also between *Cathy* and *her* in the same sentence.

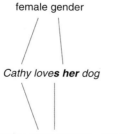

female gender

*Cathy lov**es her** dog*

third person singular, present tense, active voice

Figure 7.1 Agreement

Grammatical Gender

The type of biological distinction based on "natural gender" in English is quite different from the more common distinction found in languages that use **grammatical gender**. Whereas natural gender is based on sex (male and female), grammatical gender is based on the type of noun (masculine and feminine) and is not tied to sex. In this system, nouns are classified according to their gender class and articles and adjectives have different forms to "agree with" the nouns' gender.

Spanish, for example, has two grammatical genders, masculine and feminine, as in the expressions *el sol* ("the sun") and *la luna* ("the moon"). German uses three genders, masculine *der Mond* ("the moon"), feminine *die Sonne* ("the sun") and neuter *das Feuer* ("the fire"). The different forms of the articles in both the Spanish (*el* or *la*) and German (*der, die* or *das*) correspond to differences in gender class.

We should emphasize that this gender distinction is not based on a distinction in sex. The French noun in *le livre* ("the book") is grammatically masculine, but neither we nor the French people consider a book to be biologically male. Grammatical gender is an important category in many languages. (For more on gender, see Chapter 20.)

Traditional Analysis

The notion of appropriateness of analytic categories for a particular language has not always been a consideration. In traditional grammar books, tables such as the following were often presented for the analysis of English verbs, constructed by analogy with tables in Latin grammar, in this case for the verb *amare* ("to love").

TABLE 7.1 GRAMMATICAL CATEGORIES: PRESENT TENSE, ACTIVE VOICE

First person singular	*(I)*	*love*	*amo*
Second person singular	*(you)*	*love*	*amas*
Third person singular	*(she)*	*loves*	*amat*
First person plural	*(we)*	*love*	*amamus*
Second person plural	*(you)*	*love*	*amatis*
Third person plural	*(they)*	*love*	*amant*

Each Latin verb form is different, based on the categories of person and number, yet the English verbs are (with one exception) mostly the same. Thus, in Latin, these descriptive categories characterize verb forms, but that is not the case in English. In English, the categories actually describe different forms of pronouns.

The Prescriptive Approach

It is one thing to adopt the grammatical labels (e.g. "noun," "verb") to categorize words in English sentences; it is quite another thing to go on to claim that the structure of English sentences should be like the structure of sentences in Latin. That was an approach taken in eighteenth-century England by grammarians who set out rules for the "proper" use of English. This view of grammar as a set of rules for the proper use of a language is still found today and is best characterized as the **prescriptive approach**. Some old-style prescriptive rules for English are:

> *You must not split an infinitive.*
> *You must not end a sentence with a preposition.*

Following these types of rules, traditional teachers would correct sentences like <u>Who did you go with?</u> to <u>With whom did you go?</u> (so that the preposition *with* was not at the end of the sentence). And *Mary runs faster than me* would be corrected to *Mary runs faster than I*. And one should never begin a sentence with *and*!

It may, in fact, be a valuable part of one's education to be made aware of this "linguistic etiquette" for the use of language in certain contexts. Yet it is worth considering the origins of some of these rules and asking whether they have to be followed in English. Let's look at one example: "You must not split an infinitive."

Captain Kirk's Infinitive

The infinitive in English has the form *to* + the base form of the verb, as in *to go*, and can be used with an adverb such as *boldly*. At the beginning of each of the older televised *Star Trek* episodes, one of the main characters, Captain Kirk, always used the expression *To boldly go* ... This is an example of a split infinitive. Captain Kirk's teacher might have expected him to say *To go boldly* or *Boldly to go*, so that the adverb didn't split the infinitive. If Captain Kirk had been a Roman space traveler, speaking Latin, he would have used the expressions *ire* ("to go") and *audacter* ("boldly"). Now, in saying *Ire audacter* ... in Latin, Capitaneus Kirkus would not even have the opportunity to split his infinitive (*ire*), because Latin infinitives are single words and just do not split.

If it is a typical feature of the use of English that speakers and writers regularly produce forms such as *to boldly go, to solemnly swear* or *to never ever get back together*, then we may simply wish to note that there are structures in English that differ from those found in Latin, rather than think of the English forms as "bad" because they don't follow a rule of Latin grammar.

The Descriptive Approach

It may be that using a well-established grammatical description of Latin is a useful guide for European languages (e.g. Spanish), is less useful for others (e.g. English), and may be absolutely misleading for non-European languages. This last point became clear to linguists trying to describe the structure of the native languages of North America toward the end of the nineteenth century. Because the categories of traditional grammar did not seem to fit these languages, a different method, called the **descriptive approach**, was adopted. Analysts collected samples of the language they were interested in and attempted to describe regular structures of that language as it was used, not according to some view of how it should be used.

Structural Analysis

One type of descriptive approach is called **structural analysis** and its main concern is to investigate the distribution of forms in a language. The method involves the use of "test-frames," which can be sentences with empty slots in them.

> The _____ makes a lot of noise.
>
> I heard a _____ yesterday.

There are a lot of forms that can fit into these slots to produce good grammatical sentences of English (e.g. *car, child, donkey, dog, radio*). As a result, we can propose that, because all these forms fit in the same test-frame, they are likely to be examples of the same grammatical category, a "noun" (or N).

However, there are many forms that do not fit those test-frames. Examples would be *Cathy, someone, the dog, a car* and many others. (That is, we wouldn't say **The Cathy* or **The the dog.*) For these forms, we require different test-frames:

> _____ makes a lot of noise.
>
> I heard _____ yesterday.

Among other forms that comfortably fit these test-frames are *it, the big dog, an old car, Ani Difranco, the professor with the Scottish accent* and many other examples of the same grammatical category, a "noun phrase" (or NP).

Observing that *it* fits only in this second set of test-frames (**The it makes a lot of noise*), allows us to improve on the Latin-influenced, analysis of pronouns in English. Pronouns were described as "words used in place of nouns." We now see that it is better to say that pronouns are used in place of noun phrases (not just nouns).

Constituent Analysis

An approach with the same descriptive aims is called **constituent analysis**. The technique employed in this approach is designed to show how small constituents (or components) go together to form larger constituents. One basic step is determining how words go together to form phrases. In the following sentence, we can identify nine constituents at the word level: *The old woman brought a large snake from Brazil.* How do those nine constituents go together to form constituents at the phrase level? Does it seem appropriate to put the words together as follows?

> *The old   woman brought   brought a large   snake from   Brazil*

We don't normally think of these combinations as phrases in English. We are more likely to say that the phrase-like constituents here are combinations of the following types: *The old woman, a large snake, Brazil* (noun phrases), *from Brazil* (a prepositional phrase) and *brought* (a verb).

This analysis of the constituent structure of the sentence can be represented in a diagram (Figure 7.2) showing the distribution of the constituents at different levels.

The	old	woman	brought	a	large	snake	from	Brazil

Figure 7.2 Distribution of constituents

Using this kind of diagram we can determine the types of forms that can be substituted for each other at different levels of constituent structure. One advantage of this type of analysis is that it shows rather clearly that pronouns (*she, it*) and proper nouns or names (*Brazil*), though they are single words, can be used as noun phrases and fill the same constituent space as longer phrases (e.g. *the old woman* or *a large snake*). Figure 7.3 presents an analysis of the common constituent structure of many English sentences.

Noun phrase	Verb	Noun phrase	Prepositional phrase
The old woman	brought	a large snake	from Brazil
She	kept	it	in a cage

Figure 7.3 Constituent analysis

Subjects and Objects

In Figure 7.3, not only can we see how small constituents combine to form larger constituents as phrases; we can also work out the different grammatical functions of those phrases. We use the term "noun phrase" when we describe the form of the expression (i.e. it has a noun or a pronoun in it). We use the terms "subject" and "object" to describe the different functions of noun phrases in a sentence. Since English uses position in the sentence to indicate grammatical function, we can normally identify the **subject** as the first noun phrase before the verb and the **object** as the noun phrase after the verb. The other phrase at the end of our example sentence is an **adjunct**, often a prepositional phrase, which typically provides additional information such as where, when or how the subject verb-*ed* the object. Figure 7.4 displays this analysis.

Subject	Verb	Object	Adjunct
The old woman She	brought kept	a large snake it	from Brazil in a cage

Figure 7.4 Grammatical functions

There are a number of ways in which we can distinguish between noun phrases used as subjects versus objects. In addition to position differences, the subject is frequently the person or thing that the sentence is about and often the one that performs the action of the verb, whereas the object more typically represents the person or thing that undergoes the action. The subject noun phrase determines the form of the verb as singular or plural. English also makes a clear distinction between pronouns used as subjects (*I, he*) and those used as objects (*me, him*). These differences between subjects and objects are summarized in Table 7.2.

TABLE 7.2 SUBJECTS AND OBJECTS

Subjects	Objects
• the first noun phrase	• the noun phrase after the verb
• controls the verb (singular or plural)	• no influence on verb
• often performs the action	• often undergoes the action
• pronouns: *I, he, she, we, they*	• *me, him, her, us, them*

Word Order

The basic linear order of constituents in English is Noun Phrase–Verb–Noun Phrase (or NP V NP) and their typical grammatical functions are Subject–Verb–Object (or SVO), as shown in Table 7.3. Although we are actually talking about constituent order, this type of analysis is traditionally discussed in terms of **word order**. The English word order sequence is not the only possible, or even the most common word order among languages. The most common pattern is actually Subject–Object–Verb (SOV), as illustrated in the Japanese sentence in Table 7.3, with the verb at the end of the sentence. Japanese is a verb-final language.

In verb-initial languages, the sentence begins with the verb. As illustrated in Table 7.3, Scottish Gaelic has a Verb–Subject–Object (VSO) order and Malagasy (spoken in Madagascar) has a Verb–Object–Subject (VOS) order. Note that in Gaelic and Malagasy the adjective is placed after the noun (literally translated as "dog big").

TABLE 7.3 WORD ORDER

(SVO)	Subject	Verb	Object
	NP	V	NP
English	*John*	*saw*	*the big dog*
(SOV)	Subject	Object	Verb
	"John"	"big dog"	"saw"
Japanese	*Jon ga*	*ookii inu o*	*mita*
(VSO)	Verb	Subject	Object
	"Saw"	"John"	"the dog big"
Gaelic	*Chunnaic*	*Iain*	*an cu mor*
(VOS)	Verb	Object	Subject
	"Saw"	"the dog big"	"John"
Malagasy	*Nahita*	*ny alika be*	*Rajaona*

Language Typology

The use of word order patterns such as SVO or VOS to talk about different "types" of languages is part of a more general area of study known as **language typology**. This is the study of similarities in the grammatical structures of languages that allow them to be classified as members of the same type or group. The four main types are shown in Table 7.3. The other two possibilities, OSV and OVS, have been documented in a small number of languages in South America.

Why Study Grammar?

We began this chapter with the observation that in the grammar of English there are strict rules for combining words in a specific order to create phrases and sentences. In Table 7.3, we have expanded the analysis of those ordering rules to capture the different basic patterns that exist in most of the world's languages. One advantage of having this information is that it may help explain some of the problems second language learners face when they try to acquire a language that simply does not have the same structural organization as their first language. If you are used to referring to *the dog big* or *a bottle of wine red*, you may unthinkingly employ those structures in a language that expects *the big dog* or *a bottle of red wine*. By helping students and teachers notice critical grammatical differences of this type between languages, we may be able to develop better awareness of what the learning task is and what might be beneficially included in language teaching materials.

Throughout this discussion we have focused on the linear order of constituents in grammatical structures. However, there is a lot of evidence to suggest that the linear order we observe is based on a set of underlying structures that are more abstract and organized in a more hierarchical way. We will explore the nature of this more abstract system in Chapter 8.

Study Questions

1   Identify all the parts of speech used in this sentence (e.g. *woman* = noun):

   The woman kept a large snake in a cage, but it escaped recently.

2   How many adverbs are there in the following sentence?

   Really large objects move very slowly.

3   What is the tense and voice of the verb in the following sentence?

   My parents were married in Rome.

4   What is the difference between grammatical gender and natural gender?

5   How does Spanish differ from German in the number of grammatical genders?

6   What prescriptive rules for the "proper" use of English are not obeyed in the following sentences and how would they be "corrected"?

   (a)   *The old theory consistently failed to fully explain all the data.*
   (b)   *I can't remember the name of the person I gave the book to.*

7   How many noun phrases are there in the following sentence?

   Robert brought a small puppy to the party and we all wanted to keep it.

8   What was wrong with the older Latin-influenced definition of English pronouns?

9   What is the grammatical function of the proper noun in the following sentence?

   The professor and her students visited Berlin during the summer.

10   What is the most common word order in the languages of the world: verb-initial, verb-medial or verb-final?

11   Is Malagasy a VSO language or something else?

12   Given these other Gaelic words, translate the following sentences into English:
   beag ("small")   *bhuail* ("hit")   *dubh* ("black") *duine* ("man")   *gille* ("boy")

   (a)   *Bhuail an gille beag an cu dubh.*
   (b)   *Chunnaic an cu an duine mor.*

Tasks

A   Another term used in the description of the parts of speech is "determiner." What are determiners? How many examples were included in this chapter?

B In this chapter, we discussed "correction" in grammar. What is "hypercorrection"?

C All the underlined words in the following sentences are adverbs. On the basis of these sentences, formulate a simple rule of adverb position in English that would exclude the ungrammatical forms.

(1) *Do you <u>usually</u> wake up hungry?*
(2) *<u>Normally</u> I don't eat breakfast.*
(3) *I'd rather sleep <u>longer</u>.*
(4) *I <u>always</u> have a cup of green tea to start my day.*
(5) *I'll have some fruit juice <u>occasionally</u>.*
(6) *Of course I'm <u>often</u> starving by lunchtime.*
(7) **I might have <u>later</u> a small snack or something.*
(8) **If I feel tired, I'll drink <u>sometimes</u> coffee at work.*

D What is aspect? How is it used to describe the underlined forms here?

> *I hope no one calls while <u>I'm eating</u> lunch.*
> *<u>She's writing</u> a story about her dog.*
> *<u>I've eaten</u> lunch already, thanks.*
> *<u>She's written</u> a story about her cat and the cat next door.*
> *<u>I was eating</u> lunch, so I didn't answer.*
> *<u>She had written</u> a story about her goldfish before that.*
> *As a child, <u>she used to write</u> stories about the insects in the garden.*

E There are two constructions in English used to indicate possession, not only in the sense of "owning," but more generally in the sense of "having." They are the "*s*-genitive" (<u>Bob's</u> book) and the "*of*-genitive" (*the pages <u>of the book</u>*).

(i) Look at the following set of examples and try to work out when each of the constructions is preferred.

(ii) In the *s*-genitive construction, to which constituent is the **'s** added (article, noun, noun phrase, verb or verb phrase)?

(1) **My friend's father's ex-wife** *came to the ceremony, which was a bit weird.*
(2) *He emphasized* **the public's need** *for safe transportation.*
(3) *Do you watch* **CNN's special reports***?*
(4) *Our house is much smaller than* **Henry's***.*
(5) *She didn't say anything at* **last week's meeting***.*
(6) *They actually made it to* **the top of Mount Everest***.*
(7) *There's an entrance at* **the side of the building***.*
(8) *I'll love you till* **the end of time***.*

(9)   We didn't recognize **the size of the problem**.

(10) Do you remember **the name of that actor who played President Lincoln in the film**?

F What is the basis of the categorization of English verbs as transitive, intransitive or ditransitive? Can you use this categorization to explain why these sentences are ungrammatical?

(1)   *I thought I had lost my sunglasses, but Ali found in his car.

(2)   *Mark didn't win, but he didn't care that.

(3)   *They had a problem so we discussed.

(4)   *Suzy needed a jacket so I lent mine.

(5)   *We're always waiting you because you're late.

(6)   *I didn't have a pen so Anne gave one.

(7)   *When it's your birthday, people bring you.

(8)   *She smiled me yesterday when I saw her, so I think she really likes.

G If people typically say *little plastic forks* (and not *plastic little forks)*, there must be a preferred order of adjectives before nouns in the grammar of English. In this case, the adjective describing the size (*little*) goes before the adjective describing the material (*plastic*) of the noun (*forks*). How are other categories of adjectives ordered?

(i)   Using the underlined examples in the following sentences, identify the other categories and complete the chart in Table 7.4 below to capture the preferred order of descriptive adjectives in evidence here.

(ii) If we wanted to add those adjectives that express a subjective "opinion" to the chart (e.g. *beautiful, cute, horrible*), where would we put them relative to the other types?

(1)   <u>Japanese silk</u> scarves were very popular for many years.

(2)   The plant has <u>small round pink</u> flowers.

(3)   The <u>recent European</u> results were not very encouraging.

(4)   They had uncovered some <u>ancient square</u> stones with carvings on them.

(5)   It looked like <u>squiggly Arabic</u> writing on the back of the card.

(6)   She was wearing a <u>white cotton</u> blouse with a <u>short green</u> skirt.

(7)   Her ring had an <u>oval red</u> ruby surrounded by <u>tiny wedge-shaped</u> diamonds.

(8)   Eric still drives that <u>big old American</u> car.

(9)   The windows had <u>dated Victorian-style lace</u> curtains.

(10)   I was wearing my <u>brand-new black leather</u> shoes.

(11)   Yuri works downtown in one of those <u>huge modern glass</u> buildings.

(12)   The best bowls have <u>circular blue Chinese</u> designs in the middle.

TABLE 7.4 ADJECTIVE ORDER IN ENGLISH

Size					Material
little					*plastic*

H   There are two *-en* suffixes in English with quite different functions.

(i)   If you compare *harden* with *wooden* in terms of the parts of speech involved, can you describe what those different *-en* suffixes do?

(ii)   Does your description of the difference apply to all the following English words?

awaken	earthen	shorten
blacken	flatten	silken
dampen	golden	threaten
darken	moisten	woolen

I   The sample sentences below are from (a) Latin and (b) Amuzgo, a language of Mexico (adapted from Merrifield *et al.*, 2003).

(i)   Using what you have learned about Latin, carefully translate this sentence: *The doves love the small girl.*

(ii)   How would you write *A big woman is reading the red book* in Amuzgo?

(iii)   In terms of basic word order, which of these languages is most similar to Amuzgo: English, Gaelic, Japanese, Latin or Malagasy?

(a) Latin

puellae aquilas portant	"The girls carry the eagles"
feminae columbas amant	"The women love the doves"
puella aquilam salvat	"The girl saves the eagle"
femina parvam aquilam liberat	"The woman frees the small eagle"
magna aquila parvam columbam pugnat	"The big eagle fights the small dove"

(b) Amuzgo

macei'na tyocho kwi com	"The boy is reading a book"
kwil'a yonom kwi w'aa	"The men are building a house"

nnceihnda yusku kwi com we   "The woman will buy a red book"
kwil'a yonom ndee meisa   "The men are making three tables"
macei'na kwi tyocho com t'ma   "A boy is reading the big book"

J The following examples are from a variety of Nahuatl (Michoacán Nahuatl) spoken on the Pacific coast of Mexico. In these examples (adapted from Merrifield *et al.*, 2003), there are grammatical markers distinguishing present and past tense, first and second person, and the definite and indefinite articles.

(i)   Can you analyze the first set of examples and complete the second set?
(ii) What is the definite article in Nahuatl?

kochi in siwal ("the woman sleeps")   *nikochik* ("I slept")
maltik se sholul ("a child bathed")   *timaltik* ("you bathed")
molaluk in tunchi ("the cat ran")   *nimolaluk* ("I ran")
wala se lakal ("a man comes")   *tikita* ("you see him")

(1) _____ ("I came")   (4) _____ ("a cat comes")
(2) _____ ("you slept")   (5) _____ ("the child ran")
(3) _____ ("a woman bathed")   (6) _____ ("I see him")

K In this chapter we described Japanese word order as SOV, while English is SVO.

(i)   Looking at the examples below (based on Inoue, 1979), can you find another way in which Japanese word order is noticeably different from English?
(ii) Given the forms *tabemashita* ("ate"), *ringo* ("apple") and *-ni* ("in"), how would you translate sentences (4) and (5)?

(1) *Jakku-ga*   *gakkoo-e*   *ikimasu*
     Jack   school-to   go
     ("Jack goes to school")

(2) *Jon-ga*   *shinbun-o*   *yomimasu*
     John   newspaper   read
     ("John reads a newspaper")

(3) *Kazuko-ga*   *gakkoo-de*   *eigo-o narrateimasu*
     Kazuko   school-at   Englishlearn   be
     ("Kazuko is learning English at school")

(4) _____

     ("Jack ate an apple")

(5) _____

     ("Masuda is in school")

L The following examples are from Lotuko, spoken in South Sudan, East Africa, as described in Raglan (1922), and adapted here from Yule and Overstreet (2017: 55). The language is also known as Otuho.

(i) After analyzing the grammatical structure of the examples, try to complete sentences (1)–(8).

(ii) Which of these languages has the same word order as Lotuko: English, Japanese, Gaelic or Malagasy?

awak odwoti eito ("the girl loves the child")
amata lodole nali ("the baby is drinking milk")
amata atulo nabalu ("the man is drinking beer")
abang ezok odwoti ("the dog is afraid of the girl")
aghala nangoru aari ("the women are selling water")
ohonya nangote nawai ("the woman is eating sweet potato")

(1) _____ ("the dog loves the man")
(2) _____ ("the girl is drinking beer")
(3) _____ ("the man loves the child")
(4) _____ ("the woman loves the baby")
(5) _____ ("the child is afraid of the dog")
(6) _____ ("the woman is drinking water")
(7) _____ ("the girl is afraid of the women")
(8) _____ ("the man is eating sweet potato")

M Malagasy is spoken in Madagascar, a large island off the coast of East Africa.

These examples from Malagasy are mostly based on Keenan and Ochs (1979). After analyzing the structures in (1)–(5) and (9)–(15), can you complete examples (6)–(8) and (16)–(18)?

(1) *gaga aho*   ("I'm surprised")
(2) *noana izy*   ("he's hungry")
(3) *faly ianao*   ("you're happy")
(4) *mangetaheta izahay*   ("we're thirsty")
(5) *mihira izy*   ("he's singing")
(6) _____   ("I'm singing")
(7) _____   ("we're happy")
(8) _____   ("you're surprised")
(9) *nihira ny vehivavy*   ("the woman sang")
(10) *namaky boky ny mpianatra*   ("the student read a book")
(11) *tsy nisotro kafe ianao*   ("you didn't drink coffee")

(12)	*mihinana vary ny zaza*	("the child eats rice")
(13)	*tsy tia ny hena izy*	("he doesn't like the meat")
(14)	*misotro dite izahay*	("we drink tea")
(15)	*nahita ny vehivavy izay nihinana ny mofo aho*	("I saw the woman who ate the bread")
(16)	*tia kafe ny mpianatra*	(" _____ ")
(17)	*tsy mihinana hena izahay*	(" _____ ")
(18)	*nahita ny zaza izay nisotro ny dite ianao*	(" _____ ")

Discussion Topics/Projects

I In this chapter, we briefly mentioned the grammatical category of tense and illustrated the difference between past tense (*loved*) and present tense (*loves*). Using the examples below, and any others that you think are relevant, try to describe the "future tense" in English.

(1) *We may forgive, but we shall never forget.*

(2) *We'll leave if you want.*

(3) *Jenny's arriving at eight o'clock tonight.*

(4) *Your plane leaves at noon tomorrow.*

(5) *They were about to leave when I got there.*

(6) *We're going to visit Paris next year.*

(7) *She said Jim was leaving next Wednesday.*

(8) *I wish I had a million dollars.*

(9) *The president is to visit Japan in May.*

(10) *Water will freeze at zero degrees centigrade.*

(For background reading, see the section on "Future" in Hurford, 1994.)

II In the descriptive approach, "ungrammatical" simply means "not well-formed" in purely structural terms. However, the word "ungrammatical" is also used with a more general meaning. Which of the following sentences should be considered "ungrammatical" in your opinion and why?

(1) *There's hundreds of students waiting outside.*

(2) *Who's there? It's me and Lisa.*

(3) *Ain't nobody gonna tell me what to do.*

(4) *You wasn't here when he come looking for you.*

(5) *I hate lobsters anymore.*

(6) *Are y'all coming to see us soon?*

(7)   *That chair's broke, so you shouldn't ought to sit on it.*

(8)   *I can't remember the name of the hotel that we stayed in it.*

(9)   *I never seen anything.*

(10)   *If you'd have come with, we'd have had more fun.*

(For background reading, see chapter 8 of Napoli and Lee-Schoenfeld, 2010 or Favilla, 2017.)

Further Reading

Basic Treatments

Altenberg, E. and R. Vago (2010) *English Grammar: Understanding the Basics* Cambridge University Press

Swan, M. (2005) *Grammar* Oxford University Press

More Detailed Treatments

Hurford, J. (1994) *Grammar: A Student's Guide* Cambridge University Press

Kroeger, P. (2005) *Analyzing Grammar: An Introduction* Cambridge University Press

Grammatical Terms

Peters, P. (2013) *The Cambridge Dictionary of English Grammar* Cambridge University Press

Parts of Speech

Sakel, J. (2015) *Study Skills for Linguistics* (chapter 4) Routledge

On the Prescriptive Approach

Cameron, D. (1995) *Verbal Hygiene* Routledge

Greene, R. (2011) *You Are What You Speak* Delacorte Press

Pullum, G. (2009) "50 years of stupid grammar advice" *The Chronicle of Higher Education: The Chronicle Review* 55 (32): B15 (available online at http://chronicle.com Section: The Chronicle Review volume 55, issue 32, page B15)

Constituent Analysis

Payne, T. (2006) *Exploring Language Structure* (chapter 6) Cambridge University Press

Subjects and Objects

Culpeper, J., F. Katamba, P. Kerswill, R. Wodak and T. McEnery (2009) *English Language* (chapter 8) Palgrave Macmillan

Word Order and Typology

Haspelmath, M., M. Dryer, D. Gil and B. Comrie (eds.) (2005) *The World Atlas of Language Structures* Oxford University Press (available online at http://wals.info/)

Moravcsik, E. (2013) *Introducing Language Typology* (chapter 3) Cambridge University Press

English Word Order

Williams, P. (2016) *Word Order in English Sentences* (2nd edition) English Lessons Brighton

Gaelic Sentence Structure

Brown, K. and J. Miller (1991) *Syntax: A Linguistic Introduction to Sentence Structure* (2nd edition) Routledge

English Grammar Courses

Celce-Murcia, M. and D. Larsen-Freeman (2015) *The Grammar Book* (3rd edition) Heinle & Heinle

Yule, G. (1998) *Explaining English Grammar* Oxford University Press

English Reference Grammars

Huddleston, R. and G. Pullum (2005) *A Student's Introduction to English Grammar* Cambridge University Press

Quirk, R., S. Greenbaum, G. Leech and J. Svartvik (1985) *A Comprehensive Grammar of the English Language* Longman

Other References

Favilla, E. (2017) *A World without "Whom": The Essential Guide to Language in the BuzzFeed Age* Bloomsbury

Inoue, K. (1979) "Japanese" In T. Shopen (ed.) *Languages and Their Speakers* (241–300) Winthrop Publishers

Keenan, E. and E. Ochs (1979) "Becoming a competent speaker of Malagasy" In T. Shopen (ed.) *Languages and their Speakers* (113–158) Winthrop Publishers

Merrifield, W., C. Naish, C. Rensch and G. Story (2003) *Laboratory Manual for Morphology and Syntax* (7th edition) Summer Institute of Linguistics

Napoli, D. and L. Lee-Schoenfeld (2010) *Language Matters* (2nd edition) Oxford University Press

Raglan, L. (1922) "The Lotuko language" *Bulletin of the School of Oriental Studies* (University of London) 2 (2): 267–296

Yule, G. and M. Overstreet (2017) *Puzzlings* Amazon Books

8 | Syntax

Time flies like an arrow; fruit flies like a banana.

Oettinger (1966)

In an early observation on the difficulties of getting computers to process natural language, Anthony Oettinger used the example above to illustrate how we tend to interpret sentences based on an expected structure and when we arrive at a problematic interpretation, we are able to go back and try to use a different structure. This process brings to light the importance of recognizing the underlying structure of sentences in order to make sense of them. If we keep thinking that the structure of the second expression is the same as the first in the example, we will definitely miss something. (For a helpful analysis, see Figure 8.9, on page 127.)

In Chapter 7, we moved from the general categories of traditional grammar to more specific methods of describing the structure of phrases and sentences. When we concentrate on the structure and ordering of components within a sentence, we are studying the **syntax** of a language. The word "syntax" comes originally from Greek and literally means "a putting together" or "arrangement." In earlier approaches, there was an attempt to produce an accurate description of the sequence or ordering "arrangement" of elements in the linear structure of the sentence. In more recent attempts to analyze structure, there has been a greater focus on the underlying rule system that we use to produce or "generate" sentences.

Syntactic Rules

When we set out to provide an analysis of the syntax of a language, we try to adhere to the "all and only" criterion. This means that our analysis must account for *all* the grammatically correct phrases and sentences and *only* those grammatically correct phrases and sentences in whatever language we are analyzing. In other words, if we write rules for the creation of well-formed structures, we have to check that those rules, when applied logically, won't also lead to ill-formed structures.

For example, we might say informally that, in English, we put a preposition (*near*) before a noun (*London*) to form a prepositional phrase (*near London*). This will describe a large number of phrases, but does it describe all (and only) the prepositional phrases in English? Note that, if we use this as a rule of the grammar to create structures involving a preposition and a noun, we will end up producing phrases like *near tree* or *with dog*. These don't seem to be well-formed English structures, so we mark them with an asterisk *, indicating that they are ungrammatical.

We clearly need to be more careful in forming the rule that underlies the structure of prepositional phrases in English. We might have more success with a rule stating that we put a preposition before a noun phrase (not just a noun). In Chapter 7, we saw that a noun phrase can consist of a proper noun (*London*), a pronoun (*me*) or the combination of an article (*a, the*) with a noun (*tree, dog*), so that the revised rule can be used to produce these well-formed structures: *near London, with me, near a tree, with the dog*.

A Generative Grammar

When we have an effective rule such as "a prepositional phrase in English consists of a preposition followed by a noun phrase," we can imagine an extremely large number of English phrases that could be produced using this rule. In fact, the potential number is unlimited. This reflects another goal of syntactic analysis, which is to have a small and finite (i.e. limited) set of rules that will be capable of producing a large and potentially infinite (i.e. unlimited) number of well-formed structures. This small and finite set of rules is sometimes described as a **generative grammar** because it can be used to "generate" or produce sentence structures and not just describe them.

This type of grammar should also be capable of revealing the basis of two other phenomena: first, how some superficially different phrases and sentences are closely related and, second, how some superficially similar phrases and sentences are in fact different.

Deep and Surface Structure

Our intuitions tell us that there must be some underlying similarity involving these two superficially different sentences: *Charlie broke the window* and *The window was broken by Charlie*. In traditional grammar, the first is called an active sentence, focusing on what *Charlie* did, and the second is a passive sentence, focusing on *The window* and what happened to it. The distinction between them is a difference in their **surface structure**, that is, the different syntactic forms they have as individual English sentences. However, this superficial difference in form disguises the fact that the two sentences are closely related, even identical, at a less superficial level.

This other "underlying" level, where the basic components (Noun Phrase + Verb + Noun Phrase) shared by the two sentences can be represented, is called their **deep structure**. The deep structure is an abstract level of structural organization in which all the elements determining structural interpretation are represented. That same deep structure can be the source of many other surface structures such as *It was Charlie who broke the window* and *Was the window broken by Charlie?*. In short, the grammar must be capable of showing how a single underlying abstract representation can become different surface structures.

Structural Ambiguity

Let's say we have two distinct deep structures. One expresses the idea that "Annie had an umbrella and she bumped into a man with it." The other expresses the idea that "Annie bumped into a man and the man happened to be carrying an umbrella." Now, these two different versions of events can actually be expressed in the same surface structure form: *Annie bumped into a man with an umbrella*. This sentence provides an example of **structural ambiguity**. It has two distinct underlying interpretations that have to be represented differently in deep structure. Note that this is not the type of ambiguity that we experience in hearing *Their child has grown another foot*, which illustrates lexical ambiguity mainly because the word *foot* has more than one meaning. (See Task E, page 122, for further analysis.)

The comedian Groucho Marx knew how to have fun with structural ambiguity. In the film *Animal Crackers*, he first says *I once shot an elephant in my pajamas*, then follows it with *How he got into my pajamas I'll never know*. In the non-funny interpretation, part of the underlying structure of the first sentence could be something like: "I shot an elephant (while I was) in my pajamas." In the other (ho, ho) interpretation, part of the underlying structure would be something like: "I shot an elephant (which was) in my pajamas." There are two different underlying structures with the same surface structure, revealed by syntactic analysis.

Syntactic Analysis

In syntactic analysis we use some conventional abbreviations for the parts of speech identified in Chapter 7. Examples are N (= noun), Art (= article), Adj (= adjective) and V (= verb). We also use abbreviations for phrases, such as NP (= noun phrase) and VP (= verb phrase). In English, the verb phrase (VP) consists of the verb (V) plus the following noun phrase (NP). We can take the simple sentence from Table 7.3 (page 101) and label the constituents using these categories, as in Figure 8.1.

NP	VP	
	V	NP
John	saw	the big dog

Figure 8.1 Sentence structure

Figure 8.1 presents a static analysis of a single sentence. We would like to be able to represent the same syntactic information in a more dynamic format. One way of presenting the concept "consists of" is with an arrow (→), also interpreted as "rewrites as." The following rule states that a noun phrase (NP) such as *the dog* consists of or rewrites as (→) an article (*the*) and a noun (*dog*). This simple formula is the underlying structure of millions of different English phrases.

NP → Art N

However, it is not the only form a noun phrase can take. We want to be able to include another constituent (Adj) in the rule so that it is good for not only phrases like *the dog*, but also *the big dog*. This constituent is *optional* in a noun phrase, so we use round brackets to indicate that Adj is an optional constituent, as shown here:

NP → Art (Adj) N

Another common symbol is in the form of curly brackets {}. These indicate that *only one* of the elements enclosed within the curly brackets must be selected. We have already seen, in Figure 7.3, on page 99, that a noun phrase can also contain a pronoun (*it*), or a proper noun (*John*). Using the abbreviations "Pro" (for pronoun) and "PN" (for proper noun), we can write three separate rules, as shown on the left, but it is more succinct to write one rule, on the right, using curly brackets.

NP → Art (Adj) N
NP → Pro   NP → {Art (Adj) N, Pro, PN}
NP → PN

Phrase Structure Rules

What we have started to create is a set of syntactic rules called **phrase structure rules**. As the name suggests, these rules state that the structure of a phrase of a specific type will consist of one or more constituents in a particular order.

The first rule in the following set of simple (and necessarily incomplete) phrase structure rules captures a very general rule of English sentence structure: "a sentence (S) rewrites as a noun phrase (NP) and a verb phrase (VP)." The second rule states that "a noun phrase rewrites as either an article plus an optional adjective plus a noun, or a pronoun, or a proper noun." In the third rule, a verb phrase rewrites as a verb plus a noun phrase.

S → NP VP
NP → {Art (Adj) N, Pro, PN}
VP → V NP

Lexical Rules

Phrase structure rules generate structures. In order to turn those structures into recognizable English, we also need **lexical rules** that specify which words can be used when we rewrite constituents such as PN. The first rule in the following set states that "a proper noun rewrites as *John* or *Mary*." (It is a very small world.)

PN → {*John, Mary*}   Art → {*a, the*}
N → {*girl, dog, boy*}   Adj → {*big, small*}
V → {*followed, helped, saw*}   Pro → {*it, you*}

We can rely on these rules to generate the grammatical sentences shown below in (1)–(6), but not the ungrammatical sentences shown in (7)–(12).

(1) *A dog followed the boy.*   (7) **Dog followed boy.*
(2) *You saw it.*   (8) **You it saw.*
(3) *John saw the big dog.*   (9) **John Mary small dog*
(4) *It followed Mary.*   (10) **Followed Mary the dog big.*
(5) *The small boy helped you.*   (11) **The helped you boy*
(6) *Mary helped John.*   (12) **Mary John helped.*

Tree Diagrams

One of the best ways to create a visual representation of underlying syntactic structure is through **tree diagrams**. We can use the symbols introduced earlier to label parts of the tree when we create a representation of how each part fits into the underlying structure of phrases. The information in a phrase structure rule, on the left, can be expressed in a tree diagram, on the right, as in Figure 8.2.

NP → Art N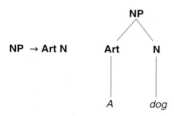

Figure 8.2 Noun phrase tree diagram

Although this kind of "tree," with its "branches," on the right, seems to grow down rather than up, it functions rather well as a diagram representing all the grammatical information found in the other analysis on the left. It also shows very explicitly that there are different levels in the analysis. That is, there is a level of analysis at which a constituent such as NP is represented and a different, lower, level at which a constituent such as N is represented.

We can use a similar tree diagram to represent the more complex structure of an English verb phrase (VP), as shown in Figure 8.3. Once again, this type of diagram provides a way of representing the hierarchical nature of underlying structure. In this hierarchy, the verb phrase (VP) in higher than and contains the verb (V) and a noun phrase (NP). The noun phrase (NP) is higher than and contains the article (Art) and the noun (N).

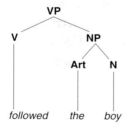

Figure 8.3 Verb phrase tree diagram

Tree Diagrams of English Sentences

We can now put together tree diagrams for whole sentences, hierarchically organized, as shown in Figure 8.4. Notice that essentially the same basic tree diagram structure is the foundation for all the different sentences (1)–(6), from page 116, with variable constituents included in each one.

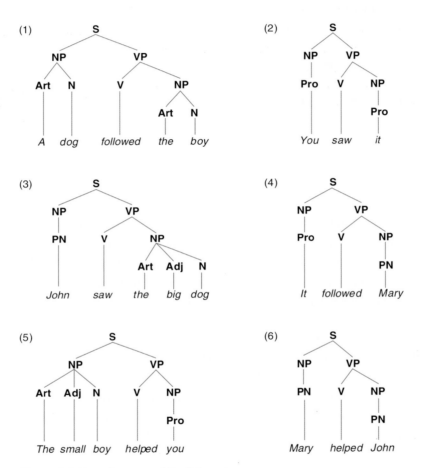

Figure 8.4 Tree diagrams of English sentences

Just Scratching the Surface

At the bottom of all the trees in Figure 8.4 are surface structure variations of a single underlying deep structure, revealing the generative power of the phrase structure rules involved. There are other phrase structure rules involved in the composition of more complex sentences. Some are presented in Task C on page 121 and Task K on page 125 for English, and Tasks F and G, on page 123 for other languages. As we try to develop better ways of analyzing the syntactic structure of complex sentences, we inevitably need a larger analytic framework. (We have barely scratched the surface structures.) However, having explored some of the basic issues, terminology, representations and methods of syntactic analysis in order to talk about basic structures in the English language, we will now move on to consider how we might incorporate the analysis of meaning in the study of language.

Study Questions

1 What was the original literal meaning of *syntax* in Greek?

2 What is wrong with the following rule of English syntactic structure? "A prepositional phrase rewrites as a preposition followed by a noun."

3 What is the main difference between a generative grammar and a traditional grammar?

4 At what level of structure are these two sentences different?

A large dog attacked us.   We were attacked by a large dog.

5 Which of the following expressions are structurally ambiguous and in what way?

 (a) *These are designed for small boys and girls.*
 (b) *The parents of the bride and groom were waiting outside.*
 (c) *How come a bed has four legs, but only one foot?*
 (d) *We met an English history teacher.*
 (e) *Flying planes can be dangerous.*
 (f) *The students complained to everyone that they couldn't understand.*

6 What part of speech is *lovely* in the following sentence?

We saw a lovely rainbow yesterday.

7 How many noun phrases are there in the following sentence?

George saw a small dog in the park near the fountain and it followed him when he left the park.

8 Which part of the following sentence is the VP?

None of the people in the building supported the proposed rent increase.

9 Which of the following expressions would be generated by this phrase structure rule: NP → {Art (Adj) N, Pro, PN}?

(a) *a lady*   (c) *her*   (e) *the widow*
(b) *the little girl*   (d) *Annie*   (f) *she's an old woman*

10 What kind of generative rule is this: N → {*girl, dog, boy*}?

11 Do phrase structure rules represent deep structure or surface structure?

12 Complete the following tree diagrams.

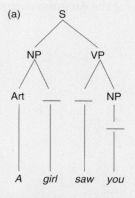 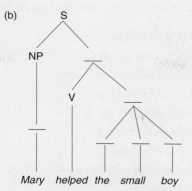

Figure 8.5 Tree diagrams

Tasks

A   What is the distinction made between "competence" and "performance" in the study of syntax?

B   What is meant by the expression "an embedded structure"? Were there any examples in this chapter?

C   In some versions of syntactic analysis there are also "movement" rules that move parts of structures to different positions. For example, the statement *You can see it* becomes the question *Can you see it?* by moving one element (*can*) to the front. This element is an auxiliary (or "helping") verb, as are *could, should, will, would*. They attach to verbs (*follow, help, see*) in the basic tree, as on the left in Figure 8.6, and are moved to the front to create a new tree, as on the right in Figure 8.6. In some descriptions, this change is called "inversion."

A special arrow (⇒) is used to indicate that a constituent can be moved, as shown in this rule for **Aux-movement**: NP Aux VP ⇒ Aux NP VP.

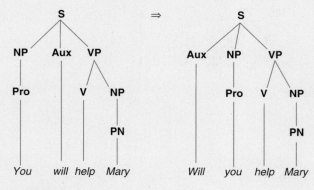

Figure 8.6 Aux-movement

Which of these structures would result from applying the Aux-movement rule?

(1)   *John will follow Mary.*
(2)   *Can you see the dog?*
(3)   *Could it follow you?*
(4)   *The girl helped you.*
(5)   *Could you help the dog?*
(6)   *Mary should see it.*
(7)   *Will the boy see you?*
(8)   *Would John help the girl?*
(9)   *It can see you.*
(10) *Can't you follow it?*

D   In spoken English, the sequence *want to* is sometimes contracted to *wanna*, as in *I don't wanna go* or *What do you wanna do tonight?*. However, as illustrated in the following set of sentences, there are some structures where *want to* cannot be contracted. English-speaking children know how to use *wanna* in the right places (and none of the wrong places) at a very early age. Can you work out what it is that they know about using *wanna*?

(1)   *Who do you **want to** or **wanna** visit?*
(2)   *Who would you **want to** or **wanna** go out with?*
(3)   *How many of your friends do you **want to** or **wanna** invite to the wedding?*
(4)   *Who do you **want to** (*wanna) win the game?*
(5)   *Who would you **want to** (*wanna) look after your pets?*
(6)   *How many of your friends do you **want to** (*wanna) stay with us?*

E   Which of the following two tree diagrams could be used to represent the underlying structure of the sentence: *George saw the boy with a telescope?*

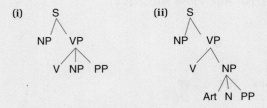

Figure 8.7 Underlying structure

F The following simplified set of phrase structure rules describes part of the syntax of a language called Ewe, spoken in West Africa. Based on these rules, which of the following sentences (1)–(10) should have an asterisk * before them?

S→ NP VP   N → {oge, ika, amu}

NP→ N (Art)   Art → ye

VP→ V NP   V → {xa, vo}

(1) *Oge xa ika*   (6) *Vo oge ika*
(2) *Ye amu vo oge*   (7) *Amu ye vo ika*
(3) *Ika oge xa ye*   (8) *Ye ika xa ye oge*
(4) *Oge ye vo ika ye*   (9) *Xa amu ye*
(5) *Amu xa oge*   (10) *Oge ye xa amu*

G Using these simple phrase structure rules for Scottish Gaelic, identify (with *) the ungrammatical sentences and draw tree diagrams for the grammatical sentences.

S→ V NP NP   NP→ {Art N (Adj), PN}

Art→ *an*   Adj→ {*ban, beag, mor*}

N→ {*cu, duine, gille*}   V→ {*bhuail, chunnaic, fhuair*}

PN→ {*Calum, Mairi, Tearlach*}

(1) *Calum chunnaic an gille.*
(2) *Bhuail an beag cu Tearlach.*
(3) *Bhuail an gille mor an cu.*
(4) *Chunnaic Tearlach an gille.*
(5) *Ban an cu an duine beag.*
(6) *Fhuair Mairi an cu ban.*

H The basic structure of a sentence in Tamasheq, spoken in north-west Africa, is illustrated as (1) in the sentences below, but an emphasized element can be moved to front position, as shown in the other examples. All these examples are from Sudlow (2001: 47), with minor changes.

(i) After looking at the syntactic structure of each Tamasheq sentence, can you add these English translations to appropriate places in the chart?

"It isn't men who cook porridge."

"Porridge, men aren't the ones who cook it."

"Men don't cook porridge?"

"Men aren't the ones who cook porridge."

(ii) Using information from Chapters 7 and 8, can you decide which of these languages has the same basic sentence structure as Tamasheq, as shown in example (1): English, Ewe, Gaelic, Japanese, Latin?

(1) *War   səkədiwan   meddan   asink*   "Men don't cook porridge."
     (not)   (cook)   (men)   (porridge)
(2) *meddan a waren isəkədiw asink*   _____
(3) *asink, meddan a waren t-isəkədiw* _____
(4) *wadde medan a isakadawan asink*_____
(5) *meddan war səkədiwan asink?*   _____

I In English prepositional phrases (PP) the preposition is placed before the noun phrase (prep + NP). In other languages, the PP is constructed differently with what is sometimes called a "postposition."

One of these languages is Arabana, an Aboriginal language that was spoken in the Lake Eyre region of South Australia. Below are some examples of PPs from Arabana, based on Hercuse (1994).

(i)   How would you write a phrase structure rule for PPs in Arabana?
(ii) Choose appropriate forms of Arabana PPs to fill the spaces (1)–(6) below.

kuthapadni ("without water")   *makanga* ("close to the fire")
nguraru ("out of the camp")   *karlaruku* ("to the river")
tyalpapurru ("with food")   *nguranganha* ("from the camp")
karlanga ("close to the river")

wadlhuru, nguranga, makapurru, karlanganha, nguraruku, tyalpapadni

(1) _____ ("from the river")
(2) _____ ("to the camp")
(3) _____ ("out of the ground")
(4) _____ ("without food")
(5) _____ ("close to the camp")
(6) *kutha* _____ ("with boiling water")

J In a **serial verb construction**, two or more verbs are used together in succession, typically describing a single event. These examples are from Yoruba, a West African language spoken in Nigeria and Benin, described in Bamgbose (2010).

(i)   Can you complete examples (7)–(10)?
(ii) Which of these phrase structure rules best describes the Yoruba structures in 1–10?

S → NP V NP   S → NP V VP
S → NP VP VP   S → NP VP NP

(1) *mo mú ìwé wá ilé*
I-take-book-come-house
("I brought a book home")

(2) *Olú fi ada ge igi náà*
Olu-put-machete-cut-tree-the
("Olu used a machete to cut the tree")

(3) *wón á sonwó fún mi*
they-will-pay money-give-me
("they will pay me")

(4) *ó se isu je*
she-cooked-yam-ate
("she cooked yam and ate it")

(5) *ó ti omó náà subú*
she-pushed-child-the-fall
("she pushed the child down")

(6) *mo á gbé wá bá*
I-will-carry-come-meet
("I will bring it to you")

(7) *ó mú ada wá*
____ ____ ____ ____ (" _____ ")

(8) *mo se isu náà je*
____ ____ ____ ____ ____ (" _____ ")

(9) *wón fi ìwé náà fún mi*
____ ____ ____ ____ ____ ____ (" _____ ")

(10) *omó náà á gbé ìwé wá*
____ ____ ____ ____ ____ ____ (" _____ ")

K The concept of **recursion** is used in syntax to describe the repeated application of a rule to the output of an earlier application of the rule. For example, we can use the terms "complementizer" (**C**) for the English word *that*, and "complement phrase" (**CP**) for *that Mary helped you* as part of the sentence *Cathy knew that Mary helped you*. In the complement phrase, the part *Mary helped you* represents a sentence (**S**), so there must be a rule: **CP → C S**, or "a complement phrase rewrites as a complement and a sentence."

This provides us with a small set of rules incorporating recursion. (Note that when you reach the end of this set of rules, you can keep going back to the beginning and repeating the sequence. That is the essence of recursion.)

S   → NP VP
VP → V CP
CP → C S

Using these rules, fill in the missing elements in the tree diagram in Figure 8.8.

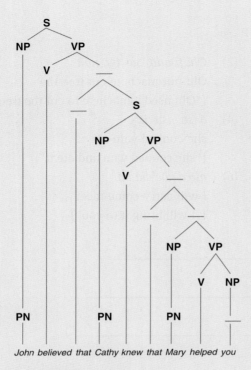

Figure 8.8 Recursion

Discussion Topics/Projects

I There is a principle of syntax called "structure dependency" that is often used to show that the rules of language structure depend on hierarchical organization and not on linear position. For example, someone trying to learn English might be tempted to think that questions of the type in (2) are formed simply by moving the second word in a statement (1) to become the first word of a question (2).

(1) *Shaggy **is** tired.*   (2) ***Is** Shaggy tired?*
    *You **will** help him.*   ***Will** you help him?*

Using the sentences in (3)–(6), try to decide if this is the best way to describe how all of these English questions are formed and, if it is not, try to formulate a better rule.

(3)   *Are the exercises in this book too easy?*
(4)   *Is the cat that is missing called Blackie?*
(5)   *Will the price of the new book you've ordered be really expensive?*
(6)   *Was the guy who scored the winning goal in the final playing for love or money?*

(For background reading, see chapter 3 of Fromkin, Rodman and Hyams, 2018.)

II   We could propose that passive sentences (*George was helped by Mary*) are derived from active structures (*Mary helped George*) via a rule such as the following:

(active) NP1 V NP2 = > NP2 *be* V-*ed by* NP1 (passive)

Note that the tense, past or present, of the V (e.g. *helped*) in the active structure determines the tense of *be* in the passive structure (e.g. **was** *helped*). Which of the following active sentences can be restructured into passive sentences using this rule? What prevents the rule from working in the other cases?

(1)   *The dog chased the cat.*
(2)   *Snow White kissed Grumpy.*
(3)   *He loves them.*
(4)   *Betsy borrowed some money from Christopher.*
(5)   *The team played badly.*
(6)   *The bank manager laughed.*
(7)   *They have two children.*
(8)   *The duckling became a swan.*
(9)   *Someone mentioned that you played basketball.*
(10)   *The police will arrest violent demonstrators.*

(For background reading, see Morenberg, 2013.)

Note: The different underlying structures in Oettinger's (1966: 168) example, *Time flies like an arrow; fruit flies like a banana*, cited at the beginning of this chapter, can be represented in the following tree diagrams. The different structures depend on some lexical ambiguity since *flies* is a verb in the first part and a noun in the second part. Also *like* is a preposition in the first part and a verb in the second part.

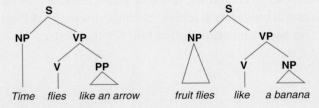

Figure 8.9 Analysis of the "Time flies" example

Further Reading

Basic Treatments

Casagrande, J. (2018) *The Joy of Syntax* Ten Speed Press

Miller, J. (2012) *An Introduction to English Syntax* (2nd edition) Edinburgh University Press

Thomas, L. (1993) *Beginning Syntax* Blackwell

More Detailed Treatments

Morenberg, M. (2013) *Doing Grammar* (5th edition) Oxford University Press

Tallerman, M. (2014) *Understanding Syntax* (4th edition) Routledge

Specifically on English Syntax

Burton-Roberts, N. (2016) *Analyzing Sentences: An Introduction to English Syntax* (4th edition) Routledge

Jonz, J. (2014) *An Introduction to English Sentence Structure* Equinox Publishing

On Generative Grammar

Baker, M. (2002) *The Atoms of Language: The Mind's Hidden Rules of Grammar* Basic Books

On Phrase Structures

Finegan, E. (2014) *Language: Its Structure and Use* (chapter 5) (7th edition) Cengage

On Structural Ambiguity

Pinker, S. (1994) *The Language Instinct* (chapter 4) William Morrow

Tree Diagrams

Carnie, A. (2012) *Syntax* (3rd edition) Wiley-Blackwell

Other References

Bamgbose, A. 2010) *A Grammar of Yoruba* Cambridge University Press

Fromkin, V., R. Rodman and N. Hyams (2018) *An Introduction to Language* (11th edition) Wadsworth

Hercuse, L. (1994) *A Grammar of the Arabana-Wangkangurru Language, Lake Eyre Basin, South Australia* The Australian National University, Canberra: Pacific Linguistics Series C 128

Oettinger, A. (1966) "The uses of computers in science" *Scientific American* 215 (September): 168

Sudlow, D. (2001) *The Tamasheq of North-East Burkina Faso* R. Köppe Verlag

9 | Semantics

This one time I was flying out of SFO (San Francisco) and I happened to have a jar of home-made quince preserves in my carry-on. A TSA (Transportation Security Administration) agent stopped me, saying that the quince preserves couldn't come aboard because no gels, liquids, or aerosols were allowed past the checkpoint. I asked him politely which of those quince preserves were: gel, liquid, or aerosol, because they seemed a lot like fruit. His response, and I kid you not, was "Sir, I'm not going to argue semantics with you."

Bergen (2012)

Semantics is the study of the meaning of words, phrases and sentences. In semantic analysis, there is always an attempt to focus on what the words conventionally mean, rather than on what an individual speaker might think they mean, or want them to mean, on a particular occasion. This approach is concerned with linguistic meaning that is shared by all competent users of the language. Doing semantics is attempting to spell out what it is we all know when we behave as if we share knowledge of the meaning of a word, a phrase, or a sentence in a language.

Meaning

While semantics is the study of meaning in language, there is more interest in certain aspects of meaning than in others. We have already ruled out special meanings that one individual might attach to words or what TSA agents believe words mean, as in Ben Bergen's story quoted earlier. That is, our main interest is in what we might describe as the widely accepted objective or factual meaning of words and not their subjective or personal meaning. This distinction is generally presented in terms of **referential meaning** as opposed to **associative** or **emotive meaning**, such as feelings or reactions to words that may be found among some individuals or groups but not others.

Referential meaning covers those basic, essential components of meaning that are conveyed by the literal use of a word. It is the type of meaning that dictionaries are designed to describe. Some of the basic components of a word like *needle* in English might include "thin, sharp, steel instrument." These components would be part of the referential meaning of *needle*. However, different people might have different associations or connotations attached to a word like *needle*. They might associate it with "pain," or "illness," or "blood," or "drugs," or "thread," or "knitting," or "hard to find" (especially in a haystack), and these associations may differ from one person to the next. These associations can't be part of the word's referential meaning.

One way in which the study of basic referential meaning might be helpful would be as a means of accounting for the "oddness" we experience when we read sentences such as the following:

> *The hamburger ate the boy.*
> *The table listens to the radio.*
> *The horse is reading the newspaper.*

We should first note that the oddness of these sentences does not derive from their syntactic structure. According to the basic syntactic rules for forming English sentences (presented in Chapter 8), we have well-formed structures.

> NP   V   NP
> *The hamburger   ate   the boy*

This sentence is syntactically good, but semantically odd. Since the sentence *The boy ate the hamburger* is perfectly acceptable, we may be able to identify the source of the problem. The components of the referential meaning of the noun *hamburger* must be significantly different from those of the noun *boy*, allowing one, not the other, to "make sense" with the verb *ate*. Quite simply, the kind of noun used with *ate* must denote a living or "animate" entity that is capable of "eating." The noun *hamburger* doesn't have this property and the noun *boy* does.

Semantic Features

We can also say that in addition to [+ animate], *boy* has the feature [+ human] and *horse* has [-human]. These examples illustrate a way of analyzing the meaning of words in terms of **semantic features**.

We can then characterize which semantic feature is required in a noun in order for it to appear as the subject of a particular verb. In this way we can predict which nouns (*boy, horse, hamburger*) would fit in a sentence appropriately and which would be odd, as in the following two. Both *boy* and *horse* would work in the first example, only *boy* would work in the second, and *hamburger* would be odd in both.

The _____ ate all the food.
          N [+ animate]

The _____ is reading the newspaper.
          N [+ human]

Componential Analysis

Semantic features have been used to analyze how words in a language are (or are not) connected to each other. Features such as [+ human] or [+ adult] can be treated as basic elements or components of meaning in an approach called **componential analysis**, as illustrated with one set of connected words in Table 9.1. If we replace [human] with [equine], we can analyze the set *colt, filly, stallion, mare* in the same way.

TABLE 9.1 COMPONENTIAL ANALYSIS

	boy	girl	man	woman
human	+	+	+	+
adult	–	–	+	+
female	–	+	–	+

Words as Containers of Meaning

The approach just outlined is a start on analyzing the basic components of word meaning, but it is not without problems. For many words in a language it may not be as easy to come up with neat components of meaning. If we try to think of the components or features we would use to differentiate the nouns *advice, threat* and *warning*, for example, we may not be very successful. Part of the problem seems to be that the approach involves a view of words in a language as some sort of "containers" that carry meaning components. This approach seems to be too restrictive and very limited in terms of practical use. There is more to the meaning of words than these basic types of features.

Semantic Roles

Instead of thinking of words as containers of meaning, we can look at the "roles" they fulfill within the situation described by a sentence. If the situation is a simple event, as in *The boy kicked the ball*, then the verb describes an action (*kick*). The noun phrases in the sentence describe the roles of entities, such as people and things, involved in the action. We can identify a small number of **semantic roles** (also called "thematic roles" or "case roles") for these noun phrases.

Agent and Theme

In our example sentence, one role is taken by the noun phrase *The boy* as "the entity that performs the action," technically known as the **agent**. Another role is taken by *the ball* as "the entity that is involved in or affected by the action," which is called the **theme** (or sometimes the "patient"). The theme can also be an entity (*The ball*) that is simply being described (i.e. not performing an action), as in *The ball was red*.

Agents and themes are the most common semantic roles. Although agents are typically human (*The boy*), as in (1) below, they can also be non-human entities that cause actions, as in noun phrases denoting a natural force (*The wind*), a machine (*A car*), or a creature (*The dog*), all of which affect *the ball* as theme in examples (2)–(4). The theme is typically non-human, but can be human (*the boy*), as in the last sentence (5).

(1) *The boy kicked the ball.*

(2) *The wind blew the ball away.*

(3) *A car ran over the ball.*

(4) *The dog caught the ball.*

(5) *The dog chased the boy.*

Instrument and Experiencer

If an agent uses another entity in order to perform an action, that other entity fills the role of **instrument**. In the sentences *The boy cut the rope with an old razor* and *He drew the picture with a crayon*, the noun phrases *an old razor* and *a crayon* are being used in the semantic role of instrument. Note that the preposition *with* is often a clue that the following noun phrase has the role of instrument in English. A related use of *with* is explored in Task G, and noun phrases marked as instruments in another language (Lakhota) can be found in Task H, both on page 143.

When a noun phrase is used to designate an entity as the person who has a feeling, perception or state, it fills the semantic role of **experiencer**. If we *feel, know, hear* or *enjoy* something, we are not really performing an action (hence we are not agents). We are in the role of experiencer. In the first sentence below, the experiencer (*The woman*) is the only semantic role. In the second example, the question is asking if (*you*) had the experience of hearing the theme (*that noise*).

The woman feels sad
Did you hear that noise?

Location, Source and Goal

A number of other semantic roles designate where an entity is in the description of an event. Where an entity is (*on the table, in the room*) fills the role of **location**. Where the entity moves from is the **source** (*from Chicago*) and where it moves to is the **goal** (*to New Orleans*), as in *We drove from Chicago to New Orleans*. When we talk about transferring money *from savings to checking*, the source is *savings* and the goal is *checking*. (Other examples are presented in Task I, page 144.)

All these semantic roles are illustrated in the following scenario. Note that a single entity (e.g. *George*) can appear in several different semantic roles.

Mary	saw	a fly	on the wall.
EXPERIENCER		**THEME**	**LOCATION**
She	borrowed	a magazine	from George.
AGENT		**THEME**	**SOURCE**
She	squashed	the bug	with the magazine.
AGENT		**THEME**	**INSTRUMENT.**
She	handed	the magazine	back to George.
AGENT		**THEME**	**GOAL**
"Gee thanks,"	said	George.	
		AGENT	

Lexical Relations

Not only can words be treated as containers of meaning, or as fulfilling roles in events, they can also have "relationships" with each other. In everyday talk, we often explain the meanings of words in terms of their relationships. If we are asked the meaning of the word *conceal*, for example, we might simply say, "It's the same as *hide*," or give the meaning of *shallow* as "the opposite of *deep*," or the meaning of *pine* as "a kind of *tree*." In doing so, we are characterizing the meaning of each word, not in terms of its component features, but in terms of its relationship to other words. This approach is used in the semantic description of language and treated as the analysis of **lexical relations**. The lexical relations we have just exemplified are synonymy (*conceal/hide*), antonymy (*shallow/deep*) and hyponymy (*pine/tree*).

Synonymy

Two or more words with very closely related meanings are called **synonyms**. They can often, though not always, be substituted for each other in sentences. In the appropriate circumstances, we can say, *What was his answer?* or *What was his reply?* with much the same meaning. Other common examples of synonyms are the following pairs:

almost/nearly	*big/large*	*broad/wide*	*buy/purchase*
cab/taxi	*car/automobile*	*couch/sofa*	*doctor/physician*
freedom/liberty	*handbag/purse*	*hard/difficult*	*sweat/perspire*

We should keep in mind that the idea of "sameness" of meaning used in discussing synonymy is not necessarily "total sameness," and it is best to think of these pairs as "close synonyms." There are many occasions when one word is appropriate in a sentence, but its synonym would be odd. For example, whereas the word *answer* fits in the sentence *Sandy had only one answer correct on the test*, the word *reply* would sound odd. Although *broad* and *wide* can both be used to describe a street in a similar way, we only talk about being *in broad agreement* (not *wide*) and *in the whole wide world* (not *broad*). There are also regional differences in the use of synonymous pairs, with *candy, chips, diaper* and *gasoline* in American English being equivalents of *sweets, crisps, nappy* and *petrol* in British English.

Synonymous forms may also differ in terms of formal versus informal uses. The sentence *My father purchased a large automobile* has virtually the same meaning as *My dad bought a big car*, with four synonymous replacements, but the second version sounds much more casual or informal than the first.

Antonymy

Two forms with opposite meanings are called **antonyms**. Some common examples are the pairs:

alive/dead	*big/small*	*buy/sell*	*enter/exit*	*fast/slow*
happy/sad	*hot/cold*	*long/short*	*male/female*	*married/single*
old/new	*raise/lower*	*rich/poor*	*smart/stupid*	*true/false*

Antonyms are usually divided into three main types, "gradable" (opposites along a scale), "non-gradable" (direct opposites) and "reversives" (one is the reverse action of the other). We can use **gradable antonyms** in comparative constructions involving adjectives, as in these underlined examples: *I'm smaller than you and slower, sadder, colder, shorter and older, but luckily quite a bit richer*. Also, the negative of one member of a gradable pair does not necessarily imply the other. For example, the sentence *My car isn't old* doesn't have to mean *My car is new*.

With **non-gradable antonyms** (also called "complementary pairs"), comparative constructions are not normally used. We don't typically describe someone as *deader* or *more dead* than another. Also, using the "negative test," we can see that the negative of one member of a non-gradable pair does imply the other member. That is, *My grandparents aren't alive* does indeed mean *My grandparents are dead*. Other non-gradable antonyms are the pairs: *male/female, married/single* and *true/false*.

Although we can use the "negative test" to identify non-gradable antonyms in a language, we usually avoid describing one member of an antonymous pair as the negative of the other. For example, while *undress* can be treated as the opposite of *dress*, it does not mean "not dress." It actually means "do the reverse of dress." Antonyms of this type are called **reversives**. Other examples are *enter/exit, pack/unpack, lengthen/shorten, raise/lower, tie/untie*. (See Tasks C and D, page 142.)

Hyponymy

When the meaning of one form is included in the meaning of another, the relationship is described as **hyponymy**. Examples are the pairs: *animal/horse, insect/ant, flower/rose*. The concept of "inclusion" involved in this relationship is the idea that if an object is a *rose*, then it is necessarily a *flower*, so the meaning of *flower* is included in the meaning of *rose*. Or, *rose* is a hyponym of *flower*.

When we investigate connections based on hyponymy, we are essentially looking at the meaning of words in some type of hierarchical relationship. Try to think quickly of a basic meaning for each of these words: *banyan, parakeet, terrier, turnip*. You can check Figure 9.1 to see if your meaning included hyponymy.

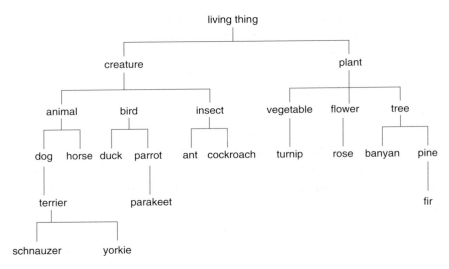

Figure 9.1 Hyponymy

Looking at the examples in Figure 9.1, we can say that "*horse* is a hyponym of *animal*," "*ant* is a hyponym of *insect*" and "*turnip* is a hyponym of *vegetable*." In these three examples, *animal, insect and vegetable* are called the **superordinate** (= higher level) terms. We can also say that two or more words that share the same superordinate term are **co-hyponyms**. So, *dog* and *horse* are co-hyponyms and the superordinate term is *animal*, while *ant* and *cockroach* are co-hyponyms with *insect* as the superordinate. Or *schnauzer* and *yorkie* are co-hyponyms, with *terrier* as one superordinate and *dog* as another at a more general level.

The relation of hyponymy captures the concept of "is a kind of," as when we give the meaning of a word by saying, "a *schnauzer* is a kind of *dog.*" Sometimes the only thing we know about the meaning of a word is that it is a hyponym of another term. That is, we may know nothing more about the meaning of the word *yorkie* other than that it is a kind of *dog* (also known as a Yorkshire terrier) or that *banyan* is a kind of *tree*.

Of course, it is not only words for "things" that are hyponyms. Words such as *punch, shoot* and *stab*, as verbs describing "actions," can all be treated as co-hyponyms of the superordinate term *injure* and the verbs *bake, boil, fry* and *grill* as co-hyponyms of the superordinate *cook*. For a lot of people, *microwave* has become another one.

Prototypes

While the words *canary, cormorant, dove, duck, flamingo, parrot, pelican* and *robin* are all equally co-hyponyms of the superordinate *bird*, they are not all considered to be equally good examples of the category "bird." According to some researchers, the most characteristic instance of the category "bird" is *robin*. The idea of "the characteristic instance" of a category is known as the **prototype**. The concept of a prototype helps explain the meaning of certain words, like *bird*, not in terms of component features (e.g. "has feathers," "has wings"), but in terms of resemblance to the clearest example. Thus, we might wonder if *ostrich* or *penguin* should be hyponyms of *bird* (technically they are), but we have no trouble deciding about *sparrow* or *pigeon*. These last two are much closer to the prototype.

Given the category label *furniture*, we are quick to recognize *chair* as a better example than *bench* or *stool*. Given *clothing*, people recognize *shirts* quicker than *shoes*, and given *vegetable*, they accept *carrot* before *potato* or *turnip*. It is clear that there is some general pattern to the categorization process involved in prototypes and that it determines our interpretation of word meaning. However, this is one area where individual experience can lead to substantial variation in interpretation. People may disagree over the categorization of words like *avocado* or *tomato* and treat them as co-hyponyms of both *fruit* and *vegetable* in different contexts.

Homophones and Homonyms

When two or more different (written) forms have the same pronunciation, they are described as **homophones**. Common English examples are:

bare/bear	*flour/flower*	*meat/meet*	*pail/pale*
pair/pear	*right/write*	*sew/so*	*to/too/two*

We use the term **homonyms** when one form (written or spoken) has two or more unrelated meanings, as in these examples:

bat (flying creature) – *bat* (used in sports)
mole (on skin) – *mole* (small animal)
pen (writing instrument) – *pen* (enclosed space)
race (contest of speed) – *race* (ethnic group)
sole (single) – *sole* (part of foot or shoe)

The temptation is to think that the two types of *bat* must be related in meaning. They are not. Homonyms are words that have separate histories and meanings, but have accidentally come to have exactly the same form.

Polysemy

When we encounter two or more words with the same form and related meanings, we have what is technically known as **polysemy**. Polysemy (from Greek *poly* "many" and *semy* "meanings") can be defined as one form (written or spoken) having multiple meanings that are all related by extension. Examples are the word *head*, used to refer to the object on top of your body, froth on top of a glass of beer, person at the top of a company or department or school and many other things. Other examples of polysemy are *foot* (of a person, of a bed, of a mountain), *mouth* (part of a face, a cave, a river) or *run* (person does, water does, colors do).

If we are not sure whether different uses of a single word are examples of homonymy or polysemy, we can check in a dictionary. If the word has multiple meanings (i.e. it is polysemous), there will be a single entry, with a numbered list of the different meanings. If two words are homonyms, they will have two separate entries. In most dictionaries, *bat*, *mail*, *mole*, and *sole* are treated as homonyms whereas *face*, *foot*, *get*, *head* and *run* are treated as examples of polysemy.

Of course, it is possible for two forms to be distinguished via homonymy and for one of the forms also to have various uses via polysemy. The words *date* (= a thing we can eat) and *date* (= a point in time) are homonyms. However, the "point in time" kind of *date* is polysemous in terms of a particular day and month (= on a letter), an arranged meeting time (= an appointment), a social meeting (= with someone we like) and even a person (= that person we like). So the question *How was your date?* could have a number of different interpretations.

Word Play

These last three lexical relations are the basis of a lot of word play, usually for humorous effect. In the nursery rhyme *Mary had a little lamb*, we think of a small animal, but in the comic version *Mary had a little lamb, some rice and vegetables*, we think of a small amount of meat. The polysemy of *lamb* allows the two interpretations. It is recognizing the polysemy of *leg* and *foot* in the riddle *What has four legs, but only one foot?* that leads to a solution (*a bed*).

We can make sense of another riddle *Why are trees often mistaken for dogs?* by recognizing the homonymy in the answer: *Because of their bark*. Shakespeare used homophones (*sun/son*) for word play in the first lines of the play *Richard III*:

Now is the winter of our discontent
Made glorious summer by this sun of York.

And if you are asked the following question: *Why is 6 afraid of 7?*, you can understand why the answer is funny (*Because 789*) by identifying the homophones.

Metonymy

The relatedness of meaning found in polysemy is essentially based on similarity. The *head* of a company is similar to the *head* of a person on top of and controlling the body. There is another type of relationship between words, based simply on a close connection in everyday experience. That close connection can be based on a container–contents relation (*bottle/water, can/juice*), a whole–part relation (*car/wheels, house/roof*) or a representative–symbol relationship (*king/crown, the President/the White House*). Using one of these words to refer to the other is an example of **metonymy**.

It is our familiarity with metonymy that makes it possible for us to understand *He drank the whole bottle*, although it sounds absurd literally (i.e. he drank the liquid, not the glass object). We also accept *The White House has announced . . .* or *Downing Street protested . . .* without being puzzled that buildings appear to be talking. We use metonymy when we talk about *filling up the car, answering the door, boiling a kettle, giving someone a hand* or *needing some wheels*. (See Task F, page 142, for more.)

Collocation

One final aspect of our knowledge of words, and how they are used, has nothing to do with any of the factors considered so far. As mature speakers of a language, we all know which words tend to occur with other words. If you ask a thousand people what they think of when you say *hammer*, more than half will say *nail*. If you say *table*, they'll mostly say *chair*, *needle* elicits *thread* and *salt* elicits *pepper*. One way we seem to organize our knowledge of words is simply on the basis of **collocation**, or frequently occurring together.

In recent years, the study of which words occur together, and their frequency of co-occurrence, has received a lot more attention in **corpus linguistics**. A corpus is a large collection of texts, spoken or written, typically stored as a database in a computer. Those doing corpus linguistics can then use the database to find out how often specific words or phrases occur and what types of collocations are most common. Some of the most common collocations are actually everyday phrases which may consist of several words used together, as in *I don't know what to do* (six words), *you know what I mean* (five words) or *they don't want to* (four words). See Task G page 257 in Chapter 16, for more examples.

We can also look into the corpus for specific words, extract a set of examples in context and arrange them in concordance lines, as illustrated in Figure 9.2.

Concordance

A **concordance** is a listing of each occurrence of a word (or phrase) in a corpus, along with the words surrounding it. The word being studied is described as the "key word in context" (KWIC). In the examples presented in Figure 9.2, from Taylor (2016: 112), the key word is *sarcastic*. From these examples, it is clear that *sarcastic* conveys an evaluation of behavior, with a range of negative terms (e.g. *abusive, condescending, hateful*) accompanying it. By far the most common collocate is the word *rude*, indicating that being *sarcastic* is frequently evaluated as a form of impoliteness, with an interpersonal meaning, adding to the referential meaning in the dictionary.

1   *I can't without being a bit **sarcastic** or rude. I'll simply photocopy and submit*
2   *to me – I mean if they were being **sarcastic** or rude, I think I would have noticed*
3   *don't wish to come across as rude, **sarcastic** or condescending. It does make*
4   *someone who is hotheaded rude **sarcastic** tactless won't give an inch etc. All your words*
5   *become more and more **sarcastic**, rude, whatever, until I respond. He's with some*
6   *words like rude, abusive and **sarcastic** keep cropping up when people deal with them*
7   *what comes out of her mouth is rude, **sarcastic** and downright mean it's hard to cope*
8   *demonstrative and hateful, rude, **sarcastic** and aggressive, I have very little support*
9   *customer service was very rude and **sarcastic**. Finally we had enough and said we*
10 *giving them an acerbic or **sarcastic** response is rude unless they were snarling in*

Figure 9.2 Concordance lines

Research of this type provides more evidence that our understanding of what words and phrases mean is tied to the contexts in which they are typically used. We will look at other aspects of the role of context in the interpretation of meaning in Chapter 10.

Study Questions

1   What semantic feature must a noun have in order to be used in this sentence?
    The _____ were discussing what to do.

2   Using semantic features, how would you explain the oddness of these sentences?

    (a)   *The television drank my water.*
    (b)   *His dog writes poetry.*

3   What phrase is used more often instead of "thematic roles" and what other term
    is used instead of "theme" in the semantic analysis of noun phrases?

4   What kind of opposites can be identified via the "negative test"?

5   How is the term "prototype" used in semantics?

6   Identify the roles of the seven noun phrases in this sentence:

    *With her new golf club, Anne Marshall whacked the ball from the woods to the
    grassy area near the hole and she suddenly felt invincible.*

7   Which of the following words are co-hyponyms?

    ant, cabbage, insect, plant, turnip, vegetable.

8   What is the basic lexical relation between each pair of words listed here?

    (a) *assemble/disassemble*   (d) *dog/schnauzer*   (g) *move/run*
    (b) *damp/moist*   (e) *furniture/table* (h) *peace/piece*
    (c) *deep/shallow*   (f) *married/single*   (i) *pen/pen*

9   Which of the following opposites are gradable, non-gradable, or reversive?

    (a) *absent/present*   (c) *fail/pass*   (e) *fill it/empty it*
    (b) *appear/disappear*   (d) *fair/unfair*   (f) *high/low*

10   What is the lexical relation between the English words *swallow* (= a small bird)
     and *swallow* (= make food or drink go down the throat).

11   What is the hierarchical relationship in the meanings of this set of words:
     bronchitis, disease, influenza, pneumonia, tuberculosis?

12   Are the underlined words in these sentences best described as examples of
     polysemy or metonymy?

     (a)   *The <u>pen</u> is mightier than the <u>sword</u>.*
     (b)   *I had to park on the <u>shoulder</u> of the road.*

(c) *Yes, I love those. I ate a whole <u>box</u> on Sunday!*

(d) *The bookstore has some new <u>titles</u> in linguistics.*

(e) *Computer <u>chips</u> created an important new technology.*

(f) *I'm going to sue your <u>ass</u>!*

(g) *I think that kind of music was called new <u>wave</u>.*

Tasks

A What is the connection between an English doctor called Peter Mark Roget and the study of lexical relations?

B In this chapter, we discussed metonymy, but not metaphor. What is the difference between these two ways of using words?

C The adjective pairs listed here are antonyms with a "marked" and "unmarked" member in each pair. Can you list the unmarked members and explain your choices?

big/small	*happy/unhappy*	*possible/impossible*
empty/full	*heavy/light*	*short/tall,*
fast/slow	*old/young*	*strong/weak*

D Which of these pairs of words are converses (also known as reciprocal antonymy)?

above/below	*doctor/patient*	*follow/precede*
asleep/awake	*dry/wet*	*husband/wife*
brother/sister	*enter/exit*	*older/younger*
buy/sell	*expensive/inexpensive*	*true/false*

E Another less common relation between word meanings is known as transferred epithet or hypallage. Why do we need to talk about this special type of meaning relation in the analysis of the meaning of the phrases listed here? Can you think of any other similar examples?

  a quiet cup of coffee   *a nude photo*   *a sleepless night*   *one of my clever days*

F Metonymy and synecdoche (/sɪnɛkdəki/) are two ways of using words with non-literal meanings. Can you identify the clear uses of synecdoche in these examples?

(1) *I read in a magazine that you shouldn't wear pink if you're a <u>redhead</u>.*

(2) *Some people expect the government to look after them from the <u>cradle</u> to the <u>grave</u>.*

(3) *There has been a significant increase in reports of <u>white-collar</u> crime.*

(4) *I was surprised when five new <u>faces</u> turned up in my first class.*

(5) *If I don't want to spend too much, I take a small amount of cash in my pocket and leave the <u>plastic</u> at home.*

(6) *The Pentagon has announced plans to upgrade their cybersecurity.*

(7) *They have something on the menu called "Surf and Turf," which consists of both fish and steak on the same plate.*

(8) *We'll never have progress as long as the greybeards remain in control.*

G   There is often a connection between English prepositions and semantic roles.

(i) Can you use an analysis based on semantic roles to explain the use of the prepositions *by* and *with* in the following examples?

(ii) Why are examples (5)–(8) treated as ungrammatical?

(1) *The walls of her room were decorated with large posters.*

(2) *One of the roads was blocked by a fallen tree.*

(3) *The store was robbed by a masked man with a gun.*

(4) *A small band of rebels was defeated by a larger force with superior weapons.*

(5) **I was surprised with the sudden bang outside my window.*

(6) **Most of his sketches were drawn by charcoal.*

(7) **Some people are embarrassed with photos from their teenage years.*

(8) **The Christmas tree was covered by ornaments and lights.*

H   In English, the semantic role of **instrument** is often expressed in a prepositional phrase (*She opened the can with a knife*; *He stopped the ball with his hand.*). In other languages the instrument may be expressed via an affix, as in the following examples from Lakhota, a Native American language spoken in North and South Dakota.

nabláza	"kick open"
nablécha	"crush something by stepping on it"
pabláska	"press out flat"
pachéka	"push aside"
pahóho	"loosen by pushing"
wabláza	"cut open"
waghápa	"cut the skin off something"
yaghápa	"bite off"
yagnáya	"tell a lie"
yuáka	"pull something up, like a fish on a line"
yughápa	"strip or pull off"
yughá	"remove the outer husk from corn"

(i) Can you identify the five affixes representing instruments in these examples and describe the type of instrument associated with each affix?

(ii)   Having identified the instrumental affixes, can you add the most appropriate affix to each of these verbs?

náchi	"raise or lift up"
óna	"push something onto something else"
xúgnaga	"to speak evil of"
kchá	"loosen by pulling"
bláza	"tear something open with the teeth"
ghápa	"kick the skin off something"
blécha	"break with a knife"
bláya	"spread out, like dough"

I   We can *pour water into a glass* and we can *fill a glass with water*, but we can't *fill water into a glass* or *pour a glass with water*. Why not?

(i)   By focusing on the meaning of the verbs and their themes ("the affected objects"), try to find a semantic reason why some of the following sentences are ungrammatical.

(1)   a. *We loaded furniture into the van.*
      b. *We loaded the van with furniture.*
(2)   a. *They sprayed paint onto the wall.*
      b. *They sprayed the wall with paint.*
(3)   a. *I poured coffee into the cup.*
      b. *I poured the cup with coffee.*
(4)   a. *She filled tissues into her pocket.*
      b. *She filled her pocket with tissues.*

(ii)   Which of the following verbs can be used in both of the (a) and (b) structures illustrated in examples (1)–(4): *attach, cram, glue, ladle, pack, paste, splash, spread*?

J   In this chapter, we looked at some examples of word play. Some other terms used to describe special ways of using words are presented in the first list and some examples in the second list. Using a dictionary if necessary, can you match each example to the appropriate descriptive term?

1 anagram	2 epigram	3 hyperbole	4 irony
5 oxymoron	6 palindrome	7 pun	8 simile

(a)   *Elvis lives!*
(b)   *Was it a car or a cat I saw?*

(c)   *His hair was white as snow.*
(d)   *Little strokes fell great oaks.*
(e)   *I feel a thousand times better today.*
(f)   *Trying to write with a broken pencil is pointless.*
(g)   (Tripping on a loose shoelace) *Well, that was clever!*
(h)   *No one goes to that restaurant anymore. It's always too crowded.*

K   Investigating a large corpus of British English, Barnbrook, Mason and Krishnamurthy (2013) reported on the frequency of a number of words occurring in collocation with the words *sun* and *moon*.

If relative frequency of collocation is part of our linguistic knowledge, we should be able to make an intuitive guess at where these words fit in appropriate positions in Table 9.2: *bright, full, light, moon, morning, planets, stars, sun.*

TABLE 9.2 COLLOCATIONS WITH *SUN* AND *MOON*

with *sun*	frequency	with *moon*	frequency
	228		228
	110		183
	103		75
	82		36

L   There is a meaning relationship between some English words that can be described as **inchoative**. In this relationship, the sense of one word "X" is incorporated in another word meaning "become X." For example, the word *die* means "become *dead*" and *grow* means "become *big*."

In some languages, this **meaning** relationship is marked by an inchoative affix. If you can identify the inchoative affix in the following examples, you should be able to fill the spaces in (1)–(6) below. These examples are from Wangkajunga, an Aboriginal language that was spoken in the Great Sandy Desert area of North Western Australia, as described in Jones (2011).

miiturriwa ("die")   *walarriwa* ("hurry")
jarlurriwa ("grow")   *putarriwa* ("decay")
yikarirriwa ("smile")   *palyarriwa* ("improve")

(1)	_____	("quick")	(4)	_____	("bad")
(2)	_____	("good")	(5)	_____	("big")
(3)	_____	("happy")	(6)	_____	("dead")

Discussion Topics/Projects

I One way to analyze the semantic structure of sentences is to start with the verb as the central element and define the semantic roles required by that verb. (This is sometimes called "theta assignment.") For example, a verb like *kill* requires an agent and a theme, as in *The cat* [agent] *killed the mouse* [theme]. A verb like *give* requires an agent, a theme and a goal, as in *The girl* [agent] *gave the flowers* [theme] *to her mother* [goal]. We can present these observations in this way:

KILL [Agent _____ Theme]
GIVE [Agent _____ Theme, Goal]

How would you define the set of semantic roles for the following verbs, using the format illustrated? Are there required roles and optional roles?

break	*build*	*die*	*eat*
fear	*kiss*	*like*	*occupy*
offer	*open*	*put*	*receive*
send	*sneeze*	*steal*	*taste*
teach	*understand*	*want*	*write*

(For background reading, see chapter 10 of Brinton and Brinton, 2010.)

II The words in the following list are all related in terms of the superordinate form *tableware*. How would you go about determining what the prototype item of "tableware" must be? Is a hierarchical diagram illustrating hyponymous relations useful? Would it be helpful to list some (or all) of the words beside a scale from 5 (= "excellent example of tableware") to 1 (= "not really an example of tableware") and ask people to indicate their choices on the scale? Do you think that the word with the highest score would indicate the prototype?

bowl	*flatware*	*ladle*	*soup spoon*
crockery	*fork*	*mug*	*spoon*
cup	*glass*	*plate*	*teaspoon*
cutlery	*glassware*	*platter*	*tumbler*
dish	*knife*	*saucer*	*wineglass*

(For background reading, see chapter 1 of Ungerer and Schmid, 2006.)

Further Reading

Basic Treatments

Birner, B. (2018) *Language and Meaning* Routledge

Cowie, A. (2009) *Semantics* Oxford University Press

Hurford, J., B. Heasley and M. Smith (2007) *Semantics: A Coursebook* (2nd edition) Cambridge University Press

More Detailed Treatments

Riemer, N. (2010) *Introducing Semantics* Cambridge University Press

Saeed, J. (2015) *Semantics* (4th edition) Wiley-Blackwell

Referential and Associative Meaning

Aitchison, J. (2012) *Words in the Mind* (4th edition) Blackwell

Pinker, S. (2007) *The Stuff of Thought* (chapter 1) Viking

Semantic Features

Goddard, C. (2009) "Componential analysis" In G. Senft, J-O. Östman and J. Verscheuren (eds.) *Culture and Language Use* (58–67) John Benjamins

Semantic Roles

Kroeger, P. (2005) *Analyzing Grammar: An Introduction* (chapter 4) Cambridge University Press

Lexical Relations

Murphy, M. (2003) *Semantic Relations and the Lexicon* Cambridge University Press

Antonymy

Jones, S. (2002) *Antonymy* Routledge

Prototypes

Taylor, J. (2004) *Linguistic Categorization* (3rd edition) Oxford University Press

Metonymy

Allan, K. (2009) *Metaphor and Metonymy* Wiley-Blackwell

Littlemore, J. (2015) *Metonymy* Cambridge University Press

Collocation and Corpus Linguistics

Anderson, W. and J. Corbett (2009) *Exploring English with Online Corpora: An Introduction* Palgrave Macmillan

Jones, C. and D. Waller (2015) *Corpus Linguistics for Grammar* Routledge

McEnery, T. and A. Hardie (2011) *Corpus Linguistics* Cambridge University Press

Other References

Barnbrook, G., O. Mason and R. Krishnamurthy (2013) *Collocation: Applications and Implications* Palgrave Macmillan

Bergen, B. (2012) *Louder Than Words* Basic Books

Brinton, L. and D. Brinton (2010) *The Linguistic Structure of Modern English* (2nd edition) John Benjamins

Jones, B. (2011) *A Grammar of Wangkajunga* (Pacific Linguistics 636) Australian National University, Canberra

Taylor, C. (2016) *Mock Impoliteness in English and Italian* John Benjamins

Ungerer, F. and H-J. Schmid (2006) *An Introduction to Cognitive Linguistics* (2nd edition) Pearson

10 | Pragmatics

In the late 1960s, two elderly American tourists who had been touring Scotland reported that, in their travels, they had come to a Scottish town in which there was a great ruined cathedral. As they stood in the ruins, they saw a small boy and they asked him when the cathedral had been so badly damaged. He replied in the war. Their immediate interpretation, in the 1960s, was that he must be referring to the Second World War which had ended only twenty years earlier. But then they thought that the ruins looked as if they had been in their dilapidated state for much longer than that, so they asked the boy which war he meant. He replied the war with the English, which, they eventually discovered, had formally ended in 1745.

Brown (1998)

In Chapter 9, we focused on referential meaning and the relationships between words. There are other aspects of meaning that depend more on context and the communicative intentions of speakers. In Gill Brown's story, the American tourists and the Scottish boy seem to be using the word *war* with essentially the same basic meaning. However, the boy was using the word to refer to something the tourists didn't expect, hence the initial misunderstanding. Communication clearly depends on not only recognizing the meaning of words in an utterance, but also recognizing what speakers mean by their utterances in a particular context. The study of what speakers mean, or "speaker meaning," is called **pragmatics**.

Invisible Meaning

In many ways, pragmatics is the study of "invisible" meaning, or how we recognize what is meant even when it is not actually said or written. In order for that to happen, speakers (or writers) must be able to depend on a lot of shared assumptions and expectations when they try to communicate. The investigation of those assumptions and expectations provides us with some insight into how we understand more than just the linguistic content of utterances. From the perspective of pragmatics, more is always communicated than is said. This pragmatic principle lies behind our ability to interpret the sign in Figure 10.1. You might think it means that we can park our "heated attendant" in this place. (They take attendants, heat them up, and this where they park them.) Alternatively, the sign may indicate a place where parking will be carried out by attendants who have been heated. (Maybe they will be more cheerful.) The words in the sign may allow these interpretations, but we prefer to think that we can park a car here, in a heated area, with an attendant to look after it. But how do we know that when the sign doesn't even have the word *car* on it?

Figure 10.1 Street sign

Context

It must be the case that we interpret the words (the "text") in a specific situation (the "context") with pre-existing assumptions about a likely message. The meaning of the text is not in the words alone, but in what we think the writer intended to communicate in that context.

A similar process is at work in making sense of the newspaper advertisement in Figure 10.2. By analogy with the expression *Furniture Sale*, we might think that someone is announcing the sale of some very young children here. But we resist that interpretation and assume that it is clothes for those children that are on sale. Yet the word *clothes* is nowhere in the message. It is part of what we bring to our interpretation in that context.

Figure 10.2 Newspaper ad

In these two examples, the influence of the context is crucial. In these cases, it is largely the **physical context**, the location "out there" where we encounter words and phrases. When we see the word *Bank* on a wall of a building, we interpret it in terms of a financial institution in that context. However, if you read about *an overgrown steep bank by the river*, you will have a different interpretation of the word *bank*. In this second interpretation it is the **linguistic context**, the surrounding words, also known as **co-text**, that helps us understand what is meant. Both physical context and linguistic context play important roles in how we make sense of any text.

Deixis

There are some very common words in our language that can't be interpreted at all if we don't know the context. These are words such as *here* and *there, this* or *that, now* or *then, yesterday, today* or *tomorrow,* as well as pronouns such as *you, me, she, him, it, them.* Some sentences of English are virtually impossible to understand if we don't know who is speaking, about whom, where and when. For example, what is the meaning of: *You'll have to bring it back tomorrow because she isn't here today?*

Out of context, this sentence is really vague. It contains a large number of expressions (*you, it, tomorrow, she, here, today*) that rely on knowledge of the local context for their interpretation. In context, we are expected to understand that the delivery driver (*you*) will have to return on February 15th (*tomorrow*) to 660 College Drive (*here*) with the long box (*it*) labeled "flowers, handle with care" addressed to Lisa Landry (*she*). For more examples, see Tasks C and D on pages 159–160.

Expressions such as *tomorrow* and *here* are technically known as **deictic** (/daɪktɪk/) **expressions**, from the Greek word **deixis**, which means "pointing" via language. We use deixis to point to people (*us, them, those idiots*), places (*here, over there*) and times (*now, last week*). All these deictic expressions are interpreted in terms of which person, place or time the speaker has in mind. As shown in Table 10.1, we also make a broad distinction between what is close to the speaker (*this, here, now*) and what is distant or not close to the speaker (*that, there, then*).

TABLE 10.1 DEICTIC EXPRESSIONS

	Close to speaker	Not close to speaker
Person deixis	*me, us, ours, this girl*	*him, them, that woman, those idiots*
Spatial deixis	*here, this bed, behind me*	*there, those hills, over yonder*
Temporal deixis	*now, today, this morning*	*then, yesterday, last week, next year*

This distinction may also be used to express emotions. If something is close, but we don't like it, we can use a "not close" term to describe it, thereby pushing it away from us by using deixis. A large bowl of cold tomato soup (which you hate) is placed in front of you (so it is close), but you find yourself saying, *I can't eat **that**.*

We can also indicate whether movement is away from the speaker (*go*) or toward the speaker (*come*). Just think about the difference between telling someone to *Go to bed* versus *Come to bed.* Deixis can even be entertaining. The bar owner who puts up a big sign that reads *Free Beer Tomorrow* (to get you to return to the bar) can always claim that you are just one day too early for the free drink.

Reference

In discussing deixis, we assumed that the use of words to refer to people, places and times was a simple matter. However, words themselves don't refer to anything. People refer. We have to define **reference** as an act by which a speaker (or writer) uses language to enable a listener (or reader) to identify something. To perform an act of reference, we can use proper nouns (*Chomsky, Jennifer, Whiskas*), other nouns in phrases (*a writer, my friend, the cat*) or pronouns (*he, she, it*). We sometimes assume that these words identify someone or something uniquely, but it is more accurate to say that, for each word or phrase, there is a "range of reference." The words *Jennifer* or *friend* or *she* can be used to refer to many entities in the world. As we observed earlier, an expression such as *the war* doesn't directly identify anything by itself, because its reference depends on who is using it.

We can also refer to things when we are not sure what to call them. We can use expressions such as *the blue thing* and *that icky stuff* and we can even invent names. For instance, there was a man who always drove his motorcycle fast and loud through my neighborhood and was locally referred to as *Mr. Kawasaki*. In this case, a brand name for a motorcycle is being used to refer to a person.

Inference

As in the "Mr. Kawasaki" example, a successful act of reference depends more on the listener/reader's ability to recognize what the speaker/writer means than on the listener's "dictionary" knowledge of a word that is used. For example, in a restaurant, one waiter can ask another, *Where's the spinach salad sitting?* and receive the reply, *He's sitting by the door*. If you're studying linguistics, you might ask someone, *Can I look at your Chomsky?* and get the response, *Sure, it's on the shelf over there*. And when you hear that *Jennifer is wearing Calvin Klein*, you avoid imagining someone called Calvin draped over poor Jennifer and recognize that they are talking about her clothing.

These examples make it clear that we can use nouns associated with things (*salad*) to refer to people, and use names of people (*Chomsky, Calvin Klein*) to refer to things. The key process here is called **inference**. An inference is additional information used by the listener to create a connection between what is said and what must be meant. In the *Chomsky* example, the listener has to operate with the inference: "if X is the name of the writer of a book, then X can be used to identify a copy of a book by that writer." Similar types of inferences are necessary to understand someone who says that *Picasso is in the museum, We saw Shakespeare in London, Mozart was playing in the background* and *The bride wore Giorgio Armani*.

Anaphora

We usually make a distinction between how we introduce new referents (*a puppy*) and how we refer back to them (*the puppy, it*).

> *We saw a funny home video about a boy washing <u>a puppy</u> in a small bath.*
> *<u>The puppy</u> started struggling and shaking and the boy got really wet.*
> *When he let go, <u>it</u> jumped out of the bath and ran away.*

In this type of referential relationship, the second (or subsequent) referring expression is an example of **anaphora** ("referring back"). The first mention is called the **antecedent**. So, in our example, *a boy, a puppy* and *a small bath* are antecedents and *The puppy, the boy, he, it* and *the bath* are anaphoric expressions.

There is a much less common pattern, called **cataphora**, which reverses the antecedent–anaphora relationship by beginning with a pronoun (*It*), then later revealing more specific information. This device is more common in stories, as in this beginning: *<u>It</u> suddenly appeared on the path a little ahead of me, staring in my direction and sniffing the air. <u>An enormous grizzly bear</u> was checking me out.*

Anaphora is, however, the more common pattern and can be defined as subsequent reference to an already introduced entity. Mostly we use anaphora in texts to maintain reference. The connection between an antecedent and an anaphoric expression is created through a pronoun (*it*), or a phrase with *the* plus the antecedent noun (*the puppy*), or another noun that is related to the antecedent in some way (*<u>The little dog</u> ran out of the room*). The connection between antecedents and anaphoric expressions is often based on inference, as in these examples:

> *We found <u>a house</u> to rent, but <u>the kitchen</u> was very small.*
> *I got on <u>a bus</u> and asked <u>the driver</u> if it went near the downtown area.*

In the first example, we must make an inference like "if X is a house, then X has a kitchen" in order to interpret the connection between antecedent *a house* and anaphoric expression *the kitchen*. In the second example, we must make an inference like "if X is a bus, then X has a driver" in order to make the connection between *a bus* and *the driver*. In some cases, the antecedent can be a verb, as in: *The victim was <u>shot</u> twice, but <u>the gun</u> was never recovered.* Here the inference is that any "shooting" event must involve a gun. We have used the term "inference" here to describe what the listener (or reader) does.

When we talk about an assumption made by the speaker (or writer), we usually talk about a "presupposition."

Presupposition

When we use a referring expression like *this, he* or *Jennifer*, we usually assume that our listeners can recognize which referent is intended. In a more general way, we design our linguistic messages on the basis of large-scale assumptions about what our listeners already know. What a speaker (or writer) assumes is true or known by a listener (or reader) can be described as a **presupposition**.

If someone tells you *Hey, your brother is looking for you*, there is an obvious presupposition that you have a brother. If you are asked the question *When did you stop smoking?*, there are at least two presuppositions involved: you used to smoke and you no longer do so. There is a test for presuppositions that involves comparing a sentence with its negative version and identifying which presuppositions remain true in both. This is called "constancy under negation." Whether you say *My car is a wreck* or the negative *My car is not a wreck*, there is an underlying presupposition (*I have a car*) that remains true. For more examples, see Task G on page 161.

Pragmatic Markers

Speakers have other ways of indicating how their utterances are to be interpreted. They can include short forms such as *you know, well, I mean, I don't know*, which are optional and loosely attached to the utterance. These are **pragmatic markers** and they can be used to mark a speaker's attitude to the listener or to what is being said. Speakers can use *you know* to indicate that knowledge is being treated as shared, and *I mean* to self-correct or to mark an attempt to clarify something.

> They had been reading something by Charles Wright, **you know**, the famous poet and **well, I mean**, he's famous in America at least, but em they didn't really understand it.

After making a statement about the poet, the speaker uses *well* to mark a shift from conveying information to commenting on it, with *I mean* introducing a clarification.

A more recent change of function has turned *I don't know* into a pragmatic marker. This phrase has evolved from a way of indicating lack of knowledge (*What's a lychee?* ~ *I don't know*) to become a marker of hesitation or uncertainty when a speaker is about to say something potentially in disagreement with another speaker.

> LEE: *I'm not very fond of Edinburgh it's so drab and it's always cold there.*
>
> JEN: **Oh, I don't know**, *I really enjoyed going to the Festival there last year.*

By appearing hesitant about disagreeing, the speaker can signal a desire not to challenge the other speaker. It seems to be a new way of being polite in interaction.

Politeness

We can think of politeness in general terms as having to do with ideas like being tactful, modest and nice to other people. In the study of linguistic politeness, the most relevant concept is "face." Your **face**, in pragmatics, is your public self-image. This is the emotional and social sense of self that everyone has and expects everyone else to recognize. **Politeness** can be defined as showing awareness and consideration of another person's face.

If you say something that represents a threat to another person's self-image, that is called a **face-threatening act**. For example, if you use a direct command to get someone to do something (*Give me that paper!*), you are behaving as if you have more social power than the other person. If you don't actually have that social power (e.g. you are not a military officer or prison warden), then you are performing a face-threatening act. An indirect request, in the form associated with a question (*Could you pass me that paper?*), removes the assumption of social power. You are only asking if it is possible. This makes your request less threatening to the other person's face. Whenever you say something that lessens the possible threat to another's face, it can be described as a **face-saving act**.

Negative and Positive Face

We have both a negative face and a positive face. (Note that "negative" doesn't mean "bad" here, it is simply the opposite of "positive.") **Negative face** is the need to be independent and free from imposition. **Positive face** is the need to be connected, to belong, to be a member of the group. So, a face-saving act that emphasizes a person's negative face will show concern about imposition (*I'm sorry to bother you . . . ; I know you're busy, but . . .*). A face-saving act that emphasizes a person's positive face will show solidarity and draw attention to a common goal (*The same thing happened to me . . . ; Let's do this together . . .*).

Ideas about the appropriate language to mark politeness differ substantially from one culture to the next. If you have grown up in a culture that has directness as a valued way of showing solidarity, and you use direct commands (*Give me that chair!*) to people whose culture is more oriented to indirectness and avoiding direct imposition, then you will be considered impolite. You, in turn, may think of the others as vague and unsure of whether they really want something or are just asking questions about it (*Are you using this chair?*). In either case, it is the pragmatics that is misunderstood and, unfortunately, more will often be communicated than is said.

The distinction between direct and indirect ways of communicating can be analyzed as different types of linguistic action, or speech acts.

Speech Acts

We use the term **speech act** to describe an action that involves language such as "requesting," "commanding," "questioning" or "informing." To take a more specific example, if you say, *I'll be there at six*, you are not just uttering a sentence, you seem to be performing the speech act of "promising." We can define a speech act as the action performed by a speaker with an utterance. (See Task E, page 160, for more.)

In order to understand how utterances can be used to perform actions that are both direct and indirect, we need to visualize a relationship between the structure of an utterance and the normal function of that utterance, as in Table 10.2.

TABLE 10.2 SPEECH ACTS

	Structures	Functions
Did you eat the pizza?	Interrogative	Question
Eat the pizza (please)!	Imperative	Command (Request)
You ate the pizza.	Declarative	Statement

Direct and Indirect Speech Acts

When an interrogative structure such as *Did you . . . ?, Is she . . . ?* or *Can you . . . ?* is used with the function of a question, it is described as a **direct speech act**. When you seriously want to know the answer to *Is she wearing a wig?*, that utterance is a direct speech act. If we really don't know something and we ask for the information (e.g. about ability), we normally use a direct speech act, as in *Can you ride a bicycle?*.

Compare that utterance with *Can you pass the salt?*. In this second example, we are not really asking a question about someone's ability. We are using an interrogative structure to make a request. This is an example of an **indirect speech act**. Whenever one of the structures in Table 10.2 is used to perform a function other than the one listed beside it on the same line, the result is an indirect speech act. For example, you can also use a declarative structure (*You left the door open*) to make a request (to the person, who just came in from the chilly outside, to close it). That is another indirect speech act.

Indirect speech acts offer fairly good evidence in support of the pragmatic principle, stated earlier, that communication depends on not only recognizing the structure and meaning of words in an utterance, but also recognizing what speakers mean by their utterances in a particular context. We will encounter more examples of this principle at work in Chapter 11.

Study Questions

1   What kinds of deictic expressions are used here (e.g. *We* = person deixis)?

    (a)   *We went there last summer.*

    (b)   *I'm busy now so you can't stay here. Come back later.*

2   How do we describe the pragmatic difference between the pair *here and now* versus *there and then*?

3   What kind of inference is involved in interpreting each of these utterances?

    (a)   TEACHER: *You can borrow my Shakespeare.*

    (b)   WAITER: *The ham sandwich left without paying.*

    (c)   NURSE: *The hernia in room 5 wants to talk to the doctor.*

    (d)   DENTIST: *My eleven-thirty canceled so I had an early lunch.*

4   What are the anaphoric expressions in the following sentence?

    Dr. Foster gave Andy some medicine after he told her about his headaches and she advised him to take the pills three times a day until the pain went away.

5   What is the technical term for the phrase *an old car* in its relationship with *it* in the following utterance?

    I have an old car, but it runs great.

6   What is the technical term used to describe the relationship between *She* and *Ginny Swisher* in the following example?

    She was born prematurely. She lost her parents at an early age. She grew up in poverty. She never completed high school. Yet Ginny Swisher overcame all these disadvantages to become one of the most successful women in America.

7   What process is involved in the connection between *cooking* and *the special meal* in the following sentence?

    The old men and women lit the fire and started cooking early in the morning so that the special meal would be ready for their guests.

8   What is one obvious presupposition of a speaker who says:

    (a)   *Your clock isn't working.*

    (b)   *Where did he find the money?*

    (c)   *We regret buying that car.*

    (d)   *The king of France is bald.*

9 How many pragmatic markers are used in the following interaction?

    MANA: *Why does everyone think he's a genius, I mean, he gets things wrong like the rest of us, doesn't he?*

    MAKA: *Well, I don't know, he got that award last year for innovation, you know, the Brill award, at the convention in New York, I think it was.*

10 In these examples, is the speaker appealing to positive or negative face?

    (a)   *If you're free, there's going to be a party at Yuri's place on Saturday.*

    (b)   *Let's go to the party at Yuri's place on Saturday. Everyone's invited.*

11 Someone stands between you and the TV set you're watching, so you decide to say one of the following. Identify which would be direct or indirect speech acts.

    (a) *Move!*   (c) *Could you please sit down?*

    (b) *You're in the way.*   (d) *Please get out of the way.*

12 In terms of speech acts, how would you explain the unusual nature of this interaction between a visitor to a city, with luggage, looking lost, and a man in the street outside the railway station.

    VISITOR: *Excuse me. Do you know where the Ambassador Hotel is?*

    RESIDENT: *Oh sure, I know where it is.* (and walks away)

Tasks

A What do you think is meant by the statement: "A context is a psychological construct" (Sperber and Wilson, 1995)?

B What is metapragmatics? What aspects of the following utterance illustrate metapragmatic awareness?

I know that Justin said, "I'll help you, darling," but he wasn't actually promising anything, I'm sure.

C Why is the concept of "deictic projection" necessary for the analysis of the following deictic expressions?

    (1)   On a telephone answering machine: *I am not here now*

    (2)   On a map/directory: YOU ARE HERE

    (3)   Watching a horse race: *Oh, no. I'm in last place.*

(4)   In a car that won't start: *Maybe I'm out of gas.*

(5)   Pointing to an empty chair in class: *Where is she today?*

D   Spatial deixis can be marked with affixes on verbs in Lolovoli (spoken on Ambae Island in the Republic of Vanuatu, in the south-west Pacific). The verbs that are used to describe the direction of movement are also deictic. Look at the following examples (based on Hyslop, 2001) and try to answer the questions that follow.

(1) *hivomai*   "come down to me"

(2) *hage*   "go away uphill"

(3) *hageatu*   "come up to you"

(4) *vano*   "go away across level space"

(5) *vanoatu*   "come to you across level space"

(6) _____   "come up to me"

(7) _____   "come down to you"

(8) _____   "come to me across level space"

(9) _____   "go away downhill"

(i)   Can you complete the set of verb forms in (6)–(9)?

(ii)   What distinction is coded in the two affixes used for spatial deixis?

(iii) Can you think of a reason for the distinctions in direction of movement, as coded in the verbs?

E   Which of these utterances contain "performative verbs" and how did you decide?

(1)   *I apologize.*

(2)   *He said he was sorry.*

(3)   *I bet you $20.*

(4)   *She won the bet.*

(5)   *I drive a Mercedes.*

(6)   *You must have a lot of money.*

F   The following phrases were all on signs advertising sales. What other words would you add to the description to make it clearer? What is the underlying structure of each phrase? For example, *Furniture Sale* means "someone is selling furniture." Would the same structure be appropriate for *Garage Sale*?

Back-to-School Sale	*Dollar Sale*	*One Cent Sale*
Bake Sale	*Foundation Sale*	*Plant Sale*
Big Screen Sale	*Furniture Sale*	*Sidewalk Sale*

Clearance Sale	*Garage Sale*	*Spring Sale*
Close-out Sale	*Labor Day Sale*	*Tent Sale*
Colorful White Sale	*Liquidation Sale*	*Yard Sale*

G Certain types of question–answer jokes or riddles seem to depend for their effect on the reanalysis of a presupposition in the question after the answer is given. For example, in the question *What two things can you never eat before breakfast?*, the phrase *two things* invites an interpretation that presupposes two "specific things," such as individual food items, as objects of the verb *eat*. When you hear the answer *Lunch and dinner*, you have to replace the first presupposition with another assuming two "general things," not individual food items, as objects of *eat*.

Identify the reanalyzed presuppositions involved in the following jokes (from Ritchie, 2002):

(1) Q: *Why do birds fly south in the winter?*
     A: *Because it's too far to walk.*

(2) Q: *Do you believe in clubs for young people?*
     A: *Only when kindness fails.*

(3) Q: *Did you know that in New York someone is knocked down by a car every ten minutes?*
     A: *No, but I imagine he must be getting really tired of it.*

(4) In a clothing store, a customer asks a salesperson:
     Q: *Can I try on that dress in the window?*
     A: *Well, maybe it would be better to use the dressing room.*

H Deictic expressions are not the only examples of vague language that require a pragmatic interpretation. All the following expressions are vague in some way. Analyze them into the categories in the chart in Table 10.3 below (based on Overstreet, 2011: 298). Can you add other examples?

and all that	*and everything*	*and stuff like that*
around seven	*heaps of*	*loads of*
maybe	*now and again*	*occasionally*
possibly	*probably*	*sevenish*
sometimes	*sort of blue*	*thingamajig*
thingy	*tons of*	*whatsisname*

TABLE 10.3 VAGUE LANGUAGE

Approximators (= "not exactly")	
General extenders (= "there is more")	
Vague nouns (= "inherently vague")	
Vague amounts (= "how many/much?")	
Vague frequency (= "how often?")	
Vague possibility (= "how likely?")	

I Using these examples, and any others you think are appropriate, try to decide if euphemisms and proverbs should be studied as part of pragmatics. Are they, for example, similar to indirect speech acts?

(1) *She's got a bun in the oven.*
(2) *He's gone to a better place.*
(3) *Unfortunately, there was some collateral damage.*
(4) *The grass is always greener on the other side of the fence.*
(5) *If wishes were horses, beggars would ride.*
(6) *People who live in glass houses shouldn't throw stones.*

J Diminutives are words that signal "small" in some way. In Spanish, the diminutive form *perrito* (from *perro* "dog") can be used for a puppy. It can also be used to talk about any dog (even a big one) in an affectionate way, as in *mi perrito* ("my doggy"). Another use of diminutives is to weaken the force of an utterance by using the "small" concept to convey "not significant" or "not a big deal," interpreted as a form of politeness.

Consider the following utterances (based on Mendoza, 2005) and try to decide if they are more likely to reflect a strategy of positive politeness or negative politeness. The non-diminutive versions are on the right.

(1) *¿Gusta un cafecito?*   ("Would you like some coffee?") [*cafe*]
(2) *Un momentito, por favor.*   ("Just a moment, please.") [*momento*]
(3) *Tengo una casita en la cuidad.* ("I have a house in town.") [*casa*]

(4) *Cuatrito nomás tengo.*   ("I only have four.") [*cuatro*]

(5) *Dame un poquito.*   ("Give me a piece.") [*poco*]

(6) *¿Alguna otra cosita?*   ("Anything else for you?") [*cosa*]

K In our discussion of politeness, we mentioned face-threatening acts, but didn't consider those acts that clearly represent forms of **impoliteness** in English. Although the interpretation of impolite uses of language necessarily depends on the context and relationship of the participants, certain types of expressions would seem to be intentionally face-threatening. (For some special uses, see the examples in Task G in Chapter 19, page 308.)

The following analytic categories are based on Culpeper (2011).

 (i) Can you connect each example below with one of the categories?

(ii) Can you think of any special situations in which these expressions would not be treated as impolite?

(a) Threats   (d) Dismissals

(b) Sarcasm   (e) Condescension

(c) Silencers   (f) Negative personal evaluation

(1) *Get lost!*

(2) *Just sit down and be quiet.*

(3) *You can't get anything right.*

(4) *I'm going to get you for this.*

(5) *That wasn't very smart of you, was it?*

(6) *Well, thanks very much for leaving all your dirty dishes in the sink.*

Discussion Topics/Projects

I On the topic of "more gets communicated than is said," consider this situation, described in Tannen (2005).

A Greek woman explained how she and her father (and later her husband) communicated. If she wanted to do something, like go to a dance, she had to ask her father for permission. He never said no. But she could tell from the way he said yes whether or not he meant it. If he said something like "Yes, of course, go," then she knew he thought it was a good idea. If he said something like "If you want, you can go," then she understood that he didn't think it was a good idea, and she wouldn't go.

 (i) Why do you think "he never said no" (when he was communicating "No")?

(ii)   How would you analyze the two speech acts reported as responses in this passage?

(iii) What other situations are you familiar with where "more is/was communicated than is/was said"?

(For background reading, see Tannen, 2005.)

II   What counts as polite behavior can differ substantially from one group or culture to the next. Below are some basic descriptions from Lakoff (1990) of three types of politeness, called distance politeness, deference politeness and camaraderie politeness. As you read these descriptions, try to decide which type you are most familiar with and whether you have encountered the others on any occasion. What kind of language do you think is characteristic of these different types of politeness?

(1)   "Distance politeness is the civilized human analogue to the territorial strategies of other animals. An animal sets up physical boundary markers (the dog and the hydrant) to signal its fellows: My turf, stay out. We, being symbol-using creatures, create symbolic fences."

"Distancing cultures weave remoteness into their language."

(2)   "Another culture might avoid the danger of conflict by adopting a strategy of deferential politeness. If a participant decides that whatever is to happen in a conversation – both what is said and it is to mean – is up to the other person, conflict can easily be avoided."

"Where distance politeness more or less assumes equality between participants, deference works by debasing one or both."

"While distance politeness has been characteristic of the middle and upper classes in most of Europe for a very long time, deference has been typical in many Asian societies. But it is also the preferred model of interaction for women in the majority of societies, either always or only when talking to men."

(3)   "A third strategy (camaraderie) that has recently emerged in this culture makes a different assumption: that interaction and connection are good in themselves, that openness is the greatest sign of courtesy."

"In a camaraderie system, the appearance of openness and niceness is to be sought above all else. There is no holding back, nothing is too terrible to say."

(For background reading, see chapter 2 of Lakoff, 1990.)

Further Reading

Basic Treatments

Cutting, J. (2014) *Pragmatics: A Resource Book for Students* (3rd edition) Routledge

Yule, G. (1996) *Pragmatics* Oxford University Press

More Detailed Treatments

Birner, B. (2012) *Introduction to Pragmatics* Wiley-Blackwell

Cummins, C. (2018) *Pragmatics* University of Edinburgh Press

The Pragmatics of English

Culpeper, J. and M. Haugh (2014) *Pragmatics and the English Language* Macmillan

Grundy, P. (2008) *Doing Pragmatics* (3rd edition) Hodder

Context and Co-Text

Malmkjaer, K. and J. Williams (eds.) (1998) *Context in Language Learning and Language Understanding* Cambridge University Press

Widdowson, H. (2004) *Text, Context, Pretext* (chapter 4) Blackwell

Reference and Deixis

Cruse, A. (2011) *Meaning in Language* (3rd edition) (part 4) Oxford University Press

Levinson, S. (2006) "Deixis" In L. Horn and G. Ward (eds.) *The Handbook of Pragmatics* (97–121) Blackwell

Anaphora

Garnham, A. (2001) *Mental Models and the Interpretation of Anaphora* (chapter 4) Psychology Press

Presupposition

Marmaridou, S. (2010) "Presupposition" In L. Cummings (ed.) *The Pragmatics Encyclopedia* (349–353) Routledge

Schwarz, F. (ed.) (2015) *Experimental Perspectives on Presupposition* Springer

Pragmatic Markers

Aijmer, K. (2013) *Understanding Pragmatic Markers* Edinburgh University Press

Archer, D., K. Aijmer and A. Wichmann (2012) *Pragmatics: An Advanced Resource Book for Students* (Units A7 and B7) Routledge

Politeness and Face

Brown, P. and S. Levinson (1987) *Politeness* Cambridge University Press

Kádár, D. and M. Haugh (2013) *Understanding Politeness* Cambridge University Press

Mills, S. (2003) *Gender and Politeness* Cambridge University Press

Speech Acts

Fogal, D., D. Harris and M. Moss (eds.) (2018) *New Work on Speech Acts* Oxford University Press

Thomas, J. (1995) *Meaning in Interaction* (chapter 2) Longman

Other References

Culpeper, J. (2011) *Impoliteness: Using Language to Cause Offence* Cambridge University Press

Hyslop, C. (2001) *The Lolovoli Dialect of the North-East Ambae Language: Vanuatu* (Pacific Linguistics 515) Australian National University, Canberra

Lakoff, R. (1990) *Talking Power* Basic Books

Mendoza, M. (2005) "Polite diminutives in Spanish" In R. Lakoff and S. Ide (eds.) *Broadening the Horizons of Linguistic Politeness* (163–173) John Benjamins

Overstreet, M. (2011) "Vagueness and hedging" In G. Andersen and K. Aijmer (eds.) *Pragmatics of Society* (293–317) De Gruyter

Ritchie, G. (2002) *The Linguistic Analysis of Jokes* Routledge

Sperber, D. and D. Wilson (1995) *Relevance* (2nd edition) Blackwell

Tannen, D. (2005) *Conversational Style* Oxford University Press

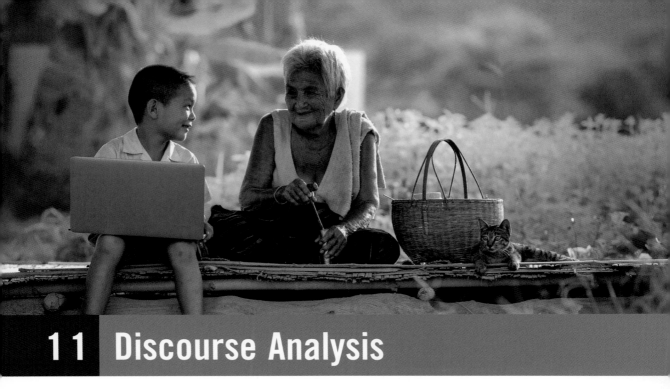

11 Discourse Analysis

There's two types of favors, the big favor and the small favor. You can measure the size of the favor by the pause that a person takes after they ask you to "Do me a favor." Small favor – small pause. "Can you do me a favor, hand me that pencil." No pause at all. Big favors are, "Could you do me a favor . . ." Eight seconds go by. "Yeah? What?"

" . . . well." The longer it takes them to get to it, the bigger the pain it's going to be.

Humans are the only species that do favors. Animals don't do favors. A lizard doesn't go up to a cockroach and say, "Could you do me a favor and hold still, I'd like to eat you alive." That's a big favor even with no pause.

Seinfeld (1993)

In the study of language, some of the most interesting observations are made, not in terms of the components of language, but in terms of the way language is used, even how pauses are used, as in Jerry Seinfeld's commentary. We have already considered some of the features of language in use when we discussed pragmatics in Chapter 10. We were, in effect, asking how it is that language-users successfully interpret what other language-users intend to convey. When we carry this investigation further and ask how we make sense of what we read, how we can recognize well-constructed texts as opposed to those that are jumbled or incoherent, how we understand speakers who communicate more than they say, and how we successfully take part in that complex activity called conversation, we are undertaking what is known as **discourse analysis**.

Discourse

The word **discourse** is usually defined as "language beyond the sentence" and so the analysis of discourse is typically concerned with the study of language in texts and conversation. In many of the preceding chapters, when we were concentrating on linguistic description, we were concerned with the accurate representation of the forms and structures. However, as language-users, we are capable of more than simply recognizing correct versus incorrect forms and structures. We can cope with fragments in newspaper headlines such as *Trains collide, two die*, and know that what happened in the first part was the cause of what happened in the second part. We can also make sense of notices like *No shoes, no service*, on shop windows in summer, understanding that a conditional relation exists between the two parts ("If you are wearing no shoes, you will receive no service"). We have the ability to create complex discourse interpretations of fragmentary linguistic messages.

Interpreting Discourse

We can even cope with texts, written in English, which we couldn't produce ourselves and which appear to break a lot of the rules of the English language. Yet we can build an interpretation. The following example, provided by Eric Nelson, is from an essay by a student learning English and contains ungrammatical forms and misspellings, yet it can be understood.

> **My Town**
>
> *My natal was in a small town, very close to Riyadh capital of Saudi Arabia. The distant between my town and Riyadh 7 miles exactly. The name of this Almasani that means in English Factories. It takes this name from the peopl's carrer. In my childhood I remmeber the people live. It was very simple. Most the people was farmer.*

This example may serve to illustrate a simple point about the way we react to language that contains ungrammatical forms. Rather than simply rejecting the text as ungrammatical, we try to make sense of it. That is, we attempt to arrive at a reasonable interpretation of what the writer intended to convey. (Most people say they understand the "My Town" text quite easily.)

It is this effort to interpret (or to be interpreted), and how we accomplish it, that are the key elements investigated in the study of discourse. To arrive at an interpretation, and to make our messages interpretable, we certainly rely on what we know about linguistic form and structure. But, as language-users, we have more knowledge than that.

Cohesion

We know, for example, that texts must have a certain structure that depends on factors quite different from those required in the structure of a single sentence. Some of those factors are described in terms of **cohesion**, or the formal ties and connections that exist within texts. There are several **cohesive ties** in this text.

> My father once bought a Lincoln convertible. He did it by saving every penny he could. That car would be worth a fortune nowadays. However, he sold it to help pay for my college education. Sometimes I think I'd rather have the convertible.

We can identify connections here in the use of words to maintain reference to the same people and things throughout. There are also connections created by terms that share a common element of meaning, such as "money" and "time." The verb tenses in the first four sentences are in the past, creating a connection between those events, in contrast to the present tense of the final sentence marking a change in time and focus. These cohesive ties are listed in Table 11.1. See Task B on page 178 for more.

TABLE 11.1 COHESIVE TIES

People	*My father – He – he – he; My – my – I – I*
Things	*A Lincoln convertible – That car – it – the convertible*
Money	*bought – saving every penny – worth a fortune – sold – pay*
Time	*once – nowadays – sometimes*
Tenses	past (*bought*) – past (*did*) – past (*could*) – past (*sold*) – present (*think*)

Analysis of these cohesive ties gives us some insight into how writers structure what they want to say. However, by itself, cohesion is not sufficient to enable us to make sense of what we read. It is quite easy to create a text that has a lot of cohesive ties, but is difficult to interpret. Note that the following text has these connections in *Lincoln – the car, red – that color, her –she* and *letters – a letter.*

> My father bought a Lincoln convertible. The car driven by the police was red. That color doesn't suit her. She consists of three letters. However, a letter isn't as fast as a telephone call.

It becomes clear from this type of example that the "connectedness" we experience in our interpretation of normal texts is not simply based on connections between words. There must be another factor that helps us distinguish connected texts that make sense from those that do not. This factor is usually described as "coherence."

Coherence

The key to the concept of **coherence** ("everything fitting together well") is not something that exists in the words or structures of discourse, like cohesion, but something that exists in people. It is people who "make sense" of what they read and hear. They try to arrive at an interpretation that is in line with their experience of the way the world is. You may have tried quite hard to make the last example fit some situation that accommodated all the details (involving a red car, a woman and a letter) into a single coherent interpretation. In doing so, you would necessarily be involved in a process of bringing other information to the text. This process is not restricted to trying to understand "odd" texts. It seems to be involved in our interpretation of all discourse.

For example, you pick up a newspaper and see this headline: *Woman robs bank with sandwich*. As you try to build a coherent interpretation, you probably focus on the *sandwich* part because there is something odd about this situation. Is she just carrying a sandwich, or is she eating the sandwich (taking occasional bites), or is she acting as if the sandwich is a weapon (concealed in a bag perhaps)? Deciding which interpretation is appropriate cannot be accomplished based on only the words in the headline. We need to bring information from our experience to create a plausible situation. If you decided on the "pretend gun in bag" situation, then your coherence-creating mind would appear to be in good working order.

We also depend on coherence in coping with everyday conversation. We are continually taking part in conversational interactions where a great deal of what is meant or communicated cannot actually be found in what is said. In this brief interaction (from Widdowson, 1978), there are no cohesive ties connecting the three utterances, so we must be using some other means to make sense of it. One way to understand what is going on is to consider the three parts of the interaction in terms of speech acts (introduced in Chapter 10). These are listed on the right, providing a way of analyzing the interaction by identifying what makes it coherent for the participants.

HER: *That's the telephone.*   (She makes a request of him to perform action)
HIM: *I'm in the bath.*   (He states reason why he cannot comply with request)
HER: *OK.*   (She accepts reason)

If this is a reasonable analysis of what took place in the brief interaction, then it is clear that language-users must have a lot of knowledge of how conversation works that is not simply knowledge of words and sentences, but must involve familiarity with a lot of other types of structures and their typical functions.

Conversation Analysis

In simple terms, English conversation can be described as an activity in which, for the most part, two or more people take **turns** at speaking. Typically, only one person speaks at a time and there tends to be an avoidance of silence between speaking turns. (This is not true in all situations or societies.) If more than one participant tries to talk at the same time, one of them usually stops, as in the following example, where A stops until B has finished.

A: *Didn't you* [*know wh-*

B: [*But he must've been there by two*

A: *Yes but you knew where he was going*

(A small square bracket [is conventionally used to indicate a place where simultaneous or overlapping speech occurs.)

For the most part, participants wait until one speaker indicates that he or she has finished, usually by signaling a **completion point**. Speakers can mark their turns as complete in a number of ways: by asking a question, for example, or by pausing at the end of a completed syntactic structure like a phrase or sentence. Other participants can indicate that they want to take the speaking turn, also in a number of ways. They can start to make short sounds, usually repeated, while the speaker is talking, and often use body shifts or facial expressions to signal that they have something to say. (For more on conversation, see Task C, on page 179, and Task F on page 180)

Turn-Taking

There are different expectations of conversational style and different strategies of partici-pation in conversation, which may result in slightly different conventions of **turn-taking**. One strategy, which may be overused by "long-winded" speakers or those who are used to "holding the floor," is designed to avoid having normal completion points occur. We all use this strategy to some extent, usually in situations where we have to work out what we are trying to say while actually saying it.

If the normal expectation is that completion points are marked by the end of a sentence and a pause, then one way to "keep the turn" is to avoid having those two markers occur together. That is, don't pause at the end of sentences; make your sentences run on by using connectors like *and, and then, so, but*; place your pauses at points where the message is clearly incomplete; and preferably "fill" the pause with a hesitation marker such as *er, em, uh, ah*.

Pauses and Filled Pauses

In the following example, note how the pauses (marked by . . .) are placed before and after verbs rather than at the end of sentences, making it difficult to get a clear sense of what this person is saying until we hear the part after each pause.

> A: *that's their favorite restaurant because they . . . enjoy French food and when they were . . . in France they couldn't believe it that . . . you know that they had . . . that they had had better meals back home*

In the next example, speaker X produces **filled pauses** (with *em, er, you know*) after having almost lost the turn at his first brief hesitation.

> X: *well that film really was . . . [wasn't what he was good at*
> Y: *[when di-*
> X: *I mean his other . . . em his later films were much more . . . er really more in the romantic style and that was more what what he was . . . you know . . . em best at doing*
> Y: *so when did he make that one*

Adjacency Pairs

That last example would seem to suggest that conversation is a problematic activity where speakers have to pay close attention to what is going on. That is not normally the case because a great deal of conversational interaction follows some fairly well established patterns. When someone says *Hi* or *Hello*, we usually respond with a similar greeting. This type of almost automatic sequence is called an **adjacency pair**, which consists of a first part and a second part, as found in greetings, question–answer (Q ~ A) sequences, thanking and leave-taking.

First part	**Second part**
YOU: *Good mornin'.*	ME: *Good mornin'.*
YOU: *Where's Mary?*	ME: *She's at work already.*
YOU: *Thanks for your help yesterday.*	ME: *Oh, you're welcome.*
YOU: *Okay, talk to you later.*	ME: *Bye.*

These examples illustrate the basic pattern, but not all first parts are immediately followed by second parts. For example, one question may not receive its answer until after another question–answer sequence. (See Task E, on page 179, for more.)

Insertion Sequences

In the following example, the sequence Q2 ~ A2 comes between the first question (Q1) and its answer (A1). This is called an **insertion sequence**, that is, an adjacency pair that comes between the first and second parts of another pair.

YOU: *Do you want some milk?*   (= Q1)
ME: *Is it soy milk?*   (= Q2)
YOU: *Of course.*   (= A2)
ME: *Okay, thanks.*   (= A1)

In some situations, a complex structure can emerge from the effect of insertion sequences. This is often the case in "service encounters," as in our next example. Notice how it is only in the middle of this interaction (Q3 ~ A3) that we have an adjacency pair together, while insertion sequences delay the occurrence of second parts for each of the other first parts.

BUD: *Can I order pizza to go?*   (= Q1)
DAN: *What kind would you like?*   (= Q2)
BUD: *Do you have any special deals?*   (= Q3)
DAN: *Well, you can get two veggie supremes for the price of one.*   (= A3)
BUD: *Okay, I'd like that deal.*   (= A2)
DAN: *Sure thing. We'll have that ready for you in no time.*   (= A1)

We are not normally aware of most of these aspects of conversational structure, but speakers sometimes draw attention to the need for a second part once a first part has been uttered. In the following interaction, originally analyzed by Sacks (1972: 341), a mother immediately notices the absence of a spoken return greeting by her daughter and draws attention to the social expectation involved.

WOMAN: *Hi, Annie.*
MOTHER: *Annie, don't you hear someone say hello to you?*
WOMAN: *Oh, that's okay, she smiled hello.*
MOTHER: *You know you're supposed to greet someone, don't you?*
ANNIE: [Hangs head] *Hello.*

The expectations we all have that certain patterns of turn-taking will occur in conversation are connected to a more general aspect of socially situated interaction, that it will be "co-operative." This observation is actually a principle of conversation.

The Co-operative Principle

An underlying assumption in most conversational exchanges is that the participants are co-operating with each other. This principle, plus four elements, or "maxims," were first described by the philosopher Paul Grice (1975: 45), and are often referred to as the "Gricean maxims," as presented in Table 11.2.

TABLE 11.2 GRICEAN MAXIMS

The Co-operative Principle: Make your conversational contribution such as is required, at the stage at which it occurs, by the accepted purpose or direction of the talk exchange in which you are engaged.
The **Quantity** maxim: Make your contribution as informative as is required, but not more, or less, than is required.
The **Quality** maxim: Do not say that which you believe to be false or for which you lack adequate evidence.
The **Relation** maxim: Be relevant.
The **Manner** maxim: Be clear, brief and orderly.

In simple terms, we expect our conversational partners to make succinct, honest, relevant and clear contributions to the interaction and to signal to us in some way if these maxims are not being followed. It is certainly true that, on occasion, we can experience conversational exchanges in which the co-operative principle may not seem to be in operation. However, this general description of the normal expectations we have in conversation helps to explain a number of regular features in our talk. For example, during their lunch break, one woman asks another how she likes the sandwich she is eating and receives the following answer.

Oh, a sandwich is a sandwich.

In logical terms, this reply appears to have no communicative value since it states something obvious and hence would appear to be a **tautology**. Repeating a phrase that adds nothing would hardly count as an appropriate answer to a question. However, if the woman is being co-operative and adhering to the Quantity maxim about being "as informative as is required," then the listener must assume that her friend is communicating something. Given the opportunity to evaluate the sandwich, her friend has responded without an explicit evaluation, thereby implying that she has no opinion, good or bad, to express. That is, her friend has communicated that the sandwich is not worth talking about. (See Task D, on page 179, for more.)

Hedges

We can use certain types of expressions, called **hedges**, to show that we are concerned about following the maxims while being co-operative speakers. Hedges can be defined as words or phrases used to indicate that we are not really sure that what we are saying is sufficiently correct or complete. We can use *sort of* or *kind of* as hedges on the accuracy of our statements, as in descriptions such as *His hair was kind of long* or *The book cover is sort of yellow*. These are examples of hedges on the Quality maxim. Other examples would include the following expressions that people sometimes use as they begin a conversational contribution.

> *As far as I know . . .*
> *Correct me if I'm wrong, but . . .*
> *I'm not absolutely sure, but . . .*

We also take care to indicate that what we report is something we *think* or *feel* (not *know*), is *possible* (not *certain*), and *may* (not *must*) happen. Hence the difference between saying *Jackson is guilty* and *I think it's possible that Jackson may be guilty*. In the first version, people will assume you have very good evidence for the statement.

Implicatures

When we try to analyze how hedges work, we usually talk about speakers implying something that is not said. Similarly, in considering what the woman meant by *a sandwich is a sandwich*, we decided that she was implying that the sandwich was not worth talking about. With the co-operative principle and the maxims as guides, we can start to work out how people actually decide that someone is "implying" something in conversation. Consider the following example.

> CAROL: *Are you coming to the party tonight?*
> LARA: *I've got an exam tomorrow.*

On the face of it, Lara's statement is not an answer to Carol's question. Lara doesn't say *Yes* or *No*. Yet Carol will interpret the statement as meaning "No" or "Probably not." How can we account for this ability to grasp one meaning from a sentence that, in a literal sense, means something else? It seems to depend on the assumption that Lara is being relevant (Relation) and informative (Quantity). Given that Lara's original answer contains relevant information, Carol can work out that "exam tomorrow" involves "study tonight," and "study tonight" precludes "party tonight." Thus, Lara's answer is not just a statement about tomorrow's activities, it contains an **implicature** (an additional conveyed meaning) concerning tonight's activities.

Background Knowledge

It is noticeable that, in order to analyze the conversational implicature involved in Lara's statement, we had to describe some background knowledge (about exams, studying and partying) that must be shared by the conversational participants. Investigating how we use our background knowledge to arrive at interpretations of what we hear and read is a critical part of doing discourse analysis.

The processes involved in using background knowledge can be illustrated in the following exercise (from Sanford and Garrod, 1981). Begin with these sentences:

> *John was on his way to school last Friday.*
> *He was really worried about the math lesson.*

Most readers report that they think John is probably a schoolboy. Since this piece of information is not directly stated in the text, it must be an inference. Other inferences, for different readers, are that John is walking or that he is on a bus. These inferences are clearly derived from our conventional knowledge, in our culture, about "going to school," and no reader has ever suggested that John is swimming or on a boat, though both are physically possible interpretations.

An interesting aspect of the reported inferences is that readers can quickly abandon them if they do not fit in with some subsequent information.

> *Last week he had been unable to control the class.*

On encountering this sentence, most readers decide that John must be a teacher and that he is not very happy. Many report that he is probably driving a car to school.

> *It was unfair of the math teacher to leave him in charge.*

Suddenly, John reverts to his schoolboy status, and the inference that he is a teacher is quickly abandoned. The final sentence of the text contains a surprise.

> *After all, it is not a normal part of a janitor's duties.*

This type of text and manner of presentation, one sentence at a time, is rather artificial, of course. Yet the exercise does provide us with some insight into the ways in which we "build" interpretations of what we read by using more information than is presented in the words on the page. We actually create what the text is about, based on our expectations of what normally happens. To describe this phenomenon, researchers often use the concept of a "schema" or a "script."

Schemas and Scripts

A **schema** is a general term for a conventional knowledge structure that exists in memory. We were using our conventional knowledge of what a school classroom is like, or a "classroom schema," as we tried to make sense of the previous example. We have many schemas (or schemata) that are used in the interpretation of what we experience and what we hear or read about. If you hear someone describe what happened during a visit to a supermarket, you don't have to be told what is in a supermarket. You already have a "supermarket schema" (food displayed on shelves, arranged in aisles, shopping carts and baskets, check-out counter and so on).

Similar in many ways to a schema is a **script**. A script is essentially a dynamic schema. That is, instead of the set of typical fixed features in a schema, a script has a series of conventional actions that take place. You have a script for "Going to the dentist" and another script for "Going to the movies." We all have versions of an "Eating in a restaurant" script, which we can activate to make sense of this text.

> *Trying not to be out of the office for long, Suzy went into the nearest place, sat down and ordered an avocado sandwich. It was quite crowded, but the service was fast, so she left a good tip. Back in the office, things were not going well.*

On the basis of our restaurant script, we would be able to say a number of things about the scene and events briefly described in this short text. Although the text doesn't have this information, we would assume that Suzy opened a door to get into the restaurant, that there were tables there, that she ate the sandwich, then she paid for it and so on. The fact that information of this type can turn up in people's attempts to remember the text is further evidence of the existence of scripts. It is also a good indication of the fact that our understanding of what we read doesn't come directly from what words and sentences are on the page, but the interpretations we create, in our minds, of what we read.

Indeed, information is sometimes omitted from instructions on the assumption that everybody knows the script. This instruction is from a bottle of cough syrup.

> *Fill measure cup to line and repeat every 2 to 3 hours.*

No, you've not just to keep filling the measure cup every 2 to 3 hours. Nor have you to rub the cough syrup on your neck or in your hair. You are expected to know the script and *drink* the stuff from the measure cup every 2 or 3 hours.

Clearly, our understanding of what we read is not only based on what we see on the page (language structures), but also on other things that we have in mind (knowledge structures) as we go about making sense of discourse.

Study Questions

1   How is the word "discourse" usually defined?

2   What is the basic difference between cohesion and coherence?

3   What do you think the slogan "No gap, no overlap" refers to in the analysis of English conversation?

4   How do speakers mark completion points at the end of a turn?

5   What is a "filled pause"?

6   How do we describe these regular conversational patterns?

    Hi ~ Hello and *Bye ~ See you later*

7   What is an "insertion sequence"?

8   Which maxim involves not saying things you believe to be false?

9   Which maxim does this speaker seem to be particularly careful about?
    I won't bore you with all the details, but it wasn't a pleasant experience.

10   What are hedges in discourse?

11   What is an implicature?

12   In the study of discourse understanding, what are scripts?

Tasks

A   In the analysis of discourse, what is "intertextuality"?

B   (i)   Identify the main cohesive ties in this first paragraph of a novel (Faulkner, 1929).
    (ii)   What do you think "they" were hitting?

Through the fence, between the curling flower spaces, I could see them hitting. They were coming toward where the flag was and I went along the fence. Luster was hunting in the grass by the flower tree. They took the flag out, and they were hitting. Then they put the flag back and they went to the table, and he hit and the other hit. They went on, and I went along the fence. Luster came away from the flower tree and we went along the fence and they stopped and we stopped and I looked through the fence while Luster was hunting in the grass.

C In conversation analysis, what is the difference between a "preferred" response and a "dispreferred" response? How would you characterize the responses by *She* in these two examples?

(i)   HE: *How about going for some coffee?*

   SHE: *Oh . . . eh . . . I'd love to . . . but you see . . . I . . . I'm supposed to get this thing finished . . . you know.*

(ii)   HE: *I think she's really sexy.*

   SHE: *Well . . . er . . . I'm not sure . . . you may be right . . . but you see . . . other people probably don't go for all that . . . you know . . . all that make-up . . . so em sorry but I don't think so.*

D The following extract is from a conversation between two women chatting about people they both knew in high school (Overstreet, 1999: 112–113). In this extract, Crystal uses the phrase *or something* twice. Is she adhering to the Co-operative Principle and the Quality maxim or not? How did you decide?

JULIE: *I can't remember any ge- guys in our grade that were gay.*

CRYSTAL: *Larry Brown an' an' John Murphy. I – huh I dunno, I heard John Murphy was dressed – was like a transvestite or something.*

JULIE: *You're kidding.*

CRYSTAL: *I – I dunno. That was a – an old rumor, I don't even know if it was true.*

JULIE: *That's funny.*

CRYSTAL: *Or cross-dresser or something.*

JULIE: *Larry – Larry Brown is gay?*

E We analyzed a regular turn-taking pattern in terms of the two parts found in adjacency pairs, but what about three-part and four-part exchanges? Can you suggest a way of analyzing the following exchanges that would account for the conversation structure(s) involved?

(1)   JOE: *Did you need anything from the store?*

   TOM: *No thanks.*

   JOE: *Okay.*

(2)   TEACHER: *So, who knows where Tripoli is?*

   STUDENT: *In Libya.*

   TEACHER: *That's right.*

(3)   PASSENGER: *Are there any early morning flights to Edinburgh?*

   AGENT: *When do you want to go?*

   PASSENGER: *Oh, any time after 6 a.m.*

   AGENT: *Well, there's a 6:45.*

(4) SUE: *Do you have any idea what time it is?*

JEN: *Em, it's just after 4.*

SUE: *Thanks.*

JEN: *No problem.*

F In his insightful study of conversation, Enfield (2017) lists some observations on how we talk to each other. Based on your own experience of conversational interaction, where would you add the following items to reconstruct Enfield's list?

60 84 200 "um" "uh" "no" "yes" "Huh?" "Who?" one-second

- The average time that people take to respond to a question is about the same time that it takes to blink the eye: (1) _____ milliseconds.
- A (2) _____ answer to a question will come slower than a (3) _____ answer, no matter which language is spoken.
- There is a standard (4) _____ time window for responding in conversation: it helps us gauge whether a response is fast, on time, late, or unlikely to arrive at all.
- Every (5) _____ seconds in conversation, someone will say (6) _____, (7) _____, or something similar to check on what someone just said.
- One out of every (8) _____ words we say is (9) _____ or (10) _____.

G This is a version of a story described in Widdowson (2007). When most people first read this story, they find it confusing. Can you identify the source of this confusion in terms of background knowledge or assumptions?

A man and his son were crossing the street one day when a car suddenly came towards them and hit the boy, knocking him down. In less than ten minutes an ambulance came and took the boy to the nearest hospital. As the boy was being taken into the emergency room, one of the surgeons saw him and cried out, "Oh no. This is my son!"

H (i)   What is Critical Discourse Analysis?

(ii) How might the following text be analyzed using that approach? This text originally appeared in the British newspaper the *Sun* (February 2, 1989) and is cited in van Dijk (1996: 98) and Cameron (2001: 127).

Britain Invaded by Army of Illegals
Britain is being swamped by a tide of illegal immigrants so desperate for a job that they will work for a pittance in our restaurants, cafés and nightclubs.

Immigration officers are being overwhelmed with work. Last year, 2,191 "illegals" were nabbed and sent back home. But there were tens of thousands more, slaving behind bars, cleaning hotel rooms and working in kitchens . . .

Illegals sneak in by:

- DECEIVING *immigration officers when they are quizzed at airports*
- DISAPPEARING *after their entry visas run out*
- FORGING *work permits and other documents*
- RUNNING *away from immigration detention centres*

I (i) What is studied in "Stylistics"?

(ii) The following text (quoted in Verdonk, 2002: 7–8) appeared on the back cover of a book of short stories by the writer Margaret Atwood. Which aspects of this text would be discussed in a stylistic analysis?

This splendid volume of short fiction testifies to Margaret Atwood's startlingly original voice, full of rare intensity and exceptional intelligence. Each of the fourteen stories shimmers with feelings, each illuminates the unexplored interior landscape of a woman's mind. Here men and women still miscommunicate, still remain separate in different rooms, different houses, or even different worlds. With brilliant flashes of fantasy, humor, and unexpected violence, the stories reveal the complexities of human relationships and bring to life characters who touch us deeply, evoking terror and laughter, compassion and recognition – and dramatically demonstrate why Margaret Atwood is one of the most important writers in English today.

Discussion Topics/Projects

I In the study of discourse, a distinction is often made between "new information" (treated as new for the reader or listener) and "given information" (treated as already known by the reader or listener). Read through the following recipe for bread sauce and identify the ways in which given information is presented. (Try to think carefully about carrying out the instructions in the Method section and how many unmentioned things you are assumed to have and use.)

Ingredients: *1 small onion   3 oz. fresh breadcrumbs*
                    2 cloves   1 oz. butter
                    1 cup of milk   Pepper and salt

Method: Peel the onion and push cloves into it. Simmer gently with the milk and butter for at least twenty minutes. Remove the onion, pour the milk over the breadcrumbs. Let this stand to thicken and reheat before serving.

(For background reading, see chapter 5 of Brown and Yule, 1983.)

II   According to Deborah Schiffrin, "the analysis of discourse markers is part of the more general analysis of discourse coherence" (1987: 49). Looking at the use of discourse markers (in bold) in the following extract from a conversation, do you think that they help to make this discourse more coherent? If any of them were omitted, would it become less coherent? Given these examples, how would you define discourse markers? Are they the same as pragmatic markers, as described in Chapter 10 on page 155? Do you think the word *like* (used twice here) should be treated as a discourse marker?

I believe in that. Whatever's gonna happen is gonna happen. I believe ... that ... **y'know** *it's fate. It really is.* **Because** *eh my husband has a brother, that was killed in an automobile accident,* **and** *at the same time there was another fellow, in there, that walked away with not even a scratch on him.* **And** *I really fee- I don't feel y'can push fate,* **and** *I think a lot of people do.* **But** *I feel that you were put here for so many, years or whatever the case is,* **and** *that's how it was meant to be.* **Because** *like when we got married, we were supposed t'get married uh like about five months later. My husband got a notice t'go into the service* **and** *we moved it up.* **And** *my father died the week ... after we got married. While we were on our honeymoon.* **And** *I just felt, that move was meant to be,* **because** *if not, he wouldn't have been there.* **So** *eh* **y'know** *it just s- seems that that's how things work.*

(For background reading, see chapter 3 of Schiffrin, 1987.)

Further Reading

Basic Treatments

Sutherland, S. (2016) *A Beginner's Guide to Discourse Analysis* Palgrave

Widdowson, H. (2007) *Discourse Analysis* Oxford University Press

More Detailed Treatments

Johnstone, B. (2018) *Discourse Analysis* (3rd edition) Wiley-Blackwell

Paltridge, B. (2012) *Discourse Analysis* (2nd edition) Bloomsbury

Jones, R. (2012) *Discourse Analysis: A Resource Book for Students* Routledge

Specifically on Spoken Discourse

Cameron, D. (2001) *Working with Spoken Discourse* Sage

Specifically on Written Discourse

Hoey, M. (2001) *Textual Interaction: An Introduction to Written Discourse Analysis* Routledge

Different Approaches to Discourse Analysis

Schiffrin, D. (1994) *Approaches to Discourse* Blackwell

Conversation Analysis

Have, P. (2007) *Doing Conversation Analysis* (2nd edition) Sage

Liddicoat, A. (2011) *An Introduction to Conversation Analysis* (2nd edition) Continuum

Adjacency Pairs and Turn-taking

Clift, R. (2016) *Conversation Analysis* Cambridge University Press

Enfield, N. (2017) *How We Talk: The Inner Workings of Conversation* Basic Books

The Gricean Maxims

Grice, P. (1989) *Studies in the Way of Words* Harvard University Press

Sperber, D. and D. Wilson (1995) *Relevance* (2nd edition) Blackwell

Implicature

Kasher, A. (2009) "Implicature" In S. Chapman and C. Routledge (eds.) *Key Ideas in Linguistics and the Philosophy of Language* (86–92) Edinburgh University Press

Background Knowledge

Gibbons, A. and S. Whitely (2018) *Contemporary Stylistics: Language, Cognition and Interpretation* Edinburgh University Press

Schemas and Scripts

Brown, G. and G. Yule (1983) *Discourse Analysis* (chapter 7) Cambridge University Press

Other References

Faulkner, W. (1929) *The Sound and the Fury* Jonathan Cape

Grice, P. (1975) "Logic and conversation" In P. Cole and J. Morgan (eds.) *Syntax and Semantics 3: Speech Acts* (41–58) Academic Press

Overstreet, M. (1999) *Whales, Candlelight and Stuff Like That: General Extenders in English Discourse* Oxford University Press

Sacks, H. (1972) "On the analyzability of stories by children" In J. Gumperz and D. Hymes (eds.) *Directions in Sociolinguistics* (325–345) Holt, Rinehart and Winston

Sanford, A and S. Garrod (1981) *Understanding Written Language* Wiley

Schiffrin, D. (1987) *Discourse Markers* Cambridge University Press

van Dijk, T. (1996) "Discourse, power and access" In C. Caldas-Coulthard and M. Coulthard (eds.) *Texts and Practices: Readings in Critical Discourse Analysis* (84–104) Routledge

Verdonk, P. (2002) *Stylistics* Oxford University Press

Widdowson, H. (1978) *Teaching Language as Communication* Oxford University Press

12 Language and the Brain

I once had a patient who suffered a right hemisphere stroke and fell to the ground, unable to walk because of a paralyzed left leg. She lay on the floor for two days, not because no one came to her aid, but because she kept blithely reassuring her husband that she was fine, that there was nothing wrong with her leg. Only on the third day did he bring her in for treatment. When I asked her why she could not move her left leg, and held it up for her to see, she said indifferently that it was someone else's leg.

Flaherty (2004)

In the preceding chapters we have reviewed in some detail the various features of language that people use to produce and understand linguistic messages. Where is this ability to use language located? The obvious answer is "in the brain." However, it can't be just anywhere in the brain. For example, it can't be where damage was done to the right hemisphere of the patient's brain in Alice Flaherty's description. The woman could no longer recognize her own leg, but she could still talk about it. The ability to talk was unimpaired and hence clearly located somewhere else in her brain.

Neurolinguistics

The study of the relationship between language and the brain is called **neurolinguistics**. Although this is a relatively recent term, the field of study dates back to the nineteenth century. Establishing the location of language in the brain was an early challenge, but one event incidentally provided a clue.

In September 1848, near Cavendish, Vermont, a construction foreman called Phineas P. Gage was in charge of a construction crew blasting away rocks to lay a new stretch of railway line. As Mr. Gage pushed an iron tamping rod into the blasting hole in a rock, some gunpowder accidentally exploded and sent the meter-long tamping rod up through his upper left cheek and out from the top of his forehead. The rod landed about fifty meters away. Mr. Gage suffered the type of injury from which, it was assumed, no one could recover. However, a month later, he was up and about, with no apparent damage to his senses or his speech.

The medical evidence was clear. A huge metal rod had gone through the front part of Mr. Gage's brain, but his language abilities were unaffected. He was a medical marvel, and even sat for his portrait, with the tamping rod, reproduced on page 184. The point of this rather amazing tale is that, while language may be located in the brain, it clearly is not situated right at the front.

Language Areas in the Brain

Since that time, a number of discoveries have been made about the specific parts in the brain that are related to core language functions. We now know that the most important parts are in areas around the left ear. In order to describe them in greater detail, we need to look more closely at some of the gray matter. So, take a head, remove hair, scalp, skull, then disconnect the brain stem (connecting the brain to the spinal cord) and cut the corpus callosum (connecting the two hemispheres). If we disregard a certain amount of other material, we will basically be left with two parts, the left hemisphere and the right hemisphere. If we put the right hemisphere aside for now, and place the left hemisphere down so that we have a side view, we'll be looking at something close to the illustration in Figure 12.1 (adapted from Geschwind, 1991).

The shaded areas in Figure 12.1 indicate the general locations of those language functions involved in speaking and listening. We have come to know that these areas exist largely through the examination, in autopsies, of the brains of people who, in life, were known to have specific language disabilities. That is, we have tried to determine where language abilities for normal users must be by finding areas with specific damage in the brains of people who had identifiable language disabilities. More brain images are presented in Task G, on page 196.

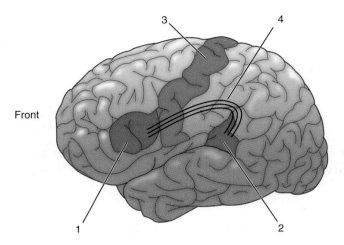

Figure 12.1 Language areas in the brain

Broca's Area

The part shown as (1) in Figure 12.1 is technically described as the "anterior speech cortex" or, more usually, as **Broca's area**. Paul Broca, a French surgeon, reported in the 1860s that damage to this specific part of the brain was related to extreme difficulty in producing spoken language. It was noted that damage to the corresponding area on the right hemisphere had no such effect. This finding was first used to argue that language ability must be located in the left hemisphere and since then has been treated as an indication that Broca's area is crucially involved in the generation of spoken language.

Wernicke's Area

The part shown as (2) in Figure 12.1 is the "posterior speech cortex," or **Wernicke's area**. Carl Wernicke was a German doctor who, in the 1870s, reported that damage to this part of the brain was found among patients who had speech comprehension difficulties. Significantly, this area is close to the part of the brain, the auditory cortex, that processes what we hear. This finding confirmed the left hemisphere location of language ability and led to the view that Wernicke's area is part of the brain crucially involved in the understanding of spoken language.

The Motor Cortex and the Arcuate Fasciculus

The part shown as (3) in Figure 12.1 is the **motor cortex**, an area that generally controls movement of the muscles (for moving hands, feet, arms, etc.). The part of the motor cortex that is close to Broca's area controls the articulatory muscles of the face, jaw, tongue and larynx and hence the physical articulation of speech. In the 1950s, two neurosurgeons, Penfield and Roberts (1959) found that, by applying small amounts of electrical current to specific parts of the brain, they could identify areas where the electrical stimulation would interfere with speech production.

The part shown as (4) in Figure 12.1 is a bundle of nerve fibers called the **arcuate fasciculus ("the curved bundle")**. This was also one of Wernicke's discoveries and is now known to form a crucial connection between Wernicke's and Broca's areas.

The Localization View

Having identified these four components, it is tempting to conclude that specific aspects of language ability can be accorded specific locations in the brain. This is called the **localization view** and it has been used to suggest that the brain activity involved in hearing a word, understanding it, then saying it, would follow a definite pattern. The word is heard and comprehended via Wernicke's area. This signal is then transferred via the arcuate fasciculus to Broca's area where preparations are made to generate a spoken version of the word. A signal is then sent to part of the motor cortex to physically articulate the word.

This is certainly an oversimplified version of what may actually take place, but it is consistent with much of what we understand about simple language processing in the brain. It is probably best to think of any proposal concerning processing pathways in the brain as some form of metaphor that may turn out to be inadequate once we learn more about how the brain functions. The "pathway" metaphor seems quite appealing in an electronic age when we are familiar with the process of sending signals through electrical circuits. In an earlier age, dominated more by mechanical technology, Sigmund Freud subtly employed a "steam engine" metaphor to account for aspects of the brain's activity when he wrote of the effects of repression "building up pressure" to the point of "sudden release." Even earlier, Aristotle's metaphor was of the brain as a cold sponge that kept the blood cool.

In a sense, we are forced to use metaphors mainly because we cannot obtain direct physical evidence of linguistic processes in the brain. Because we have no direct access, we generally have to rely on what we can discover through indirect methods. Traditionally, these methods have involved attempts to work out how the system is working from clues picked up when the system has problems or malfunctions.

Tongue Tips and Slips

We have all experienced difficulty, on some occasion(s), in getting brain and speech production to work together smoothly. (Some days are worse than others, of course.) Minor production difficulties of this sort may provide possible clues to how our linguistic knowledge is organized within the brain.

The Tip of the Tongue Phenomenon

There is, for example, the **tip of the tongue** phenomenon in which we feel that some word is just eluding us. We know the word, but it just won't come to the surface. Studies of this phenomenon have shown that speakers generally have an accurate phonological outline of the word, can get the initial sound correct and mostly know the number of syllables in the word. This experience also mainly occurs with uncommon words and names. It suggests that our "word-storage" system may be partially organized on the basis of some phonological information and that some words in the store are more easily retrieved than others.

When we make mistakes in this retrieval process, there are often strong phonological similarities between the target word we are trying to say and the mistake we produce. For example, speakers produced *secant, sextet* and *sexton* when asked to name a particular type of navigational instrument (*sextant*). Other examples are *fire distinguisher* (for "extinguisher") and *transcendental medication* (instead of "meditation"). Mistakes of this type are sometimes referred to as **malapropisms** after a character called Mrs. Malaprop (in a play by Sheridan) who consistently produced "near-misses" for words, with great comic effect. Another comic character in a TV program who was known for his malapropisms was Archie Bunker, who once suggested that *We need a few laughs to break up the monogamy.*

Slips of the Tongue

Another type of speech error is commonly described as a **slip of the tongue**. This produces expressions such as *a long shory stort* (instead of "make a long story short"), *use the door to open the key* and *a fifty-pound dog of bag food*. Slips of this type are sometimes called **spoonerisms** after William Spooner, an Anglican clergyman at Oxford University, who was renowned for his tongue-slips. Most of the slips attributed to him involve the interchange of two initial sounds, as when he addressed a rural group as *noble tons of soil*, attempted to refer to the queen as *our queer old dean*, described God as *a shoving leopard to his flock*, or in this complaint to a student who had been absent from classes: *You have hissed all my mystery lectures.*

Slips of the Brain

Other examples are often simply word substitutions as a similar, but inappropriate word is used instead of the target. In talking about his relationship with a former president, one US president had to quickly correct himself when he said: *we've had some triumphs . . . made some mistakes . . . we've had some sex . . . eh . . . setbacks*. Most everyday slips, however, are not as entertaining. There are three general types. **Perseveration** is when one sound is carried over to the next word, so that *my favorite song* comes out as *my favorite fong*. **Anticipation** is when a sound is used before its occurrence in the next word, so that *roman numeral* comes out as *noman numeral*. **Exchange** is when sounds change places, so that *feel better* comes out as *beel fetter*. Although these slips are mostly treated as errors of articulation, they may actually result from **slips of the brain** as it tries to organize and generate linguistic messages. The different types of slips are listed in Table 12.1.

TABLE 12.1 SLIPS OF THE TONGUE

Perseveration	sound carried over to next word	*black bloxes, my favorite fong*
Anticipation	sound used before next word	*noman numeral, a tup of tea*
Exchange	initial sounds change places	*shu flots, beel fetter*
	final sounds change places	*stick neff, loop before you leak*

Slips of the Ear

One other type of slip may provide some clues to how the brain tries to make sense of the auditory signal it receives. These have been called **slips of the ear** and can result, for example, in our hearing *great ape* and wondering why someone should be looking for one in his office. (The speaker actually said "gray tape.") During a conversation about dogs, one five-year-old announced *My uncle has a pimple*, which turned out to be her misheard version of a "pit bull." A similar type of misunderstanding seems to be behind a child's report that in Sunday school, everyone was singing about a bear called "Gladly" who was cross-eyed. The source of this slip turned out to be a line from a religious song that went *Gladly the cross I'd bear*. It may also be the case that some malapropisms (e.g. *transcendental medication*) originate as slips of the ear. For more slips, see Task C on page 195.

Some of these humorous examples of slips may give us a clue to the normal workings of the human brain as it copes with language. However, some problems with language production and comprehension are the result of much more serious disorders in brain function.

Aphasia

If you have experienced any of those "slips" on occasion, then you will have a small hint of the types of experience that some unfortunate individuals have to live with constantly. Those people suffer from different types of language disorders, generally described as "aphasia." **Aphasia** is defined as an impairment of language function due to localized brain damage that leads to difficulty in understanding and/or producing linguistic forms.

The most common cause of aphasia is a stroke (when a blood vessel in the brain is blocked or bursts), though traumatic head injuries from violence or an accident may have similar effects. Those effects can range from mild to severe reduction in the ability to use language. Someone who is aphasic often has interrelated language disorders, in that difficulties in understanding can lead to difficulties in production, for example. Consequently, the classification of different types of aphasia is usually based on the primary symptoms of someone having difficulties with language.

Broca's Aphasia

The serious language disorder known as **Broca's aphasia** (also called "expressive aphasia") is characterized by a substantially reduced amount of speech, distorted articulation and slow, often effortful speech. What is said often consists almost entirely of lexical morphemes (mostly nouns, verbs and adjectives, as described in Chapter 6). The frequent omission of functional morphemes (e.g. articles, prepositions) and inflectional morphemes (e.g. plural -*s*, past tense -*ed*) has led to the characterization of this type of aphasic speech as lacking grammatical forms, or "agrammatic." In **agrammatic speech**, the grammatical markers are missing.

An example of speech produced by someone whose aphasia was not severe is the following answer to a question regarding what the speaker had for breakfast:

I eggs and eat and drink coffee breakfast.

However, this type of disorder can be quite severe and result in speech with lots of hesitations and really long pauses (marked by . . .):

My cheek . . . very annoyance . . . main is my shoulder . . . achin' all round here.

Some patients can also have lots of difficulty in articulating single words, as in this attempt to say "steamship": *a stail . . . you know what I mean . . . tal . . . stail.* In Broca's aphasia, comprehension is typically much better than production.

Wernicke's Aphasia

The type of language disorder that results in difficulties in auditory comprehension is sometimes called "receptive aphasia," but is more commonly known as **Wernicke's aphasia**. Someone suffering from this disorder can actually produce very fluent speech which is, however, often difficult to understand. Very general terms are used, even in response to specific requests for information, as in this sample:

> *I can't talk all of the things I do, and part of the part I can go alright, but I can't tell from the other people.*

Difficulty in finding the correct word, sometimes referred to as **anomia**, also happens in Wernicke's aphasia. To overcome their word-finding difficulties, speakers use different strategies such as trying to describe objects or talking about their purpose, as in *the thing to put cigarettes in* (for "ashtray"). In the following example (from Lesser and Milroy, 1993), the speaker tries a range of strategies when he can't come up with the word ("kite") for an object in a picture.

> *it's blowing, on the right, and er there's four letters in it, and I think it begins with a C – goes – when you start it then goes right up in the air – I would I would have to keep racking my brain how I would spell that word – that flies, that that doesn't fly, you pull it round, it goes up in the air.*

Conduction Aphasia

One other, much less common, type of aphasia has been associated with damage to the arcuate fasciculus and is called **conduction aphasia**. Individuals suffering from this disorder sometimes mispronounce words, but typically do not have articulation problems. They are fluent, but may have disrupted rhythm because of pauses and hesitations. Comprehension of spoken words is normally good. However, the task of repeating a word or phrase (spoken by someone else) creates major difficulty, with forms such as *vaysse* and *fosh* being reported as attempted repetitions of the words "base" and "wash." What the speaker hears and understands can't be transferred very successfully to the speech production area.

It should be emphasized that many of these symptoms (e.g. word-finding difficulty) can occur in all types of aphasia. They can also occur in more general disorders such as dementia and Alzheimer's disease. Difficulties in speaking can also be accompanied by difficulties in writing. Impairment of auditory comprehension tends to be accompanied by reading difficulties. These language disorders are almost always the result of injury to the left hemisphere. The left hemisphere dominance for language has also been demonstrated by another research method.

Dichotic Listening

An experimental technique that has demonstrated a left hemisphere dominance for syllable and word processing is called the **dichotic listening test**. This technique uses the generally established fact that anything experienced on the right-hand side of the body is processed in the left hemisphere, and anything on the left side is processed in the right hemisphere. As illustrated in Flaherty's (2004) description at the beginning of this chapter, a stroke in the right hemisphere resulted in paralysis of the left leg. So, a basic assumption would be that a signal coming in the right ear will go to the left hemisphere and a signal coming in the left ear will go to the right hemisphere.

With this information, an experiment is possible in which a subject sits with a set of earphones on and is given two different sound signals simultaneously, one through each earphone. For example, through one earphone comes the syllable *ga* or the word *dog*, and through the other earphone at exactly the same time comes *da* or *cat*. When asked to say what was heard, the subject more often correctly identifies the sound that came via the right ear. The process involved is best understood with the help of Figure 12.2. (You are looking at the back of this head.)

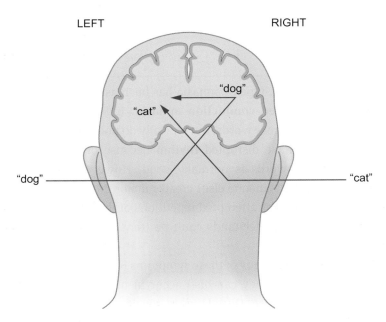

Figure 12.2 Dichotic listening process

Left Brain, Right Brain

In this process, the language signal received through the left ear is first sent to the right hemisphere and then has to be sent to the left hemisphere (language center) for processing. This non-direct route takes longer than a linguistic signal received through the right ear, which goes directly to the left hemisphere. First signal to get processed wins because of what is generally known as the **right-ear advantage** for speech sounds. In contrast, the right hemisphere appears to have primary responsibility for processing a lot of other incoming signals that are non-linguistic. In the dichotic listening test, it can be shown that non-verbal sounds (e.g. music, coughs, traffic noises, birds singing) are recognized more often via the left ear, meaning they are processed faster via the right hemisphere.

In our analysis so far, we have concentrated on the basic linguistic processing of the left hemisphere, mainly because "abstract concepts and words, along with complex syntax, are left-hemisphere-dependent" (McGilchrist, 2009: 51). However, we can't process linguistic communication without the right hemisphere, which specializes in contextual understanding, using intonation and phrasing, and non-literal meaning with inferences and all that is involved in pragmatics. Without the right hemisphere, we would never understand a joke.

We might say that the essential distinction is between narrowly focused analytic processing, such as recognizing the smaller details of sounds, words and phrase structures in rapid sequence, done with the "left brain," and contextually oriented holistic processing, such as identifying more general aspects of language and experience, done with the "right brain."

The Critical Period

The apparent specialization of the left hemisphere for language is usually described in terms of lateral dominance or **lateralization** (one-sidedness). Since the human child does not emerge from the womb as a fully articulate language user, it is generally thought that the lateralization process begins in early childhood. It coincides with the period during which language acquisition takes place. During childhood, there is a period when the human brain is most ready to receive input and learn a particular language. This is sometimes called the "sensitive period" for language acquisition, but is more generally known as **the critical period**.

Though there is increasing evidence that it may actually start earlier in the womb, the general view is that the critical period for language acquisition lasts from birth until puberty. If children do not acquire language during this period, for any one of a number of reasons, then they will find it almost impossible to learn language later on. In one unfortunate but well-documented case, we have gained some insight into what happens when the critical period passes without adequate linguistic input.

Genie

In 1970, a girl who became known as "Genie" was admitted to a children's hospital in Los Angeles. She was thirteen years old and had spent most of her life tied to a chair in a small closed room. Her father was intolerant of any kind of noise and had beaten her whenever she made a sound as a child. There had been no radio or television, and Genie's only other human contact was with her mother who was forbidden to spend more than a few minutes with the child to feed her. Genie had spent her whole life in a state of physical, sensory, social and emotional deprivation.

As might be expected, Genie was unable to use language when she was first brought into care. However, within a short period of time, she began to respond to the speech of others, to try to imitate sounds and to communicate. Her syntax remained very simple. The fact that she went on to develop some speaking ability and understand a fairly large number of English words provides some evidence against the notion that language cannot be acquired at all after the critical period. Yet her diminished capacity to develop grammatically complex speech does seem to support the idea that part of the left hemisphere of the brain is open to accepting a language program during childhood and, if no program is provided, as in Genie's case, then the facility is closed down.

In Genie's case, tests demonstrated that she had no left hemisphere language facility. So, how was she able to learn any part of language, even in a limited way? Those same tests appeared to indicate the quite remarkable fact that Genie was using the right hemisphere of her brain for basic language functions. In dichotic listening tests, she showed a very strong left ear advantage for verbal as well as non-verbal signals. Such a finding, supported by other studies of right brain function, raises the possibility that our capacity for language is not limited to only one or two specific areas, but is based on more complex connections extending throughout the whole brain.

When Genie was beginning to use speech, it was noted that she went through some of the same early "stages" found in normal child language acquisition. In Chapter 13, we will look at what these normal stages are.

Study Questions

1 What is a more common name for the posterior speech cortex?

2 What kind of difficulty did Wernicke identify among his patients?

3 Which part of the brain has been described as "the curved bundle"?

4 Is the use of *fire distinguisher* instead of *fire extinguisher* a spoonerism or a malapropism?

5 What type of slip is illustrated by: *I like pop porn* (for *popcorn*)?

6 If someone says *wistwatch* (for "wristwatch"), what kind of slip is that?

7 What is aphasia?

8 Which type of aphasia results from damage to the arcuate fasciculus?

9 Which type of aphasia is characterized by speech like this: *speech . . . two times . . . read . . . wr . . . ripe, er, rike, er, write . . .* ?

10 What happens in a dichotic listening test?

11 What is the critical period?

12 What did researchers discover from Genie's dichotic listening tests?

Tasks

A We made no distinction between the left and right hemispheres in terms of shape or size, assuming they were symmetrical. However, on closer inspection, there is some asymmetry in the lateralization of the brain. What seems to be the main source of this difference between the physiology of the two hemispheres? Does this difference support the "phrenology" model of human brain organization?

B What is meant by the "bathtub effect" in descriptions of features of speech errors? Do any examples of speech errors in this chapter illustrate this effect?

C The following examples produced by young children (from Jaeger, 2005) illustrate the three kinds of slips described in Table 12.1 on page 189. The words in brackets are what we assume the child was trying to say. Can you identify which ones should be analyzed as anticipations, perseverations or exchanges?

(1) *three, four, sive, six, seven* (five)   (7) *turn the wot hotter on* (hot water)

(2) *the shun is sining* (sun shining)   (8) *Winnie the Pooh pook* (book)

(3) *Frosted Frakes* (Flakes)

(4) *Fentucky Fried chicken* (Kentucky)

(5) *mashed matatoes* (potatoes)

(6) *Hi, fredi pace* (pretty face)

(9) *three little bigs and a big bad wolf* (pigs)

(10) *call Bost Gusters* (Ghost Busters)

(11) *not now, another nay* (day)

(12) *I have a snore neck* (sore)

D In this chapter we focused on the left hemisphere and how it is affected by impairments. What happens to the language of an individual after damage in the right hemisphere?

E How would you go about analyzing the following extract from Radford *et al.* (2009) as more likely to be indicative of agrammatism or paragrammatism? (The speaker is trying to talk about a lady's shoe.)

> *Now there there I remember. I have you there what I thought was the . . . a lady one. Another. With a very short. Very very clever done. Do that the one two. Go. But there's the liver. And there is the new. And so on.*

F What happens in "brain imaging" procedures such as CAT scans, fMRI scans and PET scans that might help in the study of language and the brain?

G Using what you learned from the discussion of language areas in the brain, try to match each description (A–D) to one of the four diagrams (1)–(4) in Figure 12.3, with a brief explanation of your choices. Each diagram is a representation of information from a PET scan showing how blood flow in the brain is concentrated in different areas during different activities. More intense activity is shown in brighter colors.

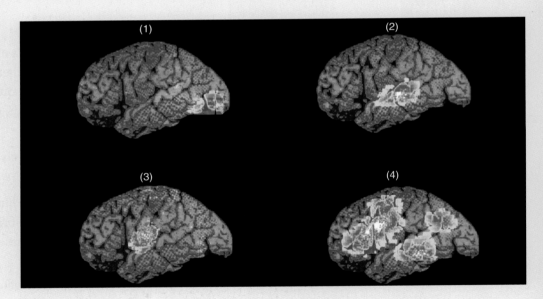

Figure 12.3 PET scans

A Hearing/processing words

B Speaking/articulating words

C Generating/preparing to speak words

D Seeing/Reading words

H The following extract from Buckingham and Kertesz (1976: 21) is discussed in Obler and Gjerlow (1999: 59) as an illustration of "neologistic jargon aphasia." Can you identify any characteristics of this condition that show up in the language used by this speaker? Is the syntax badly impaired? Are morphological features such as inflections used normally or not? Does the speaker have word-finding difficulties? Would you say that this aphasia is more likely to be associated with Broca's area or Wernicke's area? (The speaker is responding to the question, "Who is running the store now?")

> *I don't know. Yes, the bick, uh, yes I would say that the mick daysis nosis or chpickters. Course, I have also missed on the carfter teck. Do you know what that is? I've, uh, token to ingish. They have been toast sosilly. They'd have been put to myafa and made palis and, uh, myadakal senda you. That is me alordisdus. That makes anacronous senda.*

I A group of researchers (Huth *et al.*, 2016) created a visual representation of where words are processed in the brain, described as "semantic maps." A video of these maps was produced in cooperation with the journal *Nature* as "The Brain Dictionary." Try to view this video and consider the following questions.

(1) How was brain activity monitored?

(2) Did the participants have to listen to single words, sentences, or stories?

(3) Did the research find that word processing mostly takes place in the left or right hemisphere?

(4) Did all participants process the same words in the same areas of the brain?

(5) Were there special regions for particular groups of words, such as numbers or words for social categories (*wife, mother, family*)?

(6) What do these findings tell us about the connection between brain and language?

Discussion Topics/Projects

I The story of Genie is full of remarkable episodes. The following extract is from Rymer (1993), quoting Susan Curtiss, a linguist who worked with Genie for many years. How would you explain events like this?

> *"Genie was the most powerful nonverbal communicator I've ever come across," Curtiss told me. "The most extreme example of this that comes to mind: Because of her obsession, she would notice and covet anything plastic that anyone had.*

One day we were walking – I think we were in Hollywood. I would act like an idiot, sing operatically, to get her to release some of that tension she always had. We reached the corner of this very busy intersection, and the light turned red, and we stopped. Suddenly, I heard the sound – it's a sound you can't mistake – of a purse being spilled. A woman in a car that had stopped at the intersection was emptying her purse, and she got out of the car and ran over and gave it to Genie and then ran back to the car. A plastic purse. Genie hadn't said a word."

(For background reading, see chapter 17 of Rymer, 1993.)

II   One aphasia patient was asked to read aloud the written words on the left below and, in each case, actually said the words on the right. Is there any pattern to be found in these errors? Does this type of phenomenon provide any clues to the way words may be stored and accessed in the brain?

ambition	→	*career*	commerce	→	*business*
anecdote	→	*narrator*	mishap	→	*accident*
applause	→	*audience*	parachute	→	*balloon*
apricot	→	*peach*	thermometer	→	*temperature*
arithmetic	→	*mathematics*	victory	→	*triumph*

(For background reading, see Allport, 1983, the source of these examples.)

Further Reading

Basic Treatments

Ahlsén, E. (2006) *Introduction to Neurolinguistics* John Benjamins
Heilman, K. (2002) *Matter of Mind* (chapter 2) Oxford University Press
Obler, L. and K. Gjerlow (1999) *Language and the Brain* Cambridge University Press

More Detailed Treatments

Friederici, A. (2017) *Language in Our Brain* MIT Press
Ingram, J. (2007) *Neurolinguistics* Cambridge University Press
Whitaker, H. (2010) *Concise Encyclopedia of Brain and Language* Elsevier

On Phineas Gage

Damasio, A. (1994) *Descartes' Error* Putnam

Brain Structure

Carter, R., S. Aldridge, M. Page and S. Parker (2009) *The Human Brain Book* DK Publishing
Springer, S. and G. Deutsch (2001) *Left Brain, Right Brain* (6th edition) W. H. Freeman

Brain Imaging

Petrides, M. (2014) *Neuroanatomy of Language Regions of the Human Brain* Elsevier

Slips

Bond, Z. (1999) *Slips of the Ear* Academic Press

Poulisse, N. (1999) *Slips of the Tongue* John Benjamins

Language Disorders

Caplan, D. (1996) *Language: Structure, Processing and Disorders* MIT Press

Vinson, B. (2012) *Language Disorders across the Lifespan* (3rd edition) Thomson Delmar Learning

Aphasia

Lesser, R. and L. Milroy (1993) *Linguistics and Aphasia* Longman

Spreen, O. and A. Risser (2003) *Assessment of Aphasia* Oxford University Press

A Personal Account of Broca's Aphasia

Schwyter, J. (2018) "Ten years after the stroke: me talk slightly less funny" *English Today* 34 (2): 35–38

Conduction Aphasia

Bernal, B. and A. Ardila (2009) "The role of the arcuate fasciculus in conduction aphasia" *Brain* 132: 2309–2316

Dichotic Listening

Hugdahl, K. and R. Davidson (2004) *The Asymmetrical Brain* (441–476) MIT Press

The Critical Period

Singleton, D. and L. Ryan (2004) *Language Acquisition: The Age Factor* (2nd edition) Multilingual Matters

Genie

Curtiss, S. (1977) *Genie: A Psycholinguistic Study of a Modern-day Wild Child* Academic Press

Rymer, R. (1993) *Genie* HarperCollins

Other References

Allport, G. (1983) "Language and cognition" In R. Harris (ed.) *Approaches to Language* (80–94) Pergamon Press

Buckingham, H. and A. Kertesz (1976) *Neologistic Jargon Aphasia* Swets and Zeitlinger

Flaherty, A. (2004) *The Midnight Disease* Houghton Mifflin

Geschwind, N. (1991) "Specializations of the human brain" In W. Wang (ed.) *The Emergence of Language* (72–87) W. H. Freeman

Huth, A., W. de Heer, T. Griffiths, F. Theunissen and J. Gallant (2016) "Natural speech reveals the semantic maps that tile human cerebral cortex" *Nature* (April 28) doi:10.1038/nature 17637

Jaeger, J. (2005) *Kids' Slips* Lawrence Erlbaum

McGilchrist, I. (2009) *The Master and his Emissary* Yale University Press

Penfield, W. and L. Roberts (1959) *Speech and Brain Mechanisms* Princeton University Press

Radford, A., M. Atkinson, D. Britain, H. Clahsen and A. Spencer (2009) *Linguistics: An Introduction* (2nd edition) Cambridge University Press

13 First Language Acquisition

CHILD: Want other one spoon, Daddy.
FATHER: You mean, you want the other spoon.
CHILD: Yes, I want other one spoon, please Daddy.
FATHER: Can you say "the other spoon"?
CHILD: Other . . . one . . . spoon.
FATHER: Say "other."
CHILD: Other.
FATHER: "Spoon."
CHILD: Spoon.
FATHER: "Other spoon."
CHILD: Other . . . spoon. Now give me other one spoon?

Braine (1971)

First language acquisition is remarkable for the speed with which it takes place. Long before a child starts school, he or she has become an extremely sophisticated language-user, operating a system for self-expression and communication that no other creature, or computer, comes close to matching. In addition to the speed of acquisition, the fact that it generally occurs, without overt instruction, for all children, regardless of great differences in their circumstances, provides strong support for the idea that there is an innate predisposition in the human infant to acquire language. We can think of this as a special capacity for language with which each newborn child is endowed. By itself, however, this inborn language capacity is not enough.

Acquisition

The process of language acquisition has some basic requirements. During the first two or three years of development, a child requires interaction with other language-users in order to bring the general language capacity into contact with a particular language such as English. We have already seen, in the case of Genie (Chapter 12), that a child who does not hear or is not allowed to use language will learn no language. We have also identified the importance of cultural transmission (Chapter 2), meaning that the particular language a child learns is not genetically inherited, but is acquired in a particular language-using environment.

The child must also be physically capable of sending and receiving sound signals in a language. All infants make "cooing" and "babbling" noises during their first year, but congenitally deaf infants stop after about six months. So, in order to speak a language, a child must be able to hear that language being used. By itself, however, hearing language sounds is not enough. One case, reported by Moskowitz (1991), demonstrated that, with deaf parents who gave their normal-hearing son ample exposure to TV and radio programs, the boy did not acquire an ability to speak or understand English. What he did learn very effectively, by the age of three, was the use of American Sign Language, that is, the language he used to interact with his parents. A crucial requirement appears to be interaction with others via language.

Input

Under normal circumstances, human infants are certainly helped in their language acquisition by the typical behavior of older children and adults in the home environment who provide language samples, or **input**, for the child. Adults such as mom, dad and the grandparents tend not to address the little creature before them as if they are involved in normal adult-to-adult conversation. There is not much of this: *Well, John Junior, shall we invest in blue chip industrials, or would grain futures offer better short-term prospects?* However, there does seem to be a lot of this: *Oh, goody, now Daddy push choo choo?*

The characteristically simplified speech style adopted by someone who spends a lot of time interacting with a young child incorporates a lot of forms associated with "baby talk." These are either simplified words (*tummy, nana*) or alternative forms, with repeated simple sounds and syllables, for things in the child's environment (*choo-choo, poo-poo, pee-pee, wa-wa*). This type of speech style is also characterized by the frequent use of questions, often using exaggerated intonation, extra loudness and a slower tempo with longer pauses. Sometimes described as "motherese" or "child-directed speech," this style is more generally known as "caregiver speech."

Caregiver Speech

Built into a lot of caregiver speech is a type of conversational structure that seems to assign an interactive role to the young child even before he or she becomes a speaking participant. If we look at an extract from the speech of a mother to her child (aged 1 year 11 months) as if it were a two-party conversation, then this type of structuring becomes apparent. Notice how the mother reacts to the child's actions and vocalizations as if they were turns in this conversation (from Bruner, 1983).

MOTHER: *Look!*
CHILD: (touches pictures)
MOTHER: *What are those?*
CHILD: (vocalizes a babble string and smiles)
MOTHER: *Yes, there are rabbits.*
CHILD: (vocalizes, smiles, looks up at mother)
MOTHER: (laughs) *Yes, rabbit.*
CHILD: (vocalizes, smiles)
MOTHER: *Yes.* (laughs)

Caregiver speech is also characterized by simple sentence structures and a lot of repetition and paraphrasing, with reference largely restricted to the here and now. If the child is indeed in the process of working out a system of putting sounds and words together, then these simplified models produced by the interacting adult may serve as good clues to the basic structural organization involved.

The Acquisition Schedule

All normal children develop language at roughly the same time, along much the same schedule. Since we can say the same thing for sitting up, crawling, standing, walking, using the hands and many other physical activities, it would seem that the language acquisition schedule has the same basis as the biologically determined development of motor skills and the maturation of the infant's brain.

We could think of the child as having the biological capacity to identify aspects of linguistic input at different stages during the early years of life. Long before children begin to talk, they have been actively processing what they hear. We can identify what very young children are paying attention to by the way they increase or decrease "sucking behavior" in response to speech sounds or turn their heads in the direction of those sounds. At one month an infant is capable of distinguishing between [ba] and [pa]. During the first three months, the child produces big smiles in response to a speaking face, and starts to create distinct vocalizations.

Cooing

The earliest use of speech-like sounds has been described as **cooing**. During the first few months of life, the child gradually becomes capable of producing sequences of vowel-like sounds, particularly high vowels similar to [i] and [u]. By four months of age, the developing ability to bring the back of the tongue into regular contact with the back of the palate allows the infant to create sounds similar to the velar consonants [k] and [g], hence the common description as "cooing" or "gooing" for this type of production. Speech perception studies have shown that by the time they are five months old, babies can already hear the difference between the vowels [i] and [a] and discriminate between syllables like [ba] and [ga].

Babbling

Between six and eight months, the child is sitting up and producing a number of different vowels and consonants, as well as combinations such as *ba-ba-ba* and *ga-ga-ga*. This type of sound production is described as **babbling**. In the later babbling stage, around nine to ten months, there are recognizable intonation patterns to the consonant and vowel combinations being produced, as well as variation in the combinations such as *ba-ba-da-da*. Nasal sounds also become more common and certain syllable sequences such as *ma-ma-ma* and *da-da-da* are inevitably interpreted by parents as versions of "mama" and "dada" and repeated back to the child.

As children begin to pull themselves into a standing position during the tenth and eleventh months, they become capable of using their vocalizations to express emotions and emphasis. This late babbling stage is characterized by more complex syllable combinations (*ma-da-ga-ba*), a lot of sound-play and attempted imitations. This "prelanguage" use of sound provides the child with some experience of the social role of speech because adults tend to react to the babbling, however incoherent, as if it is actually the child's contribution to social interaction. By the time most children are twelve months old, they are also producing distinct gestures, such as pointing with an outstretched hand or holding out an object toward the caregiver, that accompany their vocalizations, suggesting a close physical connection between using the hand and using the vocal organs.

One note of caution should be sounded at this point. Child language researchers certainly report very carefully on the age of any child whose language they study. However, they are also very careful to point out that there is substantial variation among children in terms of the age at which particular features of linguistic development occur. So, we should always treat statements concerning development stages such as "by six months" or "by the age of two" as general approximations and subject to variation in individual children.

The One-Word Stage

Between twelve and eighteen months, children begin to produce a variety of recognizable single-unit utterances. This period, traditionally called the **one-word stage**, is characterized by speech in which single terms are used for objects such as "milk," "cookie," "cat," "cup" and "spoon" (usually pronounced [pun]). Other forms such as [ʌsæ] may occur in circumstances that suggest the child is producing a version of *What's that*, so a term such as "single-unit" is more accurate. We use the term **holophrastic** speech (meaning a single form functioning as a phrase or sentence) to describe an utterance that could be a word, a phrase, or a sentence.

While many of these holophrastic utterances seem to be used to name objects, they may also be produced in circumstances that suggest the child is already extending their use. An empty bed may elicit the name of a sister who normally sleeps in the bed, even in the absence of the person named. During this stage, then, the child may be able to refer separately to *Karen* and *bed*, but isn't ready yet to put the forms together in a more complex phrase. Well, it is a lot to expect from someone who can only walk with a stagger and has to come down stairs backwards.

The Two-Word Stage

Depending on what we count as an occurrence of two distinct words used together, the **two-word stage** can begin around eighteen to twenty months, as the child's vocabulary moves beyond fifty words. By the time the child is two years old, a variety of combinations, similar to *baby chair, mommy eat, cat bad*, will usually have appeared. The adult interpretation of such combinations is, of course, very much tied to the context of their utterance. The phrase *baby chair* may be taken as an expression of possession (= this is baby's chair), or as a request (= put baby in chair), or as a statement (= baby is in the chair), depending on different circumstances. Here are some other examples reported from the two-word stage:

> *big boat doggie bark hit ball mama dress more milk shoe off*

Whatever it is that the child actually intends to communicate through such expressions, the significant functional consequences are that the adults or, more often, older children behave as if communication is taking place. That is, the child not only produces speech, but also receives feedback confirming that the utterance worked as a contribution to the interaction. Moreover, by the age of two, whether the child is producing 200 or 300 distinct "words," he or she will be capable of understanding five times as many.

Telegraphic Speech

Between two and two and a half years old, the child begins producing a large number of utterances that could be classified as "multiple-word" speech. The salient feature of these utterances ceases to be the number of words, but the variation in word forms that begins to appear. Before we investigate this development, we should note a stage that is described as **telegraphic speech**. This is characterized by strings of words (lexical morphemes) in phrases or sentences such as *this shoe all wet, cat drink milk* and *daddy go bye-bye*. The child has clearly developed some sentence-building capacity by this stage and can get the word order correct. While this type of telegram-format speech is being produced, inflections (*-ing*) begin to appear in some word forms and simple prepositions (*in, on*) are also used.

By the age of two and a half, the child's vocabulary is expanding rapidly and the child is initiating more talk while increased physical activity includes running and jumping. By three, the vocabulary has grown to hundreds of words and pronunciation has become clearer. At this point, it is worth considering what kind of influence the adults have in the development of the child's speech.

The Acquisition Process

As the linguistic repertoire of the child increases, it is often assumed that the child is, in some sense, being "taught" the language. This idea is not really supported by what the child actually does. For the vast majority of children, no one provides any instruction on how to speak the language. A more accurate view would have the children actively constructing, from what is said to them and around them, possible ways of using the language. The child's linguistic production appears to be mostly a matter of trying out constructions and testing whether they work or not.

It is simply not possible that the child is acquiring the language principally through adult instruction. Certainly, children imitate what adults say and they are clearly in the process of adopting a lot of vocabulary from the speech they hear (the input). However, adults simply do not produce many of the expressions that turn up in children's speech. Notice how, in the following extract (Clark, 1995), the child creates a new verb (*to Woodstock*) in the context.

NOAH (picking up a toy dog):   *This is Woodstock.*
                                (He bobs the toy in Adam's face)
ADAM: *Hey Woodstock, don't do that.*
                                (Noah persists)
ADAM: *I'm going home so you won't Woodstock me.*

Learning through Imitation?

Similar evidence against "imitation" as the major source of the child's speech production comes from studies of the structures used by young children. They may repeat single words or phrases, but not the sentence structures. In the following two examples, the children were asked to repeat what the adult said (on the left).

> *The dogs are hungry*   ~ *dog hungry*
> *The owl who eats candy runs fast*   ~ *owl eat a candy and he run fast.*

It is likely that the children understand what the adults are saying in these examples. They just have their own way of expressing what they understand.

Learning through Correction?

It is also unlikely that adult "corrections" are a very effective determiner of how the child speaks. One example of attempted correction (*other one spoon*) was quoted at the beginning of the chapter. Even when the correction is attempted in a subtle manner, the child will continue to use a personally constructed form, despite the adult's repetition of what the correct form should be. Note that in the following dialog (from Cazden, 1972) the child, a four-year-old, is neither imitating the adult's speech nor accepting the adult's correction.

CHILD: *My teacher **holded** the baby rabbits and we patted them.*

MOTHER: *Did you say your teacher **held** the baby rabbits?*

CHILD: *Yes*

MOTHER: *What did you say she did?*

CHILD: *She **holded** the baby rabbits and we patted them.*

MOTHER: *Did you say she **held** them tightly?*

CHILD: *No, she **holded** them loosely.*

One factor that seems to be important in the child's acquisition process is the use of sound and word combinations, either in interaction with others or in word play, alone. One two-year-old, described in Weir (1966), was tape-recorded as he lay in bed alone and could be heard playing with words and phrases, *I go dis way . . . way bay . . . baby do dis bib . . . all bib . . . bib . . . dere.* Word play seems to be an important element in the development of the child's linguistic repertoire. When we look more closely at development beyond the telegraphic stage, we can trace specific linguistic features that turn up in the steady stream of speech from the little chatterbox.

Developing Morphology

By the time a child is two and a half years old, he or she is going beyond telegraphic speech forms and incorporating inflectional and functional morphemes. The first to appear is the *-ing* form in expressions such as *cat sitting* and *mommy reading book*. This is usually followed by the prepositions *in* and *on*, in either order.

The next morphological development is typically the marking of regular plurals with the *-s* form, as in *boys* and *cats*. The acquisition of the plural marker is often accompanied by a process of **overgeneralization**. The child overgeneralizes the apparent rule of adding *-s* to form plurals and will talk about *foots* and *mans*.

Irregular plurals such as *men* and *feet* appear next (sometimes overgeneralized, as in *some mens* or *two feets*), along with irregular past tense forms such as *came* and *went*. Not long after we see different forms of the verb "to be," such as *is* and *are*. At about the same time as these new verb forms appear, and sometimes before them, the possessive inflection *-'s* becomes part of noun phrases such as *Karen's bed* and *mommy's book*. Also in noun phrases, the articles *a* and *the* start to be used.

Finally, the regular past tense forms with *-ed*, as in *it opened* or *he walked*, become common, with some overgeneralization in examples such as *he goed* and *you comed here*, and also forms like *walkeded* and *wented*. The final inflectional morpheme to be used, present tense *-s*, occurs first on verbs (*comes, knows*), then with auxiliary verbs (*does, has*). There may be some variability in individual cases, but the general acquisition sequence is presented in Table 13.1 (based on Brown, 1973).

TABLE 13.1 ACQUISITION OF MORPHEMES

Stage	Morpheme	Examples
1	*-ing*	cat sitting, mommy reading book
2=	*in*	in bag, not in that
3=	*on*	on bed, that on top
4	plural *-s*	boys, cats
5=	irregular past tense	he came, it went away
6=	possessive *-s*	Karen's bed, mommy's book
7	verb "to be" (*is, are*)	this is no, you are look
8	articles (*a, the*)	a cat, the dog
9	past tense *-ed*	it opened, he walked
10	present tense *-s*	it comes, she knows

("=") Note that Stages 2 and 3 can be exchanged, similarly Stages 5 and 6.

Developing Syntax

There have been numerous studies of the development of syntax in children's speech. We will look at the development of two structures that seem to be acquired in a regular way by most English-speaking children. In the formation of questions and the use of negatives, there appear to be three identifiable stages. The ages at which children go through these stages can vary quite a bit, but the general pattern seems to be that Stage 1 occurs between 18 and 26 months, Stage 2 between 22 and 30 months, and Stage 3 between 24 and 40 months. (The overlap in the periods is a reflection of the different rates at which different children normally develop.)

Forming Questions

In forming questions, the child's first stage has two procedures. Simply add a *wh*-form (*Where*) to the beginning of the expression (*Where kitty?*) or utter the expression with a rise in intonation toward the end (*Sit chair?*).

In the second stage, more complex expressions can be formed, but the rising intonation strategy continues to be used (*You want eat?*). It is noticeable that more *wh*-forms, such as *What* and *Why*, come into use (*Why you smiling?*).

In the third stage, the change in position of the auxiliary verb in English questions, called **inversion**, becomes evident in the child's speech (*I can have . . . ⇒ Can I have . . . ?*), but doesn't automatically spread to all *wh*-question types. In fact, some children beginning school may still prefer to form *wh*-questions (especially with negatives) without the type of structure found in adult speech. They tend to say *Why kitty can't do it?* instead of *Why can't kitty do it?*. Apart from these problems with *wh*-questions and continuing trouble with the morphology of verbs (e.g. *Did I caught it?* instead of *Did I catch it?*), Stage 3 questions are generally quite close to the adult model.

These observations are summarized in Table 13.2.

TABLE 13.2 ACQUISITION OF QUESTIONS

Stage 1	(1 or 2 words + rising intonation)	*Doggie?*	*Sit chair?*
	(add *Where*)	*Where kitty?*	*Where that?*
Stage 2	(2 or 3 words + rising intonation)	*You want eat?*	*See my doggie?*
	(add *What* and *Why*)	*What book name?*	*Why you smiling?*
Stage 3	(3 or 4 words + inversion)	*Can I have a piece?*	*Will you help me?*
	(add *Who* and *How*)	*Who did you go?*	*How is that open?*
	(non-adult forms)	*Why kitty can't do it?*	*Did I caught it?*

Forming Negatives

In the case of negatives, Stage 1 seems to involve a simple strategy of putting *No* or *Not* at the beginning. In some cases (e.g. *No doing it*), the negative may be used for a denial (= *I am not doing it*), while in other circumstances, it may be used to express a desire (= *I don't want to do it*), but the utterance doesn't change. At this stage, both *no* and *not* can be attached to nouns (*no mitten*) and verbs (*not sit there*).

In the second stage, the additional negative forms *don't* and *can't* appear, and, with *no* and *not*, are increasingly used in front of the verb rather than at the beginning of the utterance. At this stage, children seem to be using the form *don't* as a single unit, with no connection to the alternative *do not*, probably because the contracted form of *not* (*n't*) is simply not heard as a distinct element in speech.

The third stage sees the incorporation of other auxiliary forms such as *didn't* and *won't* while the typical Stage 1 forms disappear. A very late acquisition is the negative form *isn't*, with the result that some Stage 2 forms (with *not* instead of *isn't*) continue to be used for quite a long time, as exemplified in *This not ice cream*. These observations are summarized in Table 13.3.

The study of children's use of negative forms has revealed some entertaining cases where the children involved clearly had their own rules for negative sentences. One famous example (from McNeill, 1966) also shows the futility of overt adult "correction" of children's speech.

CHILD: *Nobody don't like me.*
MOTHER: *No, say "nobody likes me."*
CHILD: *Nobody don't like me.*
          (Eight repetitions of this dialog)
MOTHER: *No, now listen carefully; say "nobody likes me."*
CHILD: *Oh! Nobody don't likes me.*

TABLE 13.3 ACQUISITION OF NEGATIVES

Stage 1	(add *No* or *Not* to beginning)	*No mitten*	*Not a teddy bear*
		No doing it	*Not sit there*
Stage 2	(add *no* or *not* to verb)	*He no bite you*	*That not touch*
	(add *don't* or *can't* to verb)	*I don't want it*	*You can't dance*
Stage 3	(add *didn't* or *won't* to verb)	*I didn't caught it*	*She won't let go*
	(non-adult forms)	*This not ice cream*	*He not taking it*

Developing Semantics

The anecdotes that parents retell about their child's early speech (to the intense embarrassment of the grown-up child) usually involve examples of the strange use of words. Having been warned that flies bring germs into the house, one child was asked what "germs" were and the answer was "something the flies play with." It is not always possible to determine so precisely the meanings that children attach to the words they use. It seems that during the holophrastic stage many children use their limited vocabulary to refer to a large number of unrelated objects. One child first used *bow-wow* to refer to a dog and then to a fur piece with glass eyes, a set of cufflinks and even a bath thermometer. The word *bow-wow* seemed to have a meaning like "object with shiny bits." Other children often extend *bow-wow* to refer to cats, cows and horses.

This process is called **overextension**. The most common pattern is for the child to overextend the meaning of a word on the basis of similarities of shape, sound and size, and, to a lesser extent, movement and texture. Thus the word *ball* is extended to all kinds of round objects, including a lampshade, a doorknob and the moon. Or, a *tick-tock* is initially used for a watch, but can also be used for a bathroom scale with a round dial. On the basis of size, presumably, the word *fly* was first used for the insect and then came to be used for specks of dirt and even crumbs of bread. Apparently due to similarities of texture, the expression *sizo* was first used by one child for scissors, and then extended to all metal objects. The semantic development in a child's use of words is usually a process of overextension initially, followed by a gradual process of narrowing down the application of each term as more words are learned.

Although overextension has been well documented in children's speech production, it isn't necessarily used in speech comprehension. One two-year-old used *apple*, in speaking, to refer to a number of other round objects like a tomato and a ball, but had no difficulty picking out *the apple*, when asked, from a set of round objects including a ball and a tomato.

One interesting feature of the young child's semantics is the way certain lexical relations are treated. In terms of hyponymy, the child will almost always use the "middle" level term in a hyponymous set such as *animal – dog – terrier*. It would seem more logical to learn the most general term (*animal*), but all evidence indicates that children first use *dog* with an overextended meaning close to the meaning of "animal." This may be connected to a similar tendency in adults, when talking to young children, to refer to *flowers* (not the more general *plants*, or the more specific *tulips*).

Later Developments

Some types of antonymous relations are acquired fairly late (after the age of five). In one study, a large number of kindergarten children pointed to the same heavily laden apple tree when asked *Which tree has more apples?* and also when asked *Which tree has less apples?*. They just seem to think the correct response will be the larger one, disregarding the difference between *more* and *less*. The distinctions between a number of other pairs such as *before/after* and *buy/sell* also seem to be later acquisitions. The ability to produce certain types of complex structures and extended discourse are also much later developments.

Despite the fact that children are still in the process of acquiring a number of other aspects of their first language through the later years of childhood, it is normally assumed that, by the age of five, they have completed the greater part of the basic language acquisition process. They have become accomplished users of a first language. According to some, the child is then in a good position to start learning a second (or foreign) language. However, most people don't start trying to learn another language until much later. The question that always arises is: if first language acquisition was so straightforward and largely automatic, why is learning a second language so difficult for so many people? We will try to answer that question in Chapter 14.

Study Questions

1 Describe four typical features of caregiver speech.

2 At what age is an infant capable of distinguishing between [ba] and [pa]?

3 Why are some of the infant's first sounds described as "cooing"?

4 Describe two gestures that one-year-olds produce along with babbling.

5 During which period do children produce holophrastic speech?

6 During which stage do children typically first produce syllable sequences similar to *mama* and *dada* and how old are they?

7 At about what age do children typically begin producing varied syllable combinations such as *ma-da-ga-ba*?

8 Which of these utterances would be described as telegraphic speech?

   (a) *hit ball*   (c) *daddy go bye-bye*
   (b) *what's that*   (d) *my teacher holded the baby rabbits*

9 Which of these expressions is likely to be used before the others?

   mommy books or *mommy's book* or *mommy reading* or *mommy goed*

10 Which of these expressions is likely to be used before the others?

   What book name? or *How that opened?* or *Where kitty go?*

11 Which of these two utterances was produced by the older child and why?

   (a) *I not hurt him*

   (b) *No the sun shining*

12 What is the term used to describe the process involved when a child uses one word like *ball* to refer to an apple, an egg, a grape and a ball?

Tasks

A The "sucking behavior" of infants was mentioned in this chapter in connection with early speech perception. How can it be measured and what can we learn from these measurements?

B It has been proposed that very young children acquiring English are able to identify the primary stress in words they hear and often use a trochaic stress pattern in their early attempts to produce those words.

(i)   What is a trochaic stress pattern?

(ii) Which of the following examples of children's versions of the English words (in brackets) might be taken as evidence that these children have a preference for trochaic structure in creating words?

æməl ("animal")   laɪ ("butterfly")

nana ("banana")   putə ("computer")

baba ("bottle")   dædæ ("daddy")

bʌbʌ ("bunny")   raɪsə ("eraser")

C   The connection between the early development of motor skills and the development of speech for an average child in an English-speaking environment was described in detail by Lenneberg (1967: 128–130) and recently elaborated by Iverson (2010). Can you complete Table 13.4 below by adding appropriate descriptions of motor skills and speech skills at each age, showing how they develop together? (There are two descriptive phrases for some levels.)

Motor Skills

- can walk with support
- can sit, bend forward and reach for objects
- can move easily on hands and feet
- can lift head and hands from a lying position
- can sit up with support
- can grasp with thumb and fingers
- puts objects such as toys or fingers in mouth while making sounds
- can pull self into standing position

Speech Skills

- produces more consonant-like sounds as well as vowels
- produces squealing, gurgling and cooing sounds
- produces sound play, bubbles and syllable combinations (e.g. [da da ba ba])
- turns head to human speech sounds
- produces longer vowels and babbling sounds, some like syllables (e.g. [da], [mu])
- recognizes different sounds (e.g. [ba] versus [ga])
- easily produces repeated syllables with different consonants (e.g. [ba da ma])
- produces more vocalizations with regular rhythm of syllables (e.g. [ba ba ba])

TABLE 13.4 MOTOR SKILLS AND SPEECH SKILLS

	Motor skills	Speech skills
4 months		
5 months		
6 months		
8 months		
10 months		
12 months		

D The following examples are from the speech of three children. Identify which child is at the earliest stage, which is next in order, and which is at the most advanced stage. Describe those features in the examples from each child's speech that support your ordering.

CHILD X: *You want eat?*
I can't see my book.
Why you waking me up?

CHILD Y: *Where those dogs goed?*
You didn't eat supper.
Does lions walk?

CHILD Z: *No picture in there.*
Where momma boot?
Have some?

E There are two distinct theoretical perspectives on how first language acquisition takes place, generally labeled the "rational" perspective and the "empirical" perspective. We can characterize each perspective with a number of tenets or principles, as illustrated in the following statements. Divide these statements into two sets, one representing the rational perspective and the other representing the empirical perspective. Which perspective do you prefer?

(1) Acquisition proceeds in a piecemeal fashion, building on what is already there.

(2) Acquisition takes places along a predetermined path.

(3)   Children begin life with some knowledge of the possible units of language.

(4)   Children learn to say things unrelated to input.

(5)   General learning mechanisms account for language learning.

(6)   It takes time to integrate new linguistic information with existing knowledge.

(7)   Language learning is independent of other kinds of learning.

(8)   New linguistic knowledge is acquired very quickly.

(9)   Speech is perceived from the start as distinct from any other physical stimuli.

(10)   There are only a few fixed possibilities of language structures to learn.

(11)   There are many possible language structures to be learned.

(12)   There is no initial distinction between speech and any other physical stimuli.

(13)   There is no pre-programmed knowledge of language.

(14)   What children learn to say is directly related to input.

F   Do boys and girls develop language differently in the early stages? Have any differences been documented in how they speak and how they are spoken to?

G   What is meant by MLU ("Mean Length of Utterance") in child language studies? Can you work out the MLU of this small sample of utterances?

no big box	*no eating that*
daddy eat red apple	*that mommy's book*
daddy eats apples	

Discussion Topics/Projects

I   In our discussion of developing semantics, we focused mainly on the use of nouns. In the following examples, a young child (age shown as year; month) seems to be using verbs in a way that is not based on typical adult uses and hence unlikely to be "imitations." Is there any consistent pattern in these examples? Can you suggest an explanation for this child's choice of words for the kinds of actions being described?

(2; 3) *I come it closer so it won't fall* (= bring it closer)

(2; 6) *Mommy, can you stay this open?* (= keep this open)

(2; 8) *Daddy, go me round* (= make me go round)

(2; 9) *I'm gonna fall this on her* (= drop this on her)

(2;11) *How would you flat it?* (= flatten it)

(3; 1) *I'm singing him* (= making him sing)

(For background reading, see chapter 6 of Clark, 2016.)

II   Which of these three metaphors of first language acquisition (from Valian, 1999) would you agree with and why?

(a) According to the copy metaphor, "the child gradually aligns her speech with that of her language community" and "the focus is on an active role for input."

(b) According to the hypothesis testing metaphor, "the child forms and tests hypotheses about what structures exist in the language" and "the child is not copying the input."

(c) According to the trigger metaphor, "the child neither copies the input nor evaluates it" and "a given piece of input triggers the correct parametric value," assuming the child has innate knowledge of a small set of possible parametric values.

(For background reading, see Valian, 1999.)

Further Reading

Basic Treatments

Apel, K. and J. Masterson (2012) *Beyond Baby Talk* (revised edition) Three Rivers Press

Clark, E. (2017) *Language in Children* Routledge

O'Grady, W. (2005) *How Children Learn Language* Cambridge University Press

More Detailed Treatments

Clark, E. (2016) *First Language Acquisition* (3rd edition) Cambridge University Press

Lust, B. (2006) *Child Language* Cambridge University Press

Speech Perception in Infants

Jusczyk, P. (1997) *The Discovery of Spoken Language* MIT Press

Vihman, M. (2013) *Phonological Development: The First Two Years* Wiley

Babbling

Oller, D. (2000) *The Emergence of the Speech Capacity* Lawrence Erlbaum

Gesture and Early Speech

Clancy, P. (2014) "First language acquisition" In C. Genetti (ed.) *How Languages Work* (318–350) Cambridge University Press

Olson, J. and E. Masur (2011) "Infants' gestures influence mothers' provision of object, action and internal state labels" *Journal of Child Language* 38: 1028–1054

The One-Word Stage

Rodgon, M. (2009) *Single-Word Usage, Cognitive Development and the Beginnings of Combinatorial Speech* Cambridge University Press

Morphological Development

Moskowitz, B. (1991) "The acquisition of language" In W. Wang (ed.) *The Emergence of Language* (131–149) W. H. Freeman

Syntactic Development

O'Grady, W. (1997) *Syntactic Development* University of Chicago Press

Semantic Development

Bloom, P. (2002) *How Children Learn the Meanings of Words* MIT Press

Rational and Empirical Perspectives (in that order)

Pinker, S. (1994) *The Language Instinct* William Morrow

Tomasello, M. (2003) *Constructing a Language* Harvard University Press

Other References

Brown, R. (1973) *A First Language* Harvard University Press

Bruner, J. (1983) *Child's Talk: Learning to Use Language* Norton

Cazden, C. (1972) *Child Language and Education* Holt

Clark, E. (1995) *The Lexicon in Acquisition* Cambridge University Press

Iverson, J. (2010) "Developing language in a developing body: the relationship between motor development and language development" *Journal of Child Language* 37: 229–261

Lenneberg, E. (1967) *The Biological Foundations of Language* John Wiley

McNeill, D. (1966) "Developmental psycholinguistics" In F. Smith and G. Miller (eds.) *The Genesis of Language* (15–84) MIT Press

Valian, V. (1999) "Input and language acquisition" In W. Ritchie and T. Bhatia (eds.) *Handbook of Child Language Acquisition* (497–530) Academic Press

Weir, R. (1966) "Questions on the learning of phonology" In F. Smith and G. Miller (eds.) *The Genesis of Language* (153–168) MIT Press

14 Second Language Acquisition/ Learning

"Easter is a party for to eat of the lamb," the Italian nanny explained. "One too may eat of the
  chocolate."
"And who brings the chocolate?" the teacher asked.
I knew the word, so I raised my hand, saying, "The rabbit of Easter. He bring of the chocolate."
"A rabbit?" The teacher, assuming I'd used the wrong word, positioned her index fingers on top
of her head, wriggling them as though they were ears. "You mean one of these? A *rabbit* rabbit?"
"Well, sure," I said. "He come in the night when one sleep on a bed. With a hand he have a basket
  and foods."
The teacher sighed and shook her head. As far as she was concerned, I had just explained everything
  that was wrong with my country. "No, no," she said. "Here in France the chocolate is brought by
  a big bell that flies in from Rome."
I called for a time-out. "But how do the bell know where you live?"
"Well," she said, "how does a rabbit?"

Sedaris (2000)

Some children grow up in a social environment where more than one language is used and
are able to acquire a second language in circumstances similar to those of first language
acquisition. Those fortunate individuals are bilingual (see Chapter 18). However, most of us
are not exposed to a second language until much later and, like David Sedaris, our ability to
use a second language, even after years of study, rarely matches ability in our first language.

Second Language Learning

There is something of an enigma in this situation, since there is apparently no other system of "knowledge" that we can learn better at two or three years of age than at thirteen or thirty. A number of reasons have been suggested to account for this enigma, and a number of different approaches have been proposed to help learners become as effective communicating in a foreign or second language (L2) as they are in their first language (L1).

A distinction is sometimes made between learning in a "foreign language" setting (learning a language that is not generally spoken in the surrounding community) and a "second language" setting (learning a language that is spoken in the surrounding community). That is, Japanese students in an English class in Japan are learning English as a foreign language (EFL) and, if those same students were in an English class in the USA, they would be learning English as a second language (ESL). In either case, they are simply trying to learn another language, so the expression **second language learning** is used more generally to describe both situations.

Acquisition and Learning

A more significant distinction is made between acquisition and learning. The term **acquisition** describes the gradual development over time of ability in a language by using it naturally in communicative situations with others who know the language. Acquisition normally takes place without a teacher and without much attention to the details of what is being acquired. The term **learning**, however, applies to a more conscious process of accumulating knowledge through analysis of features of a language, such as vocabulary and grammar, typically in an institutional setting, with teachers. (Mathematics, for example, is learned, not acquired.)

Activities associated with learning have traditionally been used in second language teaching in schools and have a tendency, when successful, to result in more knowledge "about" the language (as demonstrated in tests) than fluency in actually using the language (as demonstrated in social interaction). Activities associated with acquisition are those experienced by the young child and, by analogy, those who "pick up" a second language from long periods spent in interaction, constantly using the language, with native speakers of the language. (Native speakers are those who speak the language as their L1.) This distinction is also sometimes equated with preferred learning styles; some individuals prefer an analytic approach while others prefer a holistic approach. However, individuals whose L2 exposure is primarily a learning type of experience tend not to develop the same kind of general proficiency as those who have had more of an extended acquisition type of experience.

Acquisition Barriers

For most people, the experience with an L2 is fundamentally different from their L1 experience and it is hardly conducive to acquisition. They usually encounter the L2 during their teenage or adult years, in a few hours each week of school time (rather than via the constant interaction experienced as a child), with a lot of other things going on (young children have little else to do). They also have developed an unconscious commitment to the sounds and structures of an already known language that has been in use for most of their daily communicative requirements for many years. Despite the fact that insufficient time, focus and incentive undermine many L2 learning attempts, there are some individuals who seem to be able to overcome the difficulties and develop an ability to use the L2 quite effectively, though not usually sounding like a native speaker.

However, even in ideal acquisition situations, very few adults seem to reach native-like proficiency in using an L2. There are individuals who can achieve great expertise in the written language, but not the spoken language. One example is Joseph Conrad (1857–1924), who wrote novels in English that became classics of English literature, but whose English speech retained the strong Polish accent of his L1. This might suggest that some features of an L2, such as vocabulary and grammar, are easier to learn than others, such as pronunciation. Indeed, without early experience using the sounds and intonation of the L2, even highly proficient adult learners are likely to be perceived as having an "accent" of some kind.

The Age Factor

This type of observation is sometimes taken as evidence that, after the critical period for language acquisition has passed, around the time of puberty, it becomes very difficult to acquire another language fully (see Chapter 12). We might think of this process in terms of our inherent capacity for language being taken over by features of the L1, with a resulting loss of openness to receive the features of another language. Given the example of Joseph Conrad and many others, we might note that the dominance of the L1 is particularly strong in terms of pronunciation.

Against this view, it has been demonstrated that students in their early teens are quicker and more effective L2 learners in the classroom than, for example, seven-year-olds. It may be, of course, that the effective learning of an L2 (even with a trace of an accent) requires a combination of factors. The optimum age for learning may be during the years from about ten to sixteen when the flexibility of our inherent capacity for language has not been completely lost, and the maturation of cognitive skills allows a more effective analysis of the regular features of the L2 being learned.

Affective Factors

Yet even during this proposed optimum age for L2 learning, there may exist an acquisition barrier of quite a different kind. Teenagers are typically much more self-conscious than younger children. If there is a strong element of unwillingness or embarrassment in attempting to produce the different sounds of another language, then it may override whatever physical and cognitive abilities there are. If this self-consciousness is accompanied by a lack of empathy with the other culture (for example, feeling no identification with its speakers or their customs), then the subtle effects of not really wanting to sound like a Russian or a German or an American may strongly inhibit the learning process.

This type of emotional reaction, or "affect," may also be the result of dull textbooks, unpleasant classroom surroundings or an exhausting schedule of study and/or work. All these negative feelings or experiences are **affective factors** that can create a barrier to acquisition. Basically, if we are stressed, uncomfortable, self-conscious or unmotivated, we are unlikely to learn very much. In contrast, learners who have other personality traits, such as self-confidence, low anxiety and a positive self-image, seem better able to overcome difficulties in the learning space.

Children are generally less constrained by affective factors. Descriptions of L2 acquisition in childhood are full of instances where young children quickly overcome their inhibitions as they try to use new words and phrases. Adults can sometimes overcome their inhibitions too. In one intriguing study, a group of adult L2 learners volunteered to have their self-consciousness levels reduced by having their alcohol levels gradually increased. Up to a certain point, the pronunciation of the L2 noticeably improved, but after a certain number of drinks, as we might expect, pronunciations deteriorated rapidly. Courses introducing "French with cognac" or "Russian with vodka" may provide a partial solution, but the inhibitions are likely to return with sobriety.

Focus on Teaching Method

Despite all these barriers, the need for instruction in other languages has led to a variety of educational approaches and methods aimed at fostering L2 learning. As long ago as 1483, William Caxton used his newly established printing press to produce a book of *Right good lernyng for to lerne shortly frenssh and englyssh*. He was not the first to compile exercise material for L2 learners and his phrase-book format with customary greetings (*Syre, god you kepe. I haue not seen you in longe tyme*) has many modern counterparts. More recent approaches to L2 learning have tended to reflect different theoretical views on how an L2 might best be learned.

The Grammar–Translation Method

The most traditional approach is to treat L2 learning in the same way as any other academic subject. Vocabulary lists and sets of grammar rules are used to define the target of learning, memorization is encouraged, and written language rather than spoken language is emphasized. This method has its roots in the traditional teaching of Latin and is described as the **grammar–translation method**. This emphasis on learning about the L2 often leaves students quite ignorant of how the language might be used in everyday conversation. The method clearly produced many successful L2 users over the centuries, but students often leave school, having achieved high grades in French class via this method, yet find themselves at a loss when confronted by the way the French in France actually use their language.

The Audiolingual Method

A very different approach, emphasizing the spoken language, became popular in the middle of the twentieth century. It involved a systematic presentation of the structures of the L2, moving from the simple to the more complex, in the form of drills that the student had to repeat. This approach, called the **audiolingual method**, was strongly influenced by a belief that the fluent use of a language was essentially a set of "habits" that could be developed with a lot of practice. This practice involved hours spent in a language lab repeating oral drills. Versions of this approach are still used in language teaching, but critics have noted that isolated practice in drilling language patterns bears no resemblance to the interactional nature of actual spoken language use. Moreover, it can be incredibly boring.

Communicative Approaches

More recent revisions of the L2 learning experience can best be described as **communicative approaches**. They are partially a reaction against the artificiality of "pattern-practice" and also against the belief that consciously learning the grammar rules of a language will result in an ability to use the language. Although there are different versions of this approach, they are all based on a belief that the functions of language (what it is used for) should be emphasized rather than the forms of the language (correct forms and structures). Classroom lessons are likely to be organized around concepts such as "asking for things" in different social settings, rather than "the forms of the past tense" in different sentences. These changes have coincided with attempts to provide more appropriate materials for L2 learning that has a specific purpose, as in "English for medicine" or "Japanese for business."

Focus on the Learner

The most fundamental change in the area of L2 studies in recent years has been a shift from concern with the teacher, the textbook and the method to an interest in the learner and the acquisition process. For example, one radical feature of most communicative approaches is the toleration of "errors" produced by students. Traditionally, "errors" were regarded negatively and they had to be avoided or eradicated. The more recent acceptance of such errors in learners' use of the L2 is based on a fundamental shift in perspective from the more traditional view of how L2 learning takes place.

Rather than consider a Spanish (L1) speaker's production of *in the room there are three womens* as simply a failure to learn correct English (which can be remedied through extra practice of the correct form), we can look at this utterance as an indication of the natural L2 acquisition process in action. An "error," then, is not something that hinders a student's progress, but is probably a clue to the active learning progress being made by the student as he or she tries out ways of communicating in the new language. Just as children acquiring their L1 produce certain types of ungrammatical forms at times, so we might expect the L2 learner to produce similar forms at certain stages (see Chapter 13). The example of *womens* might be seen as a type of overgeneralization (of *-s* as the plural marker), used by the learner based on the most common way of making plural forms in English.

Transfer

Of course, some errors may be due to "transfer" (also called "crosslinguistic influence"). **Transfer** means using sounds, expressions or structures from the L1 when performing in the L2. For example, a Spanish (L1) speaker who produces *take it from the side inferior* may be trying to use the Spanish adjective *inferior* (= *lower* in English) and placing it after the noun, as is typical in Spanish constructions. If the L1 and L2 have similar features (e.g. marking plural on the ends of nouns), then the learner may be able to benefit from the **positive transfer** of L1 knowledge to the L2. On the other hand, transferring an L1 feature that is really different from the L2 (e.g. putting the adjective after the noun) results in **negative transfer** and it may make the L2 expression difficult to understand. The impact of negative transfer on communicative success tends to be greater when the L1 and L2 are really different types of languages, making the task of becoming proficient in English more demanding for Chinese than for German speakers. We should remember that negative transfer (also called "interference") is more common in the early stages of L2 learning and decreases as the learner develops greater familiarity with the L2.

Interlanguage

On close inspection, the language produced by L2 learners contains a large number of "errors" that seem to have no connection to the forms of either the L1 or L2. For example, the Spanish L1 speaker who says in English *She name is Maria* is producing a form that is not used by adult speakers of English, does not occur in English L1 acquisition by children, and is not based on a structure in Spanish. Evidence of this sort suggests that there is an in-between system used in the L2 acquisition process that certainly contains aspects of the L1 and L2, but which is an inherently variable system with rules of its own. This system is called an **interlanguage** and it is now considered to be the basis of all L2 production. (Task H on page 230 has examples.)

If some learners develop a fairly fixed repertoire of L2 expressions, containing many forms that do not match the target language, and seem not to be progressing any further, their interlanguage is said to have "fossilized." The process of **fossilization** in L2 pronunciation seems to be the most likely basis of what is perceived as a foreign accent. However, an interlanguage is not designed to fossilize. It will naturally develop and become a more effective means of L2 communication given appropriate conditions. Discovering just what count as the appropriate conditions for successful L2 learning is an ongoing area of investigation.

Motivation

There are several factors that combine in a profile of a successful L2 learner. Obviously, the motivation to learn is important. Many learners have an **instrumental motivation**. That is, they want to learn the L2 in order to achieve some other goal, such as completing a graduation requirement or being able to read scientific publications, but they have no plans to engage in much social interaction using the L2. In contrast, those learners with an **integrative motivation** want to learn the L2 for social purposes, to take part in the social life of a community using that language and to become an accepted member of that community.

It is also worth noting that those who experience some success in L2 communication are among the most motivated to learn. So, motivation may be as much a result of success as a cause. A language-learning situation that provides support and encourages students to try to use whatever L2 skills they have in order to communicate successfully must consequently be more helpful than one that dwells on errors, corrections and a failure to be perfectly accurate. Indeed, the learner who is willing to guess, risks making mistakes and tries to communicate in the L2 will tend, given the opportunity, to be more successful. An important part of that opportunity is the availability of "input."

Input and Output

The term **input** is used, as in L1 acquisition (see Chapter 13), to describe the language that the learner is exposed to. To be beneficial for L2 learning, that input has to be comprehensible, because we can't process what we don't understand. Input can be made comprehensible by being simpler in structure and vocabulary, as in the variety of speech called **foreigner talk**. Native speakers of English may try to ask an international student *How are you getting on in your studies?*, but, if not understood, may switch to *English class, you like it?* This type of foreigner talk may be beneficial, not only for immediate communication, but also for providing the learner with comprehensible examples of the basic structure of the L2 as input.

As the learner's interlanguage develops, however, there is a need for more interaction and some kind of "negotiated input." **Negotiated input** is L2 material that the learner can acquire in interaction through requests for clarification while active attention is being focused on what is said. In the following interaction (from Pica *et al.*, 1991), notice how the learner, a non-native speaker (NNS) of English, and the English native speaker (NS) negotiate meaning together. The comprehensible input (i.e. using the word *triangle* to describe a shape) is provided at a point where the learner needs it and is paying attention to the meaning in context.

NS: *like part of a triangle?*
NNS: *what is triangle?*
NS: *a triangle is a shape um it has three sides*
NNS: *a peak?*
NS: *three straight sides*
NNS: *a peak?*
NS: *yes it does look like a mountain peak, yes*
NNS: *only line only line?*
NS: *okay two of them, right? one on each side? a line on each side?*
NNS: *yes*
NS: *little lines on each side?*
NNS: *yes*
NS: *like a mountain?*
NNS: *yes*

In this type of interaction, the learner experiences the benefits of both receiving input (hearing the L2) and producing output (speaking the L2). The opportunity to produce comprehensible **output** in meaningful interaction seems to be another important element in the learner's development of L2 ability, yet it is one of the most difficult things to provide in large L2 classes.

Task-Based Learning

One solution has been to create different types of tasks and activities in which learners have to interact with each other, usually in small groups or pairs, to exchange information or solve problems. The assumption in using tasks such as "describe a way to get from A to B so that your partner can draw the route on a map" or "plan a shopping trip with your partner by making a shopping list" is that students will improve their ability, especially their fluency, by using the L2 in an activity that focuses on getting meaning across and has a clear goal. Despite fears that learners will simply learn each other's "mistakes," the results of such **task-based learning** provide overwhelming evidence of more and better L2 use by more learners. The goal of such activities is not that the learners will know more about the L2, but that they will develop communicative competence in the L2.

Communicative Competence

Communicative competence can be defined as the general ability to use language accurately, appropriately and flexibly. The first component is **grammatical competence**, which involves the accurate use of words and structures. Concentration on grammatical competence only, however, will not provide the learner with the ability to interpret or produce L2 expressions appropriately.

The ability to use appropriate language is the second component, called **sociolinguistic competence**. It enables the learner to know when to say *Can I have some water?* versus *Give me some water!* in the social context. Much of what was discussed in terms of pragmatics (see Chapter 10) has to become familiar in the cultural context of the L2 if the learner is to develop sociolinguistic competence.

The third component is called **strategic competence**. This is the ability to organize a message effectively and to compensate, via strategies, for any difficulties. In L2 use, learners inevitably experience moments when there is a gap between communicative intent and their ability to express that intent. Some learners may just stop talking (bad idea), whereas others will try to express themselves using a **communication strategy** (good idea). For example, a Dutch L1 speaker wanted to refer to *een hoefijzer* in English, but didn't know the English word. So, she used a communication strategy with vocabulary she already knew, saying *the things that horses wear under their feet, the iron things* and the listener understood immediately what she meant (*horseshoes*). This flexibility is a key element in communicative success and those learners who develop their strategic competence in order to overcome potential communication problems in interaction will inevitably have more success as L2 speakers. See Task F on page 229 for more strategies.

Study Questions

1   Which of these students are studying English in an EFL setting: Chinese students in Beijing or English students in Paris or Japanese students in London?

2   Why do we say that mathematics is learned, not acquired?

3   What are four typical barriers to acquiring an L2 as an adult compared to L1 acquisition as a child?

4   What aspect of language learning do you think "the Joseph Conrad phenomenon" refers to?

5   What are two affective factors that can create a barrier in classroom language learning?

6   What is one personality trait that is a positive factor in language learning?

7   Which approach to language teaching is characterized by oral drills?

8   What is the difference between positive and negative transfer?

9   What happens when an interlanguage fossilizes?

10   What is the difference between the two types of motivation to learn another language?

11   What kind of input is necessary for acquisition?

12   What are the three components of communicative competence?

Tasks

A   What is the difference between "input" and "intake" in L2 learning?

B   What arguments are presented in support of "the output hypothesis" in L2 studies?

C   What is meant by a "stylistic continuum" in the study of interlanguage?

D   In the acquisition of English as a second language, some "developmental sequences" have been observed that are present in the output of learners with different first languages and do not differ substantially from the output of children acquiring English as their first language. For example, in the acquisition of negation, certain structures appear before others in a fixed sequence, not unlike the one described for first language acquisition in Chapter 13 (see Table 13.3, page 210). Given the following five examples of negatives, what do you think would be the likely developmental sequence, beginning with the earliest form?

I no like you can't like it he doesn't like she don't like it no like that

E Quite distinct from the study of English language learning is an expanding new field devoted to English as a lingua franca. In an increasing number of interactions, English is used as a lingua franca (a shared language of communication) by individuals who have different L1s and who are generally concerned with meeting interactive goals rather than being formally correct according to native-speaker norms. Can you find other examples to add to Table 14.1 (based on Jenkins (2007) and Seidlhofer (2011))?

TABLE 14.1 ENGLISH AS A LINGUA FRANCA

Neologisms	*angriness*
New uses of words	*we <u>back</u> to Singapore Monday*
Zero third-person marking	*one woman <u>come</u> every morning*
Use of *which* for people	*customers <u>which</u> order online*
Zero article preferred	*doctor explained patient about treatment*
New uses of prepositions	*we discussed <u>about</u> finance*
All nouns are countable	*she say she need more <u>informations</u>*
New idioms	*they'll get in <u>hot soup</u>* (= "hot water")

F Classroom activities in communicative language teaching create situations in which L2 learners produce different types of communication strategies. Can you match each type of strategy (a)–(f) with one of the examples (1)–(6)? How would you rank them from least to most effective?

(a) appeal for assistance (d) message abandonment
(b) approximation (e) mime or gesture
(c) circumlocution (f) sound imitation

(1) *the color is dark and … the size is just as a hand … it is made of … la-leather* (talking about a glove)
(2) *how do you say in English that word … we say in Spanish "bujía"* (talking about a candlestick)
(3) *the man he play a … you know … it makes a [whistles] like that* (talking about a small musical pipe)

(4) *the first you . . . like put together and you . . . do the next step . . . I can't . . . I'm sorry*
(talking about a plunge coffee maker)

(5) *maybe is something like a rope* (talking about an electrical cord)

(6) *the oval is the big one and the other part is what take to* [demonstrates holding the handle of a brush] (talking about a Christmas tree stand)

G In recent studies of classroom second language learning, there has been a lot more attention paid to how teachers provide feedback to students.

(i) Using the descriptions of different types of feedback provided in (a)–(e), try to analyze the teacher reactions presented in (1)–(5) as responses to the student who said: *I should be student now.*

(ii) Do you think that any of these types of feedback would be more effective or more beneficial than the others?

(1) *You know, you have to include an article here and say "a student."*
(2) *I'm sorry, could you say that again?*
(3) *No, say, "I should be studying now."*
(4) *Do you mean that you want to be a student now?*
(5) *You're saying you should be studying now?*

(a) Clarification request: checking if the teacher has heard/understood the student

(b) Elicitation: trying to get the student to make another attempt or rephrase without the perceived mistake

(c) Explicit correction: clearly changing the student utterance to correct a perceived mistake

(d) Explicit mention of a rule: stating a rule that is involved in the correction of a perceived mistake

(e) Recasts: reformulating the student's utterance without the perceived mistake

H One feature of interlanguage grammars is the apparent existence of temporary rules that don't match the rules of the L1 or the L2, as described in Gass, Behney and Plonsky (2013). The following examples are from a speaker whose L1 was Arabic. Can you describe the rule(s) he seems to be using for the use of plural -*s*?

(1) *How many brother you have?*
(2) *The streets are very wide.*
(3) *I finish in a few day.*
(4) *Here is a lot of animal in the houses.*
(5) *Many people live in villages.*

(6) *There are two horses in the picture.*
(7) *Both my friend from my town.*
(8) *Seven days in a week.*

I What is contrastive analysis and how might it help us understand the following types of L2 errors in English produced by students whose L1 is Spanish?

(1) *He must wear the tie black.*
(2) *My study is modernes languages.*
(3) *He no understand you.*
(4) *It was the same size as a ball of golf.*
(5) *We stayed at home because was raining.*
(6) *I eat usually eggs for breakfast.*

J The general field of study called "Applied Linguistics" came into being in the 1940s in connection with attempts to improve second/foreign language education.

(i)   Why isn't it called "Linguistics Applied"?
(ii) What areas of study are now included in the field?

Discussion Topics/Projects

I Which of the following statements do you agree with? What reasons would you give to support your opinions?

(1) People with high IQs are good language learners.
(2) Most mistakes in the L2 are due to interference from the L1.
(3) L2 learners should not be allowed to hear mistakes or they will learn them.
(4) Teachers should teach simple L2 structures before complex ones.
(5) Teachers should teach only one L2 grammatical rule at a time and practice it thoroughly before introducing the next rule.

(For background reading, see chapter 7 of Lightbown and Spada, 2013.)

II "Communicative Language Teaching is premised on the assumption that learners do not need to be taught grammar before they can communicate but will acquire it naturally as part of the process of learning to communicate. In some versions of Communicative Language Teaching, then, there is no place at all for the direct teaching of grammar." (Ellis, 1997)

(a) Do you believe that second language learning is possible with only a focus on function ("communication") and no focus on form ("grammar")?

(b)   Why do you think that there are renewed calls for "form-focused instruction" after many years of Communicative Language Teaching?

(For background reading, see chapter 9 of Ellis, 1997.)

Further Reading

Basic Treatments

Ellis, R. (1997) *Second Language Acquisition* Oxford University Press

Lightbown, P. and N. Spada (2013) *How Languages Are Learned* (4th edition) Oxford University Press

More Detailed Treatments

Cook, V. (2016) *Second Language Learning and Language Teaching* (5th edition) Hodder Education

Hawkins, R. (2019) *How Second Languages Are Learned* Cambridge University Press

Saville-Troike, M. and K. Barto (2016) *Introducing Second Language Acquisition* (3rd edition) Cambridge University Press

Theoretical Perspectives

Cook, V. and D. Singleton (2014) *Key Topics in Second Language Acquisition* Multilingual Matters

Mitchell, R., F. Myles and E. Marsden (2013) *Second Language Learning Theories* (3rd edition) Routledge

Ortega, L. (2014) *Understanding Second Language Acquisition* Routledge

VanPatten, B. and J. Williams (eds.) (2015) *Theories in Second Language Acquisition* (2nd edition) Routledge

Translation

Bellos, D. (2011) *Is That a Fish in Your Ear? Translation and the Meaning of Everything* Faber & Faber

Bilingual Acquisition

Murphy, V. (2014) *Second Language Learning in the Early School Years* Oxford University Press

Yip, M. and S. Matthews (2007) *The Bilingual Child* Cambridge University Press

Comparing First and Second Language Acquisition

Meisel, J. (2011) *First and Second Language Acquisition: Parallels and Differences* Cambridge University Press

Culicover, P. and E. Hume (2017) *Basics of Language for Language Learners* (2nd edition) The Ohio State University

The Effects of Age

Dekeyser, R. and J. Larson-Hall (2005) "What does the critical period really mean?" In J. Kroll and A. De Groot (eds.) *Handbook of Bilingualism* (88–108) Oxford University Press

Singleton, D. and L. Ryan (2004) *Language Acquisition: The Age Factor* (2nd edition) Multilingual Matters

Focus on Method

Richards, J. and T. Rodgers (2014) *Approaches and Methods in Language Teaching* (3rd edition) Cambridge University Press

Focus on the Learner

VanPatten, B. (2003) *From Input to Output: A Teacher's Guide to Second Language Acquisition* McGraw-Hill

Pronunciation with Wine

Guiora, A., B. Beit-Hallahmi, R. Brannon, C. Dull and T. Scovel (1972) "The effects of experimentally induced change in ego states on pronunciation ability in a second language: an exploratory study" *Comprehensive Psychiatry* 13: 5–23

The Horseshoe Example

Kellerman, E., T. Ammerlan, T. Bongaerts and N. Poulisse (1990) "System and hierarchy in L2 compensatory strategies" In R. Scarcella, E. Anderson and S. Krashen (eds.) *Developing Communicative Competence in a Second Language* (163–178) Newbury House

Task-Based Learning

Samuda, V. and M. Bygate (2008) *Tasks in Second Language Learning* Palgrave Macmillan
Willis, D. and J. Willis (2007) *Doing Task-Based Teaching* Oxford University Press

Other References

Gass, S., J. Behney and L. Plonsky (2013) *Second Language Acquisition: An Introductory Course* (4th edition) Routledge
Jenkins, J. (2007) *English as a Lingua Franca: Attitude and Identity* Oxford University Press
Pica, T., L. Holliday, N. Lewis, D. Berducci and J. Newman (1991) "Language learning through interaction: what role does gender play?" *Studies in Second Language Acquisition* 11: 63–90
Seidlhofer, B. (2011) *Understanding English as a Lingua Franca* Oxford University Press

15 Gestures and Sign Languages

This old lady, in her nineties, but sharp as a pin, would sometimes fall into a peaceful reverie. As she did so, she might have seemed to be knitting, her hands in constant complex motion. But her daughter, also a signer, told me she was not knitting but thinking to herself, thinking in Sign. And even in sleep, I was further informed, the old lady might sketch fragmentary signs on the counterpane. She was dreaming in Sign.

Sacks (1989)

When we considered the process of language acquisition, we concentrated on the fact that what is naturally acquired by most children is speech. Yet this is not the only way that a first language can be acquired. Just as most children of English-speaking or Spanish- speaking parents naturally acquire English or Spanish at a very early age, so the deaf children of deaf parents naturally acquire **sign** (or **sign language**). Later in life, as Oliver Sacks observed, they may even use sign when they "talk" in their sleep. If those children grow up in American homes, they will typically acquire American Sign Language, also known as Ameslan or **ASL**, as their version of sign. With a signing population of at least half a million, and perhaps as many as two million, ASL is a widely used language in the United States. The size of this population is quite remarkable since, until relatively recently, the use of ASL was discouraged in most educational institutions for the deaf. In fact, historically, very few teachers of the deaf learned ASL, or even considered it to be a "real" language at all. For many people, sign wasn't language, it was "merely gestures."

Gestures

Although both sign and **gestures** involve the use of the hands (with other parts of the body), they are rather different. Sign is like speech and is used instead of speaking. Gestures are mostly used while speaking. Examples of gestures are making a downward movement with one hand while talking about not doing very well in a class or making a twisting motion with one hand as you describe trying to open a bottle or jar. The gestures are just part of the way in which meaning is expressed and can be observed while people are speaking and signing.

In the study of non-verbal behavior, a distinction can be drawn between gestures and emblems. **Emblems** are signals such as "thumbs up" (= things are good) or "shush" (= keep quiet) that function like fixed phrases and do not depend on speech. Emblems are conventional and depend on social knowledge (e.g. what is and isn't considered offensive in a particular situation). In Britain, the use of two fingers (the index and middle fingers) raised in a V-shape represents one emblem (= victory) when the back of the hand faces the sender and a quite different emblem (= I insult you in a very offensive way) when the back of the hand faces the receiver of the signal. It is important, when in different places, not to mix up the local emblems.

Iconics

Within the set of gestures that accompany speech, we can distinguish between those that echo, in some way, the content of the spoken message and those that indicate something being referred to. **Iconics** are gestures that seem to be a reflection of the meaning of what is said, as when we trace a square in the air with a finger while saying *I'm looking for a small box*. By itself, an iconic gesture doesn't "mean" the same as what is said, but it may add "meaning." In one particularly clear example (from McNeill, 1992), a woman was moving her forearm up and down, with a closed hand, as if holding a weapon, while saying *and she chased him out again*. The message, with weapon (an umbrella), was created via speech and gesture combined.

Deictics

Another common group of gestures are described as **deictics**. As noted in Chapter 10, the term "deictic" means "pointing." We can use deictics in the current context, as when we use a hand to indicate a table (with a cake on it) and ask someone *Would you like some cake?*. We can also use the same gesture and the same table (with cake no longer on it) when we later say *That cake was delicious*. In this case, the gesture and the speech combine to accomplish reference to something that only exists in shared memory rather than in the current physical space.

Beats

There are other gestures, such as those described as **beats**, which are short quick movements of the hand or fingers. These gestures accompany the rhythm of talk and are often used to emphasize parts of what is being said or to mark a change from describing events in a story to commenting on those events. As with other gestures, these hand movements accompany speech, but are not typically used as a way of speaking. When hand movements are used in order to "speak," we can describe them as part of a sign language. (See Tasks A and B, page 243, for more on gestures.)

Types of Sign Languages

There are two general categories of language that involve the use of signs: alternate sign languages and primary sign languages. An **alternate sign language** is a system of hand signals developed by speakers for limited communication in a specific context where speech cannot be used. These signals are also described as gestural communication to make it clear they are not the same as languages. In some religious orders where there are rules of silence, restricted alternate sign languages are used. The use of signs by monks in Benedictine monasteries during periods of silence has been documented since the Middle Ages. Among some Australian Aboriginal groups, there are periods (e.g. times of bereavement) when speech is avoided completely and quite elaborate alternate sign languages are used instead.

Less elaborate versions are to be found in some special working circumstances. Bookmakers at British racecourses used a system of gestures called "tic-tac" to communicate with each other (and not with the betting public) and whenever there is discussion of commodity prices, the television news usually shows traders in commodity exchanges signaling wildly to each other. In all these examples, the users of alternate sign languages have another first language that they can speak.

In contrast, a **primary sign language** is the first language of a group of people who do not use a spoken language with each other. British Sign Language (BSL) and French Sign Language (Langue des Signes Française or LSF), as used for everyday communication among members of the deaf communities of Britain and France, are primary sign languages. Contrary to popular belief, these different primary sign languages do not share identical signs and are not mutually intelligible. British Sign Language is also very different from American Sign Language (ASL), which, for historical reasons, has more in common with French Sign Language.

We will focus our attention on ASL in order to describe some features of a primary sign language, but first, we have to account for the fact that, until fairly recently, it was not treated as a possible language at all.

Oralism

It was not until the 1960s that any serious consideration was given to the status of ASL as a natural language, following the work of William Stokoe (1960). Before that, it was genuinely believed by many well-intentioned teachers that the use of sign language by deaf children (being too "easy") would inhibit the acquisition of the English language. Since spoken English was what those teachers believed the children really needed, a teaching method generally known as **oralism** dominated deaf education during most of the twentieth century. This method required that the students practice English speech sounds and develop lip-reading skills. Despite its resounding lack of success, the method was never seriously challenged, perhaps because of an insidious belief among many during this period that, in educational terms, most deaf children were not going to achieve very much anyway.

Whatever the reasons, the method produced few students who could speak intelligible English (less than 10 per cent) and even fewer who could lip-read (around 4 per cent). While oralism was failing, the use of ASL was flourishing. Many deaf children of hearing parents actually acquired the banned language at schools for the deaf, not from the teachers, but from other children. Since only one in ten deaf children had deaf parents from whom they acquired sign language, the cultural transmission of ASL has been mostly carried out from child to child.

Signed English

Substantial changes in deaf education have taken place in recent years, but there is still an emphasis on the learning of English, written rather than spoken. As a result, many institutions promote the learning of what is known as **Signed English** (also called Manually Coded English or MCE). This is essentially a means of producing signs that correspond to the words in an English sentence, in English word order. In many ways, Signed English is designed to facilitate interaction between the deaf and the hearing community. Its greatest advantage is that it seems to present a much less formidable learning task for the hearing parent of a deaf child and provides the parent with a communication system to use with the child.

For similar reasons, hearing teachers in deaf education can make use of Signed English when they sign at the same time as they speak. It is also easier for those hearing interpreters who produce a simultaneous translation of public speeches or lectures for deaf audiences. Many deaf people actually prefer interpreters to use Signed English because they say there is a higher likelihood of understanding the message. Unless they learned ASL in childhood, few hearing people are proficient enough to translate fairly rapid English speech into idiomatic ASL.

Origins of ASL

It would be very surprising if ASL really was "a sort of gestured version of English," as some have claimed. Historically, ASL developed from the French Sign Language used in a Paris school founded in the eighteenth century. Early in the nineteenth century, a teacher from this school, named Laurent Clerc, was brought to the United States by an American minister called Thomas Gallaudet who was trying to establish a school for deaf children. Clerc not only taught deaf children, he also trained other teachers. During the nineteenth century, this imported version of sign language, incorporating features of indigenous natural sign languages used by the American deaf, evolved into what became known as ASL. Such origins help to explain why users of ASL and users of BSL (in Britain) do not share a common sign language.

The Structure of Signs

As a natural language functioning in the visual mode, ASL is designed for the eyes, not the ears. In producing linguistic forms in ASL, signers use four key aspects of visual information. These are described as the **articulatory parameters** of ASL in terms of shape, orientation, location and movement. We can describe these parameters in the use of the common sign for THANK-YOU.

Figure 15.1 Signing THANK-YOU

Shape and Orientation

To describe the articulation of THANK-YOU in ASL, we start with the **shape**, or configuration of the hand(s), used in forming the sign. The shape may differ in terms of which fingers are used, whether the fingers are extended or bent, and the general configurations of the hand(s). The configuration shown in Figure 15.1 is a "flat hand" (not a "fist hand" or a "cupped hand").

The **orientation** of the hand is "palm up" rather than "palm down" when signing THANK-YOU. In other signs, the hand may be oriented in a number of other ways such as the "flat hand, palm towards signer" form used to indicate MINE.

Location

Each sign has a **location** in relation to the head and body of the signer. In THANK-YOU, the sign begins near the mouth and is completed at chest level. Some signs can only be distinguished on the basis of location, as in the difference between SUMMER (above the eyes) and UGLY (below the eyes) because hand shape, palm orientation and movement are the same in both. In some two-handed signs (e.g. MEDICINE, SHIP), one hand acts as the base location while the other hand moves on or above it.

Movement

The **movement** element in THANK-YOU is "out and downward" toward the receiver. The difference between faster and slower movement in signing also has an effect on meaning. In a story recounted by Stokoe (2001), the director of public relations at Gallaudet College (for the deaf) noticed two employees signing one day about a former president who had been very ill. She saw a sign she interpreted as DEAD and phoned the Washington Post, where an obituary for the ex-president appeared the following day. Rather prematurely, as it turned out. The same hand movements, used fairly quickly for DEAD, had actually been used with a much slower rotation to communicate DYING. The difference in movement creates a difference in meaning. Just as there are "slips of the ear" (Chapter 12), there can also be "slips of the eye."

Primes

The contrasting elements within these four general parameters can be analyzed into sets of features or **primes**. We say that "flat hand" is a prime in terms of shape and "palm up" is a prime in terms of orientation. Identifying each of these primes allows us to create a complete feature analysis of every sign in much the same way as we can analyze the phonological features of spoken language (see Chapter 4).

Facial Expressions and Finger-Spelling

The fact that a sign language exploits the visual medium in quite subtle ways makes it difficult to represent accurately on the page. As Lou Fant (1977) has observed, "strictly speaking, the only way to write Ameslan is to use motion pictures." There are important functions served by non-manual components such as head-movement, eye-movement and several specific types of facial expressions. Under normal circumstances, THANK-YOU is articulated with a head nod and a smiling face.

Also, if a new term or name is encountered, signers can use **finger-spelling**, which is a system of hand configurations used to represent the letters of the alphabet.

The majority of signs are located around the neck and head. If a sign is made near the chest or waist, it tends to be a two-handed sign. One of the key features of visual messages is that they can incorporate a number of distinct elements simultaneously. Spoken language production is linear, while in the visual medium multiple components can be produced at the same time in space.

Representing Signs

One of the major problems is finding a way to incorporate those aspects of facial expressions that contribute to the message. A partial solution is to write one line of manually signed words (in capital letters) and then, above this line, to indicate the nature and extent of the facial expression that contributes to the message. As shown here, the q in the transcription is used to show that the facial expression (raised eyebrows, widened eyes, head leaning forward) indicated a question function throughout the signing of what would be translated as *Can I borrow the book?*

$$\underline{\hspace{6cm}q}$$
ME BORROW BOOK

Other subtle aspects of meaning can be signaled by facial expression. In one study, it was observed that a signer, while telling a story, produced the message: MAN FISH [continuous]. The "continuous" element involves a sweeping repetitive movement of the hands. The basic translation is: *The man was fishing.* However, ASL users translated it as *The man was fishing with relaxation and enjoyment.* This extra information came from a facial expression with the lips together, pushed out a little, and the head tilted. The notation *mm* signals this element, as in the transcription:

$$\underline{\hspace{6cm}mm}$$
MAN FISH [continuous]

The Meaning of Signs

The signs of ASL are sometimes mistakenly believed to be simple visual representations or "pictures," and the language is thought to consist of a limited set of primitive gestures that look like objects or mimic actions in pantomime. Interestingly, as non-users of ASL, when we are told that a sign is used to refer to a particular thing, we can often create a symbolic connection that makes the relationship between sign and signified seem obvious. We look at the sign for THANK-YOU and see it as some appropriately symbolic version of the action of "thanking."

However, most of the time, interpretation doesn't work that way in the opposite direction. We normally find it difficult to get the meaning of a sign simply on the basis of what it looks like. Indeed, as when confronted with any unfamiliar language, we may not even be able to identify individual signs (words) in fluent signing. Most everyday use of ASL signs is not based on identifying symbolic pictures, but on recognizing familiar linguistic forms that have arbitrary status. As an experiment, try to decide what English word translates the common sign shown in Figure 15.2.

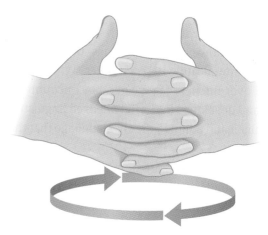

Figure 15.2 Two-handed sign

This sign involves rotating both hands together with the fingers interlocked in front of the chest. There are different ideas about the source: "it represents the stripes on a flag" or "it is a mixing pot" or "it is a coming together." To suggest that any of these images comes into the mind of a signer who uses the sign to refer to AMERICA is as absurd as proposing that in hearing the word *America*, an English speaker must be thinking about Amerigo Vespucci, the Italian whose name is the source of the modern word. The signs in ASL have their meanings within the system of signs, not through reference to some pictorial image each time they are used.

Sign Languages as Natural Languages

Investigations of ASL from a linguistic point of view are a relatively recent phenomenon. Yet it has become clear that any feature that is characteristically found in spoken languages has a counterpart in ASL. All those defining properties of human language described in Chapter 2 are present in ASL. There are equivalent levels of phonology, morphology and syntax. For example, ASL uses Subject Verb Object (SVO) word order like English, but normally puts adjectives after nouns, unlike English, but in the same way as French.

Children acquiring ASL as their first language go through developmental stages similar to children learning spoken language, though the production of signs seems to begin earlier than the production of spoken words. In the hands of witty individuals, ASL is used for a wide range of jokes and "sign play." There are different ASL dialects in different regions and historical changes in the form of signs can be traced over the past hundred years (older versions are preserved in old films).

Evidence for the natural development of a sign language among young children comes from the study of ISN (Idioma de Señas de Nicaragua), which came into being in Nicaragua, in Central America, in the 1980s. In its current form, it is now generally known as **Nicaraguan Sign Language** (NSL). When a vocational-training school was created, giving deaf students access to education for the first time, the language-teaching component relied at first on oralism. However, outside class, those young deaf students began using their own signs to communicate with each other. When groups of younger deaf children entered the school over the next few years, they encountered a sign-using system that they then expanded and developed into a fully fledged linguistic system. In the 1990s, the school abandoned oralism and adopted the sign language that the students had created.

Primary sign languages such as ASL and NSL are quite remarkable for their evolution and endurance despite prejudice, misunderstanding and bad pedagogy. They also provide examples of how humans are born to use language and how each generation has to recreate the language of their community, even when the cultural transmission involved is from child to child.

Study Questions

1   In the study of non-verbal behavior, what are emblems?

2   What is the difference between "iconics" and "deictics" in the study of gestures?

3   What is an alternate sign language?

4   Which of these sign languages share a common origin: ASL, BSL, LSF and NSL?

5   What is the major difference between ASL and Signed English?

6   What percentage of deaf students were able to develop lip-reading skills through oralism?

7   Historically, how many deaf children were born to deaf parents?

8   Why do many deaf people prefer it when interpreters use MCE?

9   What was the name of the American minister who established the first school for deaf children in the USA?

10   If the signs used in HE WATCH TV are accompanied by sweeping repetitive movement of the hands, what is the English translation?

11   Which articulatory parameters of ASL have "flat hand" and "palm up" as primes?

12   What would be the most likely English translation of:

(a)   _____ _q_

HAPPEN YESTERDAY NIGHT

(b)   neg_____ _mm_

BOY NOT WALK [continuous]

Tasks

A   In the chapter, we mentioned deictics or pointing gestures, but didn't explore how they are actually performed. Can you describe in detail the most common pointing gesture? Are there any social constraints on its use? Are there other ways of pointing, using other parts of the body?

B   Is gesture tied to self-expression or is it tied to communication with a listener? For example, do we gesture more when a listener is present in person or out of view (e.g. during a phone call)? Do blind people gesture when they're talking?

C What is the connection between deaf education and the invention of the telephone?

D What made people have such a strong commitment to oralism despite its lack of success?

E What is the basis of the distinction between "prelinguistic" and "postlinguistic" hearing impairment?

F What is "dactylology" and what is the main difference between American and British varieties?

G Unlike spoken language use where accompanying facial expressions seem to be optional most of the time, ASL is a visual language and facial expressions are an essential part of what is being communicated. What facial expressions would conventionally be associated with signing the following sentences?

(1) *Are you married?*
(2) *Where do you work?*
(3) *You like jazz, I'm surprised.*
(4) *If I miss the bus, I'll be late for work.*

H Some linguists have viewed the development of Nicaraguan Sign Language as clear evidence in support of the innateness hypothesis, described in Chapter 1. What exactly is the argument put forward by nativists such as Pinker (1994: chapter 2) concerning the development of NSL?

Discussion Topics/Projects

I Which of the following statements do you agree with and what reasons would you give to support your opinion?

(1) A shrugging gesture always indicates "helplessness" of some kind.
(2) The eyebrow flash is used everywhere as a greeting.
(3) It is easier to learn foreign gestures than foreign words.
(4) Brow lowering carries an implication of something negative whereas brow raising implies something positive.
(5) If a person uses lots of hand movements, such as smoothing the hair or touching the chin while speaking, it's an indication that the person is telling a lie.

(For background reading, see Ekman, 1999.)

II According to Corballis, "there are good reasons to suppose that much of the development of language over the past two million years took place through manual gesture rather than vocalization" (2002: 98).

What do you think of the idea that the origins of language are to be found in manual gestures and that the development of speech comes from the transfer of manual gestures to oral gestures? Is it relevant that the hands of early humans developed well before the capacity for speech? What about the fact that children communicate non-verbally (e.g. pointing) before they produce speech?

(For background reading, see chapter 5 of Corballis, 2002.)

Further Reading

Basic Treatments

Goldin-Meadow, S. (2005) *Hearing Gesture* (revised edition) Belknap Press

Lucas, C. and C. Valli (2004) "American Sign Language" In E. Finegan and J. Rickford (eds.) *Language in the USA* (230–244) Cambridge University Press

More Detailed Treatments

Kendon, A. (2004) *Gesture* Cambridge University Press

Valli, C., C. Lucas, K. Mulrooney and M. Villanueva (2011) *Linguistics of American Sign Language: An Introduction* (5th edition) Gallaudet University Press

ASL Courses

Guido, J. (2017) *Learn American Sign Language* Wellfleet Press

Humphries, T. and C. Padden (2003) *Learning American Sign Language* (plus DVD) (2nd edition) Allyn and Bacon

Stewart, D., E. Stewart and J. Little (2006) *American Sign Language the Easy Way* (2nd edition) Barron's Educational

Australian and British Sign Languages

Johnston, T. and A. Schembri (2007) *Australian Sign Language: An Introduction to Sign Language Linguistics* Cambridge University Press

Sutton-Spence, R. and B. Woll (1999) *The Linguistics of British Sign Language* Cambridge University Press

Nicaraguan Sign Language

Kegl, J. (1994) "The Nicaraguan Sign Language Project: an overview" *Signpost* 7: 24–31

Senghas, A. and M. Coppola (2001) "Children creating language: how Nicaraguan Sign Language acquired a spatial grammar" *Psychological Science* 12: 323–328

Finger-Spelling

Padden, C. and D. Gunsauls (2003) "How the alphabet came to be used in a sign language" *Sign Language Studies* 4: 10–33

Alternate Sign Languages

Kendon, A. (1988) *Sign Languages of Aboriginal Australia* Cambridge University Press
Umiker-Sebeok, D-J. and T. Sebeok (eds.) (1987) *Monastic Sign Languages* Mouton de Gruyter

Other References

Corballis, M. (2002) *From Hand to Mouth* Princeton University Press
Ekman, P. (1999) "Emotional and conversational nonverbal signals" In L. Messing and R. Campbell (eds.) *Gesture, Speech and Sign* (45–55) Oxford University Press
Fant, L. (1977) *Sign Language* Joyce Media
McNeill, D. (1992) *Hand and Mind* University of Chicago Press
Pinker, S. (1994) *The Language Instinct* William Morrow
Stokoe, W. (1960) *Sign Language Structure: An Outline of the Visual Communication Systems of the American Deaf* Studies in Linguistics, Occasional Papers 8, University of Buffalo
Stokoe, W. (2001) *Language in Hand* Gallaudet University Press

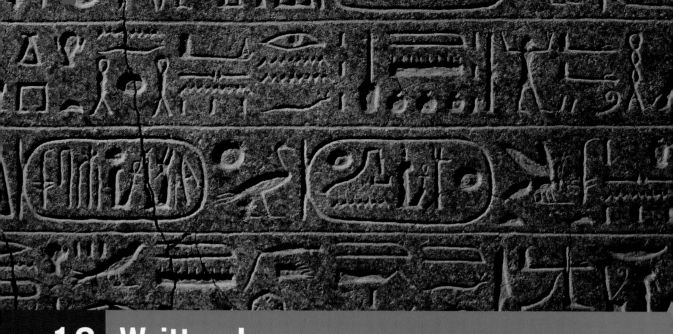

16 Written Language

Figure 16.1 A child's writing

The five-year-old child whose skills in symbolic representation are displayed here seems to be already familiar with some of the basic elements of writing. The sequence of letters goes from left to right, each letter is distinct from the next and generally well formed, and each word is separated from the next by larger spaces. The occasional spelling "mistake," a traditional problem in written English, cannot disguise the fact that this child has already learned how to write.

Writing

We can define **writing** as the symbolic representation of language through the use of graphic signs. Unlike speech, it is a system that is not simply acquired, but has to be learned through sustained conscious effort. Not all languages have a written form and, even among people whose language has a well-established writing system, there are large numbers of individuals who cannot use the system.

In terms of human development, writing is a relatively recent phenomenon. We may be able to trace human attempts to represent information visually back to cave drawings made at least 20,000 years ago, or to clay tokens from about 10,000 years ago, which appear to have been an early attempt at bookkeeping, but these artifacts are best described as ancient precursors of writing. The earliest writing for which we have clear evidence is known as "cuneiform," marked on clay tablets about 5,000 years ago. About 3,000 years ago, inscriptions were being used in an ancient script that has a more obvious connection to writing systems in use today. We know that we must have lost a lot of earlier inscriptions on perishable material, but working from the surviving inscriptions, we can trace the development of one writing tradition, lasting a few thousand years, with which humans have sought to create a more permanent record of what was going on.

Pictograms

Cave drawings may serve to record some event (e.g. Humans 3, Buffaloes 1), but they are not usually thought of as any type of specifically linguistic message. They are usually treated as part of a tradition of pictorial art. When some of the "pictures" came to represent particular images in a consistent way, we can begin to describe the product as a form of picture-writing, or **pictograms**. Modern pictograms, as in Figure 16.2, are language-independent and can be understood with the same conventional meaning in a lot of different places where a number of different languages are spoken.

Figure 16.2 Pictograms

Ideograms

Whereas the images presented in Figure 16.2 continue to reflect the physical forms of objects, we typically interpret them in a way that goes beyond simply recognizing those objects. That is, the picture of a cup (with saucer) doesn't just let us know that there is a cup in this location. That would be an odd interpretation because mostly we are not just looking for a cup, but also something to put in that cup, such as coffee or tea, and maybe something to go with it, such as cake or cookies (none of which is included in the picture). We actually interpret the images, not as objects, but as symbols of the objects, with meanings associated with the symbol that may not be tied to the object.

At some point in the early development of pictorial representation, a symbol such as ☀ came into use for referring to the sun. An essential part of this use of a representative symbol is that everyone should use a similar form to convey a roughly similar meaning. In time, this picture might develop into a more fixed symbolic form, such as ⊙, and come to be used for "heat" and "daytime," as well as for "sun." Note that as the symbol extends from "sun" to "heat," it is moving from something visible to something conceptual (and no longer a simple picture). This type of symbol is then considered to be part of a system of idea-writing, or **ideograms**. The distinction between pictograms and ideograms is essentially a difference in the relationship between the symbol and the entity it represents. The more "picture-like" forms are pictograms and the more abstract derived forms are ideograms. A key property of both pictograms and ideograms is that they do not represent words or sounds in a particular language.

It is generally thought that there were pictographic or ideographic origins for a large number of symbols that turn up in later writing systems. For example, in Egyptian hieroglyphics, the symbol ⌂ was used to refer to a house and derived from the diagram-like representation of the floor plan of a house. In Chinese writing, the character 川 was used for a river, and had its origins in the pictorial representation of a stream flowing between two banks. However, it is important to note that neither the Egyptian nor the Chinese written symbols are actually "pictures" of a house or a river. They are more abstract. When we create symbols in a writing system, there is always an abstraction away from the physical world.

When the relationship between the symbol and the entity or idea becomes sufficiently abstract, we can be more confident that the symbol is probably being used to represent words in a language. In early Egyptian writing, the ideogram for water was ≋. Much later, the derived symbol ～ came to be used for the actual word meaning "water." When symbols are used to represent words in a language, they are described as examples of word-writing, or "logograms."

Logograms

An early example of logographic writing is the system used by the Sumerians, living in Mesopotamia, in the southern part of modern Iraq, around 5,000 years ago. Because of the particular shapes used in their symbols, these inscriptions are more generally described as **cuneiform** writing. The term cuneiform (from Latin *cuneus*, "wedge") means "wedge-shaped" and the inscriptions used by the Sumerians were produced by pressing a wedge-shaped implement into soft clay tablets that created a permanent symbol when the clay hardened, resulting in forms such as ⩢⩢◁.

The form of this symbol really gives no clue to what type of entity is being referred to. The relationship between the written form and the object it represents has become arbitrary and we have a clear example of word-writing or a **logogram**. The cuneiform symbol above can be compared to a typical pictographic representation of the same fishy entity:⋈.

We can also compare the ideogram for the sun, presented earlier as ◉, with the logogram used to refer to the same entity found in cuneiform writing:⩙.

Modern logograms in English are forms such as $, 8, &, where each symbol represents one word, as is also the case with @, now one of the most commonly used logograms (in email addresses). A more elaborate writing system that is based, to a certain extent, on the use of logograms can be found in China. Many Chinese written symbols, or **characters**, are used as representations of the meaning of words, or parts of words, and not of the sounds of spoken language. In some treatments, this type of writing is technically described as "morphographic," because the symbols have come to be used for morphemes rather than words. (See Chapter 6 for the distinction between words and morphemes.) One of the advantages of such a system is that two speakers of very different dialects of Chinese, who might have great difficulty understanding each other's spoken forms, can both read the same written text. Chinese writing, with the longest continuous history of use as a writing system (i.e. 3,000 years), clearly has many other advantages for its users.

One major disadvantage is that quite a large number of different written symbols are required within this type of writing system, although the official "list of modern Chinese characters for everyday use" is limited to 2,500 characters. (Other lists contain up to 50,000 characters.) Remembering large numbers of different composite word-symbols, however, does seem to present a substantial memory load, and the history of most other writing systems illustrates a development away from logographic writing. To accomplish this, some principled method is needed to go from symbols representing words (i.e. a logographic system) to a set of symbols that represent sounds (i.e. a phonographic system).

Phonographic Writing

The development from pictographic representation to logographic writing, even among the Sumerians, did not take place without some symbols being used in a similar way if certain words had similar sounds (not meanings). Following Gelb (1963), we can observe this process taking place as the physical shape in the form of an arrow (>→—) was first used in representations of the word for "arrow" (*ti*), then later adopted for the more abstract concept "life" (*ti*), simply because both words sounded the same. Similarly, the symbol (⚹) for a physical object "reed" (*gi*) is taken over for the abstract concept "reimbursement" (*gi*) on the basis of similar pronunciations. In this development, the symbols are adopted to represent the sounds of the words, also known as **phonographic writing**.

The Rebus Principle

This general pattern of using existing symbols to represent the sounds of words in a language is often described in terms of a process known as the **rebus principle**. In this process, the symbol for one entity is taken over as the symbol for the sound of the spoken word (or part of it) used to refer to that entity. That symbol then comes to be used whenever that sound occurs in any words.

We can create an example, working with the sound of the English word *eye*. We can imagine how the pictographic representation ◁⦿▷ could have developed into the logogram ⬭. This logogram is pronounced as *eye* and, with the rebus principle at work, you could then refer to yourself as ⬭ ("I"), to one of your friends as + ⬭ ("Crosseye"), combine the form with the logogram for "deaf" to produce "defy," with the logogram for "boat" to produce "bow-tie," and so on.

A similar process is taking place in contemporary English texting where the symbol "2" is used, not only as a number, but as the sound of other words or parts of words, in messages such as the one on the left below ("(I) need to speak to you tonight"). In this message, the letter "u" also illustrates the process of rebus writing, having become the symbol for the sound of the spoken word "you," as also illustrated in the other example, with "c" and "8" also representing sounds.

 nd2spk2u2nite   *cul8r*

Let's take another, non-English, example, in which an ideogram ≋ becomes the logogram ⌣, for the word pronounced *ba* (meaning "boat"). We can then produce a symbol for the word pronounced *baba* (meaning "father"), which would be ⌣⌣. One symbol can thus be used in many different ways, with a range of meanings. This process substantially reduces the number of symbols needed in a writing system.

Syllabic Writing

In the last example, the symbol that is used for the pronunciation of parts of a word represents a unit (*ba*) that consists of a consonant sound (*b*) and a vowel sound (*a*). This unit is one type of syllable, described in Chapter 4. When a writing system employs a set of symbols, each one representing the pronunciation of a syllable, it is described as **syllabic writing**.

There are no purely syllabic writing systems in use today, but modern Japanese can be written with a set of single symbols representing spoken syllables, called "hiragana," and is consequently often described as having a (partially) syllabic writing system, or a **syllabary**.

In the early nineteenth century, a Cherokee named Sequoyah, living in North Carolina, invented a syllabic writing system that was widely used within the Cherokee community to create written messages from the spoken language. Papers with writing were described as "talking leaves." In the Cherokee examples below, we can see that the written symbol in each case does not correspond to a single consonant (C) or a single vowel (V), but to a syllable (CV).

Both the ancient Egyptian and the Sumerian writing systems evolved to the point where some of the earlier logographic symbols were being used to represent spoken syllables. However, it is not until the time of the Phoenicians, inhabiting what is modern Lebanon between 3,000 and 4,000 years ago, that we find the full use of a syllabic writing system. Many of the symbols that the Phoenicians used were taken from earlier Egyptian writing. The Egyptian form ⌐ (meaning "house") was adopted in a slightly reoriented form as ⅃. After being used logographically for the word pronounced *beth* (still meaning "house"), the symbol came to represent other syllables beginning with a *b* sound. Similarly, the Egyptian form ∿ (meaning "water") turns up as ⌐ and is used for syllables beginning with an *m* sound.

So, a word that might be pronounced as *muba* could be written as ⅃ ⌐, and the pronunciation *bima* could be written as ⌐ ⅃. Note that the direction of writing is from right to left, as it still is in the writing system of modern Arabic. By about 3,000 years ago, the Phoenicians had stopped using logograms and had a fully developed syllabic writing system.

Alphabetic Writing

If you have a set of symbols being used to represent syllables beginning with, for example, a *b* sound or an *m* sound, then you are actually very close to a situation in which the symbols can be used to represent single sound types in a language. This is, in effect, the basis of the type of writing used in an alphabet. In principle, an **alphabet** is a set of written symbols, each one representing a single type of sound or phoneme. (See Chapter 4 for a description of phonemes.) The situation just described is what occurred in the development of the writing systems of Semitic languages such as Arabic and Hebrew. Words written in these languages, in everyday use, largely consist of symbols for the consonant sounds in the word, with the appropriate vowel sounds being supplied by the reader (or rdr).

This type of writing system is sometimes called a **consonantal alphabet**. The early version of Semitic alphabetic script, originating in the writing system of the Phoenicians, is the basic source of most other alphabets to be found in the world. Modified versions can be traced to the East into Iranian, Indian and South-East Asian writing systems and to the West through Greek. The basic order of letter symbols in the first "A-B-C-D ... " was created about three thousand years ago by the Phoenicians and continues to be used as our primary ordering device for lists in everything from dictionaries to telephone directories to grades for academic performance.

The early Greeks took the alphabetizing process a stage further by using separate symbols to represent the vowel sounds as distinct entities, and so created a remodeled system with vowel symbols. This change resulted in the Phoenician consonant "alep" becoming a symbol for a vowel sound as *A* ("alpha") to go with existing symbols for consonant sounds such as *B* ("beta"), giving us single-sound writing or an "alphabet." In fact, for some scholars, it is the Greeks who should be given credit for taking the inherently syllabic system from the Phoenicians and creating a writing system with the single-symbol to single-sound correspondence fully realized as **alphabetic writing**.

From the Greeks, this revised alphabet passed to the rest of Western Europe through the Romans. As a result, we talk about the Roman alphabet as the writing system used for English. Another line of development took the same basic Greek writing system into Eastern Europe where Slavic languages were spoken. The modified version, called the Cyrillic alphabet (after St. Cyril, a ninth-century Christian missionary), is the basis of the writing system used in Russia today.

The actual form of a number of letters in modern European alphabets can be traced from their origins in Egyptian hieroglyphics through Phoenician and Greek to the symbols we use today. The examples in Figure 16.3 are based on Davies (1987).

Egyptian	Phoenician	Early Greek	Roman
			A
			B
			K
			M
			N
			T
			S

Figure 16.3 The development of letters

Written English

If indeed the origins of the alphabetic writing system were based on a correspondence between a single symbol and a single sound type, then one might reasonably ask why there is such a frequent mismatch between the forms of written English ("you know") and the sounds of spoken English ("yu no" or /ju noʊ/). Other languages (Italian, Spanish) have writing systems that stick much more closely to the one sound-one symbol principle of alphabetic writing. English is not always so consistent. As we noted in Chapter 3, there is a lot of variation in how each sound of contemporary spoken English is represented in writing. The vowel sound represented by /i/ is written in various ways, as shown in the first two columns on the left below, and the consonant sound represented by /ʃ/ has various spellings, as in the other two columns.

i (*critique*)	ee (*queen*)	s (*sugar*)	ch (*champagne*)
ie (*belief*)	eo (*people*)	ss (*tissue*)	ce (*ocean*)
ei (*receipt*)	ey (*key*)	ssi (*mission*)	ci (*delicious*)
ea (*meat*)	e (*scene*)	sh (*Danish*)	ti (*nation*)

English Orthography

As we have just seen, English **orthography** (or spelling) is subject to a lot of variation. Notice how often a single phoneme in the two lists is actually represented by more than one letter. Part of the reason for this is that the English language is full of words borrowed, often with their spelling, from other languages, as in *ph* for /f/ in the Greek borrowings *alphabet* and *orthography*, where two letters are used for a single sound. A combination of two letters consistently used for a single sound, as in *ph*/f/ and *sh*/ʃ/ is called a **digraph**.

The English writing system is alphabetic in a very loose sense. Some reasons for this irregular correspondence between sound and symbolic representation may be found in a number of historical influences on the form of written English. The spelling of written English was largely fixed in the form that was used when printing was introduced into fifteenth-century England. At that time, there were a number of conventions regarding the written representation of words that had been derived from forms used in writing other languages, notably Latin and French. For example, *qu* replaced older English *cw* in words like *queen*. Moreover, many of the early printers were native Flemish speakers and could not make consistently accurate decisions about English pronunciations, hence the change from Old English *gast* to *ghost*, with *h* derived from the Flemish version (*gheest*). Perhaps more important is the fact that, since the fifteenth century, the pronunciation of spoken English has undergone substantial changes. For example, although we no longer pronounce the initial *k* sound or the internal *gh* sound, we still include letters indicating the older pronunciation in our contemporary spelling of the word *knight*. These are sometimes called "silent letters." They also violate the one sound-one symbol principle of pure alphabetic writing, but not with as much effect as the silent final *-e* of so many English words. Not only do we have to learn that this letter is not pronounced, we also have to know the patterns of influence it has on the preceding vowel, as in the different pronunciations of *a* in the pair *hat/hate* and *o* in *not/note*.

If we then add in the fact that a large number of older written English words were actually "recreated" by sixteenth-century spelling reformers to bring their written forms more into line with what were supposed, sometimes erroneously, to be their Latin origins (e.g. *dette* became *debt, doute* became *doubt, iland* became *island*), then the sources of the mismatch between written and spoken forms begin to become clear. Further changes in the development of North American English spelling conventions are illustrated in Task D, on page 256.

In Chapter 17, we will look more closely at other aspects of the historical development of English and other ways in which languages change.

Study Questions

1 Approximately when were clay tokens first used as a means of bookkeeping?

2 Why is one early writing system called "cuneiform"?

3 What is the basic difference between a logographic writing system and a phonographic writing system?

4 What happens in the process of change based on the rebus principle?

5 What kind of writing system was invented for Cherokee?

6 Is the text message "cu@9" an example of logographic or alphabetic writing?

7 What is the name given to the writing system used for Russian?

8 Where will you find the writing system with the longest history of continuous use?

9 What is the best way to describe the written symbols used in Chinese writing: pictographic or phonographic or morphographic?

10 Which of these symbols ($, 8, ?, &) is not used as a logogram?

11 Which people created the basic order of letter symbols (A, B, C, D)?

12 What is a digraph?

Tasks

A What is boustrophedon writing and during which period was it used?

B What kind of writing system is Hangul, where is it used and how are forms written on the page?

C What kind of writing is used in texting? How would you describe the writing conventions (pictographic, ideographic, logographic, syllabic or alphabetic) that are used in the following text messages?

xlnt msg ("excellent message")	*swdyt* ("So, what do you think?")
btw ("by the way")	*ne1* ("anyone")
b42moro ("before tomorrow")	*cul8r ;-)* ("see you later, wink")

D When we reviewed English orthography, we didn't consider the differences that developed between North American and British English, exemplified in the spelling of the word *programme*, used in the UK, versus *program* in the USA.

(i) From the following list, identify the eleven words that are distinctly American in spelling, the eleven words that are distinctly British, and the six words that are spelled the same in both varieties.

(ii) Can you identify the six regular distinctions in spelling (e.g. *-mme* versus *-m*) that are illustrated in the list?

advertisement	*amour*	*analyze*	*apologise*
behaviour	*catalog*	*categorise*	*center*
counsellor	*defense*	*dialogue*	*epilogue*
favorite	*fence*	*fibre*	*filter*
humour	*jewelry*	*licence*	*liter*
modelling	*neighbor*	*offence*	*parallel*
paralyze	*pretense*	*sombre*	*traveller*

(For background reading, see Carney, 1997; chapter 7 of Cook, 2004; Micklethwait, 2000.)

E What kind of writing systems are known as abjads and abugidas and what is the basic difference between them?

F The term **palimpsest** describes the result of a particular process in the history of writing. What is this process and why was it used?

G In contemporary usage, written language is not simply spoken language written down. There are many differences between the way we create written texts and the way we have conversations, for example. Based on their corpus research, Biber *et al.* (1999) described a number of "lexical bundles," that is, sequences of four or more words that regularly occur together, some in speech and others in writing.

(i) Can you reorganize the following lexical bundles into two groups, one containing expressions that are typical of informal spoken English and the other containing expressions more typical of written English in an educational setting?

as a result of ...	*it has been suggested that* ...
do you want me to ...	*it is possible to* ...
have a look at ...	*on the other hand* ...
I don't know what ...	*that's a good idea* ...
I think I have ...	*the fact that the* ...
in the case of ...	*there's a lot of* ...
it has nothing to do with ...	*what's the matter with* ...

(ii) More generally, which version, spoken English or written English, do you think has more nouns, more verbs, more adjectives or more pronouns?

(iii) Why do you think this pattern exists?

H Consider the following examples and try to decide in which cases "X" is a symbol with a function, but without meaning, or one with an identifiable general meaning, or one with a very specific meaning. Can any of the uses be considered logographic?

(1) *The twenty-fourth letter of the English alphabet is X.*
(2) *On the map was a large X and the words "You are here."*
(3) *Most of the older men were illiterate at that time and put X where their signature was required.*
(4) *Indicate your choice by putting X next to only one of the following options.*
(5) *He wrote X – Y = 6 on the blackboard.*
(6) *There was an image of a dog with a large X across it.*
(7) *The teacher put X beside one of my sentences and I don't know why.*
(8) *We can't take the children with us to see that film because it's rated X.*
(9) *The witness known as Ms. X testified that she had heard several gunshots.*
(10) *Aren't there two X chromosomes in the cells of females?*
(11) *At the bottom of the letter, after her signature, she put X three times.*
(12) *In the XXth century, Britain's collapsing empire brought new immigrants.*

I The illustration in Figure 16.4 on page 259 is described in Jensen (1969) as a letter from a young woman of the Yukagirs who live in northern Siberia. The woman (c) is sending the letter to "her departing sweetheart" (b). What do you think the letter is communicating? Who are the other figures? What kind of "writing" is this?

Discussion Topics/Projects

I According to Florian Coulmas (2003: 201), "the present distribution of scripts testifies to the close link between writing systems and religion." Do you think that the spread of different religions (more than anything else) accounts for the different forms of writing used in the world today? What kind of evidence would you use to argue for or against this idea?

(For background reading, see chapter 10 of Coulmas, 2003.)

II Pictograms may be language-independent, but they do not seem to be culture-independent. In order to interpret many pictographic and ideographic representations, we have to be familiar with cultural assumptions about what the symbols "mean."

(i) As a simple exercise, show the twelve symbols illustrated below (Figure 16.5) to some friends and ask them if they know what each one means. (People may say they have never seen them before, but they should be encouraged to guess.)

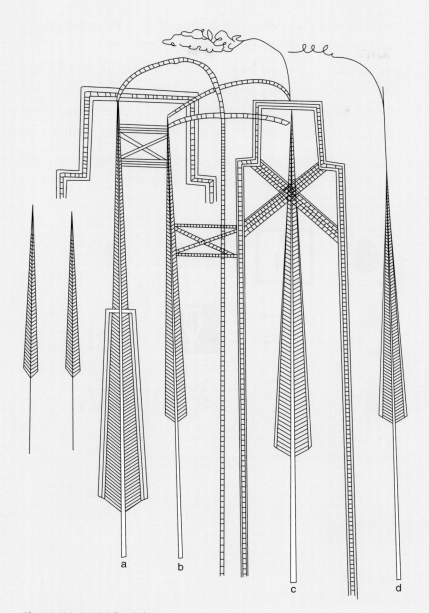

Figure 16.4 A Yukagir letter

(ii) Next, provide them with the following list of "official meanings" and ask them to decide which symbol goes with which meaning.

(a) agitate   (e) lock   (i) open door or lid

(b) blood donors   (f) lost child   (j) press, interview room

(c) dry, heat   (g) registration   (k) protection and safety equipment

(d) keep frozen   (h) telegrams   (l) turning basin maneuvring (boats)

(iii) Can you describe what kinds of cultural assumptions are involved in the interpretation of these symbols (from Ur, 2009)?

Figure 16.5 Culture-bound symbols

Further Reading

Basic Treatments

Robinson, A. (2007) *The Story of Writing* (2nd edition) Thames & Hudson

Sampson, G. (2015) *Writing Systems* (2nd edition) Equinox

More Detailed Treatments

Coulmas, F. (2003) *Writing Systems* Cambridge University Press

Rogers, H. (2005) *Writing Systems: A Linguistic Approach* Blackwell

Comprehensive Reviews

Daniels, P. and W. Bright (1996) *The World's Writing Systems* Oxford University Press

Wyse, D. (2017) *How Writing Works: From the Invention of the Alphabet to the Rise of Social Media* Cambridge University Press

Precursors of Writing

Schmandt-Besserat, D. (1996) *How Writing Came About* University of Texas Press

Ancient Languages

Woodard, R. (2003) *The Cambridge Encyclopedia of the World's Ancient Languages* Cambridge University Press

Cuneiform

Glassner, J. (2003) *The Invention of Cuneiform* Johns Hopkins University Press

Egyptian

Allen, J. (2000) *Middle Egyptian: An Introduction to the Language and Culture of Hieroglyphs* Cambridge University Press

Ancient Greek

Jeffery, L. (1990) *The Local Scripts of Archaic Greece* Clarendon Press

Cherokee

Cushman, E. (2011) *The Cherokee Syllabary* University of Oklahoma Press

Chinese, Japanese and Korean Writing

Pae, H. (ed.) (2018) *Writing Systems, Reading Processes and Cross-linguistic Influences* John Benjamins

The Alphabet

Man, J. (2000) *Alpha Beta* Wiley

Written English

Carney, E. (1997) *English Spelling* Routledge
Cook, V. (2004) *The English Writing System* Hodder Arnold
Cook, V. and D. Ryan (eds.) (2016) *The Routledge Handbook of the English Writing System* Routledge

The "Ghost" Story

Crystal, D. (2012) *Spell It Out: The Singular Story of English Spelling* (chapter 19) Profile Books

Other References

Biber, D., S. Johansson, G. Leech, S. Conrad and E. Finegan (1999) *Longman Grammar of Spoken and Written English* Longman
Davies, W. (1987) *Egyptian Hieroglyphics* British Museum / University of California Press
Gelb, I. (1963) *A Study of Writing* University of Chicago Press
Jensen, H. (1969) *Sign, Symbol and Script* (3rd edition) George Allen and Unwin
Micklethwait, D. (2000) *Noah Webster and the American Dictionary* McFarland & Company
Ur, P. (2009) *Grammar Practice Activities* (2nd edition) Cambridge University Press

17 Language History and Change

Fæder ure þu þe eart on heofonum,
si þin nama gehalgod.
Tobecume þin rice.
Gewurþe þin willa on eorðan swa swa on heofonum.
Urne gedæghwamlican hlaf syle us to dæg.
And forgyf us ure gyltas,
swa swa we forgyfað urum gyltendum.
And ne gelæd þu us in costnunge,
ac alys us of yfele.

The Lord's Prayer (c. 1000)

This barely recognizable version of the Lord's Prayer from about a thousand years ago provides a rather clear indication that the language of the "Englisc" has gone through substantial changes to become the English we use today. Investigating the features of older languages, and the ways in which they developed into modern languages, involves us in the study of language history and change, also known as **philology**. In the nineteenth century, philology dominated the study of language and one result was the creation of "family trees" to show how languages were related. Before all of that could happen, however, there had to be the discovery that a variety of languages spoken in different parts of the world were actually members of the same family.

Family Trees

In 1786, a British government official in India called Sir William Jones made this observation about Sanskrit, the ancient language of Indian law (Lehman, 1967: 10):

> The Sanskrit language, whatever be its antiquity, is of a wonderful structure; more perfect than the Greek, more copious than the Latin, and more exquisitely refined than either, yet bearing to both of them a stronger affinity, both in the roots of verbs and in the forms of grammar, than could possibly have been produced by accident.

Sir William went on to suggest, in a way that was quite revolutionary for its time, that languages from very different geographical areas must have some common ancestor. It was clear, however, that this common ancestor could not be described from any existing records, but had to be hypothesized on the basis of similar features existing in records of languages that were believed to be descendants.

During the nineteenth century, a term came into use to describe that common ancestor. It incorporated the notion that this was the original form (*Proto*) of a language that was the source of modern languages in the Indian sub-continent (*Indo*) and in Europe (*European*). With **Proto-Indo-European** established as a long ago "great-great-grandmother," scholars set out to identify the branches of the Indo-European family tree, tracing the lineage of many modern languages. Figure 17.1 shows a small selection of the Indo-European languages in their family branches.

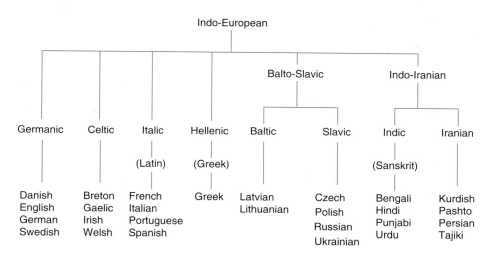

Figure 17.1 Indo-European family tree

Indo-European

Indo-European is the language family with the largest population and distribution in the world, but it is not the only one. There are about thirty such language families containing a large number of different individual languages. According to one reputable source (*Ethnologue*, 2018), there are actually 7,097 known languages in the world. Many of these languages are in danger of extinction while a few are expanding. In terms of number of speakers, Chinese has the most native speakers (over 1 billion), while Spanish (over 400 million) and English (over 330 million) are more widely used in different parts of the world. Looking at the Indo-European family tree, we might be puzzled initially by the idea that all these diverse languages are related. After all, two modern languages such as Italian and Hindi would seem to have nothing in common. One way to get a clearer picture of how they are related is through looking at records of an older generation, like Latin and Sanskrit, from which the modern languages evolved. For example, if we use familiar letters to write out the words for *father* and *brother* in Sanskrit, Latin and Ancient Greek, some common features become apparent.

Sanskrit	Latin	Ancient Greek	
pitar	pater	patēr	("father")
bhrātar	frāter	phrāter	("brother")

While these forms have clear similarities, it is extremely unlikely that exactly the same words will be found throughout the languages. However, the fact that close similarities occur (especially in the pronunciations of the words) is good evidence for proposing a family connection. For more examples, see Task C, on page 274.

Cognates

The process we have just used to establish a possible family connection between different languages involved looking at what are called "cognates." Within groups of related languages, we can often find close similarities in particular sets of words. A **cognate** of a word in one language (e.g. English) is a word in another language (e.g. German) that has a similar form and is (or was) used with a similar meaning. The English words *mother, father* and *friend* are cognates of the German words *Mutter, Vater* and *Freund*. On the basis of these cognates, we can see that Modern English and Modern German must have a common ancestor in the Germanic branch of Indo-European. We can look at similar sets in the Italic branch of Indo-European and find cognates in Spanish (*madre, padre, amigo*) and Italian (*madre, padre, amico*).

Comparative Reconstruction

Using information from sets of cognates from different (but apparently related) languages, we can embark on a procedure called **comparative reconstruction**. The aim of this procedure is to reconstruct what must have been an earlier or even the possible "proto" form in the common ancestral language. In carrying out this procedure, we can make use of two very general principles.

The **majority principle** is very straightforward. If, in a cognate set, three words begin with a [p] sound and one word begins with a [b] sound, then our best guess is that the majority have retained the original sound (i.e. [p]).

The **most natural development principle** is based on the fact that certain types of sound change are very common, as shown in Table 17.1, whereas changes in the other direction are extremely unlikely.

TABLE 17.1 SOUND CHANGES

Direction of change	Examples
1 Final vowels often disappear	*vino* → *vin*
2 Voiceless sounds become voiced, often between vowels	*muta* → *muda*
3 Stops become fricatives	*ripa* → *riva*
4 Consonants become voiceless at the end of words	*rizu* → *ris*

Comparing Cognates

If we take some examples of cognates from three languages, as shown below, we can make a start on comparative reconstruction by deciding what was the most likely form of the initial sound in the original source of all three. Since the written forms can often be misleading, we check that the initial sounds of the words in languages A and B are all [k], while in language C, the initial sound in all the words is [ʃ].

	Languages		
A	B	C	
cantare	*cantar*	*chanter*	("sing")
catena	*cadena*	*chaîne*	("chain")
caro	*caro*	*cher*	("dear")
cavallo	*caballo*	*cheval*	("horse")

Sound Reconstruction

Within the small set of languages just presented, the majority principle would be used to argue that the initial sound [k] in languages A and B is older than the [ʃ] sound in language C. Adding support to this analysis, the [k] sound is a stop consonant and the /ʃ/ sound is a fricative. According to one part of the "most natural development principle" (in Table 17.1), change occurs in the direction of stops becoming fricatives, so the [k] sound is more likely to have been the original.

We have started on the comparative reconstruction of the common origins of some words in Italian (A), Spanish (B) and French (C). In this case, we have a way of checking our reconstruction because the common origin for these three languages is known to be Latin. When we check the Latin cognates of the words listed, we find *cantare, catena, carus* and *caballus*, confirming that [k] was the initial sound.

Word Reconstruction

Looking at a non-Indo-European set of cognates, we can imagine receiving the following data from a linguist recently returned from an expedition to a remote region of the Amazon. The examples are a set of cognates from three related languages, but what would the proto-forms have looked like?

Languages

1	2	3	Protoforms	
mube	mupe	mup	_____	("stream")
abadi	apati	apat	_____	("rock")
agana	akana	akan	_____	("knife")
enugu	enuku	enuk	_____	("diamond")

Using the majority principle, we can suggest that the older forms will most likely be based on language 2 or language 3. If this is correct, then the consonant changes must have been [p] → [b], [t] → [d] and [k] → [g] in order to produce the later forms in language 1. There is a pattern in these changes: voiceless sounds became voiced between vowels. So, languages 2 and 3 have older forms than language 1.

Which of the two lists, 2 or 3, contains the older forms? Remembering one other "most natural development" type of sound change (i.e. final vowels often disappear), we can propose that the words in language 3 have consistently lost the final vowels still present in the words of language 2. Our best guess, then, is that the forms listed for language 2 are closest to what must have been the original proto-forms.

The History of English

The reconstruction of proto-forms is an attempt to determine what a language must have been like before any written records. However, even when we have written records from an older period of a language such as English, they may not bear any resemblance to the written form of the language found today. The version of the Lord's Prayer quoted at the beginning of this chapter provides a good illustration of this point. Even some of the letters seem quite alien. The older letters þ (called "thorn") and ð ("eth") were both replaced by "th" (as in *þu → thou*, *eorðan → earth*), and æ ("ash") simply became "a" (as in *to dæg → today*). To see how one language has undergone substantial changes through time, we can take a brief look at the history of English, which is traditionally divided into four periods:

Old English: before 1100

Middle English: 1100 to 1500

Early Modern English: 1500 to 1700

Modern English: after 1700

Old English

The primary sources for what developed as the English language were the Germanic languages spoken by tribes of Angles, Saxons and Jutes from northern Europe who moved into the British Isles in the fifth century. In one early account, these tribes were described as "God's wrath toward Britain." It is from the names of the first two that we have the term *Anglo-Saxons* to describe these people, and from the first tribe that we get the word for their language *Englisc* and their new home *Engla-land*.

From this early version of *Englisc*, now called **Old English**, we have many of the most basic terms in the language: *mann* ("man"), *wīf* ("woman"), *cild* ("child"), *hūs* ("house"), *mete* ("food"), *etan* ("eat"), *drincan* ("drink") and *feohtan* ("fight"). These pagan invaders did not remain pagan for long. From the sixth to the eighth century, there was a period during which these Anglo-Saxons were converted to Christianity and a number of terms from Latin (the language of the religion) came into English at that time. The origins of the contemporary English words *angel, bishop, candle, church, fever, martyr, plant, priest, school* and *temple* all date from this period.

From the eighth century through the ninth and tenth centuries, another group of northern Europeans came first to plunder and then to settle in parts of the coastal regions of Britain. They were the Vikings and it is from their language, Old Norse, that the original forms of *die, flat, get, give, law, leg, skin, sky, take, they, their* and *them* were adopted, along with the weekdays *Tiw's day* and *Thor's day*. It is from their winter festival *jól* that we have *Yule* as a term for the Christmas season.

Middle English

The event that marks the end of the Old English period, and the beginning of the **Middle English** period, is the arrival of the Norman French in England, after their victory at Hastings under William the Conqueror in 1066. These French-speaking invaders became the ruling class, so that the language of the nobility, government, law and civilized life in England for the next two hundred years was French. It is the source of words like *army, arrest, court, defense, faith, govern, marry, prison, punish* and *tax*.

Yet the language of the peasants remained English. The peasants worked on the land and reared *sheep, cows* and *swine* (words from Old English) while the upper classes talked about *mutton, beef* and *pork* (words of French origin). Hence the different terms in Modern English to refer to these creatures "on the hoof" as opposed to "on the plate." Throughout this period, French (or, more accurately, an English version of French) was the prestige language and Chaucer tells us that one of his Canterbury pilgrims could speak it.

> *She was cleped Madame Eglentyne*
> *Ful wel she song the service dyvyne,*
> *Entuned in her nose ful semely,*
> *And Frenche she spak ful faire and fetisly.*

This is an example of Middle English from the late fourteenth century. It had changed substantially from Old English, but other changes were yet to take place. Most significantly, the vowel sounds of Chaucer's time were very different from those we hear in similar words today. Chaucer lived in a "hoos," with his "weef," and "hay" might drink a bottle of "weena" with "heer" by the light of the "mona."

In the two hundred years, from 1400 to 1600, that separated Chaucer and Shakespeare, the sounds of English underwent a substantial change known as the "Great Vowel Shift." The effects of this general raising of long vowel sounds (such as long [o] moving up to long [u], as in *mōna → moon*, and [e] going up to [i], as in *hay → he*) made the pronunciation of Early Modern English, beginning around 1500, significantly different from earlier periods. The introduction of printing in 1476 brought about significant changes, but because the printers tended to standardize existing pronunciations in the spelling of words (e.g. *knee, gnaw*), later pronunciation changes are often not reflected in the way Modern English (after 1700) is written.

Those changes reflecting influences from the outside (borrowed words from Norman French or Old Norse) are examples of **external change**. Other changes (especially sound changes) are the result of processes of **internal change**.

Sound Changes

In a number of changes from Middle to Modern English, some sounds disappeared from the pronunciation of certain words, in a process simply described as **sound loss**. The initial [h] of many Old English words was lost, as in *hlud → loud* and *hlaford → lord*. Some words lost sounds, but kept the spelling, resulting in the "silent letters" of contemporary written English. Word-initial velar stops [k] and [g] are no longer pronounced before nasals [n], but we still write the words *knee* and *gnaw* with the remnants of earlier pronunciations.

Another example is a velar fricative [x] that was used in the pronunciation of the older form *niht* as [nɪxt] (closer to the modern German pronunciation of *Nacht*), but is absent in the contemporary form *night*, pronounced as [naɪt]. A remnant of this type of sound is still present in some dialects, as at the end of the Scottish word *loch*, but it is no longer a consonant in most dialects of Modern English.

Metathesis

The sound change known as **metathesis** involves a reversal in position of two sounds in a word. This type of reversal is illustrated in the changed versions of these words from their earlier forms.

acsian → ask	*frist → first*	*brinnan → beornan (burn)*
bridd → bird	*hros → horse*	*wæps → wasp*

The cowboy who pronounces the expression *pretty good* as something close to *purty good* is producing a similar example of metathesis as a dialect variant within Modern English. In some American English dialects, the form *aks*, as in *I aksed him already*, can still be heard instead of *ask*.

The reversal of position in metathesis can sometimes occur between non-adjoining sounds. The Spanish word *palabra* is derived from Latin *parabola* through the reversal in position of the [l] and [r] sounds. The pattern is exemplified in the following set.

Latin		**Spanish**	
miraculum	→	*milagro*	("miracle")
parabola	→	*palabra*	("word")
periculum	→	*peligro*	("danger")

Epenthesis

Another type of sound change, known as **epenthesis**, involves the addition of a sound to the middle of a word.

> *æmtig* → *empty*   *spinel* → *spin<u>d</u>le*   *timr* → *tim<u>b</u>er*   *þunor* → *thun<u>d</u>er*

The addition of a [p] sound after the nasal [m], as in *empty*, can also be heard in some speakers' pronunciation of *something* as "sumpthing." Anyone who pronounces the word *film* as if it were "filum," or *arithmetic* as "arithametic," is producing examples of epenthesis in Modern English.

   If you listen to the popular song "Somewhere Over the Rainbow" by Brother Iz (Israel Kamakawiwo`ole), you will hear him sing the line *High above the chim<u>i</u>ney top*, with an epenthetic vowel inside the word *chimney*.

Prothesis

One other type of sound change worth noting, though not found in English, involves the addition of a sound to the beginning of a word and is called **prothesis**. It is a common feature in the evolution of some forms from Latin to Spanish.

> *schola*   →   *escuela*   ("school")   *scribere*   →   *escribir*   ("to write")
> *spiritus*   →   *espíritu*   ("spirit")   *sperare*   →   *esperar*   ("to hope")

Spanish speakers who are starting to learn English as a second language will sometimes put a prothetic vowel at the beginning of some English words, with the result that words like *strange* and *story* may sound like "estrange" and "estory."

Syntactic Changes

Some noticeable differences between the structure of sentences in Old and Modern English involve word order. In Old English texts, we find the Subject–Verb–Object (or SVO) order most common in Modern English, but we can also find a number of different orders that are no longer used. For example, the subject could follow the verb, as in *ferde he* ("traveled *he*"), and the object could be placed before the verb, as in *he hine geseah* ("he *him* saw"), or at the beginning of the sentence, as in *him man ne sealde* ("[to] *him* man not gave [any]").

   In the last example, the use of the negative also differs from Modern English, since the sequence *not gave (ne sealde)* is no longer grammatical. A "double negative" construction was also possible, as in *ne sealdest þū næfre* ("not gave you never"), where both *ne* ("not") and *næfre* ("never") are used with the same verb. We would now say *You never gave* rather than *You not gave never*.

Loss of Inflections

In the following Old English sentence, we can see how all these distinct syntactic features result in a word order that is quite different from a Modern English version ("and you never gave me a kid"). Note that the word order is Verb–Subject–Object, or VSO, in contrast to the SVO of the contemporary language.

and	*ne*	*sealdest*	*þū*	*me*	*næfre*	*ān*	*ticcen*
(and)	(not)	(gave)	(you)	(me)	(never)	(a)	(kid)

This example also gives a hint of the most sweeping change in the form of English sentences from the older period. This was the loss of a large number of inflectional suffixes from many parts of speech. Notice that, in the previous examples, the forms *sealde* ("he gave") and *sealdest* ("you gave") are differentiated by inflectional suffixes (*-e, -est*) that are no longer used in Modern English. Nouns, adjectives, articles and pronouns all had different inflectional forms according to their grammatical function in the sentence. (For more examples of changes, see Task F, on page 274.)

Semantic Changes

The most obvious way in which Modern English differs from Old English is in the number of borrowed words that have come into the language since the Old English period. (For more on borrowing, see Chapter 5.) Less obviously, many words have ceased to be used. Since we no longer carry swords (most of us, at least), the word *foin*, meaning "the thrust of a sword," is no longer heard. A common Old English word for "man" was *were*, but it has fallen out of use, except in horror films where the compound *werewolf* occasionally appears. A number of expressions such as *lo, verily* or *egad* are immediately recognized as belonging to a much earlier period, along with names such as *Bertha, Egbert, Egfrid, Ethelbert* and *Percival*.

One type of semantic change can result in words being used with new meanings that seem to be very different. Over time, words such as *awful, dreadful, horrible* and *terrible* have undergone a shift from meanings such as "creating awe, dread, horror or terror." In modern English, these forms are now commonly used as adverbs similar to "very" or "extremely," with no hint of awe or terror, as in *The room was awfully small* or *He's always terribly polite*.

A similar transformation has occurred in the use of *literally*. Originally, this word conveyed the sense of "exactly worded or in reality," as illustrated in Chapter 5, when we described the Spanish expression *perros calientes* as literally *"dogs hot."* However, when one woman was describing a recent experience, she said, *When he said that to me, I literally died inside*. Of course, she is not describing her death (because she wouldn't be in a position to report it), but signaling a metaphorical or figurative usage. So, *literally* now means "not figuratively" and also "figuratively" in different contexts.

Broadening of Meaning

A less radical type of change is described as **broadening** of meaning, as in the change from *holy day* as a religious feast to the break from work called a *holiday*. We have broadened the use of *foda* (fodder for animals) to all kinds of *food*. Old English words such as *luflic* ("loving") and *hræd* ("quick") not only went through sound changes, they also developed more complex evaluative meanings ("wonderful" and "preferentially"), as in their modern uses: *That's a lovely idea, but I'd rather have the money*. Another example is the modern use of the word *dog*. We use it very generally to refer to all breeds, but in its older form (Old English *docga*), it was only used for one breed.

Narrowing of Meaning

The reverse process, called **narrowing**, has overtaken the Old English word *hund*, once used for any kind of dog, but now, as *hound*, used only for some specific breeds. Another example is *mete*, once used for any kind of food, which has in its modern form *meat* become restricted to only some specific types. The Old English version of the word *wife* could be used to refer to any woman, but has narrowed in its application nowadays to only married women. This type of change can take a word with a negative meaning, derived from Latin *nescius* (from *ne* + *sci*) meaning "not knowing" or "ignorant", and over time give it more positive meaning in the modern word *nice*. A different kind of narrowing can lead to a negative meaning for some words, such as *notorious* (which used to mean "widely known," but now means "known for something bad"), *vulgar* (which used to mean simply "ordinary") and *naughty* (which used to mean "having nothing").

Diachronic and Synchronic Variation

None of these changes happened overnight. They were gradual and probably difficult to discern while they were in progress. Although some changes can be linked to major social changes caused by wars, invasions and other upheavals, the most pervasive source of change in language seems to be in the continual process of cultural transmission (described in Chapter 2). In this unending process whereby each individual child has to "recreate" the language of the community, there is an unavoidable propensity to pick up some elements exactly and others only approximately. There is also the occasional desire to be different, so it should be expected that languages will not remain stable and that change and variation are inevitable.

In this chapter, we have concentrated on variation in language viewed **diachronically**, that is, from the historical perspective of change through time. The type of variation that can be viewed **synchronically**, that is, in terms of differences within one language among different groups at the same time, is the subject of Chapters 18 and 19.

Study Questions

1 What two languages did Sir William Jones think were similar to Latin?

2 To which branch of Indo-European does Gaelic belong?

3 How would you group the following languages into pairs that are closely related from a historical point of view: Bengali, Breton, Czech, English, French, Kurdish, Pashto, Portuguese, Swedish, Ukrainian, Urdu, Welsh?

4 How many language families have been identified?

5 What are cognates?

6 On the basis of the following data, what are the most likely proto-forms?

Languages

1	2	3		
cosa	*chose*	*cosa*	_____	("thing")
capo	*chef*	*cabo*	_____	("head")
capra	*chèvre*	*cabra*	_____	("goat")

7 From which language(s) did English adopt the words *die, marry* and *plant*?

8 If you learn that Brother Iz was a native speaker of Hawaiian, how might that help explain his epenthetic vowel in *chimney*?

9 Which of the following words are likely to be from Old English and which from French: *bacon, beef, calf, deer, ox, pig, veal, venison*?

10 What types of sound changes are illustrated by the following pairs?

(a) *thridda → third*   (b) *scribere → escribir*   (c) *glimsian → glimpse*

(d) *hring → ring*   (e) *slummer → slumber*   (f) *beorht → bright*

11 The Old English word *gærshoppa* underwent metathesis to become which Modern English word?

12 The Old English verb *steorfan* ("to die, from any cause") is the source of the Modern English verb *starve* ("to die, from lack of food"). What is the technical term used to describe this type of meaning change?

Tasks

A Which of these languages cannot be included in the Indo-European family tree? To which other language families do they belong?

Catalan, Chamorro, Faroese, Georgian, Hebrew, Hungarian, Marathi, Serbian, Tamil, Turkish

B A Danish linguist, Rasmus Rask, and a German writer more famous for fairy tales, Jacob Grimm, both working in the early nineteenth century, are credited with the original insights that became known as "Grimm's Law."

What is Grimm's Law and how does it account for the different initial sounds in pairs of cognates such as these from French and English (*deux/two, trois/three*) and these from Latin and English (*pater/father, canis/hound, genus/kin*)?

C We can often trace the roots of several different words in Modern English back to a single Indo-European form. Using what you learned in this chapter, can you complete the following chart, using the words provided, to illustrate several English word histories?

corage, coraticum, cord, cordialis, heorte, herton, kardia, kardiakos, kerd

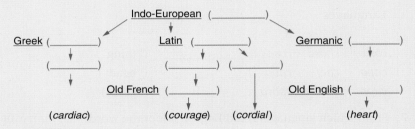

Figure 17.2 Word histories

D A famous text from the medieval period is the *Peterborough Chronicle*, which begins in the following way, with a translation from Janson (2012: 135).

Brittene igland is ehta hund mila lang & twa hund brad, & her sind on þis iglande fif gebeode: Englisc & Brittisc . . . & Scyttise & Pyhtise & Boc Leden
("Britain's island is eight hundred miles long and two hundred broad, and there are on this island five languages: English and British . . . and Scottish and Pictish and Book Latin.")

(i) A distinction is made here between English and British. If we assume that English was the language of the Angles, who were those speakers of British? Are there any modern language descendants of the British language?

(ii) What was the distinction between Scottish and Pictish? Are there any modern language descendants of these languages?

E Describe what happened in any documented case of "language death."

F These four versions of the same biblical event (Matthew 27: 73) are presented in Campbell (2013) as a way of illustrating some changes in the history of English. Can you describe the changes in vocabulary and grammar?

(i) Modern English (1961)
Shortly afterwards the bystanders came up and said to Peter, "Surely you are another of them; your accent gives you away!"

(ii) Early Modern *English* (1611)

And after a while came vnto him they that stood by, and saide to Peter, Surely thou also art one of them, for thy speech bewrayeth thee.

(iii) Middle English (1395)

And a litil aftir, thei that stooden camen, and seiden to Petir, treuli thou art of hem; for thi speche makith thee knowun.

(iv) Old English (1050)

þa æfter lytlum fyrste genēalæton þa ðe þær stodon, cwædon to petre. Soðlice þu eart of hym, þyn spræc þe gesweotolað.

(Literally: "then after little first approached they that there stood, said to Peter. Truly thou art of them, thy speech thee makes clear.")

G What happens in the process of change known as "grammaticalization"? Can you find out how the grammaticalization process made it possible for the English verb forms *go* and *will* to be used in sentences such as *I'm gonna be late* and *I'll be at work until six*?

H During the late eighteenth century when Captain Cook's voyages in the Pacific brought him to Hawai'i, he and his crew were surprised to discover that many Hawaiian words were similar to those they had learned from other Pacific island groups thousands of miles away. This similarity is now known to be a result of a number of Pacific languages having a common ancestor, called Proto-Polynesian.

(i) In Table 17.2, based on Kikusawa (2005), there are examples from five Polynesian languages. Can you work out the most likely forms of Proto-Polynesian based on these cognates? (The symbol ', as in *wa'a*, represents a consonant called a glottal stop [ʔ], described in Chapter 3.)

TABLE 17.2 POLYNESIAN LANGUAGES

	Tongan	Samoan	Rapanui	Māori	Hawaiian	Proto-forms
"eye"	*mata*	*mata*	*mata*	*mata*	*maka*	_____
"canoe"	*vaka*	*va'a*	*vaka*	*waka*	*wa'a*	_____
"water"	*vai*	*vai*	*vai*	*wai*	*wai*	_____
"sea"	*tahi*	*tai*	*vaikava*	*tai*	*kai*	_____
"seaweed"	*limu*	*limu*	*rimu*	*rimu*	*limu*	_____
"sky"	*langi*	*lagi*	*rangi*	*rangi*	*lani*	_____
"lice"	*kutu*	*'utu*	*kutu*	*kutu*	*'uku*	_____

(ii)   Given the regular differences between the forms in Tongan and Hawaiian, can you work out the most likely Hawaiian cognates of these Tongan words?

	Tongan	Hawaiian
"forbidden"	*tapu*	_____
"blood"	*toto*	_____
"fish"	*ika*	_____
"sleep"	*mohe*	_____
"hot"	*vela*	_____
"nine"	*hiva*	_____
"south"	*tonga*	_____
"name"	*hingoa*	_____
"axe"	*toki*	_____
"man"	*tangata*	_____

Discussion Topics/Projects

I   A nineteenth-century scholar named Curtius (quoted in Aitchison, 2013) described a major goal of historical linguistics in the following way:

A principal goal of this science is to reconstruct the full, pure forms of an original stage from the variously disfigured and mutilated forms which are attested in the individual languages.

Do you agree that languages decay and become worse ("disfigured and mutilated") through time? What kind of evidence would you use to argue for or against this point of view?

(For background reading, see chapter 16 of Aitchison, 2013.)

II   Using what you have learned about comparative reconstruction, try to recreate the most likely proto-forms for these cognates (from Sihler, 2000: 140).

Languages

A	B	Proto-forms
kewo ("red")	*čel* ("red")	_____
kuti ("tree")	*kut* ("wood")	_____
like ("heavy")	*lič* ("morose")	_____
waki ("sister")	*wač* ("sister")	_____
wapo ("hand")	*lap* ("hand")	_____
woli ("beam")	*lol* ("roof")	_____

(For background reading, see sections 96 to 102 of Sihler, 2000.)

Further Reading

Basic Treatments

Aitchison, J. (2013) *Language Change: Progress or Decay?* (4th edition) Cambridge University Press
Schendl, H. (2001) *Historical Linguistics* Oxford University Press

More Detailed Treatments

Campbell, L. (2013) *Historical Linguistics: An Introduction* (3rd edition) MIT Press
Crowley, T. and C. Bowern (2010) *An Introduction to Historical Linguistics* (4th edition) Oxford University Press
Janson, T. (2012) *The History of Languages* Oxford University Press

Language Families

Austin, P. (ed.) (2008) *One Thousand Languages* University of California Press
Pereltsvaig, A. (2012) *Languages of the World* Cambridge University Press

Indo-European

Fortson, B. (2010) *Indo-European Language and Culture* (2nd edition) Wiley-Blackwell
Mallory, J. and D. Adams (2006) *The Oxford Introduction to Proto-Indo-European and the Proto-Indo-European World* Oxford University Press

Language Change

Labov, W. (2001) *Principles of Linguistic Change* volume 2: *Social Factors* Blackwell
McMahon, A. (1994) *Understanding Language Change* Cambridge University Press

History of the English Language

Barber, C., J. Beal and P. Shaw (2012) *The English Language: A Historical Introduction* (Canto edition) Cambridge University Press
Crystal, D. and H. Crystal (2013) *Wordsmiths and Warriors: The English Language Tourist's Guide to Britain* Oxford University Press
Gramley, S. (2019) *The History of English: An Introduction* (2nd edition) Routledge
Tombs, R. (2014) *The English and Their History* Alfred A. Knopf

Old, Middle and Early Modern English

Baker, P. (2012) *Introduction to Old English* (3rd edition) Wiley-Blackwell
Horobin, S. and J. Smith (2002) *An Introduction to Middle English* Oxford University Press
Nevalainen, T. (2006) *An Introduction to Early Modern English* Edinburgh University Press

On Sir William Jones

Cannon, G. (1990) *The Life and Mind of Oriental Jones* Cambridge University Press

On *terribly* and *literally*

Burridge, K. and A. Bergs (2017) *Understanding Language Change* (chapter 3) Routledge

Broadening and Narrowing of Meaning

Minkova, D. and R. Stockwell (2009) *English Words: History and Structure* (2nd edition) Cambridge University Press

On *lovely* and *rather*

Adamson, S. (2000) "A lovely little example" In O. Fischer, A. Rosenbach and D. Stein (eds.) *Pathways of Change: Grammaticalization in English* (39–66) John Benjamins

Rissanen, M. (2008) "From 'quickly' to 'fairly': on the history of *rather*" *English Language and Linguistics* 12: 345–359

Other References

Ethnologue (2018) (21st edition) SIL International

Kikusawa, R. (2005) "Comparative linguistics: a bridge that connects us to languages and people of the past" In P. Lassettre (ed.) *Language in Hawai'i and the Pacific* (415–433) Pearson

Lehmann, W. (ed.) (1967) *A Reader in Nineteenth Century Historical Indo-European Linguistics* Indiana University Press

Sihler, A. (2000) *Language History: An Introduction* John Benjamins

See also www.ethnologue.com

18 Regional Variation in Language

Yesterday, I toll my dad, "Buy chocolate kine now, bumbye somebody going egg our house you know, cuz you so chang." He sed, "Sucking kine mo' bettah cuz lass mo' long. Da kids going appreciate cuz . . . " And befo' he could start his "Back in my days story" I jus sed, "Yeah, yeah, yeah, I undahstand," cuz I nevah like hea da story again ah about how he nevah have candy wen he wuz small and how wuz one TREAT fo' eat da orange peel wit sugar on top. Da orange PEEL you know. Not da actual orange, but da orange PEEL. Strong emphasis on PEEL cuz dey wuz POOR.

Tonouchi (2001)

Throughout this book, we have been talking about languages such as English, Spanish or Swahili as if there was a single variety of each in everyday use. That is, we have largely ignored the fact that every language has a lot of variation, especially in the way it is spoken. If we just look at English, we find widespread variation in the way it is spoken in different countries such as Australia, Britain and the USA. We can also find a range of varieties in different parts of those countries, with Lee Tonouchi's account of "Trick-O-Treat" in Hawai'i as just one example. In this chapter, we investigate aspects of language variation based on where that language is used, as a way of doing **linguistic geography**. First, we should identify the particular variety that we have normally assumed when we referred to a language as English, Spanish or Swahili.

The Standard Language

When we talked about the words and structures of a language in earlier chapters, we were concentrating on the features of only one variety, usually called the **standard language**. This is actually an idealized variety, because it has no specific region. It is the variety associated with administrative, commercial and educational centers, regardless of region. If we think of Standard English, it is the version we believe is found in printed English in newspapers, books and the mass media in general. It is the variety used in most works of fiction, in scientific and other technical articles, and the one taught in most schools. It is the variety we normally try to teach to those who want to learn English as a second or foreign language. It is clearly associated with education and broadcasting in public contexts and is more easily described in terms of features associated with the written language (i.e. vocabulary, spelling, grammar) than the spoken language.

If we are thinking of that general variety used in mainstream public broadcasting in the United States, we can refer more specifically to Standard American English or, in Britain, to Standard British English. In other parts of the world, we can talk about other recognized varieties such as Standard Australian English, Standard Canadian English or Standard Indian English.

Accent and Dialect

Whether we think we speak a standard variety of English or not, we all speak with an **accent**. It is a myth that some speakers have accents while others do not. We might feel that some speakers have very distinct or easily recognized types of accent while others may have more subtle or less noticeable accents, but every language-user speaks with an accent. Technically, the term "accent" is restricted to the description of aspects of pronunciation that identify where an individual speaker is from, regionally or socially. It is different from the term **dialect**, which is used to describe features of grammar and vocabulary as well as aspects of pronunciation.

We recognize that the sentence *You don't know what you're talking about* will generally "look" the same whether spoken with an American accent or a Scottish accent. Both speakers will be using forms associated with Standard English, but have different pronunciations. However, this next sentence – *Ye dinnae ken whit yer haverin' aboot* – has the same meaning as the first, but has been written out in an approximation of what a person who speaks one dialect of Scottish English might say. There are differences in pronunciation (e.g. *ye*, *whit*, *aboot*), but there are also examples of different vocabulary (e.g. *ken*, *haverin'*) and different grammatical forms (*dinnae*, *yer*).

Variation in Grammar

While differences in vocabulary are often easily recognized, dialect variations in the meaning of grammatical constructions are less frequently documented. In the following example (from Trudgill, 1983) two British English speaking visitors (B and C) are talking to a local Irish English speaker (A) in Donegal, Ireland.

A: *How long are youse here?*

B: *Till after Easter.*
(Speaker A looks puzzled.)

C: *We came on Sunday.*

A: *Ah. Youse're here a while then*

It seems that the construction *How long are youse here?*, in speaker A's dialect, is used with a meaning close to the structure "How long have you been here?" referring to past time. Speaker B, however, answers as if the question was referring to future time ("How long are you going to be here?"). When speaker C answers with a past time response (*We came on Sunday*), speaker A acknowledges it and repeats his use of a present tense (*Youse're here*) to refer to past time. Note that the dialect form *youse* (= "you" plural) seems to be understood by the visitors though it is unlikely to be part of their own dialect.

Dialectology

Despite occasional difficulties, there is a general impression of mutual intelligibility among many speakers of different dialects of English. This is one of the criteria used in the study of dialects, or **dialectology**, to distinguish between two different dialects of the same language (whose speakers can usually understand each other) and two different languages (whose speakers can't usually understand each other). This is not the only, or the most reliable, way of identifying dialects, but it is helpful in establishing the fact that each different dialect, like each language, is equally worthy of analysis. It is important to recognize, from a linguistic point of view, that none of the varieties of a language is inherently "better" than any other. They are simply different.

From a social point of view, however, some varieties do become more prestigious. In fact, the variety that develops as the standard language has usually been one socially prestigious dialect, originally associated with a center of economic and political power (e.g. London for British English and Paris for French). Yet there always continue to be other varieties of a language spoken in different regions.

Regional Dialects

The existence of different regional dialects is widely recognized and often the source of some humor for those living in different regions. In the United States, people from the Brooklyn area of New York may joke about a Southerner's definition of *sex* by telling you that *sex is fo' less than tin*, in their best imitation of someone from the Southern states. In return, Southerners can wonder aloud about what a *tree guy* is in Brooklyn, since they have heard Brooklyn speakers refer to *doze tree guys*. Some regional dialects clearly have stereotyped pronunciations associated with them.

Going beyond stereotypes, those involved in the serious investigation of regional dialects have devoted a lot of survey research to the identification of consistent features of speech found in one geographical area compared to another. These dialect surveys often involve a lot of attention to detail and operate with very specific criteria in identifying acceptable informants. After all, it is important to know if the person whose speech you are recording really is a typical representative of the region's dialect.

Consequently, the informants in the dialect surveys of the twentieth century tended to be **NORMS** or "non-mobile, older, rural, male speakers." Such speakers were selected because they were less likely to have influences from outside the region in their speech. One unfortunate consequence of using such criteria is that the resulting dialect description tends to be more accurate of a period well before the time of investigation. Nevertheless, the detailed information obtained has provided the basis for a number of Linguistic Atlases of whole countries (e.g. England) and regions (e.g. the Upper Midwest area of the United States).

Isoglosses

We can look at some examples of regional variation found in a survey that resulted in the Linguistic Atlas of the Upper Midwest of the United States. One of the aims of a survey of this type is to find a number of significant differences in the speech of those living in different areas and to be able to chart where the boundaries are, in dialect terms, between those areas. If it is found, for example, that the vast majority of informants in one area say they carry things home from the store in a *paper bag* while the majority in another area say they use a *paper sack*, then it is usually possible to draw a line across a map separating the two areas, as shown in Figure 18.1. This line is called an **isogloss** and represents a boundary between the areas with regard to that one particular linguistic item. If a very similar distribution is found for other items, such as a preference for *pail* to the north and *bucket* to the south, then other isoglosses can be drawn on the map.

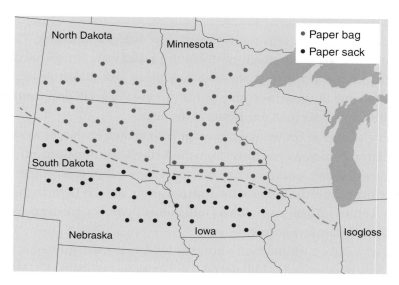

Figure 18.1 Regional variation in the Upper Midwest (USA)

 ## Dialect Boundaries

When a number of isoglosses come together in this way, a more solid line, indicating a **dialect boundary,** can be drawn. In Figure 18.1, a red dot indicates where *paper bag* was used and a black dot shows where *paper sack* was used. The broken line between the two areas is an isogloss that coincides with enough other isoglosses involving other linguistic features to be classified as a dialect boundary. Using this information, we find that in the Upper Midwest of the USA there is a Northern dialect area that includes Minnesota, North Dakota, most of South Dakota and Northern Iowa. The rest of Iowa and Nebraska show characteristics of the Midland dialect. Some of the noticeable differences are illustrated here.

	("t<u>au</u>ght")	("r<u>oo</u>f")	("cr<u>ee</u>k")	("grea<u>s</u>y")	
Northern:	[ɔ]	[ʊ]	[ɪ]	[s]	
Midland:	[ɑ]	[u]	[i]	[z]	
Northern:	*paper bag*	*pail*	*kerosene*	*slippery*	*get sick*
Midland:	*paper sack*	*bucket*	*coal oil*	*slick*	*take sick*

So, if an American English (male) speaker pronounces the word *greasy* as [grizi] and asks for a *bucket* to carry water, then he is not likely to have grown up and spent most of his life in Minnesota. While making this general claim, we shouldn't forget that a number of the features in the dialect survey won't necessarily be used by all speakers currently living in the region.

The Dialect Continuum

Another note of caution is required with regard to dialect boundaries. The drawing of dialect boundaries is quite useful in establishing a broad view of regional dialects, but it tends to obscure the fact that, in the boundary areas, one dialect or language variety merges into another. Regional variation actually exists along a **dialect continuum** rather than having sharp breaks from one region to the next.

A very similar type of continuum can occur with related languages existing on either side of a political border. As you travel from the Netherlands into Germany, you will find concentrations of Dutch speakers giving way to areas near the border where "Dutch" may sound more like "Deutsch" because the Dutch dialects and the German dialects are less clearly differentiated. Then, as you travel further into Germany, greater concentrations of distinctly German speakers occur.

Speakers who move back and forth across this border area, using different varieties with some ease, may be described as **bidialectal** (i.e. "speaking two dialects"). Most of us grow up with some form of bidialectalism, speaking one dialect "in the street" among family and friends, and having to learn another dialect "in school." However, in some places, there are two different languages involved and the people who know both languages are described as **bilingual**.

Bilingualism

In many countries, regional variation is not simply a matter of two (or more) dialects of a single language, but can involve two (or more) quite distinct and different languages. Canada, for example, is officially a bilingual country, with both French and English as official languages. This recognition of the linguistic rights of the country's French speakers, largely in Quebec, did not come about without a lot of political upheaval. For most of its history, Canada was essentially an English-speaking country, with a French-speaking minority group. In such a situation, **bilingualism** at the level of the individual tends to be a feature of the minority group. In this form of bilingualism, a member of a minority group grows up in one linguistic community, mainly speaking one language (e.g. Welsh in Britain or Spanish in the United States), but learns another language (e.g. English) in order to take part in the larger dominant linguistic community.

Indeed, many members of linguistic minorities can live their entire lives without ever seeing their native language in the public domain. It was only after protests and political activism that bilingual (English–Welsh) road signs came into widespread use in Wales. Many *henoed* never expected to see their first language on public signs in Wales, as in Figure 18.2, though they may wonder why everyone is being warned about them.

Figure 18.2 Bilingual sign in Wales

Diglossia

A rather special situation involving two distinct varieties of a language, called **diglossia**, exists in some countries. In diglossia, there is a "low" variety, acquired locally and used for everyday affairs, and a "high" or special variety, learned in school and used for important matters. A type of diglossia exists in Arabic-speaking countries where the high variety (Classical Arabic) is used in formal lectures, serious political events and especially in religious discussions. The low variety is the local version of the language, such as Egyptian Arabic or Lebanese Arabic. Through a long period in European history, a diglossic situation existed with Latin as the high variety and one of the local languages of Europe (early versions of modern Italian, French and Spanish) as the low variety or "vernacular."

Language Planning

Perhaps because bilingualism in contemporary Europe and North America tends to be found mostly among minority groups, many countries are often assumed to be monolingual. For many of those residents who are only capable of speaking one language (English), the United States would indeed seem to be a monolingual country. For others, it clearly is not, because they live in large communities where English is not the first language of the home. As one example, the majority of the population in San Antonio, Texas, will be more likely to listen to radio broadcasts in Spanish than in English. This simple fact has quite large repercussions in terms of the organization of local representative government and the educational system. Should elementary school teaching take place in Spanish or English?

Consider a similar question in the context of Guatemala, a country in Central America, where there are twenty-six Mayan languages spoken, as well as Spanish. If, in this situation, Spanish is selected as the language of education, are all those Mayan speakers put at an early educational disadvantage within the society? Questions of this type require answers on the basis of some type of **language planning**. Government, legal and educational organizations in many countries have to plan which variety or varieties of the languages spoken in the country are to be used for official business. In Israel, despite the fact that it was not the most widely used language among the population, Hebrew was chosen as the official government language. In India, the choice was Hindi, yet in many non-Hindi-speaking regions, there were riots against this decision. There were "National Language Wars" in the Philippines before different groups could agree on the name of the national language (Filipino).

The process of language planning may be seen in a better light when the full series of stages is implemented over a number of years. The adoption of Swahili as the national language of Tanzania in East Africa may serve as a good example. There still exist a large number of other languages, as well as the colonial vestiges of English, but the educational, legal and government systems have gradually introduced Swahili as the official language. The process of "selection" (choosing an official language) is followed by "codification," in which basic grammars, dictionaries and written models are used to establish the standard variety. The process of "elaboration" follows, with the standard variety being developed for use in all aspects of social life and the appearance of a body of literary work written in the standard. The process of "implementation" is largely a matter of government attempts to encourage use of the standard, and "acceptance" is the final stage when a substantial majority of the population use the standard and think of it as the national language, playing a part in not only social, but also national identity.

Pidgins

In some areas, the standard chosen may be a variety that originally had no native speakers in the country. For example, in Papua New Guinea, with more than eight hundred different languages, a lot of official business is conducted in Tok Pisin. This language is now used by over a million people, but it began many years earlier as a kind of impromptu language called a **pidgin**. A variety of a language described as a pidgin is often discussed as a "contact" language that developed for some practical purpose, such as trading, among groups of people who had a lot of contact, but who did not know each other's languages. As such, it would have no native speakers. The origin of the term "pidgin" is thought to be from a Chinese version of the English word "business."

A pidgin is described as an "English pidgin" if English is the lexifier language, that is, the main source of words adopted in the pidgin. It doesn't mean that those words will have the same pronunciation or meaning as in the source. For example, the word *gras* has its origins in the English word "grass," but in Tok Pisin it also came to be used for "hair." It is part of *mausgras* ("moustache") and *gras bilong fes* ("beard"). In Tok Pisin, a distinction developed between *yumi* ("me and you") and *mipela* ("me and others"), marking two different senses of "we" not found in standard English.

There are several English pidgins still used today. They are characterized by an absence of any complex grammatical morphology and a somewhat limited vocabulary. Inflectional suffixes such as -*s* (plural) and -*'s* (possessive) are required on nouns in standard English, but are rare in English pidgins, while structures like *tu buk* ("two books") and *di gyal place* ("the girl's place") are common. The -*ed* suffix of standard English is typically missing, so that items for sale may appear on signs as *smoke meat* and *pickle mango*. Functional morphemes often take the place of inflectional morphemes found in the source language. For example, instead of changing the form of *you* to *your*, as in the English phrase *your book*, English-based pidgins use a form like *bilong*, and change the word order to produce phrases like *buk bilong yu*, as well as *gras bilong fes*. (For more examples, see Task F, page 291.)

The syntax of pidgins can be quite unlike the languages from which terms were borrowed and modified, as in this example from an earlier stage of Tok Pisin.

Baimbai	*hed*	*bilongyu*	*i-arrait*	*gain*
by and by	head	belong you	he alright	again

"Your head will soon get well again"

There are between 6 and 12 million people still using pidgin languages and between ten and seventeen million using descendants from pidgins called "creoles."

Creoles

When a pidgin develops beyond its role as a trade or contact language and becomes the first language of a social community, it is described as a **creole**. Tok Pisin is now a creole. The first language of a large number of people in Hawai'i is also a creole and, though still locally referred to as "Pidgin," is more accurately described as "Hawai'i Creole English." (See Task D, page 291.) A creole initially develops as the first language of children growing up in a pidgin-using community and becomes more complex as it serves more communicative purposes. Unlike pidgins, creoles have large numbers of native speakers and are not restricted at all in their uses. Haiti has a French creole and Jamaica and Sierra Leone have English creoles.

The separate vocabulary elements of a pidgin can become grammatical elements in a creole. The form *baimbai yu go* ("by and by you go") in early Tok Pisin gradually shortened to *bai yu go*, and finally to *yu bigo*, with a grammatical structure not unlike that of its English translation equivalent, "you will go." (See Task C, page 290.)

The Post-Creole Continuum

In many contemporary situations where creoles evolved, there is usually evidence of another process at work. Just as there was development from a pidgin to a creole, known as **creolization**, there is now often a retreat from the use of the creole by those who have greater contact with a standard variety of the language. Where education and greater social prestige are associated with a "higher" variety (e.g. British English in Jamaica), a number of speakers will tend to use fewer creole forms and structures. This process, known as **decreolization**, leads at one extreme to a variety that is closer to the external standard model and leaves, at the other extreme, a basic variety with more local creole features. Between these two extremes may be a range of slightly different varieties, some with many and some with fewer creole features. This range of varieties, evolving after (= "post") the creole has come into existence, is called the post-creole continuum.

So, in Jamaica, one speaker may say *a fi mi buk dat*, using the basic creole variety, another may put it as *iz mi buk*, using a variety with fewer creole features, and yet another may choose *it's my book*, using a variety with only some pronunciation features of the creole, or a "creole accent." It is also very common for speakers to be able to use a range of varieties in different situations. (See Task G, page 291 for more.)

These differences are naturally connected to social values and social identity. While discussing language varieties in terms of regional differences, we have excluded the complex social factors that also determine language variation. In Chapter 19, we will investigate the influence of a number of these social variables.

Study Questions

1   Which variety of English would you say is being used in the introductory quotation from Lee Tonouchi?

2   What is the difference between an accent and a dialect?

3   In the following example from Irish English is the speaker referring to future time or past time?

How long are youse here?

4   Which of these descriptions is *not* used to identify NORMS: *male, normal, older, rural*?

5   What is one disadvantage of using NORMS in dialect surveys?

6   What does an isogloss represent in a linguistic atlas?

7   What is the difference between an isogloss and a dialect boundary?

8   If you meet some American speakers who talk about the surface of something as *slick* and say they feel they are *taking sick*, are they likely to have a Northern, Midland, or Southern dialect?

9   Name two types of discourse where a "high" variety is used in diglossia.

10   Which country adopted Swahili as the national language?

11   In what specific way is a creole different from a pidgin?

12   What is a lexifier language?

Tasks

A   Users of Standard American English and Standard British English can usually understand each other, but there are some differences in vocabulary use. Can you put the following words in the appropriate spaces below?

bill, biscuit, bonnet, boot, candy, check, cookie, crisps, dummy, estate agent, flashlight, garbage, gas, hood, jumper, pacifier, pants, petrol, potato chips, realtor, rubbish, sneakers, sweater, sweets, torch, trainers, trousers, trunk

	American	British
Example: *Would you like a chocolate _____ with your coffee?*	*cookie*	*biscuit*
(1) *He should wear a white shirt and dark _____.*	_____	_____
(2) *It's really dark outside, you'll need a _____.*	_____	_____

(3)   *I bought some new _____ in order to go running.*   _____ _____

(4)   *It's all _____, so just throw it all away.*   _____ _____

(5)   *The small child had a _____ in its mouth.*   _____ _____

(6)   *Eating a lot of _____ is bad for your teeth.*   _____ _____

(7)   *(In a restaurant) Can we have the _____, please?*   _____ _____

(8)   *Do you want some _____ with your sandwich?*   _____ _____

(9)   *You'd better bring a _____ because it's quite chilly.*   _____ _____

(10)   *What does a gallon of _____ cost these days?*   _____ _____

(11)   *The _____ thinks the house will sell quickly.*   _____ _____

(12)   *In most cars, the spare wheel is in the _____,*   _____ _____
        and not under the _____.   _____ _____

B A distinction between **rhotic** and **non-rhotic** pronunciation can be used to identify differences between international varieties, British English versus North American English, for example, and also between national varieties, such as Southern British English versus Northern British English.

(i)   What is this distinction based on?

(ii)   Looking back at Table 3.5 on page 37, is there evidence for a non-rhotic variety?

C Bislama (also known as Bichelamar) is a creole that, like Tok Pisin, became a national language, spoken in the Republic of Vanuatu, in the southwest Pacific. Look at the example sentences (from Crowley, 2004), illustrating Toktok Langwis Bislama, and try to answer the questions.

(1) *Mekanik ia bae i fiksimap trak blong mi*   ("The mechanic will fix the car.")

(2) *Bae mi imelem yu tumoro*   ("I will email you tomorrow.")

(3) *Man ia i stilim mane blong mi*   ("That man stole my money.")

(4) *Bae yumitu rusum taro*   ("We will roast taro.")

(5) *Bae mi kukum raes*   ("I will cook rice.")

(6) *Hem i stap komem hea blong hem*   ("She is combing her hair.")

(7) *Oli katemdaon stampa blong manggo*   ("They cut down the mango tree.")

(8) *Olgeta oli kilimaot ol waelpig finis*   ("They have exterminated all of the wild pigs.")

(9) *Bae yumi hipimap doti*   ("We will pile up the rubbish.")

(10) *Bae mi leftemap pikinini*   ("I will lift up the child.")

(i)   What are the suffixes *-em*, *-im* and *-um* used for?

(ii)   What is the basis for choosing each one, and not the others?

(iii) Which suffixes would you use to complete the following expressions?

bagar _____ ap ("ruin it")	kat _____ frut	("cut the fruit")
biliv_____ ("believe it")	pen _____	("paint it")
ful _____ ap ("fill it")	rid _____ buk	("read the book")
har _____ ("hear it")	wek_____ ap	("wake it up")
kar _____ ("carry it")	wil_____ ap glas	("wind up the window")

D The following example of Hawai'i Creole English (from Lum, 1990, quoted in Nichols, 2004) has some characteristic forms and structures. How would you analyze the use of *da, had, one, stay* and *wen* in this extract?

Had one nudda guy in one tee-shirt was sitting at da table next to us was watching da Bag Man too. He was eating one plate lunch and afterwards, he wen take his plate ovah to da Bag Man. Still had little bit everyting on top, even had bar-ba-que meat left. "Bra," da guy tell, "you like help me finish? I stay full awready."

E In the study of pidgins, what is meant by a "substrate" and a "superstrate" language? Which of the two is likely to be the source of intonation, syntax and vocabulary?

F The following examples are based on Romaine (1989), quoted in Holmes and Wilson (2017). Using what you learned about Tok Pisin, can you complete the translations of these examples with the following English words and phrases: *bird's feather, bird's wing, cat's fur, eyebrow, hair, weed*?

gras antap long ai gras bilong pisin gras nogut
gras bilong hed gras bilong pusi han bilong pisin

G In Creole studies, a broad distinction is made in terms of three varieties: the acrolect, the basilect and the mesolect.

(i) What is the basis of this distinction?

(ii) Which of the following ways of saying *I am eating* in Jamaican Creole (or Patois/Patwa) do you think would be an example of each of these different "lects"? These examples are adapted from Sebba and Harding (2018).

(1) /mi itɪn/
(2) /aɪ æm itɪn/
(3) /mi a nyam/
(4) /a ɪz itɪn/

H In which areas of the British Isles would we find a Brummie accent, a Geordie accent, a speaker of Scouse, the use of *bairns* (= "children"), *boyo* (= "man"), *fink* (= "think") and *Would you be after wanting some tea?* (= "Do you want some tea?")?

I   Two pioneers of dialectology were Georg Wenker and Jules Gilliéron. In what ways were their methods different and which method became the model for later dialect studies?

J   Consider the following statements about Standard English and try to decide whether you agree or disagree with them, providing a reason in each case for your decision.

    (1)   Standard English is not a language.
    (2)   Standard English is an accent.
    (3)   Standard English is a speech style.
    (4)   Standard English is a set of rules for correct usage.

Discussion Topics/Projects

I   Peter Trudgill has noted that "increased geographical mobility during the course of the twentieth century led to the disappearance of many dialects and dialect forms through a process we can call dialect levelling – the levelling out of differences between one dialect and another" (2000: 155).

Do you think that "dialect levelling" is continuing in the geographical area you are most familiar with? Does this mean that there will eventually be only one dialect? What other forces might be at work that would cause new dialects to emerge?

(For background reading, see chapter 8 of Trudgill, 2000.)

II   English is not the official language of the United States, but some insist that it should be. What are the arguments for and against the "English-Only Movement"?

(For background reading, see Wiley, 2004.)

Further Reading

Basic Treatments

Crystal, D. (2019) *The Cambridge Encyclopedia of the English Language* (3rd edition) Cambridge University Press
Kretzschmar, W. (2004) "Regional dialects" In E. Finegan and J. Rickford (eds.) *Language in the USA* (39–57) Cambridge University Press

More Detailed Treatments

Chambers, J. and P. Trudgill (1998) *Dialectology* (2nd edition) Cambridge University Press
Wardhaugh, R. (2014) *An Introduction to Sociolinguistics* (7th edition) Wiley-Blackwell

American English Dialects

Cramer, J. and D. Preston (2018) "Changing perceptions of southernness" *American Speech* 93: 3–4

Wolfram, W. and B. Ward (eds.) (2006) *American Voices: How Dialects Differ from Coast to Coast* Blackwell

British English Dialects

Hughes, A., P. Trudgill and D. Watt (2012) *English Accents and Dialects* (5th edition) Routledge

Other Varieties of English

Melchers, G. and P. Shaw (2015) *World Englishes* (3rd edition) Routledge

Trudgill, P. and J. Hannah (2017) *International English* (6th edition) Routledge

Standard Englishes

Hickey, R. (ed.) (2012) *Standards of English* Cambridge University Press

Bilingualism

Grosjean, F. (2012) *Bilingual* Harvard University Press

Myers-Scotton, C. (2005) *Multiple Voices* Wiley

Language Planning

Spolsky, B. (ed.) (2018) *The Cambridge Handbook of Language Policy* Cambridge University Press

The Language Situation in Tanzania Now

Ochieng, D. (2015) "The revival of the status of English in Tanzania" *English Today* 31 (2): 25–31

Pidgins and Creoles

Siegel, J. (2008) *The Emergence of Pidgin and Creole Languages* Oxford University Press

Velupillai, V. (2015) *Pidgins, Creoles and Mixed Languages* John Benjamins

The Dutch–German Dialect Continuum

Barbour, S. and P. Stevenson (1990) *Variation in German* Cambridge University Press

Tok Pisin (*baimbai*)

Sankoff, G. and S. Laberge (1974) "On the acquisition of native speakers by a language" In D. DeCamp and I. Hancock (eds.) *Pidgins and Creoles* (73–84) Georgetown University Press

Smith, G. (2008) *Growing up with Tok Pisin: Contact, Creolization and Change in Papua New Guinea's National Language* Battlebridge

Hawai'i Creole English

Drager, K. (2012) "Pidgin and Hawai'i English: an overview" *International Journal of Language, Translation and Intercultural Communication* 1: 61–73

Sakoda. K. and J. Siegel (2003) *Pidgin Grammar* Bess Press

Other References

Holmes, J. and N. Wilson (2017) *An Introduction to Sociolinguistics* (5th edition) Pearson Education

Lum, D. (1990) *Pass On, No Pass Back* Bamboo Ridge Press

Nichols, J. (2004) "Creole languages: forging new identities" In E. Finegan and J. Rickford (eds.) *Language in the USA* (133–152) Cambridge University Press

Romaine, S. (1989) *Pidgin and Creole Languages* Longman

Sebba, M. and L. Harding (2018) "World Englishes and English as a lingua franca" In J. Culpeper, P. Kerswill, R. Wodak, T. McEnery and F. Katamba (eds.) *English Language* (chapter 21) (2nd edition) Palgrave Macmillan

Tonouchi, L. *Da Word* Bamboo Ridge Press

Trudgill, P. (1983) *On Dialect* Blackwell

Trudgill, P. (2000) *Sociolinguistics* (4th edition) Penguin

Wiley, T. (2004) "Language planning, language policy, and the English-Only Movement" In E. Finegan and J. Rickford (eds.) *Language in the USA* (319–338) Cambridge University Press

See also

(American Dialect Society) www.americandialect.org

(British Library) sounds.bl.uk

(International Dialects of English Archive) dialectsarchive.com

19 | Social Variation in Language

When at Niagara Falls, I was escorting a young lady with whom I was on friendly terms. She had been standing on a piece of rock, the better to view the scene, when she slipped down, and was evidently hurt by the fall; she had in fact grazed her shin. As she limped a little in walking home, I said, "Did you hurt your leg much." She turned from me, evidently much shocked, or much offended; and not being aware that I had committed any very heinous offence, I begged to know what was the reason of her displeasure. After some hesitation, she said that as she knew me well, she would tell me that the word *leg* was never mentioned before ladies.

Marryat (1839)

In the preceding chapter, we focused on variation in language use found in different geographical areas. However, not everyone in a single geographical area speaks in the same way in every situation. As Captain Marryat learned, in the quotation above (cited in Mohr, 2013: 192), some individuals can have very specific views on socially appropriate language. We are also aware of the fact that people who live in the same region, but who differ in terms of education and economic status, often speak in quite different ways.

Indeed, these differences may be used, implicitly or explicitly, as indications of membership in different social groups or speech communities. A **speech community** is a group of people who share a set of norms and expectations regarding the use of language. The study of the linguistic features that have social relevance for participants in those speech communities is called "sociolinguistics."

Sociolinguistics

The term **sociolinguistics** is used generally for the study of the relationship between language and society. This is a broad area of investigation that involves the interaction of linguistics with a number of other academic disciplines that look at language in its social context such as anthropology, sociology and social psychology. We use all these connections when we analyze language from a social perspective.

Social Dialects

Whereas the traditional study of regional dialects tended to concentrate on the speech of people in rural areas, as noted in Chapter 18, the study of **social dialects** has been mainly concerned with speakers in towns and cities. In the social study of dialect, it is social class that is mainly used to define groups of speakers as having something in common. The two main groups are generally identified as "middle class," those who have more years of education and perform non-manual work, and "working class," those who have fewer years of education and perform manual work of some kind. So, when we refer to "working-class speech," we are talking about a social dialect. The terms "upper" and "lower" are used to subdivide the groups, mainly on an economic basis, making "upper-middle-class speech" another type of social dialect or **sociolect**.

As in all dialect studies, only certain features of language use are treated as relevant in the analysis of social dialects. These features are pronunciations, words or structures that are regularly used in one form by working-class speakers and in another form by middle-class speakers. In Edinburgh, Scotland, for example, the word *home* is regularly pronounced as [heɪm], as if rhyming with *fame*, among lower-working-class speakers, and as [hom], as if rhyming with *foam*, among middle-class speakers. It is a small difference in pronunciation, but it is an indicator of social status. It may also serve as a subtle indicator of social identity, used subconsciously by some speakers to mark who they are, or who they are not. A more familiar example might be the verb *ain't*, as in *I ain't finished yet*, which is more often a feature of working-class speech than middle-class speech.

When we look for other examples of language use that might be characteristic of a social dialect, we treat class as the **social variable** and the pronunciation or word as the **linguistic variable**. We can then investigate any systematic variation in usage by counting how often speakers in each class use each version of the linguistic variable. This is rarely an all-or-nothing situation, so we usually find that one group uses a certain form more or less than another and not that only one group or the other uses the form exclusively. (Task F, page 307, has examples of these variables.)

Education and Occupation

Although the unique circumstances of every life result in each of us having an individual way of speaking, a personal dialect or **idiolect**, we generally tend to sound like others with whom we share similar educational backgrounds and/or occupations. As adults, the outcome of our time in the educational system is usually reflected in our occupation and socio-economic status. The way bank executives, as opposed to window cleaners, talk to each other usually provides linguistic evidence for the significance of these social variables.

In the 1960s, sociolinguist William Labov combined elements from place of occupation and socio-economic status by looking at pronunciation differences among salespeople in three New York City department stores (see Labov, 2006). They were Saks Fifth Avenue (with expensive items, upper-middle-class status), Macy's (medium priced, middle-class status) and Klein's (with cheaper items, working-class status). Labov went into each of these stores and asked salespeople specific questions, such as *Where are the women's shoes?*, in order to elicit answers with the expression *fourth floor*. This expression contains two opportunities for the pronunciation (or not) of **postvocalic** /r/, that is, the /r/ sound after a vowel.

In the department stores, there was a regular pattern in the answers. The higher the socio-economic status of the store, the more /r/ sounds were produced, and the lower the status, the fewer /r/ sounds were produced by those who worked there. So, the frequency of this linguistic variable (r) marked the speech as upper middle class, middle class or working class.

In a British study conducted in Reading, about 40 miles west of London, Trudgill (1974) found that the social value associated with the same variable (r) was quite different. Middle-class speakers in Reading pronounced fewer /r/ sounds than working-class speakers. In this particular city, upper-middle-class speakers didn't seem to pronounce postvocalic /r/ at all. They said things like *Oh, that's mahvellous, dahling!*. The results of these two studies are shown in Table 19.1 (from Romaine, 2000).

TABLE 19.1 PERCENTAGES OF GROUPS PRONOUNCING POSTVOCALIC /r/

Social class	New York City	Reading
upper middle class	32	0
lower middle class	20	28
upper working class	12	44
lower working class	0	49

Social Markers

As shown in Table 19.1, the significance of the linguistic variable (r) can be virtually the opposite in terms of social status in two different places, yet in both places the patterns illustrate how the use of this particular speech sound functions as a **social marker**. That is, having this feature occur frequently in your speech (or not) marks you as a member of a particular social group, whether you realize it or not.

There are other pronunciation features that function as social markers. One feature that seems to be a fairly stable indication of lower class and less education, throughout the English-speaking world, is the final pronunciation of *-ing* with [n] rather than [ŋ] at the end of words such as *sitting* and *thinking*. Pronunciations represented by *sittin'* and *thinkin'* are associated with working-class speech.

Another social marker is called "[h]-dropping," which makes the words *at* and *hat* sound the same. It occurs at the beginning of words and can result in utterances that sound like *I'm so 'ungry I could eat an 'orse.* In contemporary English, this feature is associated with lower class and less education. It seems to have had a similar association as a social marker for Charles Dickens, writing in the middle of the nineteenth century. He used it as a way of indicating that the character Uriah Heep, in the novel *David Copperfield*, was from a lower class, as in this example (from Mugglestone, 1995).

> *"I am well aware that I am the umblest person going," said Uriah Heep, modestly; "My mother is likewise a very umble person. We live in a numble abode, Master Copperfield, but we have much to be thankful for. My father's former calling was umble."*

A number of grammatical features identified as social markers in British English are exemplified in Table 19.2.

TABLE **19. 2 GRAMMATICAL FEATURES AS SOCIAL MARKERS**

Working class	Middle class
we <u>was</u> too late	*were*
I don't want <u>none</u>	*any*
he <u>don't</u> know how	*doesn't*
she <u>weren't</u> too happy	*wasn't*
he's <u>went</u> to bed already	*gone*
it wasn't us <u>what done</u> that	*who did*
<u>them</u> boys <u>throwed</u> something	*those ...... threw*

Speech Style and Style-Shifting

In his department store study, Labov included another subtle element that allowed him not only to investigate the type of social stratification illustrated in Table 19.1, but also **speech style** as a social feature of language use. The most basic distinction in speech style is between formal uses and informal uses. Formal style is when we pay more careful attention to how we are speaking and informal style is when we pay less attention. They are sometimes described as "careful style" and "casual style." A change from one to the other by an individual is called **style-shifting.**

When Labov initially asked the salespeople where certain items were, he assumed they were answering in an informal manner. After they answered his question, Labov then pretended not to have heard and said, "Excuse me?" in order to elicit a repetition of the same expression, which was pronounced with more attention to being clear. This was taken as a representative sample of the speaker's more careful style. When speakers repeated the phrase *fourth floor*, the frequency of postvocalic /r/ increased in all groups. The most significant increase in frequency was among the Macy's group. In a finding that has been confirmed in other studies, middle-class speakers are much more likely to shift their style of speaking significantly in the direction of the upper middle class when they are using a careful style.

It is possible to use more elaborate elicitation procedures to create more gradation in the category of style. Asking someone to read a short text out loud will result in more attention to speech than simply asking them to answer some questions in an interview. Asking that same individual to read out loud a list of individual words taken from the text will result in even more careful pronunciation of those words and hence a more formal version of the individual's speech style.

When Labov analyzed the way New Yorkers performed in these elicitation procedures, he found a general overall increase in postvocalic /r/ in all groups as the task required more attention to speech. Among the lower-middle-class speakers, the increase was so great in the pronunciation of the word lists that their frequency of postvocalic /r/ was actually higher than among upper-middle-class speakers. As other studies have confirmed, when speakers in a middle-status group try to use a prestige form associated with a higher-status group in a formal situation, they have a tendency to overuse the form. This pattern has also been observed in studies of "hypercorrection" (see Chapter 7), where speakers can produce different forms or odd pronunciations as they shift their speech style to try to "speak better."

The concept of a "prestige" form, as perceived by members of a particular speech community, is sometimes invoked as a way of explaining the type of style-shifting that is observed in sociolinguistic studies. However, there are different ways of characterizing what is perceived as being prestigious.

Prestige

When certain individuals change their speech in the direction of a form that is more frequent in the speech of those perceived to have higher social status, we are dealing with **overt prestige**, or status that is generally recognized as "better" or more positively valued in the larger community.

There is, however, another phenomenon called **covert prestige**. This "hidden" status of a speech style as having positive value may explain why certain groups do not exhibit style-shifting to the same extent as other groups. For example, we might ask why many lower-working-class speakers do not change their speech style from casual to careful as radically as lower-middle-class speakers. The answer may be that they value the features that mark them as members of their own social group. They may value group solidarity (i.e. sounding like those around them) more than upward mobility (i.e. sounding like those above them in social terms).

Among younger middle-class speakers, there is often covert prestige attached to features of pronunciation and grammar (*I ain't doin' nuttin'* rather than *I'm not doing anything*) that are more often associated with the speech of lower-status groups.

Speech Accommodation

As we look closely at variation in speech style, we can see that it is not only based on speakers' social class and attention to speech, but is also influenced by their perception of their listeners. This type of variation is sometimes described in terms of "audience design," but is more generally known as **speech accommodation**, defined as our ability to modify our speech style toward or away from the perceived style of the person(s) we are talking to.

Convergence

We can adopt a speech style that attempts to reduce social distance, described as **convergence**, and use forms that are similar to those used by the person we are talking to. In the following examples (from Holmes and Wilson, 2017), a teenage boy is asking to see some holiday photographs. In the first example, he is talking to his friend, and in the second example, he is talking to his friend's mother. The request is essentially the same, but the style is different as the speaker converges with the speech style of the other.

(to friend) *C'mon Tony, gizzalook, gizzalook.*
(to friend's mother) *Excuse me. Could I have a look at your photos too, Mrs. Hall?*

Divergence

While we may want or try to sound like others in some social interactions to emphasize social closeness, there are other times when we may prefer to create the opposite effect. When a speech style is used to emphasize social distance between speakers, the process is called **divergence**. We can make our speech style diverge from another's by using forms that are distinctly different. In the third line of the following example, the Scottish teenager shifts to a speech style with features that differ substantially from the first line (while essentially saying the same thing).

TEENAGER: *I can't do it, sir.*

TEACHER: *Oh, come on. If I can do it, you can too*

TEENAGER: *Look, ah cannae dae it so . . . . . .*

The sudden divergence in style seems to be triggered not only by a need to add emphasis to his repeated statement, but also by the "We're the same" claim of his teacher. This teenager is using speech style to mark that they are not the same.

Register

Another influence on speech style that is tied to social identity derives from **register**. A register is a conventional way of using language that is appropriate in a specific context, which may be identified as situational (e.g. in church), occupational (e.g. among lawyers) or topical (e.g. talking about language). We can recognize specific features that occur in the religious register (*Ye shall be blessed by Him in times of tribulation*), the legal register (*The plaintiff is ready to take the witness stand*) and the linguistics register (*In this dialect there are fewer inflectional suffixes*).

Jargon

One of the defining features of a register is the use of **jargon**, which is special technical vocabulary, typically nouns (e.g. *plaintiff, suffix*), associated with a specific area of work or interest. In social terms, jargon helps to create and maintain connections among those who see themselves as "insiders" in some way and to exclude "outsiders." In many ways, it is the learning of the appropriate jargon of a profession that qualifies an individual as a valid professional within that area of expertise. This exclusive effect of specialized jargon, as in the medical register (e.g. *Zanoxyn is a nonsteroidal anti-inflammatory drug for arthritis, bursitis and tendonitis*), often leads to complaints about what may seem like "jargonitis."

Slang

Whereas jargon is specialized vocabulary used by those inside established social groups, often defined by professional status (e.g. legal jargon), **slang** is more typically used among those who are outside established higher-status groups. Slang, or "colloquial speech," describes words or phrases that are used instead of more everyday terms among younger speakers and other groups with special interests. The word *bucks* (for *dollars* or *money*) has been a slang expression for more than a hundred years in the United States, but the addition of *mega-* ("a lot of") in *megabucks* is a more recent innovation, along with *dead presidents* (whose pictures are on paper money) and *benjamins* (from Benjamin Franklin, on $100 bills).

According to one recent description, "Slang is a highly informal and unconventional type of vocabulary. It is perceived as deeply expressive, attractively catchy, and deliberately undignified" (Widawski, 2015: 8). Like clothing and music, slang is an aspect of social life that is subject to fashion, especially among adolescents. It can be used by those inside a group who share ideas and attitudes as a way of distinguishing themselves from others. As a marker of group identity during a limited stage of life such as early adolescence, slang expressions can "grow old" rather quickly. Older forms for "really good" such as *groovy, hip* and *super* were replaced by *awesome, rad* and *wicked* which gave way to *dope, kickass* and *phat*. A *hunk* ("physically attractive man") became a *hottie* and, instead of something being *the pits* ("really bad"), the next generation thought it was *a bummer, harsh!*, or said, *That's sucky!.* The difference in slang use between groups divided into older and younger speakers provides some of the clearest support for the idea that age is another important factor involved in the study of social variation in language use. Younger speakers are also much more likely to use taboo terms.

Taboo Terms

The use of slang can vary within the younger social group, as illustrated by the use of obscenities or **taboo** terms. Taboo terms are words and phrases, often involving body parts, bodily functions and sexual acts, that people avoid for reasons related to religion, politeness and prohibited behavior. They are often swear words, typically "bleeped" in public broadcasting (*What the bleep are you doing, you little bleep!*) or "starred" in print (*S**t! F*** off! You stupid f***ing a**hole!*).

In a study of the linguistic differences among "Jocks" (higher status) and "Burnouts" (lower status) in Detroit high schools, Eckert (2000) reported the regular use of taboo words among the "Burnouts," both males and females. However, among the higher status group (the "Jocks") males used taboo words only with other males, while females didn't seem to use them at all. Social class divisions, at least in the use of slang, are already well established during adolescence.

African American English

In much of the preceding discussion, we have been reviewing research on social variation based mainly on examples from British English and what we might call "European" American English. Labeling one general social variety according to the historical origins of the speakers allows us to put it in contrast with another major variety called **African American English** (**AAE**). Also known as Black English or Ebonics, AAE is a variety used by many (not all) African Americans in many different regions of the USA. It has a number of characteristic features that, taken together, form a distinct set of social markers.

In much the same way as large geographical barriers, such as oceans, rivers and mountains separating groups of people, foster linguistic differences in regional dialects, social barriers such as discrimination and segregation serve to create marked differences between social dialects. In the case of AAE, those different features have often been stigmatized as "bad" language, following a regular pattern whereby the social practices, especially speech, of dominated groups are treated as "abnormal" by those dominant groups who have decided that they are in charge of defining "normal." Although AAE speakers continue to experience the effects of discrimination, their social dialect often has covert prestige among younger members of other social groups, particularly with regard to popular music, and certain features of AAE may be used in expressions of social identity by many who are not African American.

Vernacular Language

The form of AAE that has been most studied is usually described as **African American Vernacular English (AAVE)**. The term "vernacular" has been used since the Middle Ages, first to describe early local versions of the European languages that eventually became French, Italian and Spanish (low prestige) in contrast to Latin (high prestige), then to characterize any non-standard spoken version of a language used by lower-status groups. So, the **vernacular** is a general expression for a kind of social dialect, typically spoken by a lower-status group, which is treated as "non-standard" because of marked differences from the "standard" language. (See Chapter 18 for more on the concept of the standard language.) As the vernacular language of African Americans, AAVE shares a number of features with other non-standard varieties, such as "Chicano English," spoken in some Hispanic American communities. Varieties of what has been called "Asian American English" are also characterized by some of the pronunciation features described in studies of this vernacular.

The Sounds of a Vernacular

A pervasive phonological feature in AAVE and other English vernaculars is the tendency to reduce final consonant clusters, so that words ending in two consonants (*left hand*) are often pronounced as if there is only one (*lef han*). This can affect the pronunciation of past tense *-ed* forms in certain contexts, with expressions such as *iced tea* and *I passed the test* sounding like *ice tea* and *I pass the tess*. This characteristic is shared with many pidgins and creoles, as described in Chapter 18, and has led to the suggestion that AAVE may have initially come into being in a way similar to other English creoles.

Initial dental consonants (*think, that*) are frequently pronounced as alveolar stops (*tink, dat*), with the result that the definite article (*the*) is heard as [də], as in *You da man!*. Other morphological features, such as possessive *-'s* (*John's girlfriend*) and third person singular *-s* (*she loves him*), are not typically used (*John girlfriend, she love him*). Also, when a phrase contains an obvious indication of plural number, the plural *-s* marker (*guys, friends*) is usually not included (*two guy, one of my friend*).

The Grammar of a Vernacular

It is typically in aspects of grammar that AAVE and other vernaculars are most stigmatized as being "illogical" or "sloppy." One frequently criticized element is the double negative construction, as in *He don't know nothin* or *I ain't afraid of no ghosts*. Because the negative is expressed twice, these structures have been condemned as "illogical" (since one negative supposedly cancels the other). Yet this feature of AAVE can be found in many other English dialects and in other languages such as French: *il ne sait rien* (literally, "he not knows nothing"). It was also common in Old English: *Ic naht singan ne cuðe* (literally, "I not sing not could"). There is nothing inherently illogical about these structures, which can extend to multiple negatives, allowing greater emphasis on the negative aspect of the message, as in *He don't never do nothin*.

The "sloppy" criticism focuses on the frequent absence of forms of the verb "to be" (*are, is*) in AAVE expressions such as *You crazy* or *She workin now*. It may be more accurate to say that wherever *are* and *is* can be contracted in the casual style of other varieties (*You're crazy, She's working*), they are not articulated in AAVE. Formal styles of Standard English require *are* and *is* in such expressions, but many regional varieties do not. Nor do many other languages such as Arabic and Russian require forms of "to be" in similar contexts. This aspect of the structure of AAVE speech can't be "sloppy" any more than it would be "sloppy" in the everyday talk of Arabic or Russian speakers.

TABLE 19.3 AAVE STRUCTURES

Activity or state	AAVE structures
current (= now)	*he busy*
	he playin ball
recurring or habitual (= usually)	*he **be** busy*
	*he **be** playin ball*
started or happened earlier (= from the past)	*he **bin** busy*
	*he **bin** playin ball*

While AAVE speakers don't include the auxiliary verb *is* in structures such as *She workin now*, to describe what is happening currently, they can use *be* (not *is*), as in *She be workin downtown now*, as a way of expressing habitual action, as shown in Table 19.3. That is, the presence or absence of *be* distinguishes between what is a recurring activity or state and what is currently happening. To talk about a habitual action that started or happened in the past, AAVE uses *bin* (typically stressed), not *was*, as in *She bin workin there*. In effect, the use of habitual *be* or *bin*, and the absence of forms of "to be" in present state expressions, are all consistent features in the grammar of AAVE. The negative versions of these verbs are formed with *don't* (not *doesn't*) and the verb is not used with a contracted negative. So, in AAVE, *She don't be workin* is grammatical, whereas **She doesn't be workin* and **She ben't workin* would be considered ungrammatical.

In this discussion, we have focused on the linguistic features of social dialects of different groups. Yet those groups are not only distinguished by the basic language they use, but by more general factors such as beliefs and assumptions about the world and their experience of it. This is usually discussed in terms of "culture," the subject of Chapter 20.

Study Questions

1   How would you define a "speech community"?

2   What kind of variable is class in the study of language and society?

3   Why did Labov try to elicit answers with the expression *fourth floor*?

4   Which of these expressions has the most instances of postvocalic /r/: *armed robbery* or *birth order* or *race car driver* or *red underwear*?

5   In Trudgill's study of Reading speech, which group produced the fewest instances of postvocalic /r/?

6   In what way can the pronunciation of *-ing* be a social marker?

7   Among which social group is hypercorrection more likely when more attention is paid to speech?

8   What is meant by "divergence" in analyzing speech style?

9   What kind of motivation has been identified for the existence of covert prestige in particular uses of language?

10   What is the difference between jargon and slang?

11   What is meant by a "register"?

12   In AAVE, what is communicated by *be* in *He don't be smokin now*?

Tasks

A   How does "micro-sociolinguistics" differ from "macro-sociolinguistics"?

B   In the study of social dialects, what is "the observer's paradox" and how can it be overcome?

C   What is the difference between style-shifting and code-switching?

D   What is the origin of the term "Ebonics" and how has its meaning changed?

E   Variation in language use according to social status is evident in those languages that have a system of honorifics. What are honorifics and in which languages are they most commonly used?

Using what you discover about honorifics, try to decide which speaker (A or B, C or D) in these two dialogues has superior status within the business organization in which they both work (from Shibatani, 2001: 556).

(1) A: *Konban*   *nomi*   *ni*   *ikoo*   *ka*
         tonight   drink   to   go   question
     B: *Ee,*   *iki-masyoo*
         yes,   go-honorific

(2) C: *Konban*   *nomi*   *ni*   *iki-masyoo*   *ka*
         tonight   drink   to   go-honorific   question
     D: *Un,*   *ikoo*
         yes,   let's go

F The information in Table 19.4, adapted from Cheshire (2007: 164), represents the distribution of some expressions called general extenders in the speech of teenagers (fourteen to fifteen years old) in three different English towns. Examples of general extenders are in the left column of the table and illustrated in these sentences:

> *I like watching sport <u>and stuff.</u>*
> *I cook occasionally on weekends <u>and things.</u>*
> *I think they must've broken up <u>or something.</u>*

The numbers in the table represent how often each form is used (per 10,000 words) by middle-class and working-class groups of teenagers in each town.

TABLE 19.4 SOCIOLINGUISTIC DISTRIBUTION OF GENERAL EXTENDERS

	Reading		Milton Keynes		Hull	
	Middle class	Working class	Middle class	Working class	Middle class	Working class
and that	4	49	9	44	10	66
and all that	4	14	2	4	1	4
and stuff	36	6	45	5	62	18
and things	32	0	35	0	12	5
and everything	21	16	22	18	30	31
or something	72	20	30	17	23	9

(J. Cheshire © 2007, John Wiley and Sons)

(i)   What are the three most common general extenders used by these teenagers overall?

(ii)   Which social class uses the most general extenders?

(iii) Which of the adjunctive general extenders (those beginning with *and*) is most typical of middle-class speech and which one is most typical of working-class speech?

(iv)   In which town is this class difference in speech most noticeable?

(v)   What are the three most common general extenders in use where you live?

G There is a feature of social interaction among friends in Australian English that is based on a concept called "mateship." Can you describe the basis of mateship and use it to explain the way in which the friends in the following interaction talk to each other?

Immediately prior to this interaction, Michael and Stacey have been running and Angie has just encouraged Stacey to run faster. Michael then speaks to Angie (as described in Sinkeviciute, 2014: 129).

MICHAEL:	*hey if you* were *a singer you'd be called Chubby Checker [hahaha] fat boy not so slim [hahaha]*
STACEY:	*[hahaha]*
ANGIE:	*I'm not fat and I'm not a boy so I don't understand what's happening* [Stacey pokes Angie's stomach]
MICHAEL:	*you're not slim either [hehehe]*
ANGIE:	*no but I* am *actually [ha]*
MICHAEL:	*are ya?*
ANGIE:	*yeah*
MICHAEL:	*ok*
ANGIE:	[smiling voice] *let's compare beer guts hey*
MICHAEL:	*settle down sweetheart we all know what it looks like*
ANGIE:	[smiles] [runs after Michael] *oh you little chubby red-haired man*
ANGIE AND MICHAEL:	[laugh]

H According to Fought (2003), Chicano English is spoken in the south-western region of the USA by individuals of Mexican American heritage. Read these statements about Chicano English and try to decide whether you agree or disagree with them.

(1)   Chicano English is a dialect of American English.

(2)   Chicano English is another term for "Spanglish."

(3)   Chicano English is simply ungrammatical or "broken" English, as exemplified by sentences such as *Everybody knew the Cowboys was gonna win again* and *She don't know Brenda.*

(4)   Chicano English is the second language learner's English of people from countries where Spanish is spoken.

(5)   There are no native speakers of Chicano English.

Discussion Topics/Projects

I According to Brown, Attardo and Vigliotti (2014):

If children move to an area before the age of nine, they are able to "pick up" the local dialect, which their parents do not.
Do you think this statement is true of both regional dialect and social dialect? When and how do you think people develop their social dialects?

(For background reading, see Brown, Attardo and Vigliotti, 2014.)

II From a linguistic point of view, there are no good or bad varieties of a language. However, there is a social process called "language subordination" whereby some varieties are treated as having less value than others. Can you describe how this process works in any social situation you are familiar with?

(For background reading, see Lippi-Green, 2011.)

Further Reading

Basic Treatments

Edwards, J. (2013) *Sociolinguistics: A Very Short Introduction* Oxford University Press
Spolsky, B. (1998) *Sociolinguistics* Oxford University Press

More Detailed Treatments

Holmes, J. and N. Wilson (2017) *An Introduction to Sociolinguistics* (5th edition) Pearson
Meyerhoff, M. (2018) *Introducing Sociolinguistics* (3rd edition) Routledge
Romaine, S. (2000) *Language in Society* (2nd edition) Oxford University Press

Labov's work

Gordon, M. (2013) *Labov: A Guide for the Perplexed* Bloomsbury

Speech Accommodation

Giles, H. (ed.) (2016) *Communication Accommodation Theory* Cambridge University Press

Social Markers

Kerswill, P. (2018) "Language and social class" In J. Culpeper, P. Kerswill, R. Wodak, T. McEnery and F. Katamba (eds.) *English Language* (2nd edition) (chapter 18) Palgrave Macmillan

Register

Biber, D. and S. Conrad (2009) *Register, Genre and Style* Cambridge University Press

Slang

Eble, C. (2004) "Slang" In E. Finegan and J. Rickford (eds.) *Language in the USA* (375–386) Cambridge University Press

African American English

Green, L. (2002) *African American English* Cambridge University Press

Green, L. (2011) *Language and the African American Child* Cambridge University Press

Smitherman, G. (2000) *Talkin that Talk* Routledge

Other References

Brown, S., S. Attardo and C. Vigliotti (2014) *Understanding Language Structure, Interaction and Variation* (3rd edition) University of Michigan Press

Cheshire, J. (2007) "Discourse variation, grammaticalisation and stuff like that" *Journal of Sociolinguistics* 11: 155–193

Eckert, P. (2000) *Linguistic Variation as Social Practice* Blackwell

Fought, C. (2003) *Chicano English in Context* Palgrave Macmillan

Labov, W. (2006) *The Social Stratification of English in New York City* (2nd edition) Cambridge University Press

Lippi-Green, R. (2011) *English with an Accent* (2nd edition) Routledge

Mohr, M. (2013) *Holy Shit: A Brief History of Swearing* Oxford University Press

Mugglestone, L. (1995) *Talking Proper: The Rise of Accent as Social Symbol* Clarendon Press

Shibatani, M. (2001) "Honorifics" In R. Mesthrie (ed.) *Concise Encyclopedia of Sociolinguistics* (552–559) Elsevier

Sinceviciute, V. (2014) "'When a joke's a joke and when it's too much': mateship as a key to interpreting jocular FTAs in Australian English" *Journal of Pragmatics* 60: 121–139

Trudgill, P. (1974) *The Social Differentiation of English in Norwich* Cambridge University Press

Widawski, M. (2015) *African American Slang* Cambridge University Press

20 Language and Culture

The future in Aymara is what has not been seen. We cannot see the future. In Aymara, the future is behind you. You cannot see it. In English, the future is ahead of you. You can look into it.

Miracle and Yapita Moya (1981)

The type of sociolinguistic variation described in Chapter 19 is sometimes attributed to cultural differences. It is not unusual to find aspects of language identified as characteristic features of African American culture or European culture or Japanese culture. This approach to the study of language originates in the work of anthropologists who have used language as a source of information in the general study of "culture."

Of special interest in the study of language and culture is the revelation of quite different ways of viewing the world. For speakers of Aymara (in Bolivia and Peru, South America), there is a two-part division of time into what we know (the past + the present) and what we don't yet know (the future). The English word *tomorrow*, something we can look <u>forward</u> to, is translated into Aymara as "a day <u>behind</u> one's back." This is such a stunning difference in worldview that it can only make us wonder how many other things we've been assuming are obvious and universal when they may be simply the expression of the perspective of one group of people. In this chapter, we'll try to expand that perspective and work toward a better understanding of how other people see things.

Culture

We use the term **culture** to refer to all the ideas and assumptions about the nature of things and people that we learn when we become members of social groups. It can be defined as "socially acquired knowledge." This is the kind of knowledge that, like our first language, we initially acquire without conscious awareness. We develop awareness of our knowledge, and hence of our culture, only after having developed language. The first language we learn through cultural transmission provides us initially with a ready-made system of categorizing the world around us.

With the words we acquire, we learn to recognize the types of category distinctions that are relevant in our social world. Young children may not initially think of "dog" and "horse" as different types of entities and refer to both as *bow-wow*. As they develop a more elaborated conceptual system along with English as their first language, they learn to categorize distinct types of creatures as *a dog* or *a horse*. In native cultures of the Pacific, there were no horses and, not surprisingly, there were no words for them. In order to use words such as *dog* or *horse, snow* or *snowflake, father* or *uncle, week* or *weekend*, we must have a conceptual system that includes these people, things and ideas as distinct and identifiable categories.

Categories

Although there is a lot of variation among all the individual "dogs" in our experience, we can use the word *dog* to talk about any one of them as a member of the category. A **category** is a group with certain features in common and we can think of the vocabulary we learn as a set of category labels. These are the words for referring to concepts that people in our social world have typically needed to talk about.

It is tempting to believe that there is a fixed relationship between the set of words we have learned (our categories) and the way external reality is organized. However, evidence from the world's languages would suggest that the organization of external reality actually varies to some extent according to the language being used to talk about it. Some languages may have lots of expressions for types of "rain" or kinds of "coconut" and other languages may have only one or two. Although the Dani of New Guinea can see all colors of the spectrum, they only use names for two of them, equivalents of "black" and "white." The Inuit of Greenland have names for those two, plus red, green and yellow. English has those five colors, plus blue, brown, purple, pink, orange and gray. It seems that languages used by groups with more technology have more color terms. Observing this difference in basic color terms in languages, we can say that there are conceptual distinctions that are **lexicalized** ("expressed as a single word") in one language and not in another.

Kinship Terms

Some of the clearest examples of lexicalized categories are words used to refer to people who are members of the same family, or **kinship terms**. All languages have kinship terms (e.g. *brother, mother, grandmother*), but they don't all put family members into categories in the same way. In some languages, the equivalent of the word *father* is used not only for "male parent," but also for "male parent's brother." In English, we use the word *uncle* for this other type of individual. We have lexicalized the distinction between the two concepts. Yet we also use the same word (*uncle*) for "female parent's brother." That distinction isn't lexicalized in English, but it is in other languages. In Watam (spoken in Papua New Guinea), the English word *uncle* would be translated as either *aes* (father's brother) or *akwae* (mother's brother). Speakers of Mopan Maya (in Belize, Central America) lexicalize a distinction based on a different conceptual arrangement. Each of the following words (from Danziger, 2001) is, and is not, a translation of the English word *uncle* .

> *suku'un*:   older brother and parent's younger brother
> *tataa'*:   parent's older brother and grandfather

A distinction in age among "uncles" is clearly important in Mopan Mayan culture. Other distinctions among relatives can also be lexicalized differently in the world's languages. In Norwegian, the distinction between "male parent's mother" (*farmor*) and "female parent's mother" (*mormor*) is lexicalized, but in English the word *grandmother* is generally used for both. (See Task D, page 323, and Task I, page 326, for more examples.)

Time Concepts

To take a more abstract example, when we learn a word such as *week* or *weekend*, we are inheriting a conceptual system that operates with amounts of time as common categories. Having words for units of time such as "two days" or "seven days" shows that we can think of time (i.e. something abstract, with no physical existence) in amounts, using noun phrases, in the same way as "two people" or "seven books" (i.e. something physical). In another worldview, time may not be treated in this way. In the Hopi language, spoken in Arizona, there were traditionally no terms equivalent to most of our time words and phrases (*two hours, thirty minutes*) because our terms express concepts from a culture operating on "clock time." Perhaps for a similar reason there was no term for a unit of seven days. There was no "week," nor was there a term for "Saturday and Sunday" combined as a unit of time. There really was no "weekend."

Linguistic Relativity

In these examples, we have treated differences in language use as evidence of different ways of talking about external reality. This is often discussed in terms of **linguistic relativity** because it seems that the structure of our language, with its predetermined categories, must have an influence on how we perceive the world. In its weak version, this idea simply captures the fact that we not only talk, but to a certain extent probably also think about the world of experience, using the categories provided by our language. Our first language seems to have a definite role in shaping "habitual thought," that is, the way we think about things as we go about our daily lives, without analyzing how we are thinking.

There is a stronger version of this idea, called **linguistic determinism**, which holds that "language determines thought." If language does indeed determine thought, then we will only be able to think in the categories provided by our language. For example, English speakers use one word for "snow," and generally see all that white stuff as one thing. In contrast, Eskimos look out at all the white stuff and see it as many different things because they have lots of different words for "snow." So, the category system inherent in the language determines how the speaker interprets and articulates experience. We will return to the topic of "snow," but the proposal just described provides an example of an approach to analyzing the connection between language and culture that dates back to the eighteenth century.

The Sapir–Whorf Hypothesis

The general analytic perspective we are considering is part of what became known as the **Sapir–Whorf hypothesis** during the middle of the twentieth century. At a time when American linguistics had closer ties to anthropology, Edward Sapir and Benjamin Whorf produced arguments that the languages of Native Americans, such as the Hopi, led them to view the world differently from those who spoke European languages. We have already noted a difference between Hopi and English in the treatment of time. According to Whorf, the Hopi perceive the world differently from other tribes (including the English-speaking tribe) because their language leads them to do so. In the grammar of Hopi, there is a distinction between "animate" and "inanimate," and among the set of entities categorized as "animate" are clouds and stones. Whorf claimed that the Hopi believe that clouds and stones are living entities and that it is their language that leads them to believe this. English does not mark in its grammar that clouds and stones are "animate," so English speakers do not see the world in the same way as the Hopi. In Whorf's words, "We dissect nature along lines laid down by our native languages" (see Carroll, Levinson and Lee, 2012).

Against the Sapir–Whorf Hypothesis

It is important to remember that Edward Sapir and Benjamin Whorf did not actually write a book or even an article together advocating the hypothesis that bears their names. There is also some doubt that the theoretical point of view attributed to them was as deterministic as others have argued. Nevertheless, a number of arguments have been presented against the linguistic thinking that was involved. Following Sampson (1980), let us imagine a tribe with a language in which sex differences are marked grammatically, so that the terms used for females, such as *girl* and *woman*, have special markings in the language. On close inspection, we find that these "feminine" markings are also used with the words for *stone* and *door*. Are we forced to conclude that this tribe believes that stones and doors are female entities in the same way as girls and women? This tribe is not an obscure group. They use the expressions *la femme* ("the woman"), *la pierre* ("the stone") and *la porte* ("the door"). It is the tribe that lives in France. Should we conclude that French speakers believe that stones and doors are "female" in the same way as women?

The problem with the conclusions invited in both the Hopi and French cases is that linguistic classification ("animate," "feminine") and biological classification ("living," "female") are being confused. There is frequently a correspondence in languages between these classifications, but there does not have to be. Moreover, the linguistic forms do not force us to ignore biological distinctions. While the Hopi language has a linguistic classification for the word *stone*, it does not mean that Hopi truck drivers worry about killing living creatures if they drive over some stones.

Snow

Returning to "snow" in cold places, we should first replace "Eskimo" with more accurate terms for the people, Inuit, and their language, Inuktitut. According to Martin (1986), the Inuit of West Greenland have only two basic words for "snow" (*qanik*, "snow in the air," and *aput*, "snow on the ground"). So, from one point of view, we could say that in this language there are really only two words for snow. However, in the same way as speakers of other languages, the Inuit are able to create, from these two basic elements, a large number of common expressions for different snow-related phenomena. Thus it may be more accurate to say they have lots of phrases, rather than words, for referring to snow. Yet, there seems to be no compelling reason to suppose that those expressions are controlling vision or thought among their users. Some expressions will occur frequently in the context of habitual experiences, but it is the human who is thinking about the experience and determining what will be expressed, not the language.

Non-lexicalized Categories

English does lexicalize some conceptual distinctions in the area of "snow," with *sleet, slush* and *snowflake* as examples. We might also include *avalanche* and *blizzard*. However, English speakers can also create phrases and other complex expressions, by manipulating their language, to refer to *fresh snow, powdery snow, spring snow* or *the dirty stuff that is piled up on the side of the street after the snow-plow has gone through*. These may be categories of snow for English speakers, but they are **non-lexicalized** ("not expressed as a single word"). English speakers can express category variation by making a distinction using lexicalized categories (*It's more like <u>slush</u> than <u>snow</u> outside*) and also by indicating special reference using non-lexicalized distinctions (*We decorated the windows with some <u>fake plastic snow stuff</u>*), but most of them will have a very different view of "snow" from the average speaker of Inuktitut.

We inherit a language used to report knowledge, so we would expect that language to influence the organization of our knowledge in some way. However, we also inherit the ability to manipulate and be creative with that language in order to express our perceptions. When the Hopi borrowed the word *santi* ("Sunday") from English-speaking missionaries, they used it to refer to the period beginning with one *santi* and ending with the next *santi*, essentially developing their own concept of our "week." If thinking and perception were totally determined by language, then the concept of language change would be impossible. If a young Hopi girl had no word in her language for the object known to us as a *computer*, would she fail to perceive the object? Would she be unable to think about it? What the Hopi girl can do when she encounters a new entity is change her language to accommodate the need to refer to the new entity. The human manipulates the language, not the other way round.

Cognitive Categories

As a way of analyzing cognition, or how people think, we can look at language structure for clues, not for causes. The fact that Hopi speakers inherit a language system in which clouds have "animate" as a feature may tell us something about a traditional belief system, or way of thinking, that is part of their culture and not ours. In the Yagua language, spoken in Peru, the set of entities with "animate" as a feature includes the moon, rocks and pineapples, as well as people. In the traditions of the Yagua, all these entities are treated as valued objects, so that their cultural interpretation of the feature "animate" may be closer to the concept "having special importance in life" rather than the concept "having life," as in the cultural interpretation of most English speakers.

Classifiers

We know about the classification of words in languages like Yagua because of grammatical markers called **classifiers** that indicate the type or "class" of noun involved. For example, in Swahili (spoken in East Africa), different prefixes are used as classifiers on nouns for humans (_wa-_), non-humans (_mi-_) and artifacts (_vi-_), as in <u>wa</u>toto ("children"), <u>mi</u>mea ("plants") and <u>vi</u>su ("knives"). So, a conceptual distinction exists between raw materials (<u>mi</u>ti, "trees") and artifacts made from them (<u>vi</u>ti, "chairs") based on the classifiers used. (See Task C, page 323, for more examples of classifiers.)

Classifiers are often used in connection with numbers to indicate the type of thing being counted. In the following Japanese examples, the classifiers are associated with objects conceptualized in terms of their shape as "long thin things" (_hon_), "flat thin things" (_mai_) or "small round things" (_ko_).

> _banana nihon_ ("two bananas")
> _syatu nimai_ ("two shirts")
> _ringo niko_ ("two apples")

The closest English comes to using classifiers is when we talk about a "unit of" certain types of things. There is a distinction in English between things treated as **countable** (_shirt, word, chair_) and those treated as **non-countable** (_clothing, information, furniture_). It is ungrammatical in English to use _a/an_ or the plural with non-countable nouns (i.e. *_a clothing_, *_an information_, *_two furnitures_). To avoid these forms, we use classifier-type expressions such as "item of" or "piece of," as in _an item of clothing_ and _two pieces of furniture_. The equivalent nouns in many other languages are treated as "countable," so the existence of a grammatical class of "non-countable entities" is evidence of a type of cognitive categorization underlying the expression of quantity in English. (See Task E, page 323, for more examples.)

Social Categories

Words such as _uncle_ or _grandmother_, discussed earlier, provide examples of **social categories**. These are categories of social organization that we can use to say how we are connected to others. We can provide technical definitions (e.g. "male parent's brother"), but in many situations a word such as _uncle_ is used for many people, including close friends, who are not covered by the technical definition. The word _brother_ is similarly used among many groups for someone who is not a family member. We can use these words as a means of social categorization, that is, marking individuals as members of a group defined by social connections.

Address Terms

When a man on the street asks another, *Brother, can you spare a dollar?*, the word *brother* is being used as an **address term** (a word or phrase for the person being talked or written to). By claiming the kind of closeness in relationship associated with a family member, the speaker's choice of address term is an attempt to create solidarity (i.e. being the same in social status), perhaps leading to a willingness to hand over some cash. He could have begun his request with *"Sir"* instead, indicating an unequal relationship of power (i.e. being different in social status) and, since he is the one who is clearly higher in status, perhaps *Sir* will hand over some cash.

More typically, an interaction based on an unequal relationship will feature address terms using a title (*Doctor*) or title plus last name (*Professor Buckingham*) for the one with higher status, and first name only for the one with lower status, as in: *Professor Buckingham, can I ask a question? ~ Yes, Jennifer, what is it?* More equal relationships have address terms that indicate similar status of the participants, such as first names or nicknames: *Bucky, ready for some more coffee? ~ Thanks, Jen.*

In many languages, there is a choice between pronouns used for addressees who are socially close versus distant. This is known as the **T/V distinction**, as in the French pronouns *tu* (close) and *vous* (distant). A similar type of social categorization is found in German (*du/ Sie*) and Spanish (*tú/usted*). In each of these distinctions, as in older English usage (*thou/you*), the plural form is used to indicate that the speakers do not really have a close relationship. Traditionally, these forms could be used to mark a power relationship. Lower-status individuals had to use the *vous* forms when addressing those of higher status. This usage is described as non-reciprocal, but the reciprocal use (both speakers using the same form) of the *tu* forms has generally increased in Europe among younger speakers, such as students, who may not know each other really well, but who find themselves in the same situation.

In English, people without special titles are addressed as *Mr., Mrs., Miss* or *Ms.* Only the women's address terms include information about their social status. In fact, one address term for a woman indicates that she is the wife of a particular man as in *Mrs. Dexter Smith* (or just *Mrs. Smith*). Dexter is never addressed as *Mr. (Betsy) Cuddlesworth*. When the original system was put in place, women were identified socially through their relationship to a man, either as wife or daughter. These address terms continue to function as social category labels, identifying women, but not men, as married or not. A woman using *Ms.* as part of her address term is indicating that her social categorization is not based on her marital status.

Gender

The observation that address terms for men and women are different leads us to a consideration of the most fundamental difference in social categorization, the one based on "gender." We have already noted the difference between two uses of the word **gender** in Chapter 7. Biological (or "natural") gender is the distinction in sex between the "male" and "female" of each species. Grammatical gender is the distinction between "masculine" and "feminine," which is used to classify nouns in languages such as Spanish (*el sol, la luna*). A third use is for **social gender**, which is the distinction we make when we use words like "man" and "woman" to classify individuals in terms of their social roles. Although the biological distinction ("male, female") underlies the social distinctions ("father, mother"), there is a great deal about the social roles of individuals as men or women that is unrelated to biology. It is in the sense of social gender, through the process of learning how to become a "boy" or a "girl," that we inherit a gendered culture. This process can be as simple as learning which category should wear pink versus blue, or as complex as understanding how one category was excluded (by having no vote) from the process of representative government for such a long time. Becoming a social gender also involves becoming familiar with gendered language use.

Gendered Words

In Sidamo, spoken in Ethiopia, there are some words used only by men and some used only by women, so that the translation of "milk" would be *ado* by a man, but *gurda* by a woman. In Japanese, when referring to themselves ("I"), men have traditionally used *boku* and women *watashi* or *atashi*. In Portuguese, saying "thank you" is *obrigado* if you're a man and *obrigada* if you're a woman.

These examples simply illustrate that there can be differences between the words used by men and women in a variety of languages. Many terms for referring to people, such as *chairperson* and *police officer*, have become gender neutral in contemporary English. Other terms, however, are still used with a gender bias, as in *career woman* or *working mother* (rarely "career man" or "working father").

A significant change in the direction of more "gender-neutral" language is the greater acceptance of **singular *they*** (and *their, them*) with singular antecedents that are unspecified for sex, as in *No one should be defined by the place where they are born, Each student is required to buy their own dictionary* or *One of my neighbors asked me to help them*. A singular version of the reflexive pronoun *(themself)* has also been reported to be more common, as in *You won't be the first or last man or woman who gets themself involved in a holiday romance*, cited in Mair (2006: 154).

Gendered Structures

When we reviewed social variation (Chapter 19), noting the differences between working-class and middle-class speech, we largely ignored gender differences. Yet, within each social class, there is substantial variation according to gender. Generally speaking, whenever there is a higher- versus lower-prestige variable (e.g. *talking/talkin'* or *I saw it/I seen it*), women are more likely to use the higher-prestige forms. The difference is most noticeable among middle-class speakers. In one study of double negatives (e.g. *I don't want none*) in lower-middle-class speech, substantially more men (32%) than women (1%) used the structure. This regular pattern of difference is sometimes explained in terms of women's socialization to be more aware of social status and to be more sensitive to how others may judge them. An alternative explanation appeals to the socialization of men to be strong, tough and independent. Forms which are non-standard or associated with working-class speech may be preferred by men because of their association with manual work, strength and toughness. And tough guys also have deep voices.

Gendered Speech

In general, men have longer vocal tracts, larger larynxes and thicker vocal folds than women. The result is that men speak in a lower pitch range (80–200 Herz) than women (120–400 Herz). The term **pitch** is used to describe the effect of vibration in the vocal folds, with slower vibration making voices sound lower and rapid vibration making voices sound higher. Although "normal speaking" takes place with substantial overlap in the pitch ranges of men and women, there may be a tendency to exaggerate the differences to sound more "like a man" or more "like a woman."

Among many women speaking American English, there is also generally more pitch movement, that is, more rising and falling intonation. The use of rising intonation (↑) at the end of statements (*It happened near San Diego ↑, in southern California ↑*), the more frequent use of hedges (*sort of, kind of*) and tag questions (*It's kind of cold in here, isn't it?*) have all been identified as characteristic of women's speech. **Tag questions** are short questions consisting of an auxiliary (*don't, isn't*) and a pronoun (*it, you*), added to the end of a statement (*I hate it when it rains all day, don't you?*). They are used more often by women when expressing opinions. These features of women's speech all seem to be ways of inviting agreement with an idea rather than asserting it. Men tend to use more assertive forms and "strong" language (*It's too damn cold in here!*). Other research has found that women, in same-gender groups, use more indirect speech acts (*Could I see that photo?*) rather than the direct speech acts (*Gimme that photo*) heard more often from men in same-gender groups.

Same-Gender Talk

It is important to pay attention to the concept of "same-gender" talk because much of our socialization takes place in such groups. By the time we are three years old, we have established a preference for talking to same-gender others. Throughout childhood, boys socialize in larger groups, often in competitive activities, establishing and maintaining hierarchical relationships (*I'm Spiderman and you have to follow me*). Girls socialize in smaller groups, more often in co-operative activities, establishing reciprocal relationships and exchanging roles *(You can be the doctor now and I'll be ill)*. In many societies, this pattern of same-gender socialization is reinforced through separate educational experiences and different social practices.

Gendered Interaction

Many of the features identified in women's speech seem to facilitate the exchange of turns by allowing others to speak, so that interaction becomes a shared activity. Interaction among men appears to be organized in a more hierarchical way, with "having the floor" being treated as the goal. Men generally take longer turns and, in many social contexts (e.g. religious events), are the only ones allowed to talk.

One effect of these different styles is that certain features become very salient in cross-gender interactions. For example, in same-gender discussions, there is little difference in the number of times speakers interrupt each other. However, in cross-gender interactions, men are much more likely to interrupt women. In same-gender conversations, women produce more back-channels as indicators of listening and paying attention. The term **back-channels** describes the use of words (*yeah, really?*) or sounds (*hmm, oh*) by listeners while someone else is speaking. Men not only produce fewer back-channels, but appear to treat them, when produced by others, as indications of agreement. In cross-gender interaction, the absence of back-channels from men tends to make women think the men are not paying attention to them. The more frequent production of back-channels by women may lead some men to think that the women are agreeing with what they are saying.

The differences we have documented in gendered speech may turn out to be more accurate of an older generation and less marked among younger speakers. There is accumulating evidence that in contemporary society men and women have greater opportunities to construct their own social identities rather than accept traditional roles and are less likely to conform to previous gender stereotypes. This type of social change will be reflected in language change and lead to a better understanding of the idea, noted by Cameron (2007: 152), that "speaking like a woman, or a man, is not just the automatic consequence of being one."

Study Questions

1   What is one common definition of "culture" in the study of language?

2   How many names for colors are used by the Inuit of Greenland? Is one of them "blue"?

3   What are kinship terms?

4   How do Norwegian and English differ in terms for "parent's mother"?

5   What is meant by "linguistic determinism"?

6   How many basic terms for snow are found in Inuktitut?

7   What kind of categorization is involved in the English distinction between *sleet* and *slush*: lexicalized or non-lexicalized or non-referential or social?

8   Why is this sentence ungrammatical?

    She gave me a good advice.

9   Traditionally, do you think the following sentence was more likely to be spoken by a woman or a man, and why?

    I think that golf on television is kind of boring, don't you?

10 In the Australian language Dyirbal, there are grammatical markers that distinguish different cognitive categories represented by X and Y here.

    X: "men, kangaroos, boomerangs"
    Y: "women, fire, dangerous things"

    (i)   If you learn that in Dyirbal, "the sun is the wife of the moon," in which category would you place "sun" and "moon"?
    (ii) What is the technical term for grammatical markers of this type?

11 What is the T/V distinction?

12 What is reciprocal pronoun use?

Tasks

A   What is the difference between "cross-cultural," "intercultural" and "multicultural" communication?

B We noted some differences across languages in the number of words used to describe colors. What is the "basic color term hierarchy"?

C When a number is used with a noun in Ponapean (a language spoken in the western Pacific), an appropriate classifier is also used, as described in Lynch (1998). Some classifiers used as suffixes are -*men* ("animate things"), -*pwoat* ("long things"), -*mwut* ("heaps of things"), -*sop* ("stalks of things") and -*dip* ("slices of things"). Examples of numerals are *sili-* ("three") and *pah-* ("four"). Can you complete these noun phrases with appropriate endings?

Example: *pwutak reirei silimen* ("three tall boys")

(1) *sehu* _____ ("four stalks of sugarcane")
(2) *dipen mei* _____ ("four slices of breadfruit")
(3) *mwutin dippw* _____ ("four piles of grass")
(4) *nahi pwihk* _____ ("my three pigs")
(5) *tuhke* _____ ("a tree")

D According to Foley (1997), kinship terminology in Watam (a language spoken in Papua New Guinea) is rather different from English. The word *aes* is used for both father and father's brother, while *aem* is used for both mother and mother's sister. The words *akwae* and *namkwae* are used for mother's brother and father's sister respectively.

(i) Using this information, can you complete the following comparative chart?
(ii) What would be the problems involved in translating the English words *aunt* and *uncle* into Watam?
(iii) How do English speakers make a distinction when they're talking about their father's brother versus their mother's brother or their father's sister versus their mother's sister?

English	Kinship category	Watam
Mother	female parent	_____
_____	female parent's sister	_____
_____	male parent's sister	_____
_____	male parent	_____
_____	male parent's brother	_____
_____	female parent's brother	_____

E We briefly considered a distinction that English makes between "countable" and "non-countable."

(i) Can you assign the following words to three sets, labeled "countable," "non-countable" and "both countable and non-countable"?

(ii) Which phrases referring to a "unit of" are typically used with the non-countable nouns (e.g. *a round of applause*)?

applause, business, cash, chocolate, courage, crash, equipment, hair, lesson, luck, mistake, mountain, noise, paper, party, rain, research, rubbish, salmon, sand, shopping, tennis, theft, underwear

F Which forms do you think were used in these sentences?

(1) *If Mary or Robert asked me, I would certainly help _____.*

(2) *Everyone wants _____ child to be healthy and able to take care of _____.*

(3) *One of the professors usually promises that _____ will be available in the summer.*

(4) *Someone left a message for you, but _____ didn't leave _____ name.*

(5) *A friend of my parents claimed that _____ had met Mick Jagger.*

(6) *The person who leaves _____ car unlocked has only _____ to blame if it's stolen.*

G Many languages contain "evidentials," which are markers that indicate how sure the speaker is about the truth or reliability of the information being communicated. Some of these evidential markers can be found in the following examples from Quechua, a language spoken in Peru and other countries in the Andes region of South America (adapted from Weber, 1986).

(i) Can you identify the three evidential markers being used in the following examples?

(ii) What do you think are the three levels of reliability being expressed here?

(1) *Ima-shi   kaykan   chaychaw   rikaykamunki*
what   there is   there   go see
"Go and see what's there"

(2) *Chay-ta   musya-yka-chi*
that   know   I
"I don't know anything about that"

(3) *Qam-pis   maqa-ma-shka-nki-mi*
you also   hit   me past
"I felt you hit me"

(4) *Wañu   -nqa-paq-chi*
die   it future
"Perhaps it will die"

(5)   *Chawra*   *utkupa*   *murullanta-shi tarimun*
    so   cotton   just seed   she found
    "So she found only cotton seed"

(6)   *Wañu*   *-nqa-paq-mi*
    die   it future
    "I'm sure that it will die"

(7)   *Qam-pis*   *maqa-ma-shka-nki-chi*
    you also   hit   me past
    "You may be one of a group of people who hit me"

(8)   *Wañu*   *-nqa-paq-shi*
    die   it future
    "I was told that it will die"

(9)   *Noqa*   *aywa-yka-chi*   *qam-paq-qa*
    I   going I   you-topic
    "You might have thought I was going for you, but I'm not"

(10) *Qam-pis*   *maqa-ma-shka-nki-shi*
    you also   hit   me past
    "Someone has informed me that you hit me [when I was drunk]"

H   One way in which languages encode cultural concepts differently can be found in their number systems. Some of the basic elements of the number system used in the Rotokas language (spoken on the island of Bougainville, part of Papua New Guinea) are presented in Table 20.1, based on Firchow (1987).

TABLE 20.1 ROTOKAS NUMBERS

1 = *katai*	6 = *katai vatara*	20 = *erao tau*
2 = *erao*	7 = *erao vatara*	80 = *vopeva vatara tau*
3 = *vopeva*	8 = *vopeva vatara*	100 = *katai vovota*
4 = *resiura*	9 = *resiura vatara*	200 = *erao vovota*
5 = *vavae*	10 = *katai tau*	1,000 = *katai kuku*

(i)   After looking carefully at the way expressions for numbers are constructed, can you translate this number into English?

erao kuku resiura vatara vovota vopeva tau *erao vatara*

(ii) If you learn that the word *vavae* also means "hand" in Rotokas, can you describe how the basis of this numbering system differs from English? What are the technical terms used to distinguish between these two numbering systems?

I Some kinship terms that developed in English on the basis of Norman French, including the "in-law" element (e.g. *mother-in-law*), are not very transparent in terms of which person is involved in the relationship (i.e. is that the husband's mother or the wife's mother?). In other languages, such as Wolaytta, spoken in southern Ethiopia in East Africa, the people involved in the relationship are clearly indicated. Try to match the English expressions in the list with those used in Wolaytta (from Wakasa, 2014).

mother-in-law   sister-in-law
daughter-in-law   grandmother
brother-in-law   uncle
father-in-law   nephew

aawai ("father") *aayiya* ("mother") *na`ai* ("son")
ishai ("brother") *macciya* ("wife")

aawaa ishai ("<u>uncle</u>")
aawaa aawai ("<u>grandfather</u>")

(1) *macciyo aawai* ("_____")
(2) *ishaa macciya* ("_____")
(3) *ishaa na`ai* ("_____")
(4) *aayiyo ishai* ("_____")
(5) *macciyo ishai* ("_____")
(6) *aayiyo aayiya* ("_____")
(7) *na`aa macciya* ("_____")
(8) *macciyo aayiya* ("_____")

Discussion Topics/Projects

I Why do you think there continue to be frequent references to the idea that "Eskimos have a hundred words for snow"? How would you try to convince someone who thinks this is a fact that it is best treated as a myth?

(For background reading, see chapter 19 of Pullum, 1991.)

II Is there a difference between "interruption" and "overlap" in conversation? What do you think is meant by the distinction between "report talk" and "rapport talk"? Should we distinguish between "fast-talking" and "slow-talking" styles rather than attribute certain features of interaction to men versus women?

(For background reading, see chapter 7 of Tannen, 1990.)

Further Reading

Basic Treatments

Kramsch, C. (1998) *Language and Culture* Oxford University Press

Duranti, A. (2001) *Key Terms in Language and Culture* Blackwell

More Detailed Treatments

Foley, W. (1997) *Anthropological Linguistics: An Introduction* Blackwell

Danesi, M. (2012) *Linguistic Anthropology: A Brief Introduction* Canadian Scholars Press

Culture

Kuper, A. (1999) *Culture: The Anthropologists' Account* Harvard University Press

Piller, I. (2017) *Intercultural Communication* (2nd edition) Edinburgh University Press

Categories

Taylor, J. (2003) *Linguistic Categorization* (3rd edition) Oxford University Press

Color Terms

Deutscher, G. (2010) *Through the Language Glass* Metropolitan Books

Linguistic Relativity

Boroditsky, L. (2003) "Linguistic relativity" In L. Nadel (ed.) *Encyclopedia of Cognitive Science* (917–921) Nature Publishing Group

Leavitt, J. (2011) *Linguistic Relativities* Cambridge University Press

The Sapir–Whorf Hypothesis

Carroll, J., S. Levinson and P. Lee (eds.) (2012) *Language, Thought and Reality: Selected Writings of Benjamin Lee Whorf* (2nd edition) MIT Press

McWhorter, J. (2014) *The Language Hoax* Oxford University Press

Cognitive Categories

Evans, V. (2007) *A Glossary of Cognitive Linguistics* Edinburgh University Press

Ungerer, F. and H-J. Schmid (2006) *An Introduction to Cognitive Linguistics* (2nd edition) (chapter 1) Routledge

Classifiers

Aikhenvald, A. (2000) *Classifiers* Oxford University Press

Social Categories

Mesthrie, R., J. Swann, A. Deumert and W. Leap (2009) *Introducing Sociolinguistics* (2nd edition) John Benjamins

Developing Social Gender

Maccoby, E. (1998) *The Two Sexes* Harvard University Press

Gender and Language

Coates, J. (2004) *Women, Men and Language* (3rd edition) Longman

Eckert, P. and S. McConnell-Ginet (2013) *Language and Gender* (2nd edition) Cambridge University Press

Jule, A. (2008) *A Beginner's Guide to Language and Gender* Multilingual Matters

Talbot, M. (2010) *Language and Gender* (2nd edition) Polity Press

Singular *they*

Bodine, A. (1975) "Androcentrism in prescriptive grammar: singular *they*, sex-indefinite *he*, and *he or she*" *Language in Society* 4: 129–146

Curzan, A. (2003) *Gender Shifts in the History of English* Cambridge University Press

La Scotte, D. (2016) "Singular *they*: an empirical study of generic pronoun use" *American Speech* 91: 62–80

Sources of Examples

(Aymara) Miracle, A. and J. Yapita Moya (1981) "Time and space in Aymara" In M. Hardman (ed.) *The Aymara Language in Its Social and Cultural Context* University Presses of Florida

(Dyirbal) Lakoff, G. (1987) *Women, Fire and Dangerous Things* University of Chicago Press

(Hopi) Malotki, E. (1983) *Hopi Time* Walter de Gruyter

(Inuit) Martin, L. (1986) "Eskimo words for snow: a case study in the genesis and decay of an anthropological example" *American Anthropologist* 88: 418–423

(Japanese) Frawley, W. (1992) *Linguistic Semantics* Lawrence Erlbaum

(Mopan Maya) Danziger, E. (2001) *Relatively Speaking* Oxford University Press

(Ponapean) Lynch, J. (1998) *Pacific Languages* University of Hawai'i Press

(Quechua) Weber, D. (1986) "Information perspective, profile and patterns in Quechua" In W. Chafe and J. Nichols (eds.) *Evidentiality: The Linguistic Coding of Epistemology* (137–155) Ablex

(Rotokas) Firchow, I. (1987) "Form and function of Rotokas words" *Language and Linguistics in Melanesia* 15: 5–111

(Sidamo) Hudson, G. (2000) *Essential Introductory Linguistics* Blackwell

(Swahili) Hinnebusch, T. (1987) "Swahili" In T. Shopen (ed.) *Languages and Their Status* (209–294) University of Pennsylvania Press

(Watam) Foley, W. (1997) *Anthropological Linguistics* Blackwell

(Wolaytta) Wakasa, M. (2014) "A sketch grammar of Wolaytta" *Nilo-Ethiopian Studies* 19: 31–44

Other References

Cameron, D. (2007) *The Myth of Mars and Venus* Oxford University Press

Pullum, G. (1991) *The Great Eskimo Vocabulary Hoax* University of Chicago Press

Sampson, G. (1980) *Schools of Linguistics* Stanford University Press

Tannen, D. (1990) *You Just Don't Understand* William Morrow

Glossary

AAVE: African American Vernacular English

accent: aspects of pronunciation that identify where a speaker is from, in contrast to **dialect**

acoustic phonetics: the study of the physical properties of speech as sound waves

acquisition: the gradual development of ability in a first or second language by using it naturally in communicative situations

acronym: a new word formed from the initial letters of other words (e.g. *NASA*)

active voice: the form of the verb used to say what the **subject** does (e.g. *He stole it*)

address term: a word or phrase for the person being talked or written to

adjacency pair: in conversation, an automatic sequence of a first part from one speaker and a second part from another speaker (*How are you? ~ Fine, thanks.*)

adjective (Adj): a word such as *happy* or *strange* used with a noun to provide more information

adjunct: a part of a sentence, typically an **adverb** or a **prepositional phrase**, that provides additional information about where, when or how

adverb (Adv): a word such as *slowly* or *really* used with a verb or adjective to provide more information

affective factors: emotional reactions such as self-consciousness or negative feelings that may influence learning

affix: a **bound morpheme** such as *un-* or *-ed* added to a word (e.g. *undressed*)

affricate: a **consonant** produced by stopping then releasing the airflow through a narrow opening (e.g. the first and last sounds in *church*)

African American English (AAE): a social dialect used by many African Americans in different regions of the USA

African American Vernacular English (AAVE): the casual speech style used by many African Americans as a **vernacular**

agent: the **semantic role** of the noun phrase identifying the one who performs the action of the verb in an event (*The boy kicked the ball*)

agrammatic speech: the type of speech without grammatical markers, often associated with **Broca's aphasia**

agreement: the grammatical connection between two parts of a sentence, as in the connection between a **subject** (*Cathy*) and the form of a verb (*loves chocolate*)

allomorph: one of a closely related set of **morphs**

allophone: one of a closely related set of speech sounds or **phones**

alphabet (alphabetic writing): a way of writing in which one symbol represents one sound segment

alternate sign language: a system of hand signals used in a specific context where speech cannot be used (by people who can speak), in contrast to a **primary sign language**

alveolar: a **consonant** produced with the front part of the tongue on the **alveolar ridge** (e.g. the first and last sounds in *dot*)

alveolar ridge: the rough bony ridge immediately behind the upper front teeth

Ameslan (or ASL): American Sign Language

analogy: a process of forming a new word that is similar in some way to an existing word

anaphora (anaphoric expressions): use of pronouns (*it*) and noun phrases with *the* (*the* *puppy*) to refer back to something already mentioned

anomia: a language disorder in which it is difficult to find words, often associated with **Wernicke's aphasia**

antecedent: the first mention of someone or something later referred to via **anaphora**

anticipation: a type of **slip of the tongue** in which a sound is used in a word in anticipation of that sound in a following word, as in *a tup of tea* ("cup of tea")

antonymy: the **lexical relation** in which words have opposite meanings (*"Shallow" is an antonym of "deep"*)

aphasia: an impairment of language function due to localized brain damage that leads to difficulty in understanding and/or producing language

applied linguistics: the study of a large range of practical issues involving language in general and **second language learning** in particular

arbitrariness: a property of language describing the fact that there is no natural connection between a linguistic form and its meaning

arcuate fasciculus: a bundle of nerve fibers connecting **Broca's area** and **Wernicke's area** in the left hemisphere of the brain

article (Art): a word such as *a, an* or *the* used with a noun

articulatory parameters: the four key aspects of visual information used in the description of signs (**shape, orientation, location** and **movement**)

articulatory phonetics: the study of how speech sounds are produced

ASL (or Ameslan): American Sign Language

aspiration: a puff of air that sometimes accompanies the pronunciation of a **stop**

assimilation: the process whereby a feature of one sound becomes part of another during speech production

associative meaning: the type of meaning that people might connect with the use of words (e.g. *needle* = "painful") that is not part of **referential meaning**

audiolingual method: a mid-twentieth-century approach to language teaching, with repetitive drills used to develop fluent spoken language as a set of habits

auditory phonetics: the study of the perception of speech sounds by the ear, also called "perceptual phonetics"

auxiliary verb (Aux): a verb such as *will* used with another verb

Aux-movement: in sentence structure, the movement of an **auxiliary verb** to a position before the **subject**, often at the front of the sentence

babbling: the use of syllable sequences (*baba*) and combinations (*ma-ga*) by young children in their first year

back-channels: the use of words (*yeah*) and sounds (*hmm*) by listeners while someone else is speaking

backformation: the process of reducing a word such as a noun to a shorter version and using it as a new word such as a verb (e.g. *babysit* from *babysitter*)

background knowledge: information that is not in a text, but is used from memory by a reader to understand the text

beats: **gestures** involving short quick movements of the hands or fingers that go along with the rhythm of talk

bidialectal: being capable of speaking two **dialects**

bilabial: a **consonant** produced by using both lips (e.g. the first and last sounds in *pub*)

bilingual: a term used to describe a native speaker of two languages or a country with two official languages, in contrast to **monolingual**

bilingualism: the state of having two languages

blending: the process of combining the beginning of one word and the end of another word to form a new word (e.g. *brunch* from *breakfast* and *lunch*)

borrowing: the process of taking words from other languages

bound morpheme: a **morpheme** such as *un-* or *-ed* that cannot stand alone and must be attached to another form (e.g. <u>un</u>dress<u>ed</u>)

bow-wow theory: the idea that early human speech developed from imitations of natural sounds in the environment

broadening: a semantic change in which a word is used with a more general meaning (e.g. *foda* (animal fodder) → *food* (any kind)), in contrast to **narrowing**

Broca's aphasia: a language disorder in which speech production is typically reduced, distorted, slow and missing grammatical markers

Broca's area: a part of the brain in the left hemisphere involved in speech production

calque: a type of **borrowing** in which each element of a word is translated into the borrowing language (e.g. *gratte-ciel* "scrape sky" for *skyscraper*)

caregiver speech: speech addressed to young children by the adult(s) or older children who are looking after them

cataphora: similar to **anaphora**, but reversing the antecedent–anaphora relationship, often beginning with a pronoun and a descriptive noun phrase later

category: a group with certain features in common

characters: forms used in Chinese writing

classifiers: grammatical markers that indicate the type or "class" of a **noun**

clipping: the process of reducing a word of more than one syllable to a shorter form (e.g. *ad* from *advertisement*)

closed syllable: a **syllable** that ends with a **consonant**

coarticulation: the process of making one sound virtually at the same time as the next sound

coda: the part of a syllable after the **vowel**

cognates: words in different languages that have a similar form and meaning (e.g. English *friend* and German *Freund*)

cognitive category: a **category** used in the organization of how we think

coherence: the connections that readers and listeners create in their minds to arrive at a meaningful interpretation of texts

cohesion: the ties and connections between words that exist within texts

cohesive ties: the individual connections between words and phrases in a text

co-hyponyms: words in **hyponymy** that share the same **superordinate** (*"daffodil"* and *"rose"* are co-hyponyms of *"flower"*)

coinage: the invention of new words (e.g. *xerox*)

collocation: a relationship between words that frequently occur together (e.g. *salt and pepper*)

communication strategy: a way of overcoming a gap between communicative intent and a limited ability to express that intent, as part of **strategic competence**

communicative approaches: approaches to language teaching that are based on learning through using language rather than learning about language

communicative competence: the general ability to use language accurately, appropriately and flexibly

communicative signals: behavior used intentionally to provide information

comparative reconstruction: the creation of the original form of an ancestor language on the basis of comparable forms in languages that are descendants

complementary distribution: in phonology, two different pronunciations of a phoneme always used in different places in words

complementizer (C): word such as *that* introducing a **complement phrase**

complement phrase (CP): a structure such as *that Mary helped George* used to complete a construction beginning with a structure such as *Cathy knew*

completion point: in conversation, the end of a **turn**, usually marked by a pause at the end of a phrase or sentence

componential analysis: the identification of **semantic features** [e.g. + human] as components of the meaning of a word

compounding: the process of combining two (or more) words to form a new word (e.g. *waterbed*)

concordance: a listing of each occurrence of a word or phrase in a corpus along with the words surrounding it

conduction aphasia: a language disorder associated with damage to the **arcuate fasciculus** in which repeating words or phrases is difficult

conjunction: a word such as *and* or *because* used to make connections between words, phrases and sentences

consonant: a speech sound produced by restricting the airflow in some way

consonantal alphabet: a way of writing in which each symbol represents a consonant sound

consonant cluster: two or more **consonants** in sequence

constituent analysis: a grammatical analysis of how small constituents (or components) go together to form larger constituents in sentences

context: either the **physical context** or the **linguistic context** (co-text) in which words are used

convergence: adopting a speech style that attempts to reduce social distance by using forms that are similar to those used by the person being talked to, as a type of **speech accommodation**, in contrast to **divergence**

conversation analysis: the study of turntaking in conversation

conversion: the process of changing the function of a word, such as a noun to a verb, as a way of forming new words, also known as "category change" or "functional shift" (e.g. *vacation* in *They're vacationing in Florida*)

cooing: the earliest use of speech-like sounds by an infant in the first few months

Co-operative Principle: an underlying assumption of conversation that you will "make your conversational contribution such as is required, at the stage at which it occurs, by the accepted purpose or direction of the talk exchange in which you are engaged"

corpus linguistics: the study of language in use by analyzing the occurrence and frequency of forms in a large collection of texts typically stored in a computer

co-text: the set of other words used in the same phrase or sentence, also called the **linguistic context**

countable: type of noun that can be used in English with *a/an* and the plural (e.g. *a cup, two cups*), in contrast to **non-countable**

covert prestige: the status of a speech style or feature as having positive value, but which is "hidden" or not valued similarly among the larger community, in contrast to **overt prestige**

creole: a variety of a language that developed from a **pidgin** and is used as a first language by a population of native speakers

creolization: the process of development from a **pidgin** to a **creole**, in contrast to **decreolization**

critical period: the time from birth to puberty during which normal first language acquisition can take place

cultural transmission: the process whereby knowledge of a language is passed from one generation to the next

culture: socially acquired knowledge

cuneiform: a way of writing created by pressing a wedge-shaped implement into soft clay

decreolization: the process whereby a **creole** is used with fewer distinct creole features as it becomes more like a standard variety, in contrast to **creolization**

deep structure: the underlying structure of sentences as represented by **phrase structure rules**

deictics: gestures used to point at things or people

deixis (deictic expressions): using words such as *this* or *here* as a way of "pointing" with language

dental: a **consonant** produced with the tongue tip behind the upper front teeth (e.g. the first sound in *that*)

derivation: the process of forming new words by adding **affixes**

derivational morpheme: a **bound morpheme** such as *-ish* used to make new words or words of a different grammatical category

(e.g. *boyish*), in contrast to an **inflectional morpheme**

descriptive approach: an approach to grammar that is based on a description of the structures actually used in a language, not what should be used, in contrast to the **prescriptive approach**

diachronic variation: differences resulting from change over a period of time, in contrast to **synchronic variation**

dialect: aspects of the grammar, vocabulary and pronunciation of a variety of a language, in contrast to **accent**

dialect boundary: a line representing a set of **isoglosses**, used to separate one dialect area from another

dialect continuum: the gradual merging of one regional variety of a language into another

dialectology: the study of **dialects**

dichotic listening: an experiment in which a listener hears two different sounds simultaneously, each through a different earphone

diglossia: a situation where there is a "high" or special variety of a language used in formal situations (e.g. Classical Arabic), and a "low" variety used locally and informally (e.g. Lebanese Arabic)

digraph: a combination of letters used in writing for a single sound (e.g. "ph" for /f/)

diphthong: a sound combination that begins with a **vowel** and ends with another **vowel** or a **glide** (e.g. *boy*)

direct speech act: an action in which the form used (e.g. interrogative) directly matches the function (e.g. question) performed by a speaker with an utterance, in contrast to an **indirect speech act**

discourse analysis: the study of language beyond the sentence, in text and conversation

displacement: a property of language that allows users to talk about things and events not present in the immediate environment

divergence: adopting a speech style that emphasizes social distance by using forms that are different from those used by the person being talked to, as a form of **speech accommodation**, in contrast to **convergence**

duality: a property of language whereby linguistic forms have two simultaneous levels of sound production and meaning, also called "double articulation"

Early Modern English: the form of English in use between 1500 and 1700

elision: the process of leaving out a sound segment in the pronunciation of a word

emblems: non-verbal signals such as "thumbs up" (= things are good) that function like fixed phrases with conventional interpretations

epenthesis: a sound change involving the addition of a sound to a word (e.g. *timr* → *timber*)

eponym: a word derived from the name of a person or place (e.g. *sandwich*)

etymology: the study of the origin and history of words

exchange: a type of **slip of the tongue** in which sounds in two words are switched, as in *you'll soon beel fetter* ("feel better")

experiencer: the **semantic** role of the noun phrase identifying the entity that has the feeling, perception or state described by the verb (e.g. *The boy feels sad*)

external change: influences from the outside that cause changes in a language, in contrast to **internal change**

face: a person's public self-image as described in the study of **politeness**

face-saving act: saying something that reduces a possible threat to another person's self-image

face-threatening act: saying something that represents a threat to another person's self-image

filled pause: a break in the flow of speech, using sounds such as *em* and *er*

finger-spelling: a system of hand configurations used to represent the letters of the alphabet in **sign language**

fixed reference: a property of a communication system whereby each signal is fixed as relating to one particular object or occasion

flap: a sound produced with the tongue tip briefly touching the **alveolar ridge**

foreigner talk: a way of using a language with non-native speakers that is simpler in structure and vocabulary

fossilization: the process whereby an **interlanguage**, containing many non-**L2** features, stops developing toward more accurate forms of the **L2**

free morpheme: a **morpheme** that can stand by itself as a single word

fricative: a **consonant** produced by almost blocking the airflow (e.g. the first and last sounds in *fourth*)

functional morpheme: a **free morpheme** that is used as a function word, such as a conjunction (*and*) or a preposition (*in*)

gender: a term used in three ways:

(1) a biological distinction between male and female, also called **natural gender**;

(2) a distinction between classes of nouns as masculine, feminine (or neuter), also called **grammatical gender**;

(3) a distinction between the social roles of men and women, also called **social gender**

generative grammar: a set of rules defining the possible sentences in a language

gestures: use of the hands, typically while speaking

glides: sounds produced with the tongue in motion to or from a vowel sound, also called "semi-vowels" or "approximants" (e.g. the first sounds in _wet, yes_)

glossolalia: also known as "speaking in tongues," the production of sounds and syllables in a stream of speech that seems to have no communicative purpose

glottal: a sound produced in the space between the **vocal folds** (e.g. the first sound in _hat_)

glottal stop: a sound produced when the air passing through the **glottis** is stopped completely then released

glottis: the space between the **vocal folds**

goal: the **semantic role** of the noun phrase identifying where an entity moves to (e.g. _The boy walked to the window_)

gradable antonyms: words with opposite meanings along a scale (e.g. _big–small_)

grammar: the analysis of the structure of phrases and sentences

grammar–translation method: the traditional form of language teaching, with vocabulary lists and sets of grammar rules

grammatical competence: the ability to use words and structures accurately as part of **communicative competence**

grammatical gender: a grammatical category designating the class of a noun as masculine or feminine (or neuter), in contrast to other types of **gender**

hedge: a word or phrase used to indicate that you are not really sure that what you are saying is sufficiently correct or complete

holophrastic (utterance): a single form functioning as a phrase or sentence in the early speech of young children

homonyms: two words with the same form that are unrelated in meaning (e.g. _mole_ (on skin) – _mole_ (small animal))

homophones: two or more words with different forms and the same pronunciation (e.g. _to–too–two_)

hypocorism: a word-formation process in which a longer word is reduced to a shorter form with _-y_ or _-ie_ at the end (e.g. _telly, movie_)

hyponymy: the **lexical relation** in which the meaning of one word is included in the meaning of another (e.g. _"daffodil" is a hyponym of "flower"_)

iconics: gestures that seem to echo or imitate the meaning of what is said

ideogram (ideographic writing): a way of writing in which each symbol represents a concept

idiolect: the personal **dialect** of an individual speaker

implicature: an additional meaning conveyed by a speaker adhering to the **Co-operative Principle**

indirect speech act: an action in which the form used (e.g. interrogative) does not directly match the function (e.g. request) performed by a speaker with an utterance, in contrast to a **direct speech act**

inference: additional information used by a listener/reader to create a connection between what is said and what must be meant

infix: a **morpheme** that is inserted in the middle of a word (e.g. _-rn-_ in _srnal_)

inflectional morpheme: a **bound morpheme** used to indicate the grammatical function of a word, also called an "inflection" (e.g. _dogs, walked_)

informative signals: behavior that provides information, usually unintentionally

innateness hypothesis: the idea that humans are genetically equipped to acquire language

input: the language that an acquirer/learner is exposed to, in contrast to **output**

insertion sequence: in conversation, an **adjacency pair** that comes between the first and second parts of another pair

instrument: the **semantic role** of the noun phrase identifying the entity that is used to perform the action of the verb (e.g. *The boy cut the rope with a razor*)

instrumental motivation: the desire to learn an **L2**, not to join the community of **L2**-users, but to achieve some other goal, in contrast to **integrative motivation**

integrative motivation: the desire to learn an **L2** in order to take part in the social life of the community of **L2**-users, in contrast to **instrumental motivation**

interdental: a **consonant** produced with the tongue tip between the upper and lower teeth (e.g. the first sound in *that*)

interlanguage: the interim system of **L2** learners, which has some features of the **L1** and **L2** plus some that are independent of the **L1** and the **L2**

internal change: change in a language that is not caused by outside influence, in contrast to **external change**

isogloss: a line on a map separating two areas in which a particular linguistic feature is significantly different, used in the study of **dialect**

jargon: special technical vocabulary associated with a specific activity or topic as part of a **register**

kinship terms: words used to refer to people who are members of the same family that indicate their relationship with other members

L1: first language, acquired as a child

L2: second language

labiodental: a **consonant** produced with the upper teeth and the lower lip (e.g. the first sounds in *very funny*)

language planning: choosing and developing an official language or languages for use in government and education

language typology: the identification of a language as one of a specific type, often based on **word order** such SVO or SOV

larynx: the part of the throat that contains the **vocal folds**, also called the voice box

lateralization (lateralized): divided into a left side and a right side, with control of functions on one side or the other (used in describing the human brain)

learning: the conscious process of accumulating knowledge, in contrast to **acquisition**

lexicalized: expressed as a single word, in contrast to **non-lexicalized**

lexical morpheme: a **free morpheme** that is a content word such as a noun or verb

lexical relations: the relationships of meaning, such as **synonymy**, between words

lexical rules: rules stating which words can be used for constituents generated by **phrase structure rules**

lexifier (language): the main source of words in a **pidgin**

linguistic context: the set of other words used in the same phrase or sentence, also called **co-text**

linguistic determinism: the idea that we can only think in the categories provided by our language, in contrast to **linguistic relativity**

linguistic geography: the study of language variation based on where different varieties of the language are used

linguistic relativity: the idea that, to some extent, we think about the world using categories provided by our language, in contrast to **linguistic determinism**

linguistic variable: a feature of language use that distinguishes one group of speakers from another

liquid: a sound produced by letting air flow around the sides of the tongue (e.g. the first sound in _lip_)

loan-translation: a type of **borrowing** in which each element of a word is translated into the borrowing language, also called **calque**

localization view: the belief that specific aspects of linguistic ability have specific locations in the brain

location (in semantics): the **semantic role** of the noun phrase identifying where an entity is (e.g. _The boy is sitting in the classroom_)

location (in sign language): an **articulatory parameter** of **ASL** identifying the place where hands are positioned in relation to the head and upper body of the signer

logogram (logographic writing): a way of writing in which each symbol represents a word

majority principle: in **comparative reconstruction**, the choice of the form that occurs more often than any other form in the set of descendant languages

malapropism: a speech error in which one word is used instead of another with a similar beginning, end and number of syllables (e.g. _medication_ used instead of "meditation")

Manner maxim: the assumption in conversation that we will "be clear, brief and orderly"

maxim: one of four assumptions in conversation connected to the **Co-operative Principle**

metathesis: a sound change involving the reversal in position of two sounds (e.g. _hros_ → _horse_)

metonymy: a word used in place of another with which it is closely connected in everyday experience (e.g. _He drank the whole bottle_ (= the liquid))

Middle English: the form of English in use between 1100 and 1500

minimal pair (set): two (or more) words that are identical in form except for a contrast in one **phoneme** in the same position in each word (e.g. _bad, mad_)

Modern English: the form of English in use since 1700

monolingual: having, or being able to use, only one language, in contrast to **bilingual**

morph: an actual form used as part of a word, representing one version of a **morpheme**

morpheme: a minimal unit of meaning or grammatical function

morphology: the analysis of the structure of words

most natural development principle: in **comparative reconstruction**, the choice of older versus newer forms on the basis of commonly observed types of sound change

motor cortex: a part of the brain that controls muscle movement

movement: an **articulatory parameter** in **ASL** describing the type of motion used in forming signs

narrowing: a semantic change in which a word is used with a less general meaning (e.g. _mete_ (any type of food) → _meat_ (only animal flesh)), in contrast to **broadening**

nasal: a sound produced through the nose (e.g. the first sounds in _my name_)

nasalization: pronunciation of a sound with air flowing through the nose, typically before a **nasal** consonant

natural class: a set of sounds with phonetic features in common, such as /p/, /t/ and /k/ in English, which are all **voiceless stops**

natural gender: a distinction based on the biological categories of male, female or neither, in contrast to other types of **gender**

negative face: the need to be independent and free from imposition, in contrast to **positive face**

negative transfer: the use of a feature from the **L1** (that is really different from the **L2**) while performing in the **L2**, in contrast to **positive transfer**

negotiated input: L2 material that an acquirer/learner is exposed to when active attention is drawn to that material during interaction in the **L2**

neologism: a new word

neurolinguistics: the study of the relationship between language and the brain

non-countable: type of noun that is not used in English with *a/an* or the plural (e.g. **a furniture*, **two furnitures*), in contrast to **countable**

non-gradable antonyms: words which are direct opposites (e.g. *alive–dead*)

non-lexicalized: not expressed as a single word, in contrast to **lexicalized**

NORMS: "non-mobile, older, rural, male speakers" selected as informants in dialect surveys

noun (N): a word such as *boy, bicycle* or *freedom* used to describe a person, thing or idea

noun phrase (NP): a phrase such as *the boy* or *an old bicycle*, containing a **noun** plus other constituents, or a **pronoun** such as *him* or *it*

nucleus: the vowel in a **syllable**

number: the grammatical category of **nouns** as singular or plural

object: the grammatical function of the **noun phrase** after the verb that typically undergoes the action of the verb (e.g. *The boy stole the book*)

Old English: the form of English in use before 1100

one-word stage: the period in **L1** acquisition when children can produce single terms for objects

onomatopoeia (onomatopoeic): words containing sounds similar to the noises they describe (e.g. *bang, cuckoo*)

onset: the part of the **syllable** before the **vowel**

open syllable: a **syllable** that ends with a **vowel** (or **nucleus**) and has no **coda**

oralism: a method designed to teach deaf students to speak and read lips rather than use **sign language**

orientation: the way the hand is positioned as an **articulatory parameter** of ASL

orthography: the spelling system of a language

output: the language produced by an acquirer/learner, in contrast to **input**

overextension: in **L1** acquisition, using a word to refer to more objects than is usual in the language (*ball* used to refer to the moon)

overgeneralization: in **L1** acquisition, using an **inflectional morpheme** on more words than is usual in the language (e.g. *two foots*)

overt prestige: status that is generally recognized as "better" or more positively valued in the larger community, in contrast to **covert prestige**

palate: the hard part of the roof of the mouth

palatal: a **consonant** produced by raising the tongue to the **palate**, also called "alveopalatal" (e.g. the first sounds in *ship* and *yacht*)

passive voice: the form of the verb used to say what happens to the **subject** (e.g. *The car was stolen*)

perseveration: a type of **slip of the tongue** in which a sound carries over from one word to the following word(s), as in *black bloxes* ("black boxes")

person: the grammatical category distinguishing first person (involving the speaker, *me*), second person (involving the hearer, *you*) and third person (involving any others, *she, them*)

person deixis: using words such as *him* or *them* as a way of "pointing" to a person with language

pharyngeal: a sound produced in the **pharynx**

pharynx: the area inside the throat above the **larynx**

philology: the study of language history and change

phone: a physically produced speech sound, representing one version of a **phoneme**

phoneme: the smallest meaning-distinguishing sound unit in the abstract representation of the sounds of a language

phonetic alphabet: a set of symbols, each one representing a distinct sound segment

phonetics: the study of the characteristics of speech sounds

phonographic writing: written symbols used to represent sounds of a language, either **syllables** or **phonemes**

phonology: the study of the systems and patterns of speech sounds in languages

phonotactics: constraints on the permissible combination of sounds in a language

phrase structure rules: rules stating that the structure of a phrase of a specific type consists of one or more constituents in a particular order

physical context: the situation, time or place in which words are used

pictogram (pictographic writing): a way of writing in which a picture/drawing of an object is used to represent the object

pidgin: a variety of a language that developed for a practical purpose such as trade, but which has no native speakers, in contrast to a **creole**

pitch: the effect of vibration in the **vocal folds**, making voices sound lower, higher, rising or falling

politeness: showing awareness and consideration of another person's public self-image

polysemy: a word having two or more related meanings (e.g. *foot*, of person, of bed, of mountain)

pooh-pooh theory: the idea that early human speech developed from the instinctive sounds people make in emotional circumstances

positive face: the need to be connected, to belong, to be a member of a group, in contrast to **negative face**

positive transfer: the use of a feature from the **L1** that is similar to the **L2** while performing in the **L2**, in contrast to **negative transfer**

post-creole continuum: the range of varieties that evolves in communities where a **creole** is spoken, usually as a result of **decreolization**

postvocalic: used after a vowel

pragmatic markers: short expressions such as *You know, I mean* or *Well* that indicate the speaker's attitude to the listener or the utterance

pragmatics: the study of speaker meaning and how more is communicated than is said

prefix: a **bound morpheme** added to the beginning of a word (e.g. *unhappy*)

preposition (Prep): a word such as *in* or *with* used with a **noun phrase**

prepositional phrase (PP): a phrase such as *with a dog*, consisting of a **preposition** plus a **noun phrase**

prescriptive approach: an approach to grammar that has rules for the proper use of the language, traditionally based on Latin grammar, in contrast to the **descriptive approach**

prestige: higher status

presupposition: an assumption by a speaker/writer about what is true or already known by the listener/reader

primary sign language: a sign language that is the first language of a group of people who are typically deaf and do not use a spoken language (e.g. **ASL**), in contrast to an **alternate sign language**

primes: the sets of features that form contrasting elements within the **articulatory parameters** of **ASL**

productivity: a property of language that allows users to create new expressions, also called "creativity" or "openendedness"

pronoun (Pro): a word such as *it* or *them* used in place of a **noun phrase**

proper noun (PN): a noun such as *Cathy*, with an initial capital letter, used as the name of someone or something

prothesis: a sound change involving the addition of a sound to the beginning of a word (e.g. *spiritus → espíritu*)

Proto-Indo-European: the hypothesized original form of a language that was the source of many languages in India and Europe

prototype: the most characteristic instance of a category (e.g. *"robin" is the prototype of "bird"*)

Quality maxim: the assumption in conversation that you will "not say that which you believe to be false or for which you lack adequate evidence"

Quantity maxim: the assumption in conversation that you will "make your contribution as informative as is required, but not more, or less, than is required"

rebus principle: a process used in writing in which a pictorial representation of an object is used to indicate the sound of the word for that object

recursion: the repeated application of a rule in generating structures

reduplication: the process of repeating all or part of a form

reference: an act by which a speaker/writer uses language to enable a listener/reader to identify someone or something

referential meaning: the basic components of meaning conveyed by the literal use of words, also described as "objective" or "conceptual" meaning

reflexivity: a special property of human language that allows language to be used to think and talk about language itself

register: a conventional way of using language that is appropriate in a specific situation, occupation or topic, characterized by the use of special **jargon**

relation maxim: the assumption in conversation that you will "be relevant"

reversives: antonyms in which the meaning of one is the reverse action of the other (e.g. *dress–undress*)

rhyme: the part of the **syllable** containing the **vowel** plus any following **consonant(s)**, also called "rime"

right-ear advantage: the fact that humans typically hear speech sounds more readily via the right ear

Sapir–Whorf hypothesis: the general idea that differences in language structure cause people to view the world differently, from the names of two American linguists, Edward Sapir and Benjamin Whorf

schema: a conventional knowledge structure in memory for specific things, such as a supermarket (food is displayed on shelves, arranged in aisles, etc.)

schwa: a mid central vowel /ə/, often used in an unstressed **syllable** (e.g. *afford, oven*)

script: a conventional knowledge structure in memory for the series of actions involved in events such as "Going to the dentist"

second language (L2) learning: the process of developing ability in another language, after **L1** acquisition

segment: an individual sound used in language

semantic features: basic elements such as "human," included as plus (+ human) or minus (–human), used in an analysis of the components of word meaning

semantic role: the part played by a **noun phrase**, such as **agent**, in the event described by the sentence

semantics: the study of the meaning of words, phrases and sentences

shape: the configuration of the hand(s) as an **articulatory parameter** of **ASL**

Signed English: using English sentences with signs instead of words, also called Manually Coded English or MCE

sign language (or sign): a communication system using the hands (with the face and other parts of the body)

singular they: a gender-neutral form used with singular antecedents that are unspecified for sex, as in *Each student must bring their own dictionary*

slang: words or phrases used instead of more conventional forms by those who are typically outside established higher status groups (e.g. *bucks* for *dollars*)

slip of the ear: a processing error in which one word or phrase is heard as another, as in hearing *great ape* when the utterance was "gray tape"

slip of the tongue: a speech error in which a sound or word is produced in the wrong place, as in *black bloxes* (instead of "black boxes")

social category: a **category** in which group members are defined by social connections

social dialect: a variety of a language with features that differ according to the social status (e.g. middle class or working class) of the speaker

social gender: a distinction between individuals in terms of their social roles as women and men, in contrast to other types of **gender**

social marker: a linguistic feature that marks the speaker as a member of a particular social group

social variable: a factor such as working class or middle class that is used to identify one group of speakers as different from another

sociolect: social dialect, a variety of a language that is strongly associated with one social group (e.g. working-class speech)

sociolinguistic competence: the ability to use language appropriately according to the social context as part of **communicative competence**

sociolinguistics: the study of the relationship between language and society

sound loss: a sound change in which a particular sound is no longer used in a language (e.g. the velar fricative [x], in Scottish *loch*, but not in Modern English)

source: the **semantic role** of the noun phrase identifying where an entity moves from (e.g. *The boy ran from the house*)

spatial deixis: using words such as *here* or *there* as a way of "pointing" to a location with language

speech accommodation: modifying speech style toward (**convergence**) or away from

(divergence) the perceived style of the person being talked to

speech act: an action such as "promising" performed by a speaker with an utterance, either as a **direct speech act** or an **indirect speech act**

speech community: a group of people who share a set of norms and expectations regarding the use of language

speech style: a way of speaking that is either formal/careful or informal/casual

spoonerism: a slip of the tongue in which two parts of words or two words are switched, as in *a dog of bag food* (for "a bag of dog food")

standard language: the variety of a language treated as the official language and used in public broadcasting, publishing and education

stem: the base form to which **affixes** are attached in the formation of words

stop: a **consonant** produced by stopping the airflow, then letting it go, also called "plosive" (e.g. the first and last sounds in *cat*)

strategic competence: the ability to use language to organize effective messages and to overcome potential communication problems as part of **communicative competence**

structural ambiguity: a situation in which a single phrase or sentence has two (or more) different underlying structures and interpretations

structural analysis: the investigation of the distribution of grammatical forms in a language

style-shifting: changing **speech style** from formal to informal or vice versa

subject: the grammatical function of the **noun phrase** typically used before the verb to refer to who or what performs the action of the **verb** (e.g. *The boy stole it*)

suffix: a **bound morpheme** added to the end of a word (e.g. *fainted, illness*)

superordinate: the higher-level term in **hyponymy** (e.g. *flower–daffodil*)

surface structure: the structure of individual sentences in contrast to **deep structure**

syllabic writing (syllabary): a way of writing in which each symbol represents a **syllable**

syllable: a unit of sound consisting of a vowel and optional consonants before or after the vowel

synchronic variation: differences in language form found in different places at the same time, in contrast to **diachronic variation**

synonymy: the **lexical relation** in which two or more words have very closely related meanings (e.g. *"conceal" is a synonym of "hide"*)

syntax (syntactic structures): (the analysis of) the structure of phrases and sentences

taboo terms: words or phrases that are avoided in formal speech, but are used in swearing, for example (e.g. *fuck, shit*)

tag questions: short questions consisting of an **auxiliary** (e.g. *don't*) and a **pronoun** (e.g. *you*), added to the end of a statement (e.g. *I hate it when it rains all day, don't you?*)

task-based learning: using activities involving information exchange and problem solving as a way of developing ability in language

tautology: an expression (often a saying) that seems simply to repeat an element with no apparent meaning (e.g. *Boys will be boys; A sandwich is a sandwich*)

telegraphic speech: strings of words (**lexical morphemes** without **inflectional morphemes**) in phrases (*daddy go byebye*) produced by two-year-old children

temporal deixis: using words such as *now* or *tomorrow* as a way of "pointing" to a time with language

tense: the grammatical category distinguishing forms of the **verb** as present tense and past tense

theme: the **semantic role** of the noun phrase used to identify the entity involved in or affected by the action of the verb in an event (e.g. *The boy kicked the ball*)

tip of the tongue phenomenon: the experience of knowing a word, but being unable to access it and bring it to the surface in order to say it

traditional grammar: the description of the structure of phrases and sentences based on established categories used in the analysis of Latin and Greek

transfer: using sounds, expressions and structures from the **L1** while performing in an **L2**

tree diagram: a diagram with branches showing the **hierarchical organization** of structures

turn: in conversation, the unit of talk by one speaker, ended by the beginning of the next speaker's unit of talk

turn-taking: the way in which each speaker takes a **turn** in conversation

T/V distinction: the difference between pronouns such as *tu* (socially close) and *vous* (socially distant) in French, used as **address terms**

two-word stage: a period beginning at around 18–20 months when children produce two terms together as an utterance (*baby chair*)

uvula: the small appendage at the end of the **velum**

uvular: a sound produced with the back of the tongue near the **uvula**

velar: a **consonant** produced by raising the back of the tongue to the **velum** (e.g. the first and last sounds in *geek*)

velum: the soft area at the back of the roof of the mouth, also called the "soft palate"

verb (V): a word such as *go, drown* or *know* used to describe an action, event or state

verb phrase (VP): a phrase such as *saw a dog*, containing a **verb** and other constituents

vernacular: a social dialect with low prestige spoken by a lower-status group, with marked differences from the **standard language**

vocal folds (or vocal cords): thin strips of muscle in the **larynx** which can be open, in **voiceless sounds**, or close together, creating vibration in **voiced sounds**

voiced sounds: speech sounds produced with vibration of the **vocal folds**

voiceless sounds: speech sounds produced without vibration of the **vocal folds**

vowel: a sound produced through the **vocal folds** without constriction of the airflow in the mouth

Wernicke's aphasia: a language disorder in which comprehension is typically slow while speech is fluent, but vague and missing content words

Wernicke's area: a part of the brain in the left hemisphere involved in language comprehension

word order: the linear order of constituents in a sentence (e.g. Subject–Verb–Object), used in **language typology** to identify different types of languages

writing: the symbolic representation of language through the use of graphic signs

References

Adamson, S. (2000) "A lovely little example" In O. Fischer, A. Rosenbach and D. Stein (eds.) *Pathways of Change: Grammaticalization in English* (39–66) John Benjamins

Ahlsén, E. (2006) *Introduction to Neurolinguistics* John Benjamins

Aijmer, K. (2013) *Understanding Pragmatic Markers* Edinburgh University Press

Aikhenvald, A. (2000) *Classifiers* Oxford University Press

(2008) *The Manambu Language of East Sepik, Papua New Guinea* Oxford University Press

Aikhenvald, A. and C. Genetti (2014) "Language profile 10: Manambu" In C. Genetti (ed.) *How Languages Work* (530–550) Cambridge University Press

Aitchison, J. (2000) *The Seeds of Speech* (Canto edition) Cambridge University Press

(2011) *The Articulate Mammal* Routledge Classics

(2012) *Words in the Mind* (4th edition) Wiley-Blackwell

(2013) *Language Change: Progress or Decay?* (4th edition) Cambridge University Press

Allan, K. (2015) *Linguistic Meaning* (Revised edition) Routledge

(2009) *Metaphor and Metonymy* Wiley-Blackwell

Allen, J. (2000) *Middle Egyptian: An Introduction to the Language and Culture of Hieroglyphs* Cambridge University Press

Allport, G. (1983) "Language and cognition" In R. Harris (ed.) *Approaches to Language* (80–94) Pergamon Press

Altenberg, E. and R. Vago (2010) *English Grammar: Understanding the Basics* Cambridge University Press

Anderson, S. (2004) *Doctor Dolittle's Delusion* Yale University Press

Anderson, W. and J. Corbett (2009) *Exploring English with Online Corpora: An Introduction* Palgrave Macmillan

Apel, K. and J. Masterson (2012) *Beyond Baby Talk* (Revised edition) Three Rivers Press

Archer, D., K. Aijmer and A. Wichman (2012) *Pragmatics: An Advanced Resource Book for Students* Routledge

Aronoff, M. and K. Fudeman (2011) *What Is Morphology?* (2nd edition) Blackwell

Ashby, M. and J. Maidment (2012) *Introducing Phonetic Science* (2nd edition) Cambridge University Press

Ashby, P. (2005) *Speech Sounds* (2nd edition) Routledge

Austin, P. (ed.) (2008) *One Thousand Languages* University of California Press

Baker, M. (2002) *The Atoms of Language: The Mind's Hidden Rules of Grammar* Basic Books

Baker, P. (2012) *Introduction to Old English* (3rd edition) Wiley-Blackwell

Balter, M. (2013) "Striking patterns: skill for forming tools and words evolved together" *Science/ AAS/News* (August 30, 2013) and news.sciencemag.org

Bamgbose, A. (2010) *A Grammar of Yoruba* Cambridge University Press

Barber, C., J. Beal and P. Shaw (2012) *The English Language: A Historical Introduction* (Canto edition) Cambridge University Press

Barbour, S. and P. Stevenson (1990) *Variation in German* Cambridge University Press

Barnbrook, G., O. Mason and R. Krishnamurthy (2013*) Collocation: Applications and Implications* Palgrave Macmillan

Bass, A., E. Gilland and R. Baker (2008) "Evolutionary origins for social vocalization in a vertebrate hindbrain-spinal compartment" *Science* 321 (July 18): 417–421

Bauer, L. (2003) *Introducing Linguistic Morphology* (2nd edition) Edinburgh University Press

(2015a) "English phonotactics" *English Language and Linguistics* 19: 437–475

(2015b) "Expletive insertion" *American Speech* 90: 122–127

(2017) *Compounds and Compounding* Cambridge University Press

Beaken, M. (2011) *The Making of Language* (2nd edition) Dunedin Academic Press

Bellos, D. (2011) *Is That a Fish in Your Ear? Translation and the Meaning of Everything* Faber & Faber

Bergen, B. (2012) *Louder than Words* Basic Books

Bernal, B. and A. Ardila (2009) "The role of the arcuate fasciculus in conduction aphasia" *Brain* 132: 2309–2316

Biber, D. and S. Conrad (2009) *Register, Genre and Style* Cambridge University Press

Biber, D., S. Johansson, G. Leech, S. Conrad and E. Finegan (1999) *Longman Grammar of Spoken and Written English* Longman

Bird, C. and T. Shopen (1979) "Maninka" In T. Shopen (ed.) *Languages and Their Speakers* (59–111) Winthrop

Birner, B. (2012) *Introduction to Pragmatics* Wiley-Blackwell

(2018) *Language and Meaning* Routledge

Blake, J. (2000) *Routes to Child Language* Cambridge University Press

Bloom, P. (2002) *How Children Learn the Meaning of Words* MIT Press

Bodine, A. (1975) "Androcentrism in prescriptive grammar: singular *they*, sex-indefinite *he*, and *he or she*" *Language in Society* 4: 129–146

Bond, Z. (1999) *Slips of the Ear* Academic Press

Booij, G. (2012) *The Grammar of Words: An Introduction to Morphology* (3rd edition) Oxford University Press

Boroditsky, L. (2003) "Linguistic relativity" In L. Nadel (ed.) *Encyclopedia of Cognitive Science* (917–921) Nature Publishing Group

Braine, M. (1971) "The acquisition of language in infant and child" In C. Reed (ed.) *The Learning of Language* Appleton-Century-Crofts

Brinton, L. and D. Brinton (2010) *The Linguistic Structure of Modern English* (2nd edition) John Benjamins

Brown, G. (1990) *Listening to Spoken English* (2nd edition) Longman

(1998) "Context creation in discourse understanding" In K. Malmkjær and J. Williams (eds.) *Context in Language Learning and Language Understanding* (171–192) Cambridge University Press

Brown, G. and G. Yule (1983) *Discourse Analysis* Cambridge University Press

Brown, K. and J. Miller (1991) *Syntax: A Linguistic Introduction to Sentence Structure* (2nd edition) Routledge

Brown, P. and S. Levinson (1987) *Politeness* Cambridge University Press

Brown, R. (1973) *A First Language* Harvard University Press

Brown, S., S. Attardo and C. Vigliotti (2014) *Understanding Language Structure, Interaction, and Variation* (3rd edition) University of Michigan Press

Bruner, J. (1983) *Child's Talk: Learning to Use Language* Norton

Buckingham, H. and A. Kertesz (1976) *Neologistic Jargon Aphasia* Swets and Zeitlinger

Burling, R. (2005) *The Talking Ape* Oxford University Press

Burridge, K. and A. Bergs (2017) *Understanding Language Change* Routledge

Burton-Roberts, N. (2016) *Analyzing Sentences: An Introduction to English Syntax* (4th edition) Routledge

Cameron, D. (1995) *Verbal Hygiene* Routledge

(2001) *Working with Spoken Discourse* Sage

(2007) *The Myth of Mars and Venus* Oxford University Press

Campbell, L. (2013) *Historical Linguistics: An Introduction* (3rd edition) MIT Press

Cannon, G. (1990) *The Life and Mind of Oriental Jones* Cambridge University Press

Caplan, D. (1996) *Language: Structure, Processing and Disorders* MIT Press

Carney, E. (1997) *English Spelling* Routledge

Carnie, A. (2012) *Syntax* (3rd edition) Wiley-Blackwell

Carr, P. (2013) *English Phonetics and Phonology* (2nd edition) Wiley-Blackwell

Carroll, J., S. Levinson and P. Lee (eds.) (2012) *Language, Thought and Reality: Selected Writings of Benjamin Lee Whorf* (2nd edition) MIT Press

Carstairs-McCarthy, A. (2018) *An Introduction to English Morphology* (2nd edition) Edinburgh University Press

Carter, R., S. Aldridge, M. Page and S. Parker (2009) *The Human Brain Book* DK Publishing

Casagrande, J. (2018) *The Joy of Syntax* Ten Speed Press

Cazden, C. (1972) *Child Language and Education* Holt

Celce-Murcia, M. and D. Larsen-Freeman (2015) *The Grammar Book* (3rd edition) Heinle & Heinle

Chambers, J. and P. Trudgill (1998) *Dialectology* (2nd edition) Cambridge University Press

Cheney, D. and R. Seyfarth (1990) *How Monkeys See the World* University of Chicago Press

Cheshire, J. (2007) "Discourse variation, grammaticalisation and stuff like that" *Journal of Sociolinguistics* 11: 155–193

Clancy, P. (2014) "First language acquisition" In C. Genetti (ed.) *How Languages Work* (318–350) Cambridge university Press

Clark, E. (1995) *The Lexicon in Acquisition* Cambridge University Press

(2016) *First Language Acquisition* (3rd edition) Cambridge University Press

(2017) *Language in Children* Routledge

Clift, R. (2016) *Conversation Analysis* Cambridge University Press

Coates, J. (2004) *Women, Men and Language* (3rd edition) Longman

Cole, D. (1955) *An Introduction to Tswana Grammar* Longmans

Collins English Dictionary (2018) (13th edition) Harper Collins Publishers

Cook, V. (2004) *The English Writing System* Hodder Arnold

    (2016) *Second Language Learning and Language Teaching* (5th edition) Hodder Education

Cook, V. and D. Ryan (eds.) (2016) *The Routledge Handbook of the English Writing System* Routledge

Cook, V. and D. Singleton (2014) *Key Topics in Second Language Acquisition* Multilingual Matters

Corballis, M. (2002) *From Hand to Mouth* Princeton University Press

Coulmas, F. (2003) *Writing Systems* Cambridge University Press

Cowan, W. and J. Rakušan (1999) *Source Book for Linguistics* (3rd edition) John Benjamins

Cowie, A. (2009) *Semantics* Oxford University Press

Cox, F. (2012) *Australian English: Pronunciation and Transcription* Cambridge University Press

Cramer, J. and D. Preston (2018) "Changing perceptions of southernness" *American Speech* 93: 3–4

Crowley, T. (2004) *Bislama Reference Grammar* Edinburgh University Press

Crowley, T. and C. Bowern (2010) *An Introduction to Historical Linguistics* (4th edition) Oxford University Press

Cruse, A. (2011) *Meaning in Language* (3rd edition) Oxford University Press

Cruttenden, A. (2008) *Gimson's Pronunciation of English* (7th edition) Hodder Arnold

Crystal, D. (2008) *A Dictionary of Linguistics and Phonetics* (6th edition) Blackwell

    (2012) *Spell It Out: The Singular Story of English Spelling* Profile Books

    (2019) *The Cambridge Encyclopedia of the English Language* (3rd edition) Cambridge University Press

Crystal, D. and H. Crystal (2013) *Wordsmiths and Warriors: The English Language Tourist's Guide to Britain* Oxford University Press

Culicover, P. and E. Hume (2017) *Basics of Language for Language Learners* The Ohio State University

Culpeper, J. (2011) *Impoliteness* Cambridge University Press

Culpeper, J. and M. Haugh (2014) *Pragmatics and the English Language* Macmillan

Culpeper, J., P. Kerswill, R. Wodak, T. McEnery and F. Katamba (eds.) (2018) *English Language* (2nd edition) Palgrave Macmillan

Cummins, C. (2018) *Pragmatics* Edinburgh University Press

Curtiss, S. (1977) *Genie: A Psycholinguistic Study of a Modern-day Wild Child* Academic Press

Curzan, A. (2003) *Gender Shifts in the History of English* Cambridge University Press

Cushman, E. (2011) *The Cherokee Syllabary* University of Oklahoma Press

Cutting, J. (2014) *Pragmatics: A Resource Book for Students* (3rd edition) Routledge

Damasio, A. (1994) *Descartes' Error* Putnam

Danesi, M. (2012) *Linguistic Anthropology: A Brief Introduction* Canadian Scholars Press

Daniels, P. and W. Bright (1996) *The World's Writing Systems* Oxford University Press

Danziger, E. (2001) *Relatively Speaking* Oxford University Press

Darwin, C. (1871) *The Descent of Man, and Selection in Relation to Sex* John Murray

Davenport, M. and S. Hannahs (2013) *Introducing Phonetics and Phonology* (3rd edition) Routledge

Davies, W. (1987) *Egyptian Hieroglyphics* British Museum / University of California Press

Deacon, T. (1997) *The Symbolic Species* W. W. Norton

Dekeyser, R. and J. Larson-Hall (2005) "What does the critical period really mean?" In J. Kroll and A. De Groot (eds.) *Handbook of Bilingualism* (88–108) Oxford University Press

Denning, K., B. Kessler and W. Leben (2007) *English Vocabulary Elements* (2nd edition) Oxford University Press

Deutscher, G. (2010) *Through the Language Glass* Metropolitan Books

Diniz de Figueiredo, E. (2010) "To borrow or not to borrow: the use of English loanwords as slang on websites in Brazilian Portuguese" *English Today* 26 (4): 5–12

Dixon, R. (2014) *Making New Words* Oxford University Press

Downing, B. and J. Fuller (1984) "Cultural contact and the expansion of the Hmong lexicon" Unpublished manuscript, Department of Linguistics, University of Minnesota

Drager, K. (2012) "Pidgin and Hawai'i English: an overview" *International Journal of Language, Translation and Intercultural Communication* 1: 61–73

Duanmu, S. (2008) *Syllable Structure* Oxford University Press

Duranti, A. (2001) *Key Terms in Language and Culture* Blackwell

Durkin, P. (2009) *The Oxford Guide to Etymology* Oxford University Press

(2014) *Borrowed Words: A History of Loanwords in English* Oxford University Press

Eble, C. (2004) "Slang" In E. Finegan and J. Rickford (eds.) *Language in the USA* (375–386) Cambridge University Press

Eckert, P. (2000) *Linguistic Variation as Social Practice* Blackwell

Eckert, P. and S. McConnell-Ginet (2013) *Language and Gender* (2nd edition) Cambridge University Press

Edwards, J. (2013) *Sociolinguistics: A Very Short Introduction* Oxford University Press

Ekman, P. (1999) "Emotional and conversational nonverbal signals" In L. Messing and R. Campbell (eds.) *Gesture, Speech and Sign* (45–55) Oxford University Press

Ellis, R. (1997) *Second Language Acquisition* Oxford University Press

Enfield, N. (2017) *How We Talk: The Inner Workings of Conversation* Basic Books

Erard, M. (2016) "Why Australia is home to one of the largest language families in the world" www.sciencemag.org/news/2016/09/why-australia-home-one-largest-language-families-world September 21, 2016

Espy, W. (1975) *An Almanac of Words at Play* Clarkson Potter

Ethnologue (2018) (21st edition) SIL International

Evans, V. (2007) *A Glossary of Cognitive Linguistics* Edinburgh University Press

Fant, L. (1977) *Sign Language* Joyce Media

Faulkner, W. (1929) *The Sound and the Fury* Jonathan Cape

Favilla, E. (2017) *A World without "Whom": The Essential Guide to Language in the Buzzfeed Age* Bloomsbury

Fertig, D. (2013) *Analogy and Morphological Change* Edinburgh University Press

Fiddes, I., G. Lodewijk, M. Mooring, S. Salama, F. Jacobs and D. Haussler (2018) "Human specific NOTCH2NL genes affect notch signaling and cortical neurogenesis" *Cell* 173: 1356–1369 https://doi.org/10.1016/j.cell.2018.03.051

Finegan, E. (2014) *Language: Its Structure and Use* (7th edition) Cengage

Finegan, E. and J. Rickford (eds.) (2004) *Language in the USA* Cambridge University Press

Firchow, I. (1987) "Form and function of Rotokas words" *Language and Linguistics in Melanesia* 15: 5–111

Flaherty, A. (2004) *The Midnight Disease* Houghton Mifflin

Florey, K. B. (2006) *Sister Bernadette's Barking Dog: The Quirky History and Lost Art of Diagramming Sentences* Melville House Publishing

Fogal, D., D. Harris and M. Moss (eds.) (2018) *New Work on Speech Acts* Oxford University Press

Foley, W. (1997) *Anthropological Linguistics* Blackwell

Fortson, B. (2010) *Indo-European Language and Culture* (2nd edition) Wiley-Blackwell

Fought, C. (2003) *Chicano English in Context* Palgrave Macmillan

Frawley, W. (1992) *Linguistic Semantics* Lawrence Erlbaum

Friederici, A. (2017) *Language in Our Brain* MIT Press

Friend, T. (2004) *Animal Talk* Simon and Schuster

Fromkin, V., R. Rodman and N. Hyams (2018) *An Introduction to Language* (11th edition) Wadsworth

Frommer, P. and E. Finegan (2015) *Looking at Languages* (6th edition) Wadsworth

Gardner, R., B. Gardner and T. Van Cantfort (eds.) (1989) *Teaching Sign Language to Chimpanzees* State University of New York Press

Garnham, A. (2001) *Mental Models and the Interpretation of Anaphora* Psychology Press

Gass, S., J. Behney and L. Plonsky (2013) *Second Language Acquisition: An Introductory Course* (4th edition) Routledge

Gelb, I. (1963) *A Study of Writing* University of Chicago Press

Geschwind, N. (1991) "Specializations of the human brain" In W. Wang (ed.) *The Emergence of Language* (72–87) W. H. Freeman

Gibbons, A. and S. Whiteley (2018) *Contemporary Stylistics: Language, Cognition and Interpretation* Edinburgh University Press

Giles, H. (ed.) (2016) *Communication Accommodation Theory* Cambridge University Press

Glassner, J. (2003) *The Invention of Cuneiform* Johns Hopkins University Press

Gleason, H. (1955) *Workbook in Descriptive Linguistics* Holt

Goddard, C. (2009) "Componential analysis" In G. Senft, J-O. Östman and J. Verscheuren (eds.) *Culture and Language Use* (58–67) John Benjamins

Goldin-Meadow, S. (2005) *Hearing Gesture* (revised edition) Belknap Press

Gordon, M. (2013) *Labov: A Guide for the Perplexed* Bloomsbury

Gramley, S. (2019) *The History of English: An Introduction* (2nd edition) Routledge

Green, L. (2002) *African American English* Cambridge University Press

   (2011) *Language and the African American Child* Cambridge University Press

Greene, R. (2011) *You Are What You Speak* Delacorte Press

Grice, P. (1975) "Logic and conversation" In P. Cole and J. Morgan (eds.) *Syntax and Semantics 3: Speech Acts* (41–58) Academic Press

   (1989) *Studies in the Way of Words* Harvard University Press

Griffin, D. (2001) *Animal Minds* University of Chicago Press

Grosjean, F. (2012) *Bilingual: Life and Reality* Harvard University Press

Grundy, P. (2008) *Doing Pragmatics* (3rd edition) Hodder

Guido, J. (2017) *Learn American Sign Language* Wellfleet Press

Guiora, A., B. Beit-Hallahmi, R. Brannon, C. Dull and T. Scovel (1972) "The effects of experimentally induced change in ego states on pronunciation ability in a second language: an exploratory study" *Comprehensive Psychiatry* 13: 5–23

Haiman, J. (2018) *Ideophones and the Evolution of Language* Cambridge University Press

Handbook of the International Phonetic Association (1999) Cambridge University Press

Harari, Y. (2015) *Sapiens: A Brief History of Humankind* Harper

Hardcastle, W. and N. Hewlett (2006) *Coarticulation: Theory, Data and Techniques* Cambridge University Press

Harley, H. (2006) *English Words: A Linguistic Introduction* Blackwell

Haspelmath, M., M. Dryer, D. Gil and B. Comrie (eds.) (2005*) The World Atlas of Language Structures* Oxford University Press

Hauser, M. (1996) *The Evolution of Communication* MIT Press

Have, P. (2007) *Doing Conversation Analysis* (2nd edition) Sage

Hawkins, R. (2019) *How Second Languages Are Learned* Cambridge University Press

Hayes, C. (1951) *The Ape in Our House* Harper

Heilman, K. (2002) *Matter of Mind* Oxford University Press

Herbst, T. (2010) *English Linguistics* De Gruyter

Hercuse, L. (1994) *A Grammar of the Arabana-Wangkangurru Language* (Pacific Linguistics Series C 128) Australian National University, Canberra

Hess, E. (2008) *Nim Chimpsky: The Chimp Who Would Be Human* Bantam Books

Hickey, R. (ed.) (2013) *Standards of English* Cambridge University Press

Hinnebusch, T. (1987) "Swahili" In T. Shopen (ed.) *Languages and Their Status* (209–294) University of Pennsylvania Press

Hitchings, H. (2008) *The Secret Life of Words* John Murray

Hobaiter, C. and R. Byrne (2014) "The meaning of chimpanzee gestures" *Current Biology* 24: 1596–1600

Hockett, C. (1960) "The origin of speech" *Scientific American* 203: 89–96

Hoey, M. (2001) *Textual Interaction: An Introduction to Written Discourse Analysis* Routledge

Holmes, J. and N. Wilson (2017) *An Introduction to Sociolinguistics* (5th edition) Pearson

Horobin, S. and J. Smith (2002) *An Introduction to Middle English* Oxford University Press

Huang, Y. (2000) *Anaphora: A Cross-Linguistic Approach* Oxford University Press

Huddleston, R. and G. Pullum (2005) *A Student's Introduction to English Grammar* Cambridge University Press

Hudson, G. (2000) *Essential Introductory Linguistics* Blackwell

Hugdahl, K. and R. Davidson (2004) *The Asymmetrical Brain* MIT Press

Hughes, A., P. Trudgill and D. Watt (2012) *English Accents and Dialects* (5th edition) Routledge

Humphries, T. and C. Padden (2003) *Learning American Sign Language* (2nd edition) Allyn and Bacon

Hurford, J. (1994) *Grammar: A Student's Guide* Cambridge University Press

(2014) *The Origins of Language* Oxford University Press

Hurford, J., B. Heasley and M. Smith (2007) *Semantics: A Coursebook* (2nd edition) Cambridge University Press

Huth, A., W. de Heer, T. Griffiths, F. Theunissen and J. Gallant (2016) "Natural speech reveals the semantic maps that tile human cerebral cortex" *Nature* (April 28) doi:10.1038/nature 17637

Hyslop, C. (2001) *The Lolovoli Dialect of North-East Ambae Island: Vanuatu* (Pacific Linguistics 515) Australian National University, Canberra

Ingram, J. (2007) *Neurolinguistics* Cambridge University Press

Inkelas, S. and C. Zoll (2009) *Reduplication: Doubling in Morphology* Cambridge University Press

Inoue, K. (1979) "Japanese" In T. Shopen (ed.) *Languages and Their Speakers* (241–300) Winthrop Publishers

Iverson, J. (2010) "Developing language in a developing body: the relationship between motor development and language development" *Journal of Child Language* 37: 229–261

Jaeger, J. (2005) *Kids' Slips* Lawrence Erlbaum

Jaggar, P. (2001) *Hausa* John Benjamins

Janson, T. (2012) *The History of Languages* Oxford University Press

Jeffery, L. (1990) *The Local Scripts of Archaic Greece* Clarendon Press

Jeffries, L. (2006) *Discovering Language* Palgrave Macmillan

Jenkins, J. (2007) *English as a Lingua Franca: Attitude and Identity* Oxford University Press

Jensen, H. (1969) *Sign, Symbol and Script* (3rd edition) (trans. G. Unwin) Putnam's

Jespersen, O. (1922) *Language: Its Nature, Development and Origin* George Allen & Unwin

Johnson, K. (2011) *Acoustic and Auditory Phonetics* (3rd edition) Wiley-Blackwell

Johnston, T. and A. Schembri (2007) *Australian Sign Language: An Introduction to Sign Language Linguistics* Cambridge University Press

Johnstone, B. (2018) *Discourse Analysis* (3rd edition) Wiley-Blackwell

Jolly, A. (1966) *Lemur Behavior* University of Chicago Press

Jones, B. (2011) *A Grammar of Wangkajunga* (Pacific Linguistics 636) Australian National University, Canberra

Jones, C. and D. Waller (2015) *Corpus Linguistics for Grammar* Routledge

Jones, D., P. Roach, J. Hartman and J. Setter (2011) *Cambridge English Pronouncing Dictionary* (18th edition) Cambridge University Press

Jones, R. (2012) *Discourse Analysis: A Resource Book for Students* Routledge

Jones, S. (2002) *Antonymy* Routledge

Jonz, J. (2014) *An Introduction to English Sentence Structure* Equinox Publishing

Jule, A. (2008) *A Beginner's Guide to Language and Gender* Multilingual Matters

Jusczyk, P. (1997) *The Discovery of Spoken Language* MIT Press

Kádár, D. and M. Haugh (2013) *Understanding Politeness* Cambridge University Press

Kasher, A. (2009) "Implicature" In S. Chapman and C. Routledge (eds.) *Key Ideas in Linguistics and the Philosophy of Language* (86–92) Edinburgh University Press

Keenan, E. and E. Ochs (1979) "Becoming a competent speaker of Malagasy" In T. Shopen (ed.) *Languages and Their Speakers* (113–158) Winthrop Publishers

Kegl, J. (1994) "The Nicaraguan Sign Language project: an overview" *Signpost* 7: 24–31

Kellerman, E., T. Ammerlan, T. Bongaerts and N. Poulisse (1990) "System and hierarchy in L2 compensatory strategies" In R. Scarcella, E. Anderson and S. Krashen (eds.) *Developing Communicative Competence in a Second Language* (163–178) Newbury House

Kellogg, W. and L. Kellogg (1933) *The Ape and the Child* McGraw-Hill

Kendon, A. (1988) *Sign Languages of Aboriginal Australia* Cambridge University Press
    (2004) *Gesture* Cambridge University Press

Kenneally, C. (2007) *The First Word* Viking Press

Kerswill, P. (2018) "Language and social class" In J. Culpeper, P. Kerswill, R. Wodak, T. McEnery and F. Katamba (eds.) *English Language* (2nd edition) (chapter 18) Palgrave Macmillan

Kikusawa, R. (2005) "Comparative linguistics: a bridge that connects us to languages and people of the past" In P. Lassettre (ed.) *Language in Hawai'i and the Pacific* (415–433) Pearson

Knight, R-A. (2012) *Phonetics: A Coursebook* Cambridge University Press

Kramsch, C. (1998) *Language and Culture* Oxford University Press

Kreidler, C. (2004) *The Pronunciation of English* (2nd edition) Blackwell

Kretzschmar, W. (2004) "Regional dialects" In E. Finegan and J. Rickford (eds.) *Language in the USA* (39–57) Cambridge University Press

Kroeger, P. (2005) *Analyzing Grammar: An Introduction* Cambridge University Press

Kuper, A. (1999) *Culture: The Anthropologist's Account* Harvard University Press

Labov, W. (2001) *Principles of Linguistic Change, volume 2: Social Factors* Blackwell
    (2006) *The Social Stratification of English in New York City* (2nd edition) Cambridge University Press

Ladefoged, P. and K. Johnson (2015) *A Course in Phonetics* (7th edition) Wadsworth, Cengage Learning

Lakoff, G. (1987) *Women, Fire and Dangerous Things* University of Chicago Press

Lakoff, R. (1990) *Talking Power* Basic Books

Lane, H. (1976) *The Wild Boy of Aveyron* Harvard University Press

Language Files (2016) (12th edition) Ohio State University Press

LaScotte, D. (2016) "Singular *they*: an empirical study of generic pronoun use" *American Speech* 91: 62–80

Leavitt, J. (2011) *Linguistic Relativities* Cambridge University Press

Lehmann, W. (ed.) (1967) *A Reader in Nineteenth Century Historical Indo-European Linguistics* Indiana University Press

Lenneberg, E. (1967) *The Biological Foundations of Language* John Wiley

Lesser, R. and L. Milroy (1993) *Linguistics and Aphasia* Longman

Levinson, S. (1983) *Pragmatics* Cambridge University Press
    (2006) "Deixis" In L. Horn and G. Ward (eds.) *The Handbook of Pragmatics* (97–121) Blackwell

Lewis, G. (2000) *Turkish Grammar* (2nd edition) Oxford University Press

Liddicoat, A. (2011) *An Introduction to Conversation Analysis* (2nd edition) Continuum

Lieber, R. (2016 *Introducing Morphology* (2nd edition) Cambridge University Press

Lieber, R. and P. Stekauer (2009) *The Oxford Handbook of Compounding* Oxford University Press

Lieberman, P. (1998) *Eve Spoke: Human Language and Human Evolution* W. W. Norton

Lightbown, P. and N. Spada (2013) *How Languages Are Learned* (4th edition) Oxford University Press

Lippi-Green, R. (2011) *English with an Accent* (2nd edition) Routledge

Locke, J. (1983) *Phonological Acquisition and Change* Academic Press

Long, Y. and G. Zheng (1998) *The Dong Language of Guizhou Province, China* Translated by D. Leary. The Summer Institute of Linguistics, The University of Texas at Arlington, Publication 126

Loritz, D. (1999) *How the Brain Evolved Language* Oxford University Press

Lucas, C. and C. Valli (2004) "American Sign Language" In E. Finegan and J. Rickford (eds.) *Language in the USA* (230–244) Cambridge University Press

Lum, D. (1990) *Pass On, No Pass Back!* Bamboo Ridge Press

Lust, B. (2006) *Child Language* Cambridge University Press

Lynch, J. (1998) *Pacific Languages* University of Hawai'i Press

Maccoby, E. (1998) *The Two Sexes* Harvard University Press

Mackay, D. (1970) *A Flock of Words* Harcourt

MacNeilage, P. (1998) "The frame/content theory of evolution of speech production" *Behavioral and Brain Sciences* 21: 499–546

Mallory, J. and D. Adams (2006) *The Oxford Introduction to Proto-Indo-European and the Proto-Indo-European World* Oxford University Press

Malmkjær, K. and J. Williams (eds.) (1998) *Context in Language Learning and Language Understanding* Cambridge University Press

Malotki, E. (1983) *Hopi Time* Walter de Gruyter

Mampe, B., A. Friederici, A. Christophe and K. Wermke (2009) "Newborns' cry melody is shaped by their native language" *Current Biology* 19: 1994–1997

Man, J. (2000) *Alpha Beta* John Wiley

Marciano, J. (2009) *Anonyponymous* Bloomsbury

Marmaridou, S. (2010) "Presupposition" In L. Cummings (ed.) *The Pragmatics Encyclopedia* (349–353) Routledge

Marryat, F. (1839) *"When at Niagara Falls" A Diary in America: With Remarks on Its Institutions* (154) Wm. H. Colyer

Martin, L. (1986) "'Eskimo words for snow': a case study in the genesis and decay of an anthropological example" *American Anthropologist* 88: 418–423

McCully, C. (2009) *The Sound Structure of English: An Introduction* Cambridge University Press

McEnery, T. and A. Hardie (2011) *Corpus Linguistics* Cambridge University Press

McGilchrist, I. (2009) *The Master and His Emissary* Yale University Press

McMahon, A. (1994) *Understanding Language Change* Cambridge University Press
(2002) *An Introduction to English Phonology* Edinburgh University Press

McMahon, A. and R. McMahon (2013) *Evolutionary Linguistics* Cambridge University Press

McNeill, D. (1966) "Developmental psycholinguistics" In F. Smith and G. Miller (eds.) *The Genesis of Language* (15–84) MIT Press

(1992) *Hand and Mind* University of Chicago Press

(2012) *How Language Began: Gesture and Speech in Human Evolution* Cambridge University Press

McWhorter, J. (2014) *The Language Hoax* Oxford University Press

Meisel, J. (2011) *First and Second Language Acquisition: Parallels and Differences* Cambridge University Press

Melchers, G. and P. Shaw (2015) *World Englishes* (3rd edition) Routledge

Mendoza, M. (2005) "Polite diminutives in Spanish" In R. Lakoff and S. Ide (eds.) *Broadening the Horizons of Linguistic Politeness* (163–173) John Benjamins

Merrifield, W., C. Naish, C. Rensch and G. Story (2003) *Laboratory Manual for Morphology and Syntax* (7th edition) Summer Institute of Linguistics

Mesthrie, R., J. Swann, A. Deumert and W. Leap (2009) *Introducing Sociolinguistics* (2nd edition) John Benjamins

Meyerhoff, M. (2018) *Introducing Sociolinguistics* (3rd edition) Routledge

Micklethwait, D. (2000) *Noah Webster and the American Dictionary* McFarland & Company

Miller, D. (2012) *External Influences on English: From Its Beginnings to the Renaissance* Oxford University Press

Miller, J. (2012) *An Introduction to English Syntax* (2nd edition) Edinburgh University Press

Mills, S. (2003) *Gender and Politeness* Cambridge University Press

Minkova, D. and R. Stockwell (2009) *English Words: History and Structure* (2nd edition) Cambridge University Press

Miracle, A. and J. Yapita Moya (1981) "Time and space in Aymara" In M. Hardman (ed.) *The Aymara Language in Its Social and Cultural Context* University Press of Florida

Mitchell, R., F. Myles and E. Marsden (2013) *Second Language Learning Theories* (3rd edition) Routledge

Mithen, S. (2006) *The Singing Neanderthals* Harvard University Press

Mithun, M. (2014) "Morphology: what's in a word?" In C. Genetti (ed.) *How Languages Work* (71–99) Cambridge University Press

Mohr, M. (2013) *Holy Shit: A Brief History of Swearing* Oxford University Press

Moravcsik, E. (2013) *Introducing Language Typology* Cambridge University Press

Morenberg, M. (2013) *Doing Grammar* (5th edition) Oxford University Press

Mosel, U. and E. Hovdhaugen (1992) *Samoan Reference Grammar* Scandinavian University Press

Moskowitz, B. (1991) "The acquisition of language" In W. Wang (ed.) *The Emergence of Language* (131–149) W. H. Freeman

Mugglestone, L. (1995) *Talking Proper: The Rise of Accent as Social Symbol* Clarendon Press

Murane, E. (1974) *Daga Grammar: From Morpheme to Discourse* SIL Publications

Murphy, M. (2003) *Semantic Relations and the Lexicon* Cambridge University Press

Murphy, V. (2014) *Second Language Learning in the Early School Years* Oxford University Press

Myers-Scotton, C. (2005) *Multiple Voices* Wiley

Napoli, D. and L. Lee-Schoenfeld (2010) *Language Matters* (2nd edition) Oxford University Press

Nevalainen, T. (2006) *An Introduction to Early Modern English* Edinburgh University Press

Newberg, A., N. Wintering, D. Morgan and M. Waldman (2006) "The measurement of regional cerebral blood flow during glossolalia: a preliminary SPECT study" *Psychiatry Research: Neuroimaging* 148: 67–71

Newton, M. (2002) *Savage Girls and Wild Boys: A History of Feral Children* Picador

Nichols, P. (2004) "Creole languages: forging new identities" In E. Finegan and J. Rickford (eds.) *Language in the USA* (133–152) Cambridge University Press

Norris, M. (2015) *Between You and Me* W. W. Norton

Obler, L. and K. Gjerlow (1999) *Language and the Brain* Cambridge University Press

Ochieng, D. (2015) "The revival of the status of English in Tanzania" *English Today* 31 (2): 25–31

Odden, D. (2013) *Introducing Phonology* (2nd edition) Cambridge University Press

Oettinger, A. (1966) "The uses of computers in science" *Scientific American* 215 (September): 168

Ogden, R. (2017) *An Introduction to English Phonetics* (2nd edition) Edinburgh University Press

O'Grady, W. (1997) *Syntactic Development* University of Chicago Press

    (2005) *How Children Learn Language* Cambridge University Press

O'Grady, W., J. Archibald, M. Aronoff and J. Rees-Miller (2017) *Contemporary Linguistics* (7th edition) Bedford/St. Martin's Press

Oller, D. (2000) *The Emergence of the Speech Capacity* Lawrence Erlbaum

Olson, J. and E. Masur (2011) "Infants' gestures influence mothers' provision of object action and internal state labels" *Journal of Child Language* 38: 1028–1054

Ortega, L. (2014) *Understanding Second Language Acquisition* Routledge

Overstreet, M. (1999) *Whales, Candlelight and Stuff Like That: General Extenders in English Discourse* Oxford University Press

    (2011) "Vagueness and hedging" In G. Andersen and K. Aijmer (eds.) *Pragmatics of Society* (293–317) De Gruyter

Padden, C. and D. Gunsauls (2003) "How the alphabet came to be used in a sign language" *Sign Language Studies* 4: 10–33

Pae, H. (ed.) (2018) *Writing Systems, Reading Processes and Cross-Linguistic Influences* John Benjamins

Paltridge, B. (2012) *Discourse Analysis* (2nd edition) Bloomsbury

Patel, A. (2008) *Music, Language and the Brain* Oxford University Press

Payne, T. (2006) *Exploring Language Structure* Cambridge University Press

Penfield, W. and L. Roberts (1959) *Speech and Brain Mechanisms* Princeton University Press

Pereltsvaig, A. (2017) *Languages of the World* (2nd edition) Cambridge University Press

Peters, P. (2013) *The Cambridge Dictionary of English Grammar* Cambridge University Press

Petrides, M. (2014) *Neuroanatomy of Language Regions of the Human Brain* Elsevier

Pica, T., L. Holliday, N. Lewis, D. Berducci and J. Newman (1991) "Language learning through interaction: what role does gender play?" *Studies in Second Language Acquisition* 11: 63–90

Piller, I (2017) *Intercultural Communication* Edinburgh University Press

Pinker, S. (1994) *The Language Instinct* William Morrow

    (1999) *Words and Rules* HarperCollins

    (2007) *The Stuff of Thought* Viking Press

Plag, I. (2018) *Word-formation in English* (2nd edition) Cambridge University Press

Poulisse, N. (1999) *Slips of the Tongue* John Benjamins

Premack, A. and D. Premack (1991) "Teaching language to an ape" In W. Wang (ed.) *The Emergence of Language* (16–27) W. H. Freeman

Pullum, G. (1991) *The Great Eskimo Vocabulary Hoax* University of Chicago Press

    (2009) "50 years of stupid grammar advice" *The Chronicle of Higher Education: The Chronicle Review* 55 (32): B15 Available online at http://chronicle.com Section: The Chronicle Review volume 55, issue 32, page B15

Pullum, G. and W. Ladusaw (1996) *Phonetic Symbol Guide* (2nd edition) University of Chicago Press

Quirk, R., S. Greenbaum, G. Leech and J. Svartvik (1985) *A Comprehensive Grammar of the English Language* Longman

Radford, A., M. Atkinson, D. Britain, H. Clahsen and A. Spencer (2009) *Linguistics: An Introduction* (2nd edition) Cambridge University Press

Raglan, L. (1922) "The Lotuko language" *Bulletin of the School of Oriental Studies* (University of London) 2 (2): 267–296

Richards, J. and T. Rodgers (2014) *Approaches and Methods in Language Teaching* (3rd edition) Cambridge University Press

Riemer, N. (2010) *Introducing Semantics* Cambridge University Press

Rimpau, J., R. Gardner and B. Gardner (1989) "Expression of person, place and instrument in ASL utterances of children and chimpanzees" In R. Gardner, B. Gardner and T. van Cantfort (eds.) *Teaching Sign Language to Chimpanzees* (240–268) State University of New York Press

Rissanen, M. (2008) "From 'quickly' to 'fairly': on the history of *rather*" *English Language and Linguistics* 12: 345–359

Ritchie, G. (2002) *The Linguistic Analysis of Jokes* Routledge

Roach, P. (2009) *English Phonetics and Phonology* (4th edition) Cambridge University Press

Roberts, I. (2017) *The Wonders of Language* Cambridge University Press

Robinson, A. (2007) *The Story of Writing* (2nd edition) Thames & Hudson

Rodgon, M. (2009) *Single-Word Usage, Cognitive Development and the Beginnings of Combinatorial Speech* Cambridge University Press

Rogers, H. (2005) *Writing Systems: A Linguistic Approach* Blackwell

Rogers, L. and G. Kaplan (2000) *Songs, Roars and Rituals* Harvard University Press

Roig-Marín, A. (2016) "'Blended cyber-neologisms" *English Today* 128 (32): 2–5

Romaine, S. (1989) *Pidgin and Creole Languages* Longman

    (2000) *Language in Society* (2nd edition) Oxford University Press

Rumbaugh, D. (ed.) (1977) *Language Learning by a Chimpanzee: The LANA Project* Academic Press

Rymer, R. (1993) *Genie* HarperCollins

Sacks, H. (1972) "On the analyzability of stories by children" In J. Gumperz and D. Hymes (eds.) *Directions in Sociolinguistics* (325–345) Holt, Rinehart and Winston

Sacks, O. (1989) *Seeing Voices* University of California Press

Saeed, J. (2015) *Semantics* (4th edition) Wiley-Blackwell

Sakel, J. (2015) *Study Skills for Linguistics* Routledge

Sakoda, K. and J. Siegel (2003) *Pidgin Grammar* Bess Press

Samarin, W. (1972) *Tongues of Men and Angels: The Religious Language of Pentecostalism* Macmillan

Sampson, G. (1980) *Schools of Linguistics* Stanford University Press

(2005) *The "Language Instinct" Debate* (revised edition) Continuum

(2015) *Writing Systems* (2nd edition) Equinox

Samuda, V. and M. Bygate (2008) *Tasks in Second Language Learning* Palgrave Macmillan

Sanchez-Stockhammer, C. (2018) *English Compounds and Their Spelling* Cambridge University Press

Sanford, A. and S. Garrod (1981) *Understanding Written Language* Wiley

Sankoff, G. and S. Laberge (1974) "On the acquisition of native speakers by a language" In D. DeCamp and I. Hancock (eds.) *Pidgins and Creoles* (73–84) Georgetown University Press

Savage-Rumbaugh, S. and R. Lewin (1994) *Kanzi: The Ape at the Brink of the Human Mind* John Wiley

Saville-Troike, M. and K. Barto (2016) *Introducing Second Language Acquisition* (3rd edition) Cambridge University Press

Schendl, H. (2001) *Historical Linguistics* Oxford University Press

Schiffrin, D. (1987) *Discourse Markers* Cambridge University Press

(1994) *Approaches to Discourse* Blackwell

Schmandt-Besserat, D. (1996) *How Writing Came About* University of Texas Press

Schwarz, F. (ed.) (2015) *Experimental Perspectives on Presupposition* Springer

Schwyter, J. (2018) "Ten years after the stroke: me talk slightly less funny" *English Today* 34 (2): 35–38

Sebba, M. and L. Harding (2018) "World Englishes and English as a lingua franca" In J. Culpeper, P. Kerswill, R. Wodak, T. McEnery and F. Katamba (eds.) *English Language* (2nd edition) (chapter 21) Palgrave Macmillan

Sedaris, D. (2000) *Me Talk Pretty One Day* Little Brown

Seidlhofer, B. (2011) *Understanding English as a Lingua Franca* Oxford University Press

Seinfeld, J. (1993) *SeinLanguage* Bantam Books

Senghas, A. and M. Coppola (2001) "Children creating language: how Nicaraguan Sign Language acquired a spatial grammar" *Psychological Science* 12: 323–328

Shibatani, M. (2001) "Honorifics" In R. Mesthrie (ed.) *Concise Encyclopedia of Sociolinguistics* (552–559) Elsevier

Siegel, J. (2008) *The Emergence of Pidgin and Creole Languages* Oxford University Press

Sihler, A. (2000) *Language History: An Introduction* John Benjamins

Sinceviciute, V. (2014) "'When a joke's a joke and when it's too much': mateship as a key to interpreting jocular FTAs in Australian English" *Journal of Pragmatics* 60: 121–139

Singleton, D. and L. Ryan (2004) *Language Acquisition: The Age Factor* (2nd edition) Multilingual Matters

Smith, G. (2008) *Growing up with Tok Pisin: Contact, Creolization and Change in Papua New Guinea's National Language* Battlebridge

Smitherman, G. (2000) *Talkin that Talk* Routledge

Sperber, D. and D. Wilson (1995) *Relevance* (2nd edition) Blackwell

Spolsky, B. (1998) *Sociolinguistics* Oxford University Press

  (ed.) (2018) *The Cambridge Handbook of Language Policy* Cambridge University Press

Spreen, O. and A. Risser (2003) *Assessment of Aphasia* Oxford University Press

Springer, S. and G. Deutsch (2001) *Left Brain, Right Brain* (6th edition) W. H. Freeman

Stewart, D., E. Stewart and J. Little (2006) *American Sign Language the Easy Way* (2nd edition) Barron's Educational

Stokoe, W. (1960) *Sign Language Structure: An Outline of the Visual Communication Systems of the American Deaf* Studies in Linguistics, Occasional Papers 8, University of Buffalo

  (2001) *Language in Hand* Gallaudet University Press

Sudlow, D. (2001) *The Tamasheq of North-East Burkina-Faso* R. Köppe Verlag

Sutherland, S. (2016) *A Beginner's Guide to Discourse Analysis* Palgrave

Sutton-Spence, R. and B. Woll (1999) *The Linguistics of British Sign Language* Cambridge University Press

Swan, M. (2005) *Grammar* Oxford University Press

Talbot, M. (2010) *Language and Gender* (2nd edition) Polity Press

Tallermann, M. (2014) *Understanding Syntax* (4th edition) Routledge

Tannen, D. (1990) *You Just Don't Understand* William Morrow

  (2005) *Conversational Style* (revised edition) Oxford University Press

Taylor, C. (2016) *Mock Politeness in English and Italian* John Benjamins

Taylor, J. (2003) *Linguistic Categorization* (3rd edition) Oxford University Press

Tench, P. (2011) *Transcribing the Sound of English* Cambridge University Press

Terrace, H. (1979) *Nim: A Chimpanzee Who Learned Sign Language* Alfred Knopf

Thomas, J. (1995) *Meaning in Interaction* Longman

Thomas, L. (1993) *Beginning Syntax* Blackwell

Tomasello, M. (2003) *Constructing a Language* Harvard University Press

Tombs, R. (2014) *The English and Their History* Alfred A. Knopf

Tonouchi, L. (2001) *Da Word* Bamboo Ridge Press

Trudgill, P. (1974) *The Social Differentiation of English in Norwich* Cambridge University Press

  (1983) *On Dialect* Blackwell

  (2000) *Sociolinguistics* (4th edition) Penguin

Trudgill, P. and J. Hannah (2013) *International English* (5th edition) Routledge

Umiker-Sebeok, D-J. and T. Sebeok (eds.) (1987) *Monastic Sign Languages* Mouton de Gruyter

Ungerer, F. and H-J. Schmid (2006) *An Introduction to Cognitive Linguistics* (2nd edition) Routledge

Uomini, N. and G. Meyer (2013) "Shared brain lateralization patterns in language and Acheulean stone tool production: a functional transcranial Doppler ultrasound study" *PLoS ONE* 8 (8): e72693

Ur, P. (2009) *Grammar Practice Activities* (2nd edition) Cambridge University Press

Valian, V. (1999) "Input and language acquisition" In W. Ritchie and T. Bhatia (eds.) *Handbook of Child Language Acquisition* (497–530) Academic Press

Valli, C., C. Lucas, K. Mulrooney and M. Villanueva (2011) *Linguistics of American Sign Language: An Introduction* (5th edition) Gallaudet University Press

van Dijk, T. (1996) "Discourse, power and access" In C. Caldas-Coulthard and M. Coulthard (eds.) *Texts and Practices: Readings in Critical Discourse Analysis* (84–104) Routledge

Vaneechoute, M. and J. Sloyles (1998) "The memetic origin of language: modern humans as musical primates" *Journal of Memetics* 2: 84–117

VanPatten, B. (2003) *From Input to Output: A Teacher's Guide to Second Language Acquisition* McGraw-Hill

VanPatten, B. and J. Williams (eds.) (2015) *Theories in Second Language Acquisition* (2nd edition) Routledge

Velupillai, V. (2015) *Pidgins, Creoles and Mixed Languages* John Benjamins

Verdonk, P. (2002) *Stylistics* Oxford University Press

Vihman, M. (2013) *Phonological Development: The First Two Years* Wiley

Vinson, B. (2012) *Language Disorders across the Lifespan* (3rd edition) Thomson Delmar Learning

Vise, D. and M. Malseed (2005) *The Google Story* Delacorte Press

von Frisch, K. (1993) *The Dance Language and Orientation of Bees* Harvard University Press

Wakasa, M. (2014) "A sketch grammar of Wolaytta" *Nilo-Ethiopian Studies* 19: 31–44

Wardhaugh, R. (2014) *An Introduction to Sociolinguistics* (7th edition) Wiley-Blackwell

Weber, D. (1986) "Information perspective, profile and patterns in Quechua" In W. Chafe and J. Nichols (eds.) *Evidentiality: The Linguistic Coding of Epistemology* (137–155) Ablex

Weir, R. (1966) "Questions on the learning of phonology" In F. Smith and G. Miller (eds.) *The Genesis of Language* (153–168) MIT Press

Whitaker, H. (2010) *Concise Encyclopedia of Brain and Language* Elsevier

Widawski, M. (2015) *African American Slang* Cambridge University Press

Widdowson, H. (1978) *Teaching Language as Communication* Oxford University Press
(2004) *Text, Context, Pretext* Blackwell
(2007) *Discourse Analysis* Oxford University Press

Wiley, T. (2004) "Language planning, language policy and the English-Only movement" In E. Finegan and J. Rickford (eds.) *Language in the USA* (319–338) Cambridge University Press

Williams, P. (2016) *Word Order in English Sentences* (2nd edition) English Lessons Brighton

Willis, D. and J. Willis (2007) *Doing Task-based Teaching* Oxford University Press

Wolfram, W. and B. Ward (eds.) (2006) *American Voices: How Dialects Differ from Coast to Coast* Blackwell

Woodard, R. (2003) *The Cambridge Encyclopedia of the World's Ancient Languages* Cambridge University Press

Wyse, D. (2017) *How Writing Works: From the Invention of the Alphabet to the Rise of Social Media* Cambridge University Press

Yip, V. and S. Matthews (2007) *The Bilingual Child* Cambridge University Press

Yu, A. (2007) *A Natural History of Infixation* Oxford University Press

Yule, G. (1996) *Pragmatics* Oxford University Press

(1998) *Explaining English Grammar* Oxford University Press

Yule, G. and M. Overstreet (2017) *Puzzlings* Amazon Books

Index